HOW TO CREATE

Profitable New Products

—from Mission to Market

GEORGE GRUENWALD

Foreword by Robert W. Galvin

 NTC Business Books
NTC/Contemporary Publishing Company

Library of Congress Cataloging-in-Publication Data

Gruenwald, George.
    How to create profitable new products : from mission to market /
George Gruenwald.
       p.   cm.
    Includes bibliographical references and index.
    ISBN 0-8442-3353-6 (alk. paper)
    1. New products—Management.   2. New products—Marketing.
I. Title.
HF5415.153.G766   1997
658.5′75—dc21   96-37177
                                       CIP

BK
$49.95

Some of the material in this book was previously published in
New Product Development.

In Memory of

Linus Pauling
Guy-Robert Detlefsen
Preston Townley
David Hardin

Contents

Illustrations, Tables, Graphs

Foreword

George Gruenwald's thinking has stimulated me since we were in high school together years ago. Our thoughts, always maturing, have been most congruent over the years. Lively thinking must be good for a person, because both of us continue to project ever fresher views as activists in our commercial roles today.

In this practical text George stresses such vital fundamentals as creativity and newness. These certainly have worked for us. Throughout my career, I have emphasized in person and to the organization CREATIVITY, the basic vocational thinking skill of hunting up the facts and changing what you find, as well as RENEWAL, the driving thrust that energizes everything (particularly product initiatives) that our company's customers expect and often what they never thought possible.

As with every subject he has mastered, he leaves no what, when, where, and why factor to chance. His hands-on product development experience is manifested through the instructive anecdotes and well-essayed principles and practices.

The journey he lays out for us—from mission to market—is one well worth traveling.

Robert W. Galvin
Chairman of the Executive Committee
Motorola, Inc.

Acknowledgments

For suggesting I write my fourth book on new product development, Rich Hagle, editor at NTC Business Books. For helpful input of all sorts, my outstanding past and present clients, and my son Paul. For forfeiting our vacation companionship to this project, my dear wife, Corrine.

For writing the foreword, Robert W. Galvin, whose entire career has been devoted to innovative, world-leading new products. Mr. Galvin is Chairman of the Executive Committee, Motorola, and its former President, board chairman, and CEO. He is also board chairman of Semantech, Inc., as well as a former member of Presidential and Department of Commerce advisory groups on technology and international trade. He is a Medal of Honor recipient and former president of the Electronics Industries Association and Chairman of the Illinois Institute of Technology.

World renowned as an innovator in communications technology throughout his entire career, business leader Robert W. Galvin is the most appropriate choice to inspire successful new product development, which is the mission of this book. To quote *Forbes*, Mr. Galvin's "greatest gift: anticipating change."

For their special efforts, unparalleled expertise and professional experiential contributions (listed in alphabetical order of their affiliations):

- American Brands, Charles H. McGill*
- American Formulating and Manufacturing, Nevel DeHart
- Business Development Index, John F. Dix (when at Borden)
- Campbell Mithun Esty, Steve Gordon, Howard Liszt, and Carol Weitz
- Cannondale Associates, Kenneth A. Harris, Jr.
- ConAgra, Susie Sharples Poznick of Fleishman Hillard, Inc.
- CPC International, Tom DiPiazza
- EMI Music, James G. Fifield and Michael J. Gross of Robinson Lake Sawyer Miller Communications
- General Mills, R. Craig Shulstad (Communications Director, Minnesota Public Radio)
- Gillette, Eric Kraus

* When this book went to press, American Brands was planning to change its name to Future Brands.

- Heinz, Debora S. Foster
- Kimberly Clark, Wendi Strong
- Land O' Lakes, Jack Gherty, Ron Ostby, and Kathie Mapes
- Landor Associates, Allen Adamson and Pamela Abitbol
- Macrotherm™, Donald Grieb
- Martek Biosciences, Henry "Pete" Linsert and Larry Horn
- 3M, Colleen Harris and Stephanie Hack
- Robert Mondavi Winery, Margaret Kearnes
- Motorola, George Grimsrud, Karayn L. Schingoethe, and
  Cheryl Beck-Ruff
- Packaging Digest, Michael Bordenaro
- Procter & Gamble, Charlotte R. Otto
- Sara Lee, Randy White, Jennifer Armstrong, Clover Bergman
  (via Marina Maher Communications), and Julia Gallagher
- Toro, Kendrick Melrose and Donald St. Dennis

And, for entrepreneurial input: Bodies Made New's Joan Detlefsen, Claypool Classics' Lois Claypool, I Dood It's Barbara Engberg, Sandicast's Sandra Brue, and To Market To Market's Pam Hanson.

And for other contributions from corporations, trade and public service organizations and publications, special thanks to:

The Advertising Research Foundation, American Association of Advertising Agencies, American Marketing Association, Association of National Advertisers, *Automotive News*, Leo Burnett, Booz Allen & Hamilton, Campbell Soup, The Conference Board, Daniel J. Edelman, Inc., General Motors, *Harvard Business Review*, Honeywell, Hormel, Hunter Industries, IBM, Market Facts, A.C. Nielsen, Nissan, Pillsbury, PBS, Quaker Oats, Schrello Associates, SRI, J. Walter Thompson, Troxel, Vanderbilt University.

Finally, this book is dedicated to the memories of four inspirational, recently departed friends and associates. All four left the world better for their contributions of brilliance and leadership.

Thanks for the many helpful inputs, deep understanding, and warmth of the world's only winner of two unshared Nobel Prizes (in two different fields, chemistry and peace), Linus Pauling.

Thanks for the new product partnership of the brilliant R&D leader Guy-Robert Detlefsen.

Thanks for all the helpful marketing and research input over the years from former Market Facts Inc. and American Marketing Association leader David K. Hardin.

And thanks for the memories of business leader, The Conference Board leader, nonprofit educational and cultural leader Preston "Pete" Townley.

Introduction

The Book's Mission:
Profitable New Products

More and more, new product development has become the driving source behind the most successful companies—in all business categories. Driving *force*—as well as driving *source*.

New products should account for 37 percent of total sales by the year 2000, up from 26 percent during 1990–95, reports the Product Development and Management Association, representing new-product-development professionals from 2,000 companies.

The best performers link technological innovation and the marketing/R&D interface, even in the leading international corporations.

The best performers encourage—even reward—conceptualization and inspiration from all sources, internal and external. An engineer or a chemist may inspire an original concept for which there is no assignment. A marketing communicator, who doesn't understand technology, may identify a need, may anticipate an opportunity for which there is no assignment—but which may be appropriate for the company's future. The best and the brightest corporations wisely exploit inspirational new product concepts from dedicated internal and outsources.

Business Week/Enterprise, Spring, 1996 reported: "In a recent survey of 400 fast-growing companies with revenues of $1 million to $5 million, the half that used outsourcing reported cost savings averaging 7.8 percent over the cost of providing the same services in-house. However, companies that outsourced also reported revenues 22 percent greater than those that didn't, not to mention fatter margins and healthier cash flows."

New products may not only leverage corporate growth, they can inspire corporate renewal. "New Products," of course, is a term that includes new services, as well as significantly innovated and improved basic offerings.

The use of information systems in manufacturing and the internationalization of the R&D function have also leveraged new product leadership success.

Once a company's broadly defined strategy is key to its mission, every step of the way, every possible direction and source should be utilized in the start-up phases of identifying opportunities. The world is changing so rapidly, new product leadership is more and more the key to continuing success.

Beyond that, as the Pittsburgh-based INPEX℠ May 1996 Innovation/New Product Exposition stated: "The best and the least expensive way to find new products is to let someone else invent them for you." That, of course, isn't always true—especially for innovation-driven companies. Nonetheless, to expand your product line, locate new products, improve existing products, discover new markets, save development costs, stay ahead competitively, find licensing opportunities—to be aware of new ideas—the most successful makers and marketers have open minds.

Open minds, with proper legal protection, should encourage entrepreneurs, inventors, contract manufacturers, technology marketers, and research and development groups who are attempting to find licensing or sales opportunities.

Although the guiding principles of new product development haven't changed, some of the processing technology and outsourcing have—and continue to do so. Thousands of corporations have undergone change—they have merged, joint-ventured, downsized, licensed basic patents and proprietary advantages, been acquired, spun off parts, added new areas, gone Chapter 11, or worse.

Managements, of course, adapt to or move with these tides, as well as retire, retrofit, etc. At the same time, tens of thousands of corporate management jobs have shifted, and hundreds of thousands of new and redefined products and their extensions have entered the marketplace, while other huge numbers have expired or have begun winding down. New management services and technologies have been activated, and new management viewpoints have emerged.

Other facts affecting market-driven new product development include the increasing globalization of business and technological emphasis on environmentally safe "greening" of ingredients, products, services, and easily, inexpensively recyclable packages.

New product development is becoming more and more technology based. This is being felt on all fronts—and is reflected in nearly all aspects, including consumer behavior, distribution channels, alternative media, R&D, R&E, and market research. The Internet is proliferating in interactive cyberspace.

For Whom Was This Book Written?

It was written for anyone making decisions affecting new products programs; anyone responsible for judging the process; any practitioner, consultant, student; or anyone just plain interested in how new products are conceived, born, and brought to market.

Why Was This Book Written?

Business needs new products just to survive. This has never been more true than today. The pace quickens. Consumers accept new products faster and reject them faster. Life cycles of products are shorter except for those products that are continually infused with "newness"—significant improvements that keep them in the forefront of their category.

The importance of new products is attested to by the fact that products introduced in the past five years account for the majority of sales and profits for many industry leaders.

At the same time, technology kills entire categories, while creating new problems to be solved by new products. Communications must be briefer, more single-minded. Products must have a sharpened reason to exist—computer inventory control soon sorts out undistinguished brands.

Governmental restrictions, consumerist pressures, buyer sophistication, and foreign competition draw tighter parameters, thus increasing the challenge.

Both the private and public sectors need new products and services to keep up with the demands of changing living standards, disposable income, quicker identification of problem areas, and growing venturesomeness.

Two organizational changes in industry have had profound influence on new products and services.

The first was the widespread adoption of the product manager system. Joining the product manager (or brand manager) organization was the profit center system, accountable for its own profits (and losses). This restructuring of management systems led to an emphasis on cost-effectiveness in marketing decision making—a concern for favorable investment-return ratios—and, with that, a financially oriented marketing philosophy.

The second change was the shift of new product responsibilities—a change that is continuing today. Formerly, most organized new products efforts were centered in research and development (or engineering) departments. Today, they are mostly centered in revenue divisions—marketing groups with profit responsibilities. Additionally, some companies have new products departments, and some have made progress in seeding new-products-only groups or venture teams to open up new areas. Overall coordination, including acquisitions, is often centered in a growth and development executive.

At the same time, the research and development effort has become more important through better direction: It improves quality control standards, does basic research, and is given better direction, usually through product opportunity targets provided by the marketing groups.

Because marketing powers rely on identification of market needs prior to development-fulfillment plans, computerized refinement of checkout counters and telemarketing have sophisticated prospecting, more clearly identifying users and refusers.

At the same time, every aspect of communications media has helped redefine the opportunity areas. Digital video compression and fiber optics has led to as many as 500 channels. And "rewiring" isn't necessary. Examples: Jones Intercable in Alexandria, VA, has 60 channels on a single cable. Nearby Fairfax, VA, has 120 channels with a dual cable system. Digital compression will permit multiple signals in the bandwidth of a single present channel. Systems with a bandwidth of 1 GHz are being built. The technology is evolving rapidly. And the small RCA satellite dish has proliferated.

As television and radio become even more niche-driven, many more special audience print and video/disc publications have emerged, also eating away at the long-established world of mass media.

CD-ROMs and the Internet can work hand-in-hand to provide a powerful message. New technologies leverage new product success possibilities. Whether online services or interactive kiosks, network-centric hardware, or high-tech presentation devices—marketers can craft more efficient, effective communications, whether they're targeting a narrowly defined niche or operating in the global marketplace. Marketing communications become more powerful. Direct-to-home insertions and two-way dialogues are possible. Interactive marketing gives prospects a better understanding of new product appeals.

Recognizing the market needs and leveraging the complex new world of marketing tools has shifted the perspective of new product planning and execution.

More targeted media can signal more refined new product and service opportunities.

Among the most important changes in recent years have been the increasing role of marketing management in preparing marketing plans and of very top management in approving such plans, whether they be established product or service programs or new product marketing plans.

New Product Management

A company may organize the management of its new products program along the following lines:

- **Revenue division**: Responsible for the existing product line, its customer franchise, and its expansion, by way of appropriate new additions. This development is funded by the established business unit's own revenues.

- **Capability development**: An extension of the company's strengths (whether manufacturing, sourcing of material, technology, distribution, etc.) to seed new divisions.

- **New enterprises**: An extension of company capabilities within its basic industry to achieve new strengths and to develop entirely new businesses. It often identifies acquisitions, joint ventures, licensing opportunities, or outside contract manufacturing candidates. (However, going *outside* the basic industry for new enterprises is a general management function not normally assumed in any aspect of the formalized new-products function.)

- **Long-range development**: New business program planning, which integrates forecasting of evolving scientific and technology advances; population and industry changes in composition, location, and behavior, etc.

How Does This Book Define a New Product?

For the purposes of this book, a new product also means a new service—or a "package" of services or of products and services (e.g., business machines, programs, software, and technical service may be "packaged" as a new product). To simplify presentation, "new products" will represent any or all of these possible ramifications.

Figure 1 Responsibility for Preparing Plans: 1980 vs. 1989

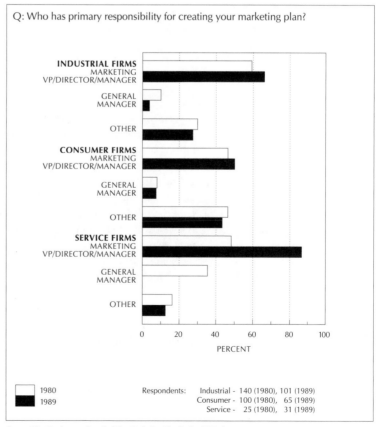

Source: The Conference Board—"The Marketing Plan in the 1990s."

Figure 2 Responsibility for Approving Plans: 1980 vs. 1989

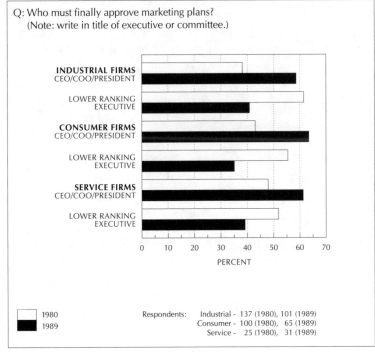

Q: Who must finally approve marketing plans?
    (Note: write in title of executive or committee.)

□ 1980
■ 1989

Respondents: Industrial - 137 (1980), 101 (1989)
                Consumer - 100 (1980), 65 (1989)
                Service -   25 (1980), 31 (1989)

Source: The Conference Board—"The Marketing Plan in the 1990s."

As for a definition, the broadest possible description is used. No one definition is precise to every need. Because of the various interpretations of what a new product constitutes, we have widely ranging assessments of new product success and failure rates. In the shelf-stable grocery field, for example, the leading new product successes are usually low-technology products that are slight variations on existing established products. Under such a definition, one would expect low capital risk and relatively high success rates, where success is related to expected performance against financial risk goals. Such successes are *marketing* successes.

An example of the financial commitment to marketing successes was cited by William D. Smithburg, chairman and chief executive officer of the Quaker Oats Company, in reference to Quaker's Chewy Granola Bars: "You would be dealing with $2 million or $3 million in research and development, as much as $15 million or $20 million of marketing development, probably $10 million or $15 million capital investment."

In some industries and scientific services, a new product may be almost entirely technology based, requiring heavy research investment and long lead time. Usually, the marketing investment is relatively low in sophisticated industrial technology successes

With that understood, what *is* a new product?

- To the maker, a new product is something the company doesn't make now.

- To the customer, a new product is something never heard of.

There are other judges of what defines a new product—from the U.S. Patent Office to the Food and Drug Administration, which may view a new product under its jurisdiction as something that does not have a long and safe use history in this country and/or has not successfully survived a range of carefully controlled testing procedures, and received the agency's approval.

The reader can think of other definitions.

In a broad sense, here is a useful classification of new products:

A. Evolution of an existing product
   1. Repositioned product
   2. Recycled product
   3. Appearance/form improvement
   4. Performance improvement
   5. Packaging construction improvement
   6. Price/value change
   7. Distribution pattern change
   8. Combination of several of the above
B. Expansion of a brand/product franchise
   1. Line extensions to the brand
   2. Flankers to the brand
   3. New category for the brand
C. New entry into an established category
D. New category
E. New business

How Is This Book Organized?

In an ideal world, perhaps, new product development would proceed in chronological order. As it is, many steps proceed at different paces; unplanned accidents spawn problems—and inspirations; outside factors exercise more control than inside planning.

This book necessarily addresses a disciplined, phased process with predetermined decision points. In fact, the seminal union of concept and practice may be a constantly regenerative process, fissured however with unpredictable divisions, splices, and clones. Effective practitioners will not lose sight of this.

The critical path to new product success is strewn with broken event bubbles. Nonetheless, a program is planned with a sense of order. The order followed by the sections of this book is:

> *Need* leads to *Commitment* leads to *Exploration* leads to *Conception* leads to *Modeling* (the beginning of the product development process) leads to *Marketing* leads to *Market Testing* leads to *Major Introduction* leads to continual commercial viability by keeping the product forever new.

At the end of each section, there is a summary afterword—a highlight outline of guideposts developed in the preceding chapters of the section.

The direction (and style) of this book is that of a new product generalist. Enough is offered to provide all of the guidance needed to design a new products marketing development program. Highly technical computer forecasting models, various research techniques to optimize successful predictability, and specific proprietary programs being offered by outside services are avoided for the most part. Plentiful literature is available in these fields for those readers with specific special interests.

Many of the examples given are from package goods manufacturers, who are widely visible, heavily chronicled in the trade press, and least esoteric for students of new product development. The procedures, however, are generally applicable to any field.

This Book Has a Bias

This book is infused with the author's more than 40 years' experience as a practitioner in the field working with more than 50 of the world's largest companies, as well as many others. The book reflects the learning gained both by participating in and by observing failures and successes in the pursuit of new products in a wide range of fields from telecommunications, business machines, and automobiles to consumer appliances, package goods, and financial services, in various roles as a maker and marketer, as a consultant and as an agent, as well as in executive positions with several major advertising agencies distinguished by their success records in new products marketing development in fields ranging across dozens of industrial and service classifications.

Research for this book was done in Western Europe, where many new product forms, processes, packaging, and marketing techniques are inspiring U.S. adaptations, and in Southern California, where life-style changes and quick trial of anything new often foretell our nation's consumer and high-tech industry trends.

For me, there is nothing more rewarding in business than the satisfaction and excitement of being party to the conception, gestation, birth, and life of a new product. Once born, the product's growing pains, its successful maturity, and then the constant search for a fountain of youth to keep the offering forever new outshine any other business experience.

The overall conclusion from these experiences is that the principles and judgments advocated herein are applicable to any new products program, with appropriate adaptation by the funding resource and to the market needs.

George Gruenwald
RANCHO SANTA FE, CALIFORNIA

NEED

1

Need for Growth and Diversification

Nowhere is Peter Drucker's statement more true than in new product development. In fact, several companies and some entire industries are based on effectiveness in this area. Their success rates have been conditioned by proven systems of procedure and event planning—well in advance of major financial commitment. The payoff, of course, depends upon the ability to *execute*, both with precision and with realistic marketplace flexibility.

Key to Sales Growth

New products are the key to a company's sales growth. According to a Booz Allen & Hamilton survey: "In the next three years alone, about 75 percent of the nation's growth in sales volume can be expected to come from new products, including new brands." In other words, if you include everything from minor innovations to major new brands, new products are the most vital fuel of our economy.

Some specific examples:

The multibillion-dollar 3M (Minnesota Mining & Manufacturing) Company leverages its technological leadership to generate new products. Today the goal is that 30 percent of annual revenues must come from products less than four years old, a goal first achieved in 1994. In 1995, 27 percent of sales came from new products introduced in the previous four years. In addition, the goal is that by 1997, 10 percent of revenues must be generated by products less than one year old.

In 1994, some $1 billion of revenues came from products launched during the year, a year in which 3M registered 543 patents—40 percent more than in 1991.

According to *The Economist* (March 18, 1995), "3M's vast portfolio of more than 60,000 different products relies on its 8,000-person research staff," which is encouraged to spend 15 percent of its time "bootlegging"—working on pet projects of their own choosing. Traditionally, 3M has spent 6 to 7 percent of its revenues on R&D—double the average for American manufacturers. *The Economist* also reports that L. D. Simone, 3M's chairman since 1991, "has perfected a system for speedy, sustained innovation. The ability to come up with madcap inventions that create new markets is a good deal harder to institutionalize." To focus the firm on would-be blockbusters, 3M uses what is called "pacing programs" to select a relatively small number of big technologies and products that it hopes will "change the basis of competition."

Under the headline "3M Puts Faith in New Products" (August 30, 1996), *International Herald Tribune* reported that 3M "expected earnings to grow 10 percent annually in the next three years . . . from innovations in several product areas, including structured abrasives and materials that would replace ozone-depleting chlorofluorocarbons. New capital investments will total about $1 billion worldwide in 1996. In the process, the company is stepping up its search for major new products. . . . The company will devote 20 percent of its annual research budget, or about $180 million based on this year's research spending, to that goal. It is estimated that the first 25 candidates in its new program will produce about $6 billion in annual sales. Most of them should reach the market by 2000, the company said . . . 3M isn't devoting any new dollars to the program, however. It instead will be reallocating part of this year's $900 million research and development budget.

"Bill Coyne, 3M's senior vice president of research and development, said each product must have large growth potential and offer a high return on investment capital."

Among new products developed will be film that enhances brightness of the screens of computers, cellular phones, pagers and other consumer electronic products flexible circuitry for use in digital photography, etc. On August 16, 1996 3M won approval for the first CFC-free asthma drug inhaler with $350 million in sales expected for that product by 2000.

Also in March 1995, Gillette Chairman Alfred M. Zeien reported: "45 percent of our sales came from products introduced in the last five years."

Some companies in new products-intensive industries, such as toys (on one extreme) and pharmaceuticals (on another), generate more than 60 percent of their income over a similar period. Even the service industries benefit.

According to a report from The Conference Board, even when classifying *only major new products* (not mere line extensions), reliance on new products for company growth is important to all classifications of industry. The Conference Board reports that of 148 companies surveyed,

> 15 percent of their current sales volume is attributable to the sale of major new products introduced by them during the past five years. This average (as measured by the median) dependence on new products is similar for manufacturers of either industrial or consumer products. The range for individual firms goes all the way from zero to more than 50 percent. As might be expected, firms in stable, commodity-type industries tend to be less dependent on new products than those in specialty businesses, where opportunities for innovation are higher or product life cycles shorter.
>
> Looking to the future, two-thirds of the reporting executives expect their companies to have an even greater dependence on new products over the next five years.

Reviewing the same corporations six years later, The Conference Board reports that they were right. Of those companies contributing to the study 35 percent got at least half their revenues from products they did not make ten years earlier.

Yet another example of the need for new products is that a key consideration of executive recruits in considering new employers is the company's new product record. This is taken to be a sure sign of a manager's growth opportunities.

New Products Sustain Company

Everyone in industry knows that new products are essential for viability: If we do not continue to grow, we die. To grow, a company must continue to learn (research) and to make a difference in its industry (pioneer).

These are not mottoes for milking cash cows; the words are prophetic for any enterprise with a long-term goal of financial and psychic rewards for its employees and shareholders.

Here, new products are the key to success.

Business, whether it sells waste management or interstellar communications, janitorial services or gene-splicing, lives through new growth—not through clones of the past.

Diversification Is Essential

Both growth and diversification are served by a well-articulated new product program. Most companies recognize that there are various means to achieve diversification.

When the need is not within the capability of your company, but fits the corporate charter that guides the activities of the company, then beneficial arrangements can be made with other companies to joint-venture, contract-supply, license/acquire, or, in rare instances, to merge—be acquired by a complementary organization. Pools of expertise can also be acquired by recruiting within the subject industry and by the use of technical and marketing consultants. If your company is not on the leading edge of a new product development, seek outside help. Beware the defensive NIH syndrome—the "not invented here" factor.

Some of the most advanced new product innovators have no such inhibitions. IBM has had cross-licensing agreements for decades, and with Japanese firms since the 1960s. As an example, the Paris-based *International Herald Tribune* reports on an accord that allowed Nippon Telephone & Telegraph and IBM "to use each other's patents on electronic switching systems, computers, and terminal equipment free of charge."

Often, different skills and organizations are needed to advance most effectively on more than one front at a time. All of the above can be part of a growth plan to enhance established capabilities—or to diversify. Most often, it is both.

The most ambitious and dynamic enterprises should carefully consider a multipronged organizational approach to every area of growth and diversification. In many cases, *all* should be adopted.

To recognize the consequences of failure to grow and to diversify, you need only to observe those industries locked into a posture controlled by outside events that have not been recognized. Geographic population shifts and changing needs, resources, and marketplace value systems dictate a review of the corporate charter. Media changes also can affect redefinition of the charter. Contemporary computerized techniques for segmentation make available discrete marketing opportunities that may have been previously inefficient and hence unaffordable. Such segmentation suggests new products opportunities, which may be characterized by the commonality of neighborhood social definition, and reached by new ZIP code sorting, by telephone, with two-way cable, or with programmatic precision over 100-channel cable.

Some savants of doom say that the era of new products marketing is fading with an oversaturation of options, efficient mass distribution, generic low-priced parity products, and a glut of inefficient media. Then along comes the next series of breakthroughs—and all evidence points to the contrary. The corporate charters, the rules of the game, and the means change, but the need for new products not only persists, it is on the increase.

2

Why New Products Fail

There are no reliable overall statistics on new product successes or failures, though there are plenty offered by industry classification. Even here, the numbers are apt to be misleading. One company's failure could be another's success (and vice versa). It depends on the goals. One chief executive of a specialty food company (flavor enhancers) said: "Bring us all those ideas you have that do not meet the large-volume goals of your giant clients—we know how to make money from special-purpose products." That's true across that entire field, from McCormick-Schilling spices to Pet Incorporated (Ac'cent) to McIlhenny's Tabasco. In other words, a failure for General Foods could be a smashing success for General Spices. And so it goes in most categories.

The Numbers

If you'd like some numbers, here are some comments and some success/failure scores from a 1980 study by The Conference Board:

> For purposes of the present study, a major new product was taken to be a success if it met management's original expectations for it in all important respects. Conversely, a major new product was taken to have been a failure if, in some important respect, it failed to have met manage-

ment's original expectations for it. Although such a product often continued to be sold, the extreme possibility was that its performance proved so disappointing that it was actually withdrawn from the market.

Half of the companies surveyed had achieved success, as defined above, with at least two-thirds of the major new products that they marketed over the past five years. The other half reported such success with fewer than two-thirds of their new products—and there were some for which each and every one of their new offerings had proved disappointing. These median values for new product success (i.e., two out of three meeting management's expectations in all important respects) were the same for manufacturers selling either to industrial or consumer markets. (Table 2-1 summarizes these findings.)

Table 2-1 Success rates for major new products over a five-year period

Successful new products	Percentage of companies selling primarily to:	
	Industrial markets	Consumer markets
All succeeded	9	18
90 to 99%	7	4
80 to 89%	16	9
70 to 79%	11	11
60 to 69%	16	12
50 to 59%	15	15
40 to 49%	4	2
30 to 39%	9	9
1 to 29%	5	4
None succeeded	8	16
	100	100

The success rate reported by each company represents the percentage of all major new products introduced to the market by the company during the previous five years that subsequently met management's expectations in all important respects.

Source: The Conference Board

(A similar poll, conducted in 1971, found that the equivalent median values for success with major new products at that time were approximately 80 percent for industrial product firms and 60 percent for consumer product firms. Especially in view of sampling differences, however, probably not too much importance should be attached to differences in the success rate between the 1971 and 1980 surveys.)

(In each of the surveys, most product failures [not having met management's expectations in some important respect] did not result in such disappointing performance as to require actually being withdrawn from the market. In the 1980 survey, the proportion of all major new products marketed by the reporting companies that later proved so disappointing that they had to be removed from the market was about 9 percent for industrial product firms and about 13 percent for consumer product firms.)

Complete success or complete failure is more common among manufacturers catering to consumer markets than among those servicing industrial markets. However, firms falling at either of these extremes include, to an above-average extent, a number that launched only relatively few major new products. A firm that sends to market only one or two major new items over a five-year period is perhaps either exceptionally cautious or exceptionally short in new product experience. In either case, the low number of products at risk increases the chances of total success or total failure.

Nevertheless, reporting firms with a perfect batting average for new products include a large manufacturer of metal components and equipment with more than 100 successful new products; a producer of electrical components with 25; a petroleum products company with nine; a paper products company with six; and two drug manufacturers each having a handful or so of consistently successful new items.

Among the firms that went scoreless for five long years are a large chemicals producer with 20 new product failures; a small manufacturer of heating equipment with 11; a producer of sports equipment with six; and two firms making office supplies and two others in packaged goods industries, each with several losers and no winners.

Management View

How do managements, in general, regard their companies' new product performances? On the whole, they are reported to be quite well satisfied. More than one-third of the total regard their rate of success with major new products as being highly acceptable, and another half of them as being disappointing, but still acceptable. Only a small minority view their new products performance as being unacceptably low. (Table 2-2 outlines these views.)

Managements in firms selling to consumer markets seem to be even more pleased with the outcome than are those concerned with industrial markets. And there is a correlation between the degree of management satisfaction and the relative degree of success actually achieved over the past five years. Thus, as many as four out of five managements of companies with success rates well above average (i.e., falling within the top quartile of those surveyed) find this result highly acceptable. In contrast, where success rates were much below average (i.e., falling within the bottom quartile in terms of success), very few managements consider the result highly acceptable. Yet managements are not uniformly discouraged even in these cases. While more than a quarter of them consider the performance unacceptably low, two-thirds view it as disappointing—but still acceptable. . . .

Table 2-2 How management views the acceptability of new product success rates achieved

Management feeling	Percentage of all reporting companies	Percentage of companies selling primarily to:		Percentage of companies whose past success rate was:			
		Industrial markets	Consumer markets	Much above average	Somewhat above average	Somewhat below average	Much below average
Highly acceptable	37	33	44	79	42	15	5
Disappointing, but still acceptable	52	57	44	21	53	73	67
Unacceptably low	11	10	12	—	5	12	28
	100	100	100	100	100	100	100

Source: The Conference Board

Dissecting the Failure Rate

The median failure rates for new products found in both the 1971 and 1980 surveys by The Conference Board are sharply lower than averages sometimes quoted and repeated by certain other observers of the new product scene. The statement has been made from time to time, for example, that typically as many as eight or nine out of every ten new products turn out to be failures.

Differences of definition probably account for most such seeming discrepancies. The board's surveys cover major new products that firms have actually introduced to the market. In contrast, some other observers have apparently referred to new product ventures that may have been abandoned at a much earlier stage in their development.

Many managements have had the experience of bringing a new product toward the point of launch, perhaps even to test market, and have then had second thoughts and held it back. Possibly some such ventures might have become winners, yet the likelihood is there were sound reasons for management to fear they would have become losers in the marketplace. And obviously behind such near-starters there are often numerous other projects, or mere proposals, that are picked up by R&D or examined by the company's marketing research unit in a preliminary way and soon dropped from further consideration. In general, the farther back along the development process it is decided to set the cutoff point for definition of a new product, the greater might be the expected proportion of failures reported.

Operating in the reverse direction, however, one could take into account "new products" of all kinds—not only major new products covered in the board's surveys, but also lesser product improvements and line extensions that characteristically have more assurance of success. In that event, the proportion of "winners" to "losers" might be expected to be higher—not lower—than the board's findings.

Acceptable Risk

The prevailing view is that it is realistic to expect an occasional loser mixed in with the winners. Most of the marketers surveyed consider some element of risk to be inherent—even desirable—in any active program of new product development.

One executive sums up for many when he declares: "A 100 percent success rate can never be assured in the marketplace, and any company that insists on this will surely see a great number of opportunities pass it by."

Acknowledging that virtually every new product inevitably carries some risk does not, however, preclude attempts to cut such risk to a minimum. The general view is that management should at least insist on maximum effort and aim for the bull's-eye every time. There is, to be sure, a minority view found in certain industrial firms, where so significant an investment is required to bring any new offering to market that no failure whatever can be countenanced.[1]

Importance of New Products

In quoting a Booz Allen & Hamilton study of the success rate of 13,311 items introduced by 700 companies between 1976 and 1981, *The Wall Street Journal* writes:

> Although success rates for new products haven't improved over the past 13 years, marketers are banking on them more than ever for future growth. New products will account for 31 percent of profits over the next five years, compared with 22 percent over the past five. These new products will account for 37 percent of total sales growth, compared with 28 percent in the earlier period.

> In contrast, acquisitions are expected to contribute just 9 percent of sales growth over the next five years; 54 percent will come from existing products. Additional evidence of the importance marketers attach to new products: companies expect to bring out a median of ten products each in the next five years, compared with half that many in the past five years.

---

[1] David S. Hopkins, "New-Product Winners and Losers," Report No. 773, © The Conference Board, Inc., New York. Reprinted by permission.

The consulting firm's study, one of the most extensive on a much-researched subject, consisted of a mail survey answered by 700 of 2,800 companies. Three-fifths of the survey respondents sell industrial goods, with the rest evenly divided between consumer durables and nondurable products. . . . Success was determined by the company's own criteria.

Although marketers may not be improving their new product batting average, they are becoming more efficient at developing products. Today only seven ideas need to be seriously evaluated to find one successful product, compared with a 58:1 ratio in a 1968 study. One reason: earlier weeding of ideas that are weak or don't fit a company's overall strategy.

New product spending also is more efficient. Today successful entries account for 54 percent of total new product expenditures, compared with 30 percent in 1968. Capital investment as a percent of total new product spending has fallen to 26 percent from 46 percent in 1968.

The external factor most likely to inhibit product introductions is the rising cost of capital. It was cited by two-thirds of the respondents. Internal obstacles mentioned by more than 40 percent of those in the survey: current business pressures that reduce attention to new products and corporate emphasis on short-term profitability. The leading stimulus to new products cited by 86 percent of respondents—technological advances.

The journal cited other findings of the Booz Allen study:

One-third of all companies don't formally measure the performance of new products. Those that do most often use sales volume, percentage of sales, profits, or return on investment.

Successful new product companies don't spend more, as a percentage of sales, than unsuccessful ones on research and development and promotion of new products.

Top corporate management devotes 7 percent of its time to new products. Marketing managers spend 21 percent; R&D and engineering managers, 42 percent.

Just 5 percent of companies surveyed pay new product executives a bonus tied to the performance of their entries.

Each time a company doubles its number of new products, its cost per introduction falls 29 percent. There's no correlation, though, between the number of new products and success rates.

Reasons for Failure

Obviously, money devoted to failures is money that might better have been spent on developing and introducing successes. Knowing causes for failure can help screen out ill-fated ventures before much time and money has been consumed.

It is instructive to look at how management appraises some of the reasons for success and failure in achievement of new product goals. As would be suspected, the reasons are similar: e.g., predictive/nonpredictive market research, good/poor timing, etc.

According to *BRANDWEEK*: "More than 22,000 'new' product introductions, including the brand equity slicing and dicing known as line extensions, occurred in 1994. Since no company, large or small, has proven itself immune to the inevitability that 90 percent or more of these will die on the vine, about $129 billion in research and development, manufacturing, and marketing expenditures will cruise toward the line item: cost of doing business."

Following is a catalog of reasons for failure, as tabulated in various studies, in various years by leading research firms. The average rate of new product failures reported by more than 1,000 firms and more than an additional 300 brands, as studied by A.C. Nielsen, A.T. Kearney, Booz Allen & Hamilton, as well as others, ranged from 35 percent to 95 percent, based on studies over 25+ years.

Of course, the research methods used by *BRANDWEEK* experts interviewed and by those firms referred to above differ primarily because of definitions, sources, methodology, etc. Differing goals play a role also. A flop for Company A could be a success for Company B. However, "the reasons for failure" are critical, no matter the statistics.

Poor Planning

It is unfortunately true that poor planning is the single biggest reason for new product failures. Too often, facts and factors that would have been foretold are either overlooked or are ignored.

Here are just a few examples:

- The product doesn't fit company strategy.
- The product doesn't fit company expertise.
- It doesn't fit company distribution strength/knowledge.
- It doesn't fit company margin, return-on-investment, or return-on-sales requirements.
- The cost of entering the category is an unsurmountable barrier.
- The diffuse category is not vulnerable to a single entry; a line assault is needed.
- The manufacturing, purchasing, and quality control standards are unfamiliar.
- The regulatory complications are unfamiliar.
- There are patent, copyright, or license infringements.

- The market analysis is inadequate.
- Development funds are inadequate.
- The company fails to face up to competitive strengths—*after* launch.
- The product has no phased critical path with clear time, budget, and go/no go decision points.
- There is no preplan guideline checklist.
- The timing is poor—too early or too late.

Poor Management

Poor planning and poor management are really interlocking failures. Management is responsible for the planning process and for authorizing the planned programs. Although managements identify poor research and poor timing as top failures in many surveys, the answer lies closer to home.

Some examples of poor management:

- The product doesn't fit the corporate or division charter guiding such activities.
- There was no management "sponsor."
- The product introduction is an unchecked management "ego trip" (i.e., the "sponsorship" is too powerful).
- There is no management information system to provide two-way communication.
- Management direction and goals are confusing and inconsistent.
- The wrong department leads the introduction program.
- Those who should have been pioneers and risk-takers are unwilling.
- There are budget and time constraints—change of signals—due to an unanticipated course of events.
- There are manufacturing, sales efforts, and communications constraints resulting from the change of signals, due to the unanticipated course of events.
- Management direction is capricious.

Needed is a balance between carefully designed critical path–planning and entrepreneurial risk-taking. Each major step in a phased program should require management to authorize termination, proceed as planned, or proceed with gap jumps or with added steps. The plan should be a living guide, subject to change with new knowledge, outside circumstances, and unforeseen breakthroughs or roadblocks. In fact, more programs tend to be carried along farther than they should be than are terminated too early or when they should be. There often tends to be a management inertia—a career identification with the project and the procedure—which is not justified by the facts. Some project managers admit that they do not want to recommend themselves "out of a job" by killing their program. Rather than fostering this wasteful attitude, management should reward pragmatic recommendations (which, after all, save dollars that may then be applied to future, hopefully successful projects). Because management of an established brand is often the career carrot for a new products manager, a premium is placed on rushing to market.

Reinforcing this view is an indictment from Gerald Schoenfeld, who heads Schoenfeld, Chapman & Pearl, Tarrytown, NY, consultancy, as reported in *The New York Times*:

> When a brand manager, who learned nothing about new products in business school, is put in charge of a new product venture and has a success, he or she is quickly plucked out of that job and thrown against existing family jewels. That's what pays the rent. A new product guy is a minister without portfolio, a brand manager without a brand.

What is needed, according to Mr. Schoenfeld, is a corporate reorganization that would make the new product team "the Marines and the Green Berets."

As a former new product brand manager, I would like to underscore that different management attitudes (and, perhaps, skills as well) are needed to be an entrepreneurial innovator than are needed to nurture institutionalized products. Yet the reward system in most companies favors those who manage the more easily forecastable fortunes of the established products—rather than the sowers and tillers of future growth.

Thorough planning requires more than doing it "by the book." No two projects are exactly alike, nor should any two plans be identical. The "real world" has different effects on the planning. The course being charted grows out of varying degrees of foreknowledge. Careful, detailed, imaginative preplanning cannot be overemphasized. Start every plan with a clean sheet of paper, an open mind—and all the help that can be mustered.

As R. Buckminster Fuller said, in discussing the planning that went into the Apollo project:

> The critical path organization of the Apollo Project disclosed some two million tasks that had to be successfully accomplished before the human astronauts were to be returned safely to Spaceship Earth. NASA's Apollo management then put a scientifically and technically competent control group to work to identify all the approximately two million tasks, a million of which required technological performances the design, production, and successful operation of which had never before been undertaken by humans.[2]

---

[2] R. Buckminster Fuller, *Critical Path*, St. Martin's Press, 1981

The time to cut and run is early, before the investment of too much money, too much time, and too much ego. Countless experiences have shown that a major percentage of failures are predictable at the planning phase. Further, a wise, noninvolved, experienced devil's advocate asking the right questions of senior management (the approvers, not the submitters) can spare later losses. Such an *éminence grise* may be a respected internal executive or an outside consultant given to candid objectivity.

Poor Concept

"Poor concept" is a relative statement. What is meant by "poor" is that the concept itself does not appeal at the time of and/or in the form of execution being evaluated, as determined by the mode of evaluation or test used. Some examples:

- The product doesn't offer a unique benefit—or one that is unique enough.
- The product offers too many benefits, unique or otherwise.
- It has no *single* strong reason for being.
- It has unique benefit(s), but fulfills little need.
- It has a unique benefit, but a poor price/value relationship.
- It has a unique benefit, but it out of synchronization with the market—in terms of demographic and psychographic realities, trends, fads, and fashion.
- It is too innovative, ahead of the market.
- It fills an unrealized need, about which it is too expensive to educate the prospect.
- The product message is too complicated—too difficult to communicate.
- The margin of benefit is not enough to break use habit, justify expense, change shopping patterns, etc.

Poor Execution

Marshall McLuhan said: "The medium is the message." That's often true. Every new product is a communication in itself. It has a face, a dress, and a personality. It has always been so.

It is even more so now, said Mel Von Smith in a lecture at the University of Chicago's Center for Continuing Education:

> It's an age where people are willing to spend money on fun, on pleasure, on me . . . we have had a lot of booms— inflation booms, divorce booms. Now we're entering a *personality boom*—and products with a positive personality are doing the booming.

In an age of "generics" (another boom), *personality* often becomes the point of difference, more important than function or intrinsic benefit. Here are a few executional problems, all related to the overall perception of the offering's personality and (hence) viability:

- There are product defects.
- There are other technical problems.
- The product is over- (under-)engineered.
- It is over (under) packaged.
- The development and introduction budget has been underspent or (not as common) overspent. There is a higher cost-of-goods than estimated.
- The product is misbranded.
- It is mistargeted.
- It is mistimed for character of market.
- It is mistimed for other reasons—it is contraseasonal, has come out amid a flurry of other introductions by company, has come out during an inventory reduction period, has come out during a trade category buying hiatus, there is insufficient purchasing lead time for a class new to manufacturing, etc.
- It is mispriced (over- or underpriced).
- It is misplaced (in the trade channel, distribution method, store section, etc.).
- It has weak distribution.
- The company has poor sales operations.
- Product benefits are miscommunicated (to the customer, to intervening trade channels).
- Insufficient and/or inappropriate media are being used.
- The product is mispositioned.
- It has an imprecise image, an indistinct personality.

Poor concept and poor execution are usually intermingled. A good concept poorly executed, a poor concept well executed—both are paths to the new product poorhouse. When the problems are identified at advanced prototype phases, the faults begin to become obvious.

Unfortunately both good and poor concepts poorly communicated at preliminary screening phases can lead to misdirection. Although concepts may originate from any quarter, it is recommended that the concept statement to be communicated to a prospective respondent be devised by a professional communicator, not necessarily an involved inventor or researcher.

The concept statement should hew to the rules, but should be single-minded, clear, concise, and prospect-directed. Further, it should be benefit-oriented, not product-descriptive. An example: One of the most successful hair-care items introduced by Gillette years ago was Dippity-

Do Hair Setting Gel. It never would have come out of the lab if this (unfortunately typical) concept statement had gone out to the mail panel: "Now, there's a new clear jelly for setting your hair. Doesn't flake or stain. Dries quickly. Washes out easily. Comes in wide-mouthed jar so it's easy to use. Choose pink or green colored gel." Rather, what the prospect wanted to know was how much fun it was to use; how it made messing permissible (thank you, Dr. Freud); how it allowed creative styling with fingers, pins, rollers, etc., that was not easy with sprays, perms, or conventional setting agents; how it was pretty, clear, bubbling, jewel-like, etc. Sensory cues were needed to induce trial.

This important fact, the appeal of sensory cues, is often lost in food products, household products, and appliance concept statements. In all of these cases of hands-on ritual, chore, self-indulgence, or prideful preparation, the sensory component is a *fact* about the product, not an embellishment. In most consumer products, this sensory appeal should be built into the product, its design, and its graphics. At the concept-sorting phase, it should be *anticipated*, e.g.:

> Now there is a word-processor typewriter that's easy and comfortable to use any place, any time. Smooth, soft-sided, weighs less than one pound—less than many books. Works on any surface—comfortable in your lap. Stores and plays back on any television screen or (with simple key switch) provides audio transcription on any radio (portable or car radio also) and delivers permanent record print-out upon command, ten copies per second.

Here, then is another intermingling of the concept and the product execution. Perhaps the example is overengineered. At the concept-sorting stage, however, this may be weeded out. Each concept can (and often should) be stated and tested in several variations. The above hypothetical example, if tested without the radio playback feature, without the multiple copy feature, etc., each at appropriate price points, might reveal appeals to various targets at various price points. If the concept scores well, then the maker can decide to market the model most appropriate to his distribution strength (commercial business machine outlets), can choose a narrower target with high margins, can concentrate on new consumer channels, or can bring out a variety of more- and less-sophisticated adaptations for all appropriate markets. Prudence would probably dictate starting with strength, then using the income generated to test other models in markets less familiar to the maker.

Poor Use of Research

Marketers often cite faulty market research as one of the most frequent causes of new product failure. Research, properly handled, can be invaluable in launching a new product. Yet, many heavily researched products have gone on to failure, and others have succeeded while apparently flying in the face of negative research findings.

There are many valid, useful applications of marketing and communications research. The problem often lies not in the research itself, but in how it is used. As The Conference Board reports:

> Marketers cite insufficient or faulty marketing research as the most frequent cause of new product failure. And lack of thoroughness in identifying real needs in the marketplace, or in spotting early signs of competitors girding up to take the offensive, are often the findings of a new-product postmortem.
>
> Thus, after a new item has failed to come up to expectations, marketers sometimes confess to a "serious misreading" of customer needs, "too little field testing," or "overly optimistic forecasts of market need and acceptance." All too often, it seems, some managements still fall into the trap described by the marketing vice president of one industrial firm, who says: "Simply stated, we decided what our marketplace wanted in this new product without really asking that market what its priorities were."

Dr. Edward M. Tauber, professor of marketing at the University of Southern California and editor of the *Journal of Advertising Research*, enlarged on this theme in an article in the August 1981 issue of *Ad Forum*. He observed:

> The elaborate systems companies have established for screening new products—evaluating every dimension of the product at every stage of development—reflects the strong *risk-averse* attitude of U.S. management . . . Marketing research does not create failures nor will it answer to a greater number of successes.
>
> Present methods of new-product screening such as concept testing, product testing, and test market simulators employ as criteria pretrial and posttrial attitudes and purchase expectations of a sample of consumers upon first exposure to the product. Test markets measure trial and repeat behavior for a relatively short time span (six months to a year) generally covering only the introductory stage of an innovative product's life cycle. Thus, early attitudes and behavior are assumed to be valid predictors of later adoption behavior. The history of truly innovative products contradicts this assumption.

Dr. Tauber cites videodisc, early television, and negative ("who needs it?") findings for other products that were not predictive. He also states that to be a valid screening device for new products, research must measure or simulate the process consumers go through both individually and collectively in adopting new products. He states that the effects of social interaction are not measured by conventional techniques, and offers as evidence the bandwagon effects common in fashion and image items—clothing, cosmetics, beer, wine, cigarettes, etc. I have seen sensitive judgments based on experience and instinct fly in the face of negative research to successfully launch fragrances, designer jeans, wave set compounds, toys, etc. Likewise, such well-researched innovations as the Edsel and Polavision did not go on to success.

Dr. Tauber concludes:

> We could reduce the failure rate of new products to zero by simply discontinuing to launch any. The need is not a lower failure *rate*; it is a greater number of major new business successes. The challenge of predicting new product performance should not focus on pretest market simulators alone. By then it is too late. No simulators ever turned a dog into a star.

> Instead, we need to understand the clues to success much earlier. We need risk-seeking research. We need brave researchers who are willing to tell management when simulators and other current research technology will not work, do not accurately simulate, and can mislead us so that we discard a potential winner. We need research suppliers who refrain from making outrageous claims about near-perfect prediction track records. And, finally, all marketers need to step back, examine history, and attempt to understand the circumstances, process, and requirements for creating a new business success.

The last sentence, of course, summarizes a mission of this book.

Predicting the future is not a certain strength of most research techniques, which are often one-time experiences (or, merely, exposures to unperfected stimulus material out of true selection and use context). Too often, early screening research is so crude as to actually discard the most promising concepts.

Two common techniques are the large-scale mail panel and the mall intercept, in both cases providing a gross impression from atypical respondents (atypical in the sense that the large-scale method purports to offer some projectability). Here, both the stimulus material and the response catalog (questionnaire or imperfect, but in-person, interviewer) generate data for evaluation that is wholly unrelated to the real world.

Another common early screening technique is the group interview. Here, a few people in one or more locations are shown some representation of the concept, and then guided (by a professional interviewer) through a discussion of its pros and cons. It's another atypical setup with atypical respondents (unless the target audience is composed of people with nothing better to do).

A supposed virtue of these popular screening techniques is low cost. In the first two techniques, fairly large numbers (hence, presumed statistical reliability) are surveyed at low cost per respondent. In the last instance, "qualitative understanding . . . in depth" is said to be the yield. Unbelievably, even these less precise responses in low numbers are sometimes quantified and passed along as research findings, rather than as explorations to uncover unanticipated pluses or minuses as well as the prospects' patois and frame of reference.

The point is to use research with knowledge of its limitations. It is all too obvious that most, if not all, techniques are available (for a price) to all competitors in a category. Given expenditures of equal amounts of money and time to evaluate similar concepts, each should find a similar success rate. It's just not that easy.

Despite these words of caution, focus groups continue to be among the most popular forms of research—in many phases of the process. That being so, here are some of the critical lessons learned and reported by the author in the May 27, 1991, issue of *Marketing News*, a publication of the American Marketing Association:

The group moderator must be in tune with the topic, be the end user of the interview service, and (most importantly) understand and appreciate a focused definition of the group to be selected. The moderator(s) selected are to do the job—no substitutes accepted.

The stimulus material, most likely prepared by the buyer of the service— but not necessarily—must be no further developed than the concept to be studied. In early phases, it must be general, even vague enough to elicit different understandings and creative suggested changes.

The group makeup should begin by being the broadest definition of the target, narrowing down as that target and the stimulus material develop specificity through later phases. Recognize that time, site, and other circumstances are not typical of the real world the group may be perceived to represent.

The group perspective must be elicited by the moderator so as to create discussion within the group, almost as if the moderator wasn't in the room. The moderator should not impose direction or refinements, except in atypical situations.

The group vocabulary should be specially noted. Often, it is discovered that the marketer's vocabulary and actual definition of generic descriptors differ from consumers' and prospects'. In refining communications, this is critically essential. You will want to use the most easily perceived common vernacular in future research and in communicating the end product.

The evaluation of results should be separately reported—before comparing notes—by the buyer of the service, who will have viewed via video conferencing (and may even have participated in an audio hookup), or through one-way glass or tapes or, in some circumstances, as an unidentified participant, and by the moderator. After all observation reports are reviewed, only then is an acceptable summary report developed. Any such report should focus on the very positive and the very negative comments that are most forcefully offered by group participants. Focusing on the middle majority of calm acceptance may not be the way to gain greatest rewards from the sessions.

Focus groups are not for decision making. They can be important input steps during the understanding phase of communications development. They can trigger creativity to help shape, improve, or bring new perspective to the assignment. They can lead you back to the drawing board, the test tube, or the information processor. Or to the bank. They should not be used as a basis for a major commitment. Other circumstances, more refined and hopefully more reflective of typical behavior, come into play here. Don't forget, the "focus" of focus groups is usually much greater (and different) attention than is given to an ordinary buying decision, as in low-cost, repeat-purchase categories.

But since collection of knowledge—correct and incorrect—is the basis for judgment, this creation of a false situation to trigger nonprojectable speculations can often yield some general guidance. (But proceed with caution!)

Poor Technology

Technical problems in design or production are the second most common cause of reported new product failures, according to The Conference Board. Such problems often occur in commercial scaling-up from R&D laboratory and pilot plant accomplishments to full-scale production. The electronics and the mechanics are often solved. Yet the quality control of materials and throughput, broader specifications for price-competitive components and ingredients, substitute materials, novel improvements, lowering of quality assurance surveillance, poor labor training, early technical obsolescence vs. more sophisticated competition, overengineering, and overbuilding are among manifestations of poor technology.

The Conference Board report cited some examples:

> We have entered the market with two new products. In both cases, they turned out to be less successful than we had hoped, basically because of inadequate pilot-plant development. In other words, our research was not complete, and therefore, caused considerable delay in modification of the process in order to produce the product quality necessary. In pilot-plant work, we were capable of producing the desired product, but not in full-scale production. We were eventually able to modify our process sufficiently to manufacture the product needed, and our sales and production since that time have been satisfactory.
> *Vice-president, sales—an industrial chemicals company*

With the encouragement of a major fiber company, we introduced a special yarn designed to replace cotton yarns. Despite assurances that the fiber had been evaluated thoroughly and was ready for commercial exploitation, processing the fiber proved more difficult than anticipated, with resultant delays and problems. Our customers became discouraged and turned to other products, leaving the program insufficient in size to justify retention.

We failed to check the claims of the producer thoroughly, yielding instead to their pressure to introduce the product to meet a market trend. We should have confined our program to one or two critical customers who would have been capable of assessing the product's virtues and market potential while affording us the opportunity of evaluating the fiber's processing characteristics in greater detail.
Marketing vice president—a textile company

One of our divisions designed a [new type of wire]. The specifications were very severe and, in a sense, pushed the technology to its outer limits. As a consequence, our product, although generally reliable in laboratory tests, experienced serious difficulties when produced on a quantity basis. After a year of extensive test work and expenditure of considerable sums of money, we are slowly solving the technical problems.

The major lesson to be learned from this incident is to make sure that we understand the limits of the materials and designs with which we are dealing, and that we do not attempt to develop products to meet specifications too rigorous for our manufacturing procedures.
Vice president, technology—a diversified manufacturer

In the not-too-distant painful past, we marketed a product to meet competition in a new area of endeavor. Our market information, return on investment, pricing and packaging were good. Unfortunately, this information caused our product development and R and D people to shortcut the requirements for quality within the product. To meet cost figures they substituted plastics for the bottle enclosure, which let the material inside evaporate and thicken. Efforts were made to overcome the product and container weaknesses, but the sales force had been burned. I removed the product from the market rather than continue to push an inferior product. The lessons are obvious.
Vice president, marketing—a commercial supplies manufacturer

A recent new product developed by our company and introduced at our industry's largest international show has turned out to be far below our expected success.

> The problem developed while our new product was on exhibit. Many people liked what they saw—with the qualifications that just a few more functional capabilities would enhance its salability. Unfortunately, we listened to too many suggestions and proceeded to adapt additional features to the product. Its original $55,000 selling price became $80,000 as a result of these added features. We found the $80,000 product put us in a more unfavorable competitive position than if we had left it in its $55,000 configuration. The lesson learned was not to overengineer a product once it is developed for a specific market need.
> *Senior vice president, marketing—a machinery producer*

As stated by one of the respondents, the lessons are obvious.

Poor Timing

The elements and economics in the late 1970s stifled a surge of new product successes by major makers of snowmobiles, snow throwers, and lawn mowers with two successive years of low precipitation and unprecedented soaring interest rates. Business had been so good for the new models the preceding several years that distributors loaded field inventories in anticipation of record sales volume. Instead, two back-to-back years of demand disappearance were generated by virtually snowless winters, dry springs, and tight money. In these instances, the timing was not wholly within the companies' control.

When time and circumstances change, a formerly unfeasible technology may suddenly become attractive. An example reported in the Sept. 23, 1981, *International Herald Tribune*:

> Experiments with coal-oil mixtures date back to the 19th century, but it took the OPEC-led spiral in the price of oil beginning in 1973 to force the substantial advance in the technology that has occurred in the United States, Japan, and Western Europe.
>
> The oil industry is working with various mixtures . . . increases in the price of crude oil have lifted the cost of industrial fuel oil for use in boilers well above that of steam coal . . . The use of a coal-oil mixture necessitates only minor modifications for the adaptation of liquid fuel boilers.

Since the 1981 report, oil prices took a drop; then "Desert Shield" and "Desert Storm" boosted them again, fluctuating with the fortunes of war and its aftermath.

Caught by the first oil-price leap, the industry raced to downsize its cars, cutting several inches and hundred of pounds to increase fuel economy. When prices were down, big, powerful cars began rolling off the lines, hoping to pick up market share.

The return to the biggies may have been mistimed. Measures to lessen the environmental effects of auto fuel, and government rules regarding sales quotas are set to go into effect in 1998. California, New York, and Massachusetts plan to require auto makers to sell some electric vehicles beginning that year, according to *The New York Times*, July 25, 1995. Already, the cost of gasoline in many foreign markets (i.e., $5 per gallon in Japan) signals downsizing of engines or fuel alternatives in the years ahead.

Other penalties of poor timing have come from moving too fast or too slow, often because of poor planning, organizational problems, or lack of suitable controls. Moving too fast on a crash project can mean overlooking vital factors. Moving too slow can mean missing a market change. The domestic U.S. auto industry, caught by the gasoline price leap, is a model example. The tattered remains of cut velvet on 7th Avenue are legendary witness to the result of being caught out of fashion.

Bringing the product out of the lab too soon or not soon enough . . . Testing that is short-cut or overdone . . . Environmental factors that change the rules of entry . . . A surprise move by competition . . . Whatever timing is out of the new product maker's control bears careful, continual monitoring from the beginning of the project assignment. It can provide a sure go/no go signal rarely on the PERT chart. (PERT is an acronym for Program Evaluation and Review Technique, which plans the dovetailed activities of various functional groups contributing to a project in proper time sequence—planning that points up those activities that are critical from a time standpoint, those that if not accomplished on schedule may delay other elements of the program and conceivably delay attainment of the program goals.)

Poor Distribution Control

In the arena of new items introduction, precise does not necessarily mean accurate. Kenneth A. Harris, Jr., Partner, Cannondale Associates, Evanston, IL, offers this example: A failed pet food launch.

Using the latest geodemographic information, the product's maker knew exactly who would buy the product. Unfortunately, the company wasn't accurate in controlling the distribution of the product and eventually lost the perceived leverage it was going to gain in distribution, promotion, merchandising, and price—ultimately leading to the failure of the new product launch.

The multibillion-dollar pet food category is one of the nine bellwether categories in the supermarket business. Bellwether categories are much like the Dow Jones Industrial Average, which retailers use to determine the overall health of their business. Beginning in 1988, alternative distribution channels began gaining headway in the pet food business. Single-focus pet supply retailers began selling pet food products unique to their stores, without offering distribution in the supermarket trade channel. Additionally, inroads by companies with veterinarian-endorsed products came to market. As the pet food category continued to grow, sales outside of the supermarkets were increasing at three and four times the rate of supermarkets. By 1991, the situation had reached the critical stage, because the pet food category in supermarkets was flat and specialty brands in pet food stores were growing in double digits.

A major pet food maker, realizing the drain on its business out of the supermarket channel, decided to retaliate in force with its own "veterinarian-endorsed" products. After reviewing the latest Nielsen information in January 1991, the decision was made to introduce a new line of pet food into supermarkets. The decision was to repackage a highly successful European pet food line and sell it in the United States. Because the products were ready to go, the timetable was collapsed significantly from a normal 6- to 8-month development period to 6 to 8 weeks.

An entire marketing plan, complete with product, pricing, package, and place (distribution channels) was written, signed, sealed, and delivered within four weeks of the decision to go. While this in itself was no small feat, the plan was sound, and the intensity by which it was put together provided great focus for the entire marketing and sales organization.

The new pet food line (both wet and dry) was to be introduced to veterinarians and receive support from key opinion leaders in the veterinarian community. The line was introduced in both dog food and cat food in most popular sizes.

The products had been rigorously tested and were not only as nutritious for pets as the specialty competitors, they were also preferred by pets in taste testing. The packaging had a professional look, and the price was competitive, or slightly more aggressive than the pet food store brands.

In total, although conventional wisdom would suggest a longer lead time would have ferreted out potential pitfalls in the introductory program, the total marketing plan was in relatively sound shape at launch time.

The ace in the hole for the launch was the use of geodemographic information to clearly indicate to the supermarket retailers where the product would be purchased. More specifically, Spectra™ data was used to identify those stores with the geodemographic makeup of consumers who would (a) be interested in buying the product and (b) live close to the retail outlet—and potentially be shopping in a store other than a supermarket to purchase pet food.

Retailers claimed they were looking for this kind of information to help them better manage the pet food category. Additionally, kiosks were set up in the special stores, which had the greatest likelihood of purchasers for the new product line, with free-standing displays in the form of pet nutrition centers. The store-within-a-store concept was provided for the most geodemographically desirable stores.

The go-to-market plan was set up so not all stores would receive the product (or, at a minimum, they would receive only a handful of items where consumers were less likely to shop for it). In theory, there was no need to have product available in stores where consumers were not going to buy it. Because retailers had said they were amenable to this approach, it was perceived that this controlled launch would be favorably viewed. This was the downfall of the new pet food line's launch.

Upon introduction, retailers decided they wanted distribution of the product in *all of the stores*. They claimed that its maker was forcing them to be selective in distribution and therefore discriminating against some stores where the retailer wanted the product. Even though data proved to them that the stores would not do well with the product, the retailers demanded distribution. As a result, the sales organization lost control quickly, and the product went into 100 percent distribution in the chains in which the product was sold. This caused a twofold problem: (1) The company did not have the capacity to produce the product quickly enough, and (2) there were not enough display vehicles provided at retail because the projected need was not anticipated. Retailers that set up introductory ads had to call off the ads because no product was available. The retailers blamed the marketer for the miscalculation, even though the original marketing plan called for only limited distribution.

The new pet food program never got off the ground. Although certain chains were able to do the kind of volumes originally forecast, there was no way to recover from the initial start-up. Interestingly, a sales organization would normally take the rap for distribution problems in a launch. However, in this case the desire was to aggressively control distribution. This miscalculation was at a much higher level and beyond sales control.

In the end, this veterinarian-endorsed pet food line was pulled from the shelves within eight months of initial launch. One could argue that the accelerated timetable caused the failure. Others might argue that miscalculating retailer desires signalled the failure. The largest issue was that even though the company had precisely calculated who and where the consumers were going to shop, using geodemographic information, the desires of the retailers were not accurately understood, and therefore beyond the power of the company's sales force to control.

In the textbook setting, geodemographic information can be one of the most powerful tools in a new product launch. However, when practicality enters the picture, the needs of the marketplace must be understood. In the case of this example, the product was sound, the need was there, and the plan potentially would have worked. Overreliance on the geodemographic technique of controlling distribution was the Achilles' heel of the program.

This example proves that precise information is not always accurate; the practical realities of a marketplace must be taken into consideration.

Other Reasons

There is an almost endless array of other reasons for new product failures, many related to the quality of management. The most successful companies have few marketplace failures, but lots of conceptual, prototype (or analog) failures at a stage where it doesn't cost so much.

Among some of the other reasons for failure are:

- Inadequate market analysis
- Poor assumptions, or misidentified opportunities
- Overpowering competitive reaction
- Over- (under-) reaction to competition
- Too many (not enough) gap jumps to market entry
- Low product awareness
- Low trial (albeit hardcore repeaters) due to underpromising or mispromising
- High trial, but few repeaters due to overpromising and underdelivery
- Regulations (e.g., FDA) that limit sales
- Unpredicted patent, license, copyright infringement by marketer or by competitor
- Foreign competition (better quality, lower price, etc.)
- Unauthorized style or name knockoff (prevalent in fashion industry)

The Flip Side— Reasons for Success

Sometimes flops provide knowledge that leads to reasons for success. "Just because the company can make it doesn't mean the consumer will have any use for it," said Kraft General Foods Chairman and CEO Michael Miles at the Gorman Conference on New Products in late 1990.

As the nation's largest food company, KGF needs to generate big numbers on new products. The goal is to increase sales by 10 percent each year before acquisitions. Based on current sales, that means a $2.75 billion gain each year. By Miles' calculations, about half of that will come from new products. Assuming that about 30—or one of every ten KGF launches—will be successful, each must deliver about $46 million each year, he estimates.

Reaching this lofty goal, Miles says, requires a six-prong strategy, as reported in the January 1991 issue of *Prepared Foods* magazine:

1. *Start with the consumer,* not with the factory. Summarized:

2. *Research.* To reach sales goals, niche products are not enough. Ideas must be big enough to chase. Group presidents are told there will be very limited credit for long runs that produce short slides.

3. *Find a competitive advantage.* For example, develop a broad technology that can reach across a range of product lines and will be difficult for competition to duplicate.

4. *Move quickly.* Shave time off the test-marketing period; leave less time for competitors to beat you to the punch, being sure to do it right the first time.

5. *Know when to hold 'em and when to fold 'em.* As soon as key indicators signal red, be ruthless about cutting your losses and moving on, even if it occasionally means a healthy baby goes out with the bathwater—because nearly every effort to fix a failing new product results in throwing good money after bad.

6. *Accept, but carefully manage, the financial risks.* Build in some safety valves. Although KGF may spend $750 million on one year's new-product development, it has built in some safety valves, including short payback plans, usually no more than 24 months.

That's an instructive point of view from one of the industry leaders.

Each example carries a different lesson. However, in most instances the lesson is to keep the communications flow going in all directions, all the way out, all the way down, and all the way up—all in the company, of course.

This usually turns into a two-way street. The information flow opens up idea sources. One example, among many I recall, was of an R&D chemist who had discovered a source for a shelf-stable ingredient not then incorporated in any shelf-stable products. And the company's R&D labs had no assignments for which it was applicable. And no budget to work on exploratory applications for such. However, I was able to outsource a concept incorporating the ingredient . . . which I presented as part of a club luncheon side dish to a member of management. He thought it delicious. I told him it was made from his product. (And to this day, it is a very successful one.)

Be accessible—outside the company, as well as inside. For example, let the trade publication reps in your field chat up with you as they do with so many of your competitors. You'll know what others in your business are up to; you may even learn of fixable flops and potential licensing opportunities that mesh with your company's growth strategy.

Top management commitment to developing new business is reportedly one of the keys to success—that coupled with the key factors of a longer-range perspective, recognition for technological creativity, and encouragement of entrepreneurship, as Figures 2-1 and 2-2 show.

Although new product success requires careful execution of research and marketing, there may also be less obvious signs that management considers the new product important. In a survey of five new product consultants, *New Product Development*, a Point Pleasant, NJ, newsletter, came up with 20 critical questions to determine if management will support the effort. According to the newsletter: "Fifteen or more affirmative answers mean the product's success is almost assured. Eleven to 14 suggest probable success and eight to ten indicate a 'coin toss.' "

Here is the quiz.

1. Has the product been in development for a year?

2. Does your company now make a similar product?

Figure 2-1 Factors associated with success in new product development

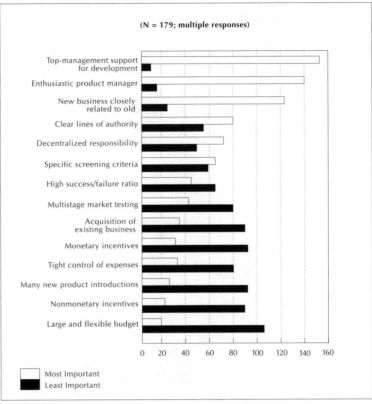

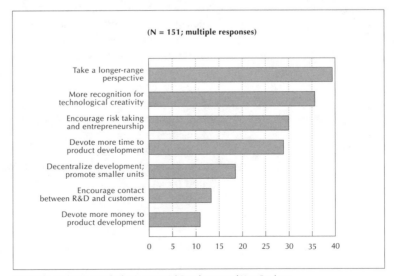

Source: The Conference Board: *The Commercial Development of New Products*

Figure 2-2 Conditions that would encourage new product development

Source: The Conference Board: *The Commercial Development of New Products*

3. Does your company now sell to a related customer market?

4. Is research and development at least one-third of the product budget?

5. Will the product be test-marketed for at least six months?

6. Does the person in charge have a private secretary?

7. Will the ad budget be at least 5 percent of anticipated sales?

8. Will a recognized brand name be on the product?

9. Would the company take a loss on it for the first year?

10. Does the company "need" the product more than it "wants" it?

11. Have three samples of advertising copy been developed?

12. Is the product really new, as opposed to improved?

13. Can the decision to buy it be made by only one person?

14. Is the product to be made in fewer than five versions?

15. Will the product not need service and repair?

16. Does the development team have a working code name?

17. Will the company president see the project leader without an appointment?

18. Did the project leader make a go of the last two projects?

19. Will the product be on the market for more than ten years?

20. Would the project leader quit and take the items with him or her if the company says it won't back it?

And so it goes. In summary, it is obvious that successful new products programs are a balanced mixture of good planning, good management, appealing concepts, research well employed but used with discretion, good timing, appropriate risk-taking—and a modicum of just plain good luck.

Whatever the reason for your new products record, a systematic review of new product management is useful. The Booz Allen & Hamilton New Products Management Scorecard shown in Figure 2-3 can help provide a quick overview.

Figure 2-3 Booz Allen & Hamilton's New Products Management Scorecard
Determine how well your company manages new products.
Rate your company from 1–10 points for each question.
(10 = "Fully meets"; 5 = "Partially meets"; and 1 = "Does not meet")

	SCORE
1. Our corporate growth plan includes an explicit strategic description on the role of internally developed new products over the next five years.	_____
2. We have a well-defined new product strategy which identifies the financial gap and strategic roles which new products must satisfy.	_____
3. We establish different hurdle rates, based on associated risk.	_____
4. We have had a systematic, yet adaptive, new products process in place for at least five years.	_____
5. Idea generation for use begins **after** we have identified external market niches and assessed our internal competitive strengths.	_____
6. We have a formalized monitoring and tracking system in place to measure cost per introduction and new product performance against established objectives.	_____
7. We have compensation programs that encourage entrepreneurship, reward risk-takers, and reinforce innovative management.	_____
8. We have a clear understanding of who is responsible for new product development.	
9. Top management provides consistent commitment to new products in terms of funds and requisite managerial know-how.	_____
10. We adapt our new products organization to match the requirements of our new products portfolio.	_____
TOTAL	======

SCORE

90–100   We are one of the best!
80–89   Improvement areas exist, but we're in good shape.
70–79   We should consider making changes to our new products program.
<70   We better get some assistance in managing new products.

By permission. ©Booz Allen & Hamilton, Inc.

3

The Hierarchy of New Products

This book hopes to be helpful in the development of new businesses that fit marketing-oriented companies—rather than those that serve the goals and prime financial orientations of holding companies and conglomerates.

A company is marketing-oriented if its organizing concept is to serve customer needs, albeit with rewards to shareholders and a demonstrated policy of social responsibility.

Earlier, we defined a progression of new business activities, building from those that were close-in slightly new product refinements to far-reaching new businesses. These broad divisions, which will be treated in some detail in this chapter, move from the evolution of existing products through the expansion of an existing brand/product franchise and new entry into an established category to the creation of new categories and new businesses.

But before we get into that, let's take a look at the role of the brand name itself.

Importance of Brand Name

A rose by any other name would smell as sweet.
—*William Shakespeare*

A rose is a rose is a rose.
—*Gertrude Stein*

If cod was rare, it would sell for more money than lobster.
—*New England fisherman*

Perceptions are key in branding. The fisherman is closer to the truth than Shakespeare or Stein.

Every day this truth hits us in the face. The name "Bruno" calls up a different image than does "Roland."

It isn't often a "Smucker" is the exception that proves the rule.

Much care should go into brand name development and, in the case of entirely new product classes, brand descriptors and generic definitions. These alternatives can be sorted in attribute tests, in cluster analysis, and within the context of winning concept statements that are screened with the name being the only variable.

The brand name, if an existing one, should be well defined and understood. If it is clearly inappropriate to the new product, it should not be used merely because it is broadly known and the alternative of establishing a new brand is costly.

The better known the brand, the tighter the image—which limits its extension, but does often provide an acceptable base for numerous line extensions and flankers close to home. Campbell Soup Company, a perennial winner of new product success scores, is a clear illustration. But the Colgate brand on food didn't work.

Evolution of Existing Product

Repositioning to Find a New Audience

Betty Crocker Potatoes, a shelf-stable convenience product in such specialties as au gratin, scalloped, creamed, sour cream and chives, hash browns, etc., were once backed by an upscale advertising presentation, in party settings, with fancy food. The product varieties dominated a relatively small market.

After being repositioned to the mass market, as "the plain meat potatoes" for everyday family meals, the entire category took wing, with the brand maintaining its dominant share. The market became so large that it attracted low-priced generic and store-brand imitations. An increased emphasis on the quality reputation of the Betty Crocker brand name was General Mills's counter, while maintaining the successful reposition—a reposition that built an entire business.

Recycling

Arm & Hammer baking soda was a staid standby household product. It could be used for baking and scouring, as a poultice, as a freshening agent, for gargling, for deodorizing laundry and diapers, etc. It was an ingredient with a multipurpose image.

Then it was firmly recycled for one prime purpose—as a refrigerator deodorizer. To do that job took an entire package, and that package had to be replaced with predictable frequency. No changes were made in the product, just the emphasis on a contemporary benefit—and business boomed!

Appearance or Form Improvement

Probably the most common change that justifies a claim of newness is an improvement in product appearance or form. This encompasses modifications in formula (new, with lemon added); color (new, blue Cheer); texture/flow (from smooth peanut butter to chunky, from regular oatmeal to creamy, from cleansing cream to lotion, from liquid shampoo to creams and gels); graphics (paper towel "prints," designer-signature fabrics, decorated reusable jelly jars, new postage stamp editions); and shape (Mrs. Butterworth pancake syrup in a bottle shaped like the lady herself, beer in barrel-shaped bottles, children's vitamins shaped like animals, dog biscuits made to look like bones, screw-in light bulbs shaped like flames).[1]

Performance Improvement

The second, and most helpful, form of newness embellishing an established product is a performance improvement. It is often accompanied by improvements in appearance and form.

To stay viable, almost any product should constantly be searching for improvement. Even a commodity such as flour has been changed by various milling methods, by bleaching, by agglomerating (Wondra), by combining with other ingredients to give it special qualities (Bisquick). Now it is being recycled to its stone-ground, unbleached origins to create other new flour products.

But let us turn to the nation's leading advertiser, generally regarded as one of the premier consumer product marketers, for an analysis of performance improvements as the path to continuing newness leading to continuing success. Edwin L. Artzt, then Procter & Gamble's chairman and chief executive, spoke at Harvard University in late 1994. He spoke of reinvigorating products to keep them new. Tide is a dramatic example. After five decades, its forever-young performance keeps it the leader in washday products. Excerpts from Artzt's Harvard speech are presented on page 59.

---

[1] For complete discussion, see Chapter 20, New Product Communications

Ingredient Change

Performance improvements come about through modifications in structure, assembly, and formulation. Often these involve new active additives, new processing techniques, substitute ingredients, and even subtraction of component parts or ingredients.

Flour was improved when the bran was removed. Now it makes news when bran is added back. Air was added to Ivory soap and it floated!—distinctive point of difference. Cocoa butter, legendary for its emollient properties on the human skin, was added to bath soap and The Dial Corporation launched TONE Soap. Spray lacquers were made water-soluble, and a spate of soft-holding hair sprays hit the market. P&G added fragrance to its Puffs brand facial tissues, and Crown-Zellerbach (now James River Corporation) incorporated skin conditioners in its Chiffon brand tissues. Bristol-Myers buffered its aspirin. Crest was the first toothpaste to include stannous fluoride. Typewriters replaced spool ribbons with cartridges, just as word processors replaced typewriters.

Packaging Improvement

Package construction improvements add newness by improving convenience of use, attractiveness, reusability, bulk, weight, portability, and by utilizing the characteristics of new materials and technological changes to modify the package to fit modern processing, recyclable disposal and life style.

A dramatic example was brought to the 7,000-year-old wine business in the summer of 1994, when Robert Mondavi Winery made the first important development in wine packaging since Dom Perignon adapted the cork from Iberian fruit juice containers to wine bottles.

The marketplace was asking for some new way to avoid foils—and Mondavi was the first to come up with an environmentally sound solution—a godsend for consumers, the restaurant trade, etc.

Mondavi wanted a dramatic, visual statement that would serve as a tribute to its outstanding Napa Valley wines, artistic as well as functional packaging. The unique, flange-top bottles are labeled and packaged with recycled and recyclable paper products. The natural deckle edge label—custom-designed, proprietary paper stock—is patterned after handmade paper samples containing vine clippings from the vineyards. A natural paper and beeswax seal closure is affixed atop the cork, replacing the usual metal or plastic capsule. With no metal capsule to cut, remove and discard, a few steps are eliminated—a cork puller is simply inserted directly into the paper and wax seal.

The bottom line is a package closure better for the consumer, better for the environment, and that is attractive, functional, and innovative.

It's called the B-Cap Seal—Mondavi's finest contribution to the art of packaging (see Figure 3-1). This recycled-paper and wax cork seal replaces lead, tin, and plastic seals, providing many added values. In addi-

Figure 3-1 Mondavi's new environmentally oriented wine corkage

A   *Source*: Michael Bordenaro   B   *Source*: Robert Mondavi Winery

"Our agricultural practices go beyond organic farming, and our new package reflects this approach," says Timothy Mondavi, managing director and "winegrower" at the winery his father established. The handsome new flange-top corkage (A) receives round B-Cap Seals applied with a custom-designed machine (B). "Using a recycled paper seal means we don't have to mine the earth," Tim Mondavi says.

tion to helping reduce the amount of materials used for packaging wine, the B-Caps also reduce costs. The paper and natural wax seals cost approximately $.05 each, while traditional seals can cost $.10 or more.

Robert Mondavi says: "The package itself should tell you there is care and consideration in the winemaking."

Another example of the integration of processing and packaging that has brought about change is the retort pouch, a foil-lined bag that acts as a shelf-stable medium for new food processing and filling technology. It replaces the tin can. An adaptation is the vacuum-sealed Tetra Brik envelope first commonly used in Europe for beverages, both fruit- and dairy-based. In the United States, the canned foods industry was revolutionized by the bi-pack, containing two separately processed recipes (one usually meat-based) marketed in cans that were packed together with an adhesive strip. The components are combined only in the homemaker's heating process before serving, to yield improved taste and texture.

A collapsible filled polybag inside a cardboard box provides a space-saving, easy-dispensing method to store and serve refrigerated wine, which achieved an important share of the popularly priced "jug" wine segment.

Price/Value Change

Price says a lot about how a company values its new products. At introduction, when marketing dollars are apt to be heaviest, it is important to establish an appropriate price point related to value delivered. It is often better to err on the high side, because it is usually easier to lower prices if necessary than to raise them, given a stable economy. Usually, the more innovative and the more specialized products can sustain the largest margins, reserving price flexibility for later stages of market development.

Such pricing flexibility might include bonus-packs, extra ounces, with little extra price; step-up prices for a premium version of a standard product (perhaps packaged as a gift, a common holiday practice in the liquor industry); banded deals, two or more similar or related products marketed together at a special price (the salt-and-pepper picnic set); introductory deals (free razor with the new blades); limited-time-only introductory price-offs; limited edition up-charges; etc.

Expansion of a Brand or Product Franchise

Line Extensions

To the Brand

Line extensions to the brand itself might include additional sizes, colors, flavors, forms, or additives. Thus, for salt, you might consider iodized salt, ice cream freezer salt, deicing salt, sea salt, kosher salt, rock salt, pickling salt. It could be packaged in boxes, jars, cylinders, shakers, and bags. Additional variations might include garlic salt, lemon salt, herbed salt, curried salt, salt with monosodium glutamate, and others in various packaging forms.

It's never too late to leverage a brand. One example is 104-year-old Cracker Jack®. This venerable brand—first introduced in 1893 at the Columbian Exposition in Chicago—made its first major brand extension in 1992 with Butter Toffee Cracker Jack®. In late 1994, Borden launched another significant category expansion with Cracker Jack® Nutty Deluxe, butter toffee–glazed popcorn with almonds & pecans (Figure 3-2). Then, in 1996, NEW Fat Free Original Cracker Jack® Caramel Coated Popcorn and NEW Fat Free Original Cracker Jack® Butter Toffee Glazed Popcorn were introduced.

For Different Brands

Similar products can be marketed under different brand names. This is a way to extend a line with new positionings in very large categories. Examples are coffee, cereals, detergents.

Flankers to the Brand

Brand flankers are additional affinity products under the same brand umbrella. Brand-name salt spawns flanker pepper—black pepper, white pepper, peppercorns (white, black, green, pink)—which goes on to inspire an ever-lengthening assortment of line-extending spices, seasonings, and flavorings. Even better examples are seen in a stroll through a hardware store's nuts-and-bolts department!

Figure 3-2 Century-old Cracker Jack® extends brand

A   B

The first significant category extension for 1893's brand and product introduction of Cracker Jack® was in 1992, with the new flavor butter-toffee and peanuts launch (A), followed in 1994 with the second new confection in more than 100 years to carry the famous brand name: Cracker Jack® Nutty Deluxe, Glazed Popcorn Clusters with Almonds & Pecans (B). Then, in 1996, two fat-free extensions were introduced: Caramel Coated Popcorn and Butter Toffee Glazed Popcorn.

A successful example of both line extensions and flankers is Land O'Lakes' entry into the table spread market.[2] About 76 years ago, the farmer cooperative introduced the first important branded sweet cream butter; then it innovated by portion-packaging it; then it introduced line extensions in unsalted sticks, whipped versions of both lightly salted and unsalted, plus various sizes and various forms (including individual serving pats) for the food-service market. In the early 1970s, the first true flanker, with its own line extensions, was introduced regionally: Land O Lakes® Margarine, in regular sticks, corn oil, and whipped. In 1981, another flanker, Land O Lakes® Country Morning Blend (a combination of butter and margarine) began its expansion out of test markets, with unsalted sticks, and salted and unsalted tub line extensions. In the early 1990s, Land O'Lakes extended its flagship butter brand by introducing Land O Lakes® Light Butter (a 40-percent-fat product).

---

[2] Land O'Lakes (with apostrophe) is the company name; Land O Lakes (without apostrophe) is the brand name.

Figure 3-3 Land O'Lakes spread extensions

Land O'Lakes dairy cooperative launched its first product—butter, of course—in 1921. It has since expanded in nearly every dairy-based area—butter, margarine and blends, cheese (dairy case and deli), sour cream, no-fat dips, and hot cocoa mix—with much more to come.

In the mid 1980s, Land O'Lakes expanded into the emerging spreads (less than 80 percent fat) segment with its test market of Land O Lakes® Spread with Sweet Cream (a soy oil–based product with 6 percent fresh sweet cream added). In the late 1980s, Land O'Lakes also introduced another line extension: Land O Lakes® Country Morning Blend Light (a 52-percent-fat spread with 25 percent butter).

Land O'Lakes has defined its market as the premium table spread category, not butter alone, but butter and non-butter products at the premium end of the category—with the resultant development and introductions of a lengthening line of products appropriate to its strong brand franchise. Land O'Lakes is the largest-selling brand of butter. In its regional marketing areas, all of Land O'Lakes non-butter products are already among the leading sellers (Figure 3-3). (See case history in Appendix 1-B.)

The best-known example of flanking and extending is found in the automobile business. General Motors has not just one car, but a line of cars for each of its target market segments. At the top end, there are not only the economic prestige divisions, but the social set definitions. A Cadillac as a Brougham d'Elegance seeks a different audience than does the Eldorado, than does the DeVille, than does the Seville. Within each model class, whether for the low-key affluent, the conspicuous consumer, established wealth, or *nouveau riche*, there are various trim options, and, in some segments, coupe and sedan models. Using the same basic chassis selection, GM has developed different lines for different targets, with slightly different price points for comparable models, and (most importantly) large numbers of entirely different dealer-franchise groups for Cadillac, Oldsmobile, Buick, Pontiac, Chevrolet, and now Saturn Corp., and its truck lines. It is the ultimate demonstration of flanking, extending, positioning, and targeting.

New Category

For the Brand

To carry the analogy along: From salt to spices is an easy affinity. A logical new category may be sauces, another may be condiments—still in the same shelf-stable section of the store. Beyond this, tread carefully into other sections, even if it appears brand-appropriate to offer frozen sauce concentrated or refrigerated salad dressings. Consumers see your qualities within a familiar competitive set. Those qualities might not rank as high in other environments where other brand franchises are well established.

Combining Different Brands under a New Category Umbrella

Manufacturers often combine different products with different brand names in a similar category with a unifying use concept. An example is Hormel's line of single-serve entrees, marketed together and positioned as "Short Orders," although branded separately as Hormel Dinty Moore Beef Stew, Mary Kitchen Corned Beef Hash, etc.

New Entry into an Established Category

Even where the product class and the store section may be home ground, an established all-American brand may not comfortably move into foreign territory. Your "Yankee" brand of spices and seasonings might be peculiarly bland and unauthentic on a spaghetti sauce label.

With the technology, materials, and distribution muscle all at hand, do not forestall the entry test. However, consider development of a new, more appropriate brand personality than your present franchise projects. This may encompass a new brand name, position, price point, distribution, and store section. For example, although it was basic in tomatoes and possessed one of the best-known of company names, Campbell Soup Company nonetheless smartly gave its spaghetti sauce an appropriately ethnic label—Prego, not Campbell.

Newness of Brand Name

When entering an established category, consider carefully the necessary brand-name attributes needed. Although a company may have all of the necessary skills and production capacity, it may find that the very strength of its brand inhibits expansion along what may appear to be entirely appropriate lines. In our example above regarding flankers and extensions for a salt company, it might appear that the appropriate reference would be Morton's. Unlikely, however. The Morton brand is so firmly identified with salt that its reputation will modify perceptions of anything else the company makes—thus limiting the world of flavorings to those that are necessarily salty (no fruits, no sweets, no citrus, no vegetables).

A lot of baby food is consumed by senior citizens—yet the preeminent name in the field would be disastrously unappealing for a line of Golden Age Meals for our rapidly increasing proportion of over-60 consumers.

It is almost axiomatic that the more explicit and stronger the brand franchise is, the more limited is its capacity to expand into wholly new categories. The very strength that buys a solid core of basic business acts as a ceiling to major expansion.

For this reason alone, it is necessary to periodically assess the meaning of the brand franchise. Entering an established category with a new product calls for an open-minded approach to branding. Remember, it's the product, not the brand name, you want to sell to the consumer.

New Position

To *position* a product is to locate it in relation to something else; another product or other products in the same class, adjunctive to an established regimen, at a point in time, against a specific target, vs. competition, in an entirely new perception from the established tradition. Examples of advertising themes that helped establish such positions: "The plain paper copier" (vs. others that use special papers or chemicals); "Nature's answer to candy" (vs. other confections that contain artificial preservatives); "The pause that refreshes" (establishes both its regimen and its benefit); "It leaves you breathless" (vs. other types of distilled spirits); "Melts in your mouth—not in your hand" (vs. conventional chocolate candies); "A taste of the country" (locates the wholesome source); "The friendly skies of United" (vs. a concern about big, impersonal carriers); "Babies are our business—our only business" (a tight target served by an established specialized authority).

Designer jeans are an example of taking a mundane utilitarian garment and positioning it as high fashion, thereby increasing the manufacturer's and the retailer's margins, while creating an entirely new demand cycle, from an entirely new market segment. This is not just *re*positioning, because the designer jeans pioneers were not the basic work clothes makers; they were new to the market.

Expanding a Category

Health foods have been around since Adam and Eve. But none so marketing wise and powerful as the first frozen dinners to meet the dietary guidelines of the American Heart Association—introduced in 1988, inspired by then ConAgra Chairman Charles Harper's heart attack: "This isn't just for people on restricted diets. This is for healthy people who like to be healthy."

Harper and his wife, Josie, invented some healthy but tasty dishes at home, convincing him that ConAgra could do the same. "Other low-calorie frozen dinner lines have some dishes that are low in fat and relatively low in salt, but ConAgra's entry is more consistently healthy, nutrition experts say," per February 1989 *Associated Press* report.

That was the beginning—Healthy Choice® was born.

From its "heart healthy" launch nine years ago, a powerful brand has been built—widely credited with pioneering the development of health-positioned foods. Today, more than 70 percent of U.S. homes have tried one or more of the line's 300-plus product varieties in more than 14 grocery categories.

Beginning in October 1995, Healthy Choice bread went into three test markets: Minneapolis, Milwaukee, and Omaha. The line featured three varieties of premium whole-grain breads, and hamburger and hot dog buns. Developed by Omaha-based ConAgra Trading and Processing Companies, the bread line for test marketing was produced by Metz Baking Company, a division of Specialty Foods Corp.

By early 1996, growing at a compound sales rate of more than 38 percent during the previous five years, sales were at a $1.4 billion-plus annual rate. The 1996 budgeted capital spending for growth was up 30

Figure 3-4 ConAgra's brand building of Healthy Choice

From its "heart healthy" launch in 1988, Healthy Choice brand has expanded its appeal to a broad empowerment to eat healthy to the personal benefits of getting taste and healthy: "Healthy Choice. Eat what you like." ConAgra leveraged all of its R&D and manufacturing strengths, starting with frozen dinners and entrees, expanding into specialty areas of many of its companies, including Beatrice Cheese, Golden Valley Microwave Foods, Hunt Wesson, Rosarita-LaChoy, Hunts, Armour Swift-Eckrich—accounting for its wide range of Healthy Choices. Additionally, adding licensing partners in key areas increased its brand power. Two examples: Kellogg, largest cereal company, and Nabisco low-fat cookies and crackers all sold under the Healthy Choice brand name.

percent—the largest percentage increase projected for all leading food and beverage companies, according to the April 1996 *Prepared Foods*. With 90 percent awareness, with a quality image of health, taste, and trust, Healthy Choice was acclaimed the "most successful new product introduction in two decades," by *Advertising Age*. And it's still growing (see Figure 3-4). In summer of 1996, Healthy Choice Recipe Creation Condensed Soups were launched—while also expanding its ready-to-serve soup line. And the healthy foods category continues to grow (see Figure 3-5).

In September, Healthy Choice's leading brand of nutritionally positioned pasta sauces expanded with Garlic Lovers™, the first line of pasta sauces to meet customers' growing preference for garlic-flavored foods. The $15 million television introduction was supported by freestanding newspaper coupons.

Also in September, Healthy Choice launched its largest product introduction and reformulation of its frozen foods line since its 1988 debut. The brand features eight new meals, overall taste improvements and several larger-portion entrees with more vegetables.

1996 was an exceptionally big year for Healthy Choice's category expansion.

Figure 3-5 Healthy Choice Soups

A

B

Healthy Choice Recipe Creations Condensed Soup—a new line of six innovative recipe soups from the makers of Healthy Choice—provides a great tasting, nutritious base for quick, easy-to-prepare homemade meals. The line became available in grocery stores nationwide in September 1996.

Healthy Choice Soups brings great taste and superior nutrition to two new low-fat, creamy soup varieties, Chicken Alfredo with Pasta and Broccoli & Cheddar. These are the first cheese-based, health-positioned ready-to-serve soups available to consumers. Each variety delivers no more than 2.5 grams of fat, 480 milligrams of sodium, 130 calories and 10 milligrams of cholesterol per serving.

Appearance or Form Difference

While a change in texture or form may be sufficient to breathe new life into an established brand—where its performance has already found acceptance, and only a marginal difference is needed to stimulate some retrial or reawaken interest—this is generally *not* an important enough base for a new product entry. The exception, of course, is when the new form is entirely new to the category.

A typical example is Softsoap brand liquid soap in a pump dispenser, which quickly captured a significant share of the toilet soap market by promising a new, non-messy form of soap and no-waste economy when compared with the conventional bar form. Its rise to a 9 percent market share caught the attention of the major soapers, who countered with their own versions.

An earlier example of a small marketer creating a new category that attracted major soapers was Lestoil cleaning agent. It took off dramatically, then was overtaken by the major soapers, e.g., Mr. Clean from P&G and Ajax from Colgate.

This is not to suggest that any new appearance or form difference launched by a nonmajor manufacturer will be overtaken by the entrenched leaders of major categories. It is, however, a consideration that must be taken into account.

While it may be sufficient for the majors to create change in a modest way, supported by major marketing investments, minor marketers need to invade the market with significant appearance and form differences. Examples include Kitchens of Sara Lee, with a new appearance, form, and standard of packaged baked goods quality; and Pearl Drops Tooth Polish from Carter Products, an exclusive special-purpose dentifrice in a new form, appearance, and package (squeeze bottle).

Performance Difference

A superior performance that is readily evident—often in a side-by-side comparison—is a powerful appeal to any customer. Examples are all around, from sustained-release medication that meters dosage over time or a choice of sunscreens that let the tanner control the result, to longer-lasting house paint and fertilizers with built-in weed killers.

One of the most dramatic performance differences is the leadership in cellular technology evolved from Motorola's broad-based participation in the communications industry dating back to the 1920s. In mid-1994, Motorola introduced the MicroTAC Elite™—the world's lightest cellular telephone, weighing a mere 3.9 ounces—less than a D-cell battery. Also introduced at same time was the Micro Digital Elite™, the latest edition to the Time Division Multiple Access (TDMA) family of phones.

As one of the world's leading providers of wireless communications, semiconductors, and advanced electronic systems and services, its equipment businesses include cellular telephone, two-way radio, paging and data communications, personal communications, automotive, defense and space electronics, and computers. Communications devices, computers, and millions of consumer products are powered by Motorola semiconductors.

"While we have continually reduced the size and weight of our family of MicroTAC personal phones, we have never forgotten that a phone must feel like a phone," says Robert N. Weisshappel, senior vice president and general manager of Motorola's Cellular Subscriber Group. "Our phones are available with a variety of beneficial features allowing consumers to stay in touch using a phone designed in a compact and convenient package."

A leader in globalization, Motorola cellular telephones are available in more than 80 countries worldwide. With an estimated 33 million cellular phone users by the year 2000, more and more people will be using cellular phones to stay in touch in their personal and business lives (Figure 3-6).

Packaging Difference

Packaging differences that become the basis for new products are more significant than those packaging improvements that contribute to more convenient product usability or novel appearance.

Figure 3-6 Motorola cellular telephones

Two Motorola mid-1994 introductions: MicroTAC Elite™—the world's lightest cellular telephone, weighing a mere 3.9 ounces—less than a D-cell battery, and (right) the Micro Digital Elite™, the latest edition to the Time Division Multiple Access (TDMA) family of phones.

Source: Motorola, Inc.

One packaging change that created entire industries was the aerosol can, which made possible fine mist sprays, instant foams, and controlled delivery of liquid and lotion streams. New aerosols continue to evolve. Low-pressure, soft-sided packages lightly spray fine powders. The Sepro can has been developed for pressure dispensing where the propellant and the ingredient should not mix. In this instance, it made possible push-button food products (such as cheese spreads).

First introduced in Europe, food products that had formerly required refrigeration to preserve quality, now are available packaged as extended-life, shelf-stable. This packaging difference has grown in popularity for dairy and various beverage combinations, such as Creative Beverages, Inc.'s "Caffe Fantastico" cappucino milk beverage, which leverages the growing popularity of flavored coffee.

Resource Difference

A different ingredient, source, and/or location of supply or technology for making a product can be the basis for an entirely new product.

By-products from one process can become a resource for making others. The sludge from paper making becomes charcoal briquets; wood pulp from lumber mills becomes plastic; garbage becomes fuel, minute quantities of silver become antiseptic preservatives.

Labor rates and special economic arrangements in less-developed countries make possible new, competitively priced products. Automation of electronic elements makes possible a change in life-style, education, and commerce for millions with the introduction of the hand-held solar-powered calculator, palmtop computers, wristwatch pager, language translator, memory bank, etc. With great advances in digital technology and compression techniques, laser-based gyroscopes and superconductivity, even more advanced, precise, automated electronics are ahead.

Price/Value Difference

A better value, a better price, or both has always been a strong new product introductory position. When this translates to lower price for comparable value, it is difficult to sustain over time, except possibly for basic commodities.

Generic consumables are a present-day example, motivated by the retailer's response to inflation effects on the grocery dollar. Here the trade-offs may be minimum (but acceptable) quality and marketing margins.

Another type of price/value difference is offering the finest quality at its consequent price, both becoming virtues to be considered by the target customer. Hallmark built an industry-dominating business in greeting cards based on the appeal: "When you care enough to give the very best." Outlets were exclusive. Nothing ever cut-price.

From Häagen-Dazs ice cream to the three-star restaurants of France, there is always a market for quality. But once that quality slips, once a maker compromises with a few changes here and there to save a dollar or two, failure follows.

If the price must be high to deliver the quality—make the price a virtue of the new product.

If the quality is compromised to make the price low, make its basic nature an acceptable virtue of the new product.

Sometimes, both high quality and low price are possible. BIC introduced its disposable lighters as the least expensive. It put the cost into the product, stripped away unnecessary features (refillable, replacement flints, etc.) to undercut the market's then-prevailing low price point.

Distribution Pattern Difference

Introducing new products through new distribution patterns can often steal a march on competition and provide a point-of-difference customer benefit.

As an example, Control Data and other business systems makers have experimented with storefront computer hardware and software outlets, convenient to independent retailers, small manufacturers, and other businesses who might ordinarily not be considered prime targets by their sales forces. Just as importantly, these prospects might not normally seek out new data processing assistance because of a fear of the complications, applicability, and price.

In a different area, impelled by the auto fuel crunch, the increase in numbers of working women, and the premium on free time, home grocery delivery has been reintroduced in several areas. Groceries are now ordered by telephone, even fax—and two-way cable makes possible electronic catalog ordering and billing.

And this ties into other forms of direct response marketing, using inquiry-stimulating print media, telephone, and the mails, which have become newly important to new-product introductions. Such methods are best suited to narrow interest categories where selective lists make it cost-efficient to solicit the prospect directly. When current experiments with credit cards inserted into telephone terminals are fully exploited, direct response marketing will really take off!

Other examples:

- Tombstone Pizza was introduced through saloons, then went to groceries as a new form of distribution.

- While most snacks and confections started out as individual servings sold at cashier counters and through vending machines, General Mills began distribution of its Nature Valley granola snacks in multiple-packs through groceries, then added counter and vending distribution for incremental sales and sampling.

New Category

When a company enters a new category, it must have a complete business development program, which includes discovering what outside expertise may be necessary. Even when the new category is relatively close, with many common characteristics, this is often necessary.

New Solution to an Old Problem

One of the most dramatic examples of a new solution to an old problem is the national introduction in late 1983 of Depend® disposable undergarments by Kimberly-Clark Corporation. The old problem is incontinence, chronically or under special circumstances. It affects at least ten million adult Americans. Until now, only makeshift solutions were available to ambulatory sufferers from this common problem—often tying them down to locations and situations that prevent their active participation in social and other recreational events remote from toilet facilities. Now this old problem has led to a new consumer benefit: disposable products with a patented absorbency system for men and women who need comfortable, discreet, and effective protection from bladder control problems. Kimberly-Clark extended its unique absorbency technology, first developed for other types of personal care products, to create an entirely new consumer disposables market.

Since Depend's introduction, the retail incontinence category has seen tremendous growth because of increased category penetration and the "graying of America." Ten years after Depend's introduction, the category had more than doubled in size, generating more than $450 million in retail sales in 1994. According to Robert D. Thibault, Kimberly-Clark's Adult Care Sector president: "By the year 2000, retail sales are expected to increase 70 percent." In 1995, it was expected to become a billion-unit category. The growth of the category in recent years has been double-digit vs. the 3 percent growth rate experienced by other health and beauty care products, Mr. Thibault reports.

While incontinence products once were sold primarily in drug stores, today they are merchandised and promoted by all major food, drug, and mass merchandise outlets.

Market segmentation has been an important key to Kimberly-Clark's new product developments and introductions in the "graying of America" field—the incontinence market, which is growing almost twice as fast as the general population. In 1994, it was estimated that about 15 million individuals in the United States are affected by incontinence, with about half experiencing nominal or very light incontinence. For the most part, that half considers its condition a nuisance and attempts to meet its needs with such products as facial and bath tissue or feminine care products. Category penetration of this segment is low. About five million consumers experience light incontinence. They use a variety of incontinent pads and undergarments, and the segment is growing rapidly.

About 2.5 million consumers have moderate to heavy incontinence and typically use undergarments and briefs. These products allow individuals suffering from a loss of bladder control to live a more normal life. Penetration of these segments is relatively high.

Kimberly-Clark breaks out sales of incontinence products by major product forms. It was the first company to recognize the need for a product for heavy incontinence. Thus, the Depend line introduced its Briefs, to provide the best protection for that category, typically much older and slightly more females than males. Household penetration of these segments is relatively high. The Depend Briefs line is offered in three sizes plus an overnight version with extra absorbence. "Despite fierce competition, Depend briefs still lead the market with a 55 percent share of the segment," Mr. Thibault reported to a financial analyst meeting in late 1994.

Undergarments represent about a third of category sales. The undergarment is the mainstay product for consumers with moderate to heavy incontinence. The overwhelming majority of these consumers are female, with a median age of 65. Category penetration is high.

Since Depend's introduction in the mid-1980s, it has been the category leader. Only Kimberly-Clark offers such a broad choice, including undergarments with elastic legs and either button straps or adjustable straps from Velcro USA and undergarments with nonelastic legs and button straps. Kimberly-Clark expects its undergarment business to grow steadily—reflecting consumer preference for Depend (Figure 3-7).

Figure 3-7   Old problem = new opportunities for Depend® and Poise®

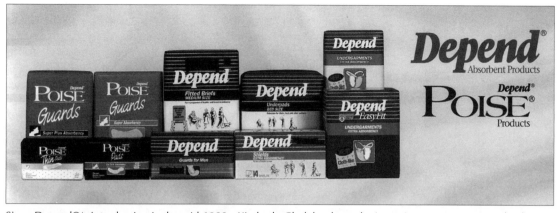

Since Depend®'s introduction in the mid-1980s, Kimberly-Clark has been the incontinence-care category leader, applying its technological expertise, its experience in absorbent tissues, pads, diapers, and more—and expanding the basic Depend product line into the many new areas of adult incontinence care: a category expected to increase to more than $750 million annual retail sales by the year 2000.

Source: Kimberly-Clark Corporation

Depend Guards represent 14 percent of category sales. Currently they are used almost exclusively by females with moderate incontinence. However, many men have the problem also—which led Kimberly-Clark to introduce a guard product designed for the male anatomy in June of 1994—an excellent example of technology transfer. (In this case, the transfer was of the technology developed for the company's disposable diaper business to its incontinence care business to better meet the needs of male consumers.)

Shields and underpads complete the Depend lineup and compete for the remaining 16 percent share of category sales.

But there are even more old problems that need new solutions.

Kimberly-Clark addressed this opportunity with Poise® incontinence pads in 1992 created to meet the needs of females with light incontinence. This segment, virtually nonexistent until very recently, is predicted to generate half of all category sales—overtaking undergarments as the largest segment.

Poise pads were another example of technology transfer. In its case, its three absorbencies combine the chassis of a Kotex maxi pad with the absorbent structure of a disposable diaper. Since the introduction of Poise pads, Kimberly-Clark's share of the incontinence market grew nearly nine points—to 88 percent, it was reported in the fall of 1994.

Advertising has been a significant factor in the growth of Kimberly-Clark's incontinence care business. Actress June Allyson, spokesperson for Depend products, played an important role in reducing the social stigma associated with incontinence. Through her, the message was delivered in a compassionate way, encouraging consumers to "Get Back Into Life With Depend" and to not let incontinence affect their quality of life.

The demographics of the pads user, female and 45 years and older, dictated a different approach than the Depend advertising. Advertising for Poise pads focuses on a trusting, one-on-one communication between a woman and the viewer.

Other factors in the Depend and Poise success have been strong brand names and superior products developed from Kimberly-Clark technology in fibers, absorbency, and nonwovens. Being first to market with innovative products and finding ways to continually reduce costs are other important elements.

"The impact of this tradition of superior products and innovation is clear: Total sales of Depend and Poise products represent more than 50 percent of category sales," Kimberly-Clark's Thibault states, adding: "We are aggressively taking the success of Depend products worldwide. The brand is available in Canada, Mexico, the United Kingdom, Germany, France, Korea, Australia, and more than 20 other countries." Globalization continues.

Solution to a New Problem

The cost of energy has made business and consumer alike alert to ways to economize. Here again 3M has identified this "new" problem and come up with a solution that becomes a new category for the company. It is the 3M Energy Savings Center, which carries a broad line of do-it-yourself, easy-to-install barriers against heat and cooling loss.

In a totally different area, smokers' clinics were spawned by the identification of health hazards created by products of another category.

Clairol and Gillette were both dominant factors in beauty aid toiletries, then entered the small electric appliance business with assortments of curlers, hot combs, and dryers. Hairstyles and habit changes created new beauty care problems that opened up the new category for exploitation.

Creation of a New Need

Fads and fashion come first to mind. These may relate to life-style, vanity, or the conventional wisdom of the moment.

As an example, many current dietary practices arose in response to newly created needs; for vitamins (natural or otherwise), low cholesterol and polyunsaturated fats, organically grown produce, and fiber-filled cereals. Health-consciousness and social self-consciousness with slimness have created spas, clinics, appliances, and entire lines of food and drug products.

Satisfying the need for aural gratification on the jog (and, accordingly, shutting out the rest—perhaps another new need—of the world) are lightweight, earphone-enclosed stereo radios.

Fitness for fitness' sake was one thing. Fitness as a fad created a new need. Today, room additions are made to house the Nautilus machine. The rumpus room has given way to the home health club.

Revival of an Outmoded or Dead/Dying Category

In new products, many opportunities come full circle. The herbs, emollients, and potions of folklore became today's newly discovered medicaments. The ancient properties of aloe vera slick the sunning skins on the sands of St. Tropez's Tahiti beach, while jetsetters (and the rest of us mere mortals) sip millions of gallons of expensive naturally gaseous mineral water from distinctively shaped pale-green bottles. Great-grandfather may have gone to Baden-Baden for the waters. Now they are contemporary chic in the home refrigerator.

Innovation

For new products definition, an innovation is an invented or discovered new use, an adjunctive feature, or a superior sophistication that is part of an already established product or category. For example: The Internet resources of the global computer network, e-mail, the World Wide Web, Lexis/Nexis, and other such tools. The CD-ROM. Floppy disk. Fax. Shelf-stable packaging of formerly refrigerated products.

A more recent innovation introduced in the United States is the Wonderbra®—the "dramatic cleavage" bra that won the 1995 Special Award from the Council of Fashion Designers of America (CFDA) "for creating a phenomenon never before experienced in this industry." Wonderbra® (Figure 3-8) was included among lists of the top ten products by *Fortune, Time, Newsweek, U.S. News & World Report, USA Today, Advertising Age*, and lots more (not to mention its humorous accolades in David Letterman's "Top Ten," Jay Leno, "Entertainment Tonight," and a *New Yorker* cartoon.)

During the product's New York launch, it sold out at the rate of one bra every 15 seconds. In Charlotte, NC, the bra sold 100 percent of its stock in 1 day. Since its launch, Wonderbra® has become the number-one-ranked push-up bra in dollar shares, holding 36.5 percent of the market.

What inspired Wonderbra®?

How does it differ from other push-ups?

It was created more than 30 years ago for a Canadian company that later became part of Sara Lee Intimates, maker of the Wonderbra®. Its creator, Louise Poirier, a talented designer, wanting to enhance her slight silhouette, designed a bra that naturally enhances the bustline and creates cleavage. Its secret: ingenious engineering that creates dramatic cleavage with a natural projection that does not compress the breasts and does not need a lot of padding. Some of the many features that set it

Figure 3-8 Daring denim—Wonderbra®

The One and Only Wonderbra® . . . "Anywear" is the perfect accessory for casual dressing—it's the newest offering from Wonderbra®, an innovation from Sara Lee Intimates.

apart from competition: Three-part cup construction, precision-angled back and underwire cups, fiberfill cups and removable pads, back support, adjustable nonstretch straps—and more.

And now Wonderbra® incorporates this ingenious engineering for swimwear, as well as innerwear/outerwear, bras that can be worn "anywear," under a blouse or all by itself.

Invention and Discovery

Research breakthroughs build businesses and whole industries. Examples are gene-splicing, space satellite communications, high-capacity memory chips, high-definition television, and laser discs—the list is almost endless, and is increasing at a geometric rate. Most companies do applied research, putting knowledge together in new ways to innovate and invent. High technology companies do basic research as well, spending billions to unlock the secrets of science.

Putting knowledge together in new ways to innovate and invent is an encouraged tradition at 3M. For example: In the early 1990s, a strategic marketing decision united the efforts of more than 80 3M marketers, scientists, and engineers. In record time, the team created the Scotch-Brite™ Never Rust™ Wool Soap Pad through a process that exemplifies 3M's commitment to innovation and customer satisfaction.

Completing a Product Line

3M decided to become a full-line supplier of cleaning pads and sponges by building on the Scotch-Brite consumer brand loyalty and established retailer relationships. Missing was a soaped product similar to steel wool pads.

Rather than introducing just another steel wool pad into the $100 million market, 3M was determined to "change the basis of competition" in a product category, where the most recent innovation was the introduction of steel wool in 1917.

Marketers assessed consumer preferences, knowing they needed a product that would draw consumers away from traditional steel wool pads. People liked steel wool pads' size, shape, and cleaning power, 3M found, but more than 90 percent of those asked objected to rust and splinters.

Soda Bottles Turned Soap Pads

The idea for the new soap pad struck a chord with inventors Ray Heyer and Connie Hubbard, who had worked on a similar project. Earlier attempts at creating a new scouring pad had failed because scientists could not work cost-effectively using conventional methods. The inventors thought about the product in environmentally responsible terms and charted a new direction.

Heyer and Hubbard worked with recycled polyethylene terephthalate (PET), a polyester plastic used for soft drink bottles and containers. Other companies were turning PET into new beverage containers, fiber-fill for sleeping bags and carpeting; using it to make soaped scrubbing pads would be a first. The Never Rust product team chose phosphorous-free detergent for the cleaning agent and designed manufacturing equipment and processes so it conserved energy and generated minimal by-products. The bright orange and yellow Never Rust boxes are made from recycled chipboard.

Turning shredded PET into a three-dimensional abrasive fiber that held soap and kept its shape through repeated scrubbing was no easy task. Heyer and Hubbard faced some unprecedented challenges. Given the freedom of trial and error, they ingeniously discovered solutions in existing 3M technologies. Making a three-dimensional abrasive pad was a tedious manual process. Heyer found a better way using old coating equipment he literally dug out of the mud in the St. Paul plant, where it had once been used to make sandpaper. The coating process he and Hubbard eventually developed was so innovative, it is now protected by a patent. The soap pad product is patented as well (Figure 3-9).

Figure 3-9 3M's Scotch-Brite™ Never Rust™ wool soap pad

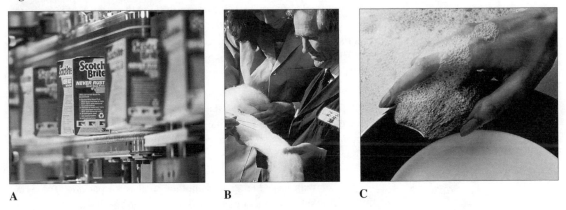

A   B   C

Never Rust™ rolling off 3M production line (A). Never Rust™ inventors Connie Hubbard and Raymond Heyer (B). Scotch-Brite™ Never Rust™ wool soap pad in action (C).

Source: 3M

If You Build It, They Will Buy

As 3M engineers translated the inventors' work into a manufacturing process, it became clear the unique soap pads required a new factory for their production. The company would make that kind of investment if the product's success was assured. The marketing team kicked into high gear.

Preliminary market research using lab-made pads showed Never Rust earned a 63 percent overall preference rating, compared to a 30 percent rating for traditional steel wool pads. A pilot plant produced enough product to support in-home testing in six cities: Minneapolis, Chicago, Milwaukee, Columbus, St. Louis, and Indianapolis. Repurchase patterns were tracked. Never Rust wool soap pads earned an unprecedented 20 percent share over 36 weeks in markets supported with television advertising. Like the *Field of Dreams* baseball diamond, 3M built a factory almost miraculously in short time in a rezoned midwestern cornfield. The facility had produced millions of pads in time for the January 1993 product launch.

The Never Rust wool soap pad epitomizes one of 3M's high-impact pacing programs, which compress the cycle time for products with strong market potential to reduce lag between concept and commercialization. The team was empowered to get the job done. Members collectively agreed on deadlines, costs, modifications, and the value of frequent communication. The team eliminated the functional boundaries that might have otherwise created roadblocks.

Strategic Global Marketing

3M's next goal with Never Rust soap pads: increase market penetration worldwide. The international marketing plan proceeded twofold: to capture share in markets such as Brazil, where steel wool pads have a large consumer base, and to attract new consumers in places where steel wool is not commonly used. Never Rust pads were introduced simultaneously in the United States, Canada, Columbia, and New Zealand, then rolled out to 20 more countries.

The development team didn't stop there. A second-generation product introduced in 1994, Scotch-Brite™ Never Scratch™ wool soap pads offer effective cleaning power for nonstick cookware. And, commercial floor polisher pads made from recycled PET are used to polish marble floors.

New Business

Accompanying all the changes in people classification, growing data banks, and computer tracking will be changes in business and industry; in politics, academia, and entertainment; in health care, food, shelter, and more.

This implies defensive strategies to maintain product franchises—and burgeoning opportunities for new products to meet consumer needs. The units of communications—at the point of sale as well as the point of preliminary exploitation—will be of greater range. This necessitates a different approach to product development.

Sheer economics dictate an optimal level of business volume for any product development, merely to sustain the efficiencies of production and the demands of the marketing chain.

Therefore, escalating costs of doing business require a new perspective on product development.

One view is that this will move the emphasis from product development to a broader emphasis on product line development and, in all but the largest categories, to a prime emphasis on new business development and long-range strategic planning. Cost of money, more sophisticated inventory management, escalating media demand and clutter all point to the need for building strong cohesive business franchises, rather than spewing out an unplanned stream of unrelated new products.

As Figure 3-10 shows, improvement of existing products demands the least in time and technology investment, but also probably provides the shortest payout period. As one moves up through product development, line development, and finally business development, each stage requires progressively more input in terms of time and technology, but also holds out the promise of increasingly greater long-term return.

This is not to say that the various aspects of new product development should all give way to long-range business development, but that there should be a balanced program wherein each aspect is given properly proportionate attention, with the shorter range, more mature, established product and category entries funding the longer-range business that will assure the future growth of the company.

Implications are that technology will become more important to those companies with primary marketing skills. Basic research will be-

Figure 3-10 Development perspective

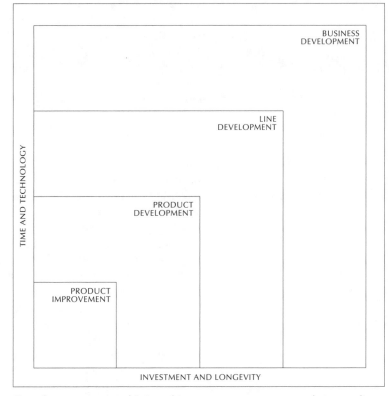

Cost of money, more sophisticated inventory management, escalating media demand, and clutter all point to the need to build strong cohesive business franchises, rather than an unplanned stream of unrelated new products.

come more important to those companies with outstanding applied research. Business differentiation will become more important to those companies with product proliferation expertise.

The accelerating net effect is that the corporate persona will be made up of major business units, each with distinctive, well-defined personalities. Each will strive for a critical mass in its competitive set. The lesser lights will compete as specialists.

In product development, this suggests a trend to two extremes— away from the middle majority where most of the action is today. On the one hand will be the major newly developed business units based on a combination of superior technology and marketing. On the other hand will be special-purpose, limited-need product development units. Between will be the utilizers of slowly evolving industry standards.

More reliable precommercialization research must emerge to meet the demands of the heavy economic risks of a business-building product development commitment.

As we have seen, there are many ways to be new.

Being new is important. Being different is important.

Being *both* new *and* different is the best start toward new product success.

And being able to sustain the impact of a successful new product over time is critical.

Product Life Cycle

In fact, the myth of the product life cycle has been successfully challenged by Procter & Gamble—as Edwin L. Artzt (former chairman/CEO of P&G, now its board's executive committee chairman) demonstrated in his October 20, 1994, address at Harvard University. Following are appropriate extracts from those pertinent examples:

> People are getting smarter about the products they buy. People have gotten more *value* conscious—more quality conscious—and more price conscious. Tastes and habits are changing all over the world, and new trends may start anywhere—in Europe, in Japan, even in California. It's harder to get into business . . . and it's easier to go out of business than at any time I remember.
>
> So . . . what does this mean? Shorter and shorter life cycles for the things we market—or not? At P&G, we don't think so. . . . Today, our worldwide sales are over $30 billion. . . . We do more than half of our business outside the U.S. We market the same types of products—including many U.S. brands—in over 140 countries. [P&G markets more than 300 brands worldwide and is the global leader in a half-dozen major product categories, including Laundry, Feminine Protection, Diapers and Shampoo.]
>
> Our business is brands.
>
> Now a word about our business strategy.
>
> We are an inventor/marketer company. We earn our profit and achieve our growth principally through internal invention . . . and the creation of new and improved products and brands. We think market leadership is important, and we plan for it. Our growth target as a company has been to double our unit volume every ten years. We increase volume by adding new brands to a healthy growing base of established brands.
>
> But the creation of a new brand is a massive investment. A new brand usually involves many years and millions of dollars of upfront research money. On top of this comes

the introductory marketing support, plus capital investment for new plant and equipment. The resulting payout period can extend well beyond any new brand's novelty phase.

A new brand represents an enormous investment and a considerable risk for the company.

How does P&G handle that risk? How do we keep revitalizing our basic business so that new inventions will be extra business—and not a replacement for business lost on dying brands? The answer lies in three basic principles:

First we try to do a thorough job of identifying consumer needs. We identify those needs through in-house and outside market research. In the U.S. alone, we do over five million interviews with consumers each year. We find out how the consumer uses the products, and what they like and dislike about products. We look for trends—even the slightest beginning of a new habit.

We also get unsolicited market research information in the form of 300,000 letters a year from consumers—and more than two and a half million phone calls per year from consumers using the toll-free 800 numbers that appear on our packaging. We keep in touch.

The second principle is a commitment to product advantage. We try to develop products that do a better job of satisfying consumer needs. And we constantly work to keep that advantage as products mature.

We look for big ideas that will bring a discontinuity to the market: compact detergents, for example, or toothpaste that reduces tartar buildup. These are the kinds of innovations that not only maintain our advantage over competition, but also revolutionize entire categories.

The third principle is consistent strategic focus. Our brands have a distinct reason for being and character when we launch them. This strategic focus rarely if ever changes . . . even as we modernize and improve the products—sometimes radically—over the years.

Like people, brands and products are presumed to be mortal. Brands pass through a typical four-phase cycle:

1. A brand is born and goes through a low-volume introductory phase.

2. Then comes the growth phase when volume and profit both rise.

3. After that, maturity. Volume stabilizes, profits start to fall, and increased spending may be needed to sustain the brand.

4. Finally, obsolescence begins, sales volume declines, and the brand quietly dies.

The length of the life cycle and the duration of each phase can vary for different products, but decline and burial eventually occur for one of three reasons:

1. The need for the product may disappear . . . as it did for buggy whips.

2. A better, cheaper, or more convenient product may be developed.

3. An existing competitive product may suddenly gain a decisive advantage.

Any brand that gets itself in one of these pickles is certainly a candidate for life cycle phase #4—obsolescence and decline.

But we don't believe that obsolescence and decline are inevitable—not as long as we anticipate the need for change in our brands.

First of all, the need for our kinds of products seldom disappears. What's more, every brand we market has the same opportunity as its competition. Every brand can become better, cheaper, even more convenient. There certainly is nothing standing in the way of our brands gaining a decisive advantage through superior marketing strategy.

Even the author of the original life cycle theory concedes that the shape and duration of a product's life cycle can be altered. He said it pretty well and I'll quote:

"The challenge of maturity in a product is not to adapt to it, but to change it by revitalizing the product through repackaging, product modifications, appealing to new users, or some combination of marketing strategy changes. Often, a successfully revitalized product offers a higher return on management time and funds invested than does a new product."

Take Tide, for example. Tide was introduced in 1946— nearly 50 years ago—five times the normal life cycle for most consumer products. During those 50 years, many laundry brands have come and gone. . . . In all, Tide has introduced more than 70 performance improvements in the last 48 years.

Tide is alive and kicking. It became the market leader 45 years ago and has remained the market leader ever since. Historically, Tide has maintained somewhere between a 20 and 30 share of market, while the closest competitor has held a six or seven share. That's an extraordinary achievement, and it's directly attributable to the fact that we've kept Tide focused on its original strategic positioning: delivering superior cleaning performance.

Good brands don't really die unless you let them. . . . This is about Procter & Gamble, about brand marketing, about the process of giving established brands the blessing of a long life. And about the debunking of product life cycles.

The next time you are in a store, notice the brands that used to be popular favorites. Notice the brands that have faded and may now be headed downhill. Ask yourself what you might do if they were your brands to:

1. Re-establish consistent strategic focus.

2. Re-establish product advantage.

3. Respond strategically to a changed competitive environment.

4. Appeal to unchanged values within the context of changed habits and lifestyles.

5. Contemporize the benefits of long-established distinctive product advantages.

If your head fills with good ideas, do like that electric shaver fellow did—buy the company.

4

Where Do New Products Come From?*

"*If you do not think about the future, you cannot have one.*"

—JOHN GALSWORTHY

"*The cleverly expressed opposite of any generally accepted idea is worth a fortune to somebody.*"

—F. SCOTT FITZGERALD

There is a constellation of conventional sources for most new product ideas. These "borrowed" ideas range from bringing foreign successes to the United States (feminine hygiene sprays, enzyme detergents) to going to the institutional trades for consumer products (jarred cheese spread and hair-setting gel) to commercializing developments by industry groups and government agencies.

Then there are outside inventors who shape ideas, but do not identify their commercial roles.

There are other, more blatant borrowings: purchased patents and competitive knockoffs.

And, most importantly, there are your own R&D or R&E, who manipulate their sciences to improve basic materials and compounds.

These represent the vast majority of new product offerings—and successes. They do not, however, represent the methods of the originators of the appropriated inspirations.

How do *they* operate—and is it reproducible?

Leaving out single accidents, but not excluding the driving ambition of a single woman, the truly *new* products require a set of attitudes—which may be identified, but not taught. However, they *can* be organized.

---

* This chapter contains material edited from *The Rountree Report* series "Meeting the Challenge of New Products," by George Gruenwald, and from the author's feature in *Marketing News*, May 8, 1995, a publication of the American Marketing Association.

To properly channel the attitudes of curiosity, skepticism, disassembly, perseverance, and perfectionism into one champion group (or being) is the requirement. Everyone knows that the venture team needs a marketing generalist, a technical generalist, and probably a financial woman—and the later appurtenances thereto (legal, production, purchasing, etc.). And everyone knows the chronology of procedures.

Even though these and other far-out categories were not part of the screening, it is important to look at the conventional major sources of new product ideas, based on an early 1986 study (Figure 4-1).

Figure 4-1 Where companies get ideas for new products and business ventures

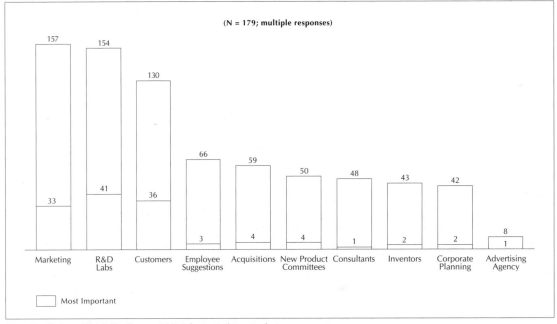

(N = 179; multiple responses)

Marketing	R&D Labs	Customers	Employee Suggestions	Acquisitions	New Product Committees	Consultants	Inventors	Corporate Planning	Advertising Agency
157 / 33	154 / 41	130 / 36	66 / 3	59 / 4	50 / 4	48 / 1	43 / 2	42 / 2	8 / 1

☐ Most Important

Source: The Conference Board: *The Commercial Development of New Products*

Why Are Some Companies More Successful?

Why, then, are some companies consistently more successful at developing new products than others?

It starts at the top—where the leader sets the tone, making it clear there is both honor and reward for the disasters of daring needed to come up with the successes.

It continues with a long-range commitment to a system—any system—that places primacy on new products and their management. It is nurtured by recognition of the imaginative champions who have the truest instincts (and viscera) for this highly frustrating field.

Although there is no ready catalog of millionaire chief executives who started as new product managers, Polaroid's Dr. Edward Land fits the attitudinal definition well. If glory alone is enough, take Leonardo da Vinci.

"The Collection Act" and "Seeing Differently"

The most fascinating mental process of the creators of truly new products is what goes on during the "collection acts." These originators seek and store vast quantities of information which they "see" and hence catalog) in quite different ways than most.

Both Buckminster Fuller and Salvador Dali were able to see a sofa in a pair of lips, and then apply it to a painting or an engineering principle. And they were self-censoring—always rejecting their own creations in search of an ideal.

The mere collection (research) and organization (cataloging) of information are not enough. Nor is the self-fulfilling prophecy of meaning, as Theodore H. White aptly uses in describing one 1972 presidential candidate:

> The mind was like a gravitational field which attracted and rearranged scattered iron shavings of fact about a hidden magnetic polarity within . . . the polarity was always that of Good and Evil.

Between the romantic extremes of white and black lie the subtle shades of success. The complexities of modern marketing do not allow for absolutes.

Taking such illustrations apart leads one to look at matters from many points of view (hence, the basis for techniques such as brainstorming and more disciplined group-think techniques, such as Synectics, developed at fuller length in Chapter 14).

With conventional wisdom, packaged goods marketers look at their opportunity targets in terms of arbitrary attributes.

Market Share (what if there is no market?);

Market Growth (what if the growing one is attracting all the competitive action, and the stable one is a bit sleepy?);

Unchallengeable Leaders Dominating a Huge Market (aren't there weaknesses to exploit against those who have so much to lose?);

Convenient Product Classifications (the industry may have bar soap divided among beauty, deodorant, and hand soaps, but have you ever seen a triple soap dish?). How about "ethnic" and "gourmet" foods—are those terms really useful?

Barriers to Entry

Then there are the advertising-intensive categories that pose cost barriers to entry for the small advertiser and the price-intensive categories that baffle the large one.

Over all this there is the cloak of industry marketing cliches—consumer sets, overpricing, overpackaging, breaking-the-dollar, odd-number sizing and pricing, push money, co-op funds, traditional trade channels, and the like.

What wonderful challenges these generalizations offer to new product marketing thinking! What opportunities!

"Inside-out" and "Outside-in" Approaches

Most marketers seek out targets within industry classifications, trade categories, and store sections—or find gaps in consumer offerings by using a cluster-grid method. This is the "inside-out" approach. The "outside-in" method is to screen consumer use habits and then to elicit responses from stimulus exhibits.

Both methods suffer from the limitations of research—the playback of past and present. Although a seer may divine what is in the future from this data, it is not yet a credible discipline. Therefore, we find the premium on pragmatic risk-takers—those who stimulate future desires.

Sometimes, as Fitzgerald implies in our opening quote, taking the opposite tack from research readings promises the most success. Often, it is both affordable and a good gamble to test a hypothesis that has a champion—even though consumer research is cautionary. Every venture team needs a devil's advocate—because one may turn out to be on the side of the gods.

This book concentrates on a relatively organized approach to new products. The emphasis is on less cautionary risk-taking and on the committed entrepreneurial perspective. It is ideal if "where new products originate" and "who is responsible" are one and the same entity—and backed by corporate commitment. Probably nowhere else in business are there fewer reliable guideposts, more risks, and more Delphic riddles than in new product work. But the payoff, when successful, can be many times greater than the cost of the disasters (which explains why the ratio of failures to successes is so high).

Admitting this admits a lot. Obviously, well-executed procedures alone do not assume success. What then? Beyond the scientific method as applied inside your company, you can look beyond, you can look outside. You can read ahead.

Some ventures are inspired by internally created atmospheres that encourage independent entrepreneuring (3M is an example)—or intrapreneurs.

Highly organized systems, specially assigned experts in R&D and engineering, prospect research, competitive analysis, satisfaction measures, entrepreneur-driven corporate commitment—there are many planned routes to new product development but unplanned discoveries happen and should be encouraged.

The Unsystematic Process

A few examples:

- When I was a new products brand and advertising manager for a major personal care products company, one of our ad agency account executives told me about a terrific cleansing lotion one of his clients had just introduced. Naturally, it was too expensive for our mass merchandise audience.

  I bought some of the lotion and took it to our lab and asked if it lived up to its claims. Later that afternoon, I found a bottle of liquid cream on my desk with a note: "This is our version. Deep cleans beautifully."

  Because we were a hair care company looking to broaden our base to skin care, I jumped at the formula and outsourced the initial manufacturing for test marketing.

  The product is still on the shelf. The upscale product no longer exists.

- Opportunities are created by strange twists of fortune—such as the law. One of my clients was a meat packer that acquired a household products company. Among the successful products it bought was a spray starch. There was one unanticipated problem: In those days, federal law prohibited meat producers from making or marketing vegetable products.

  Because starch was considered a vegetable product, the company had to drop the spray starch line. But that produced an opportunity. Instead of competing in the generic starch field—why not a better product?

  This ex-new personal products manager went to his hair spray supplier and asked if an aerosol starch substitute could be made.

  No problem. A starch substitute was launched—a pioneering spray sizing.

- Other new products inspirations abound. One source was shopping in foreign countries (first time I saw disposable bed sheets and shelf-stable dairy-fresh products), attending foreign food fairs, wine festivals, fashion shows—even auto shows and carnivals. All yield inspirations, concepts, basis for licensing agreements, U.S.-foreign partnerships, distribution rights, etc.

Inspirations are everywhere.

Follow the systematic approach to new product development, but do personal research as well. Watch what's going on in everyday life. Chat up your suppliers, so they can chat you up, and can do plenty of listening and questioning.

Follow the journalism credo: Who? What? When? Where? Why? How? Discovery is fun—and rewarding.

The independent entrepreneurs are inspirations. Their own drive, mission, need to bring to life their creations—that is encouraging to new product success, from a one person start-up to a giant corporation that encourages dedicated new product drive, independent of a carefully defined corporate objective.

5

Another Path to New Products—External Development

Although it is the mission of this text to address the process of *internal* new products development in considerable detail, it must not be overlooked that external development (i.e., acquisition, joint venture, and strategic alliance) is another path to satisfying the corporation's growth goals. For many corporations, this path has been much more successful than internal new business generation. Of course, the opposite is the more prevalent activity and represents a higher percentage of incremental new product generation for the economy. Other companies have been uniquely successful with a balanced program, addressing each new opportunity area in relationship to corporate strengths and weaknesses—evaluating outside prospects vs. internal abilities.

Even when an acquisition or other business combination appears to make sense and has been successfully negotiated, its integration may present unanticipated problems in relation to opportunities.

To clearly identify potential pitfalls, it is wise to review Peter Drucker's "Rules for Successful Acquisition," as reported by *The Wall Street Journal*.

Rules for Successful Acquisition

Peter Drucker says his rules for successful acquisition have been followed by all successful acquirers since the days of J. P. Morgan, a century ago. They include:

> 1.   An acquisition will succeed only if the acquiring company thinks through what it can contribute to the business it is buying. Not what the acquired company will contribute to the acquirer, no matter how attractive the expected "synergy" may look.
>
> 2.   Successful diversification by acquisition, like all successful diversification, requires a common core of unity. The two businesses must have in common either markets or technology, though occasionally a comparable production process has also provided sufficient unity of experience and expertise, as well as a common language, to bring companies together.
>
> 3.   No acquisition works unless the people in the acquiring company respect the product, the markets, and the customers of the company they acquire. The acquisition must be a "temperamental fit."

Drucker's fourth and fifth rules deal with the integration and cross-promotion of management necessary between the two recently combined companies, important stabilizing and motivating steps, but not the subject of this specific treatment of the external development process—new products.

Examples where the first three rules were not followed, and where the acquisitions were not successful, as cited by Drucker:

> While General Motors has done very well with the diesel businesses it bought, it could and did contribute both technology and management. It got nowhere with the two businesses to which its main contribution was money: heavy earth-moving equipment and aircraft engines . . . None of the big television networks and other entertainment companies has made a go out of the book publishers they bought. Books are not "media."

Another example of a merger not made in heaven was that of RCA Corporation acquiring Banquet Foods Corporation. An electronics and entertainment company didn't understand poultry processing and frozen foods. Subsequently, Banquet was acquired from RCA by ConAgra, a major agribusiness company. Under new ownership and management, Banquet was transformed into a highly successful line of nutritionally positioned foods: "Healthy Choice."

Now, let's take a closer look at the role of external development in corporate diversification plans. Little has been written on this subject in texts on new products—yet it is of extreme importance to any broad-ranging program of new enterprise development.

The Role of External Development in Corporate Diversification Plans*

It is appropriate to consider the option of external development as a means of achieving an organization's strategic goals of growth, new market penetration, and diversification. It is not that an external development strategy should be used in lieu of a well-developed and implemented new product strategy; rather a coordinated program of new product development and acquisitions, and joint ventures can be extremely effective in meeting management's goals for the enterprise.

Following is a brief overview of the external development process typical of many major U.S. corporations, as well as a discussion of the specific role of and issues relating to external development as part of corporate diversification.

The Organization

The external development process in most large corporations typically is controlled at senior levels. Although operating groups and subsidiaries often have their own executives dedicated to finding and evaluating potential acquisitions, joint ventures, and strategic alliances, the responsibility for coordinating and frequently for executing transactions is assigned to a centralized staff function generally regarded as part of senior corporate management. Often this function reports to the chief financial officer or a senior development officer. Occasionally it reports directly to the chief executive officer. In all cases, an *effective* external development program reflects the participation (and enthusiasm) of the chief executive officer.

The Process

The external development process itself is a flow of contiguous activities usually progressing sequentially through as many as five major phases:

1. Identification of prospects

2. Courting

3. Valuation, deal structuring, and negotiations

4. Due diligence and closing

5. Integration

Binding these phases within the acquirer corporation is a constant flow of communications generated by the acquisition team to middle management, senior management, and the corporation's board of directors.

---

*Except for "Business Extensions—Globalized," the remainder of this chapter was prepared especially for this book by Charles H. McGill, senior vice president—Corporate Development, American Brands, Inc.

Identification of Prospects

The approaches to prospect identification taken by American corporations are as varied as the nature of the corporations themselves. Generally, where the external development process is designed to achieve relatively specific strategic objectives, then the identification of prospects or leads is executed via an active program of establishing concrete, specific criteria; screening industries and industry subsegments for target candidates; and quantitatively ranking these candidates in order of desirability.

On the other hand, where expansion or diversification acquisition criteria are not clearly established, or are expressed qualitatively with little precision, then identification is passive and essentially opportunistic. This "over the transom" type of approach by its very nature can lead to interesting situations for the potential acquirer, yet it is a relatively inefficient and time-consuming way of teaching acquisition objectives.

Regardless of the active or passive nature of the external development program, prospects are identified through a broad variety of channels ranging from referrals by investment bankers and business brokers or "finders" to referrals by the candidates themselves to "cold calls" by the acquirer to prospects.

Courting

Once a prospect becomes an acquisition candidate, there begins an often elaborate process of courting or romancing with the objective of determining if a suitable "fit" exists between purchaser and seller. During this phase, the specific financial and managerial needs of the seller usually become evident and are compared for compatibility with the specific growth, return on investment, market diversification, and other business objectives of the purchaser.

The buyer's access to the seller's organization varies at this time depending upon (a) possible confidentiality; (b) likely impact on the seller's employees; and (c) the mutually perceived seriousness of discussions thus far.

Far more than a series of lunches, dinners, and other entertainment, this phase sets the groundwork for identification and assessment of the likely satisfaction of unilateral and mutual objectives.

Valuation, Deal Structuring, and Negotiations

Next comes valuation, deal structuring, and negotiations. Perceptions and understandings gained in the second phase now are incorporated into a specific financial structure oriented toward meeting the financial and other objectives of both the seller and the buyer.

This is a relatively complex and technical aspect of the external development process incorporating legal, tax, and often pension considerations as integral parts of a basic business proposition. For example the desirability/preferability of paying for a transaction with a company's stock as opposed to cash, notes, or a combination thereof impacts significantly on the plans of the seller after the acquisition is completed, i.e., immediate reinvestment of proceeds, estate diversification, long-term decision to hold stock received in the transaction for tax benefits, and similar considerations. Significantly, the price or value of a transaction usually varies depending upon the nature of payment and the attendant tax consequences for both buyer and seller.

The underlying basis of valuation is the long-term profit forecast reflecting expectations for the business on a stand-alone basis modified by the benefits of combining it with the acquirer's organization (i.e., synergies) less any revenue/profit losses that may also result from the combination. Valuation may also reflect the uneconomic pressures of competitive bidding in increasingly prevalent auction processes.

When businesses are acquired from entrepreneurs, other, less technical, considerations are also important. The ongoing involvement in the business of the entrepreneur and his management team (occasionally also members of his or her family) after acquisition is a consideration of financial and egotistical significance and frequently of paramount importance for a purchaser; the purchaser may need the "know-how" of the entrepreneurial team. This relationship is particularly important in cases where the entrepreneur negotiates an "earn-out" or "kicker" whereby the entrepreneur benefits directly, as a significant part of the total consideration, from the future growth and profitability of his or her business.

Personal considerations make their way into deal structures. It is not uncommon for entrepreneurs selling a business to require that they not be required to move their operations after acquisition from current locations. Similarly, some sellers may require that specific lines (which may be unprofitable at the time of acquisition) may not be discontinued for at least several years.

This phase of the acquisition process involves the traditional "give and take" associated with negotiations. The skills of the negotiator are augmented by lawyers and tax counsel.

The outcome of valuation, deal structuring, and negotiations is an agreement to agree, i.e., an explicit, written exposition of the structured deal. Known as a "letter of intent" or a "letter of understanding," this legal document usually does not bind either party to perform the obligations recited; however, it typically is not issued when performance is regarded as unlikely. Over time it serves as the basis or outline of the binding purchase and sale agreement.

Due Diligence and Closing

This next phase of the acquisition process is designed to permit the buyer to conduct a thorough review of the business to be acquired, including relevant financial, marketing, operating, and legal records and documents. This process, known as "due diligence," is time consuming but necessary to give the buyer sufficient comfort to proceed toward consummation.

Often the due diligence program is completed via functional teams fielded by the acquiring corporation; occasionally management consultants and auditors are engaged. There may be a human resources team, a marketing team, and teams representing the more narrow corporate functions and specialties, i.e., pensions, insurance, facilities, purchasing, management development, and training.

As due diligence proceeds, so does the drafting and negotiating of the definitive purchase and sale agreement. This purchase and sale agreement will contain all of the key elements of the transaction and serve as a permanent record of the rights and obligations of both parties. Because in many transactions the broad issues in effect have been negotiated through the courting and deal-structuring phases, narrower, more technical issues often dominate the purchase and sale agreement negotiations. Not uncommonly, phrases and even words are argued at length if they are perceived to offer either side an advantage—however improbable the likelihood of the advantages being realized. "Deal breakers" may arise here, particularly if there are contentious tax, environmental and/or indemnification issues.

At the conclusion of due diligence is the closing. In contrast to the often elaborate process that precedes it, the closing is often swift and undramatic, subject occasionally to postclosing review and adjustments. The business has now changed hands.

Integration

The final phase of the acquisition process calls for integrating the acquired business into the corporation's structure and environment. In some cases, the corporate acquisition team also is responsible for at least the initial aspects of integration; in all cases the acquirer must ensure a logical and rational transition in order to protect its newly acquired investment.

As with a new product that is being brought on stream once out of the developmental stage, this integration phase is a crucial element to (a) ensure a mutuality of objectives of the acquirer and acquiree; (b) establish appropriate operating and policy guidelines for the newly acquired business; (c) retain and motivate desired key managers; and (d) assess the long-term strategic and tactical factors that will ensure that the acquisition performs at least as well as expected.

Throughout the acquisition process, the acquirer develops quantitative models both for analysis of possible outcomes and eventually as the basis of a three-to-five-year profit plan. The likelihood of achieving the profit plan targets is enhanced significantly with successful integration of the new acquisition.

Why Diversify?

Perhaps the best answer is the retort "why not—everyone else does." In fact, large corporations (and increasingly small and medium-sized public and private companies) see diversification as a critical factor to their success and even survival. For manufacturers, a single product/single market strategy often results in a risky no-growth situation. Even service firms that are relatively undiversified compared to manufacturers succeed on the basis of new products, new services, and continual repositioning to new markets. A good example is one of the premier service companies, Marriott Corporation, which progressively diversified from a root-beer-stand business to a coffee-shop–restaurant company to a hotel company and then to a diversified service mix of restaurants, hotels, resorts, airline catering, and other institutional food businesses. (In 1993, Marriott split into two publicly traded corporations, Marriott International and Host Marriott. In 1995, Host Marriott spun off Host Marriott Services.)

In the area of consumer foods manufacturing, diversification was common during the past three decades. Some—Pillsbury, for example—stayed within the concept of agribusiness but diversified broadly into restaurants (Burger King/Steak and Ale), wines (Souverain), food service, and agricultural commodities. Acquisitions also included new product categories and new distribution systems, typified by the purchases of Häagen-Dazs and Pet, Inc.

Others diversified into restaurants but also acquired nonrelated businesses, including toy manufacturers and clothing retailers. Typically, the mid- to late-1980s saw the dismantling of these nonagribusiness moves and in the case of Pillsbury the acquisition of the company itself as the centerpiece of U.K.–based Grand Metropolitan's diversification beyond alcoholic beverages, hotels, and pubs and its geographic concentration in the United Kingdom. Seagram's recent decision to expand beyond beverages and its passive DuPont holdings into entertainment via acquisition of MCA is a dramatic diversification example.

Because diversification is a major element in corporate strategy, diversification moves typically reflect perceived opportunities and weaknesses of the corporation. Among the more common motives for diversification are:

Stimulative—improving an organization's prospects for continued and stepped-up growth in sales and particularly in earnings

Synergistic—extending an organization's strengths to another business. For example, a complementary business that can draw upon distribution and sales strengths established in the acquirer

Strategic—balancing a business portfolio for risk and investment opportunities via acquisition

Reactive—responding to competitive pressures

Supportive—using diversification as a means of retaining and further developing an in-place management team

Coordinated Product Development and External Development

In meeting diversification objectives, a coordinated approach to product development and external growth makes sense. Generally, the greater the extent of diversification, the more likely the use of acquisition(s) to reach the goal. There are situations in which only an acquisition will suffice, such as unique market positioning or proprietary technology. Conversely, there may be no opportunity to acquire a business that adequately meets defined criteria, e.g., the business is not for sale or, commonly, does not exist. It is important to recognize that product development and external growth are the "means" for achieving strategic results, not the "ends."

The remainder of this section distinguishes between these "means," but does so within the broad context of tactical versus strategic diversification. As Table 5-1 shows, the key variable is not whether the diversification is done via product development or external growth, but rather if the diversification is basically tactical or strategic in nature.

Tactical Diversification

The strength of product development lies in building upon existing businesses by applying related technology. The heart of tactical product development lies in various line extensions and product proliferations. A continual stream of new varieties, shapes, and sizes, along with ongoing profit improvement programs represents the bread-and-butter of research and development effort in consumer-oriented companies.

Tactical acquisitions follow logically from the concept of the tactical product development. Tactical acquisitions can include acquisition of directly competing products, although more typically acquisitions are likely to center on complementary products that are readily integrated into existing distribution and sales systems. Pillsbury's acquisition of Joan of Arc yams and sweet potatoes for its Green Giant business illustrates the concept.

Tactical diversification is a relatively low-risk, quick way to meet diversification objectives.

Strategic Diversification

The area of strategic product development and external development introduces new dimensions of higher diversification and higher risk.

On the surface, strategic acquisitions are appealing; they may even appear to offer a "quick fit." Such acquisitions permit a corporation to establish a commanding market position, perhaps replete with proprietary technology, overnight. They may offer entry into totally new, profitable businesses.

However, by their nature, strategic acquisitions are relatively risky and typically rely on simultaneous acquisition of a first-class management team. All of this is usually costly, albeit, to the acquirer. It is not uncommon for 30 percent or more of the purchase price to be classified

Table 5-1 Diversification approaches

COORDINATED DIVERSIFICATION APPROACHES			
Tactical		Strategic	
Product development	Acquisitions & joint ventures	Acquisitions & joint ventures	Product development
• New varieties, textures, shapes, and sizes • Synergy oriented • Draws on existing management • Utilizes existing sales and distribution • Complements existing R&D capability • Easily integrated into the organization • Relatively low risk		• New markets and products • Often not synergy oriented • Often requires new management • Often requires new sales and distribution systems, may be totally unrelated • Extends existing R&D capability; may be totally unrelated • Not easily integrated into the organization, may stand alone • Relatively high risk	

Source: Charles H. McGill, American Brands, Inc.

on the balance sheet as "goodwill" written off over 20 to 40 years depending upon accounting interpretations and management's policies.

The acquisition by General Foods of the Oscar Mayer Company is a good example of a strategic acquisition. In short order, General Foods was able not only to enter the processed meats business but also to enter as a market leader. General Foods paid for this privilege with "good will," yet in doing so was able to decrease the risk that years of product development and market introductions might not pan out at all. Similarly, Campbell Soups' decision to acquire the market leader in Mexican salsas and sauces, Pace Picante, and Quaker Oats' acquisition of Snapple beverages reflect judgments that it makes more sense to pay for management expertise, brand awareness, and market position than to attempt to build these intangibles over long periods of time.

Occasionally, major diversification objectives simply cannot be met because a business either is not available as an acquisition or simply does not exist. Then, strategic product development is the only way. The advantage of internal development in these circumstances rests with the ability to pinpoint a specific product attribute via technological application. Also, there is no explicit kind of goodwill required with internal product development.

The drawbacks to this approach are significant:

• First, it is difficult to ensure that funds expended will, in fact, have an acceptable payback (if any at all). Expensive dry holes are not at all uncommon.

- Second, strategic product development represents a long process of research, product development, test marketing, and refinements. Occasionally, the length of the process offsets some, if not all, of the perceived benefits of the original project.

- Third, there may be a need to develop an entire new management structure around a new product concept and this adds yet another element of risk and effort to the overall project.

Despite these drawbacks, the indisputable benefit of true new strategic product development lies in introducing products that are unique or at least distinctive. The various new shaving products, including Atra and Sensor, introduced by Gillette in recent years, and the highly successful ice cream bars introduced by Häagen-Dazs speak eloquently to the success of strategic product development. Some companies, such as Procter & Gamble, have long relied on strategic product development as a lifeline to sales and profitability growth . . . generally eschewing acquisitions.

Coordination: The Final Word

The key word here is coordination. Product development does not usually stand well alone without acquisitions and, occasionally, joint ventures. They complement each other. The successful chief executive is sensitive to this byplay and typically will ensure that both activities are conducted professionally, consistent with overall corporate goals and objectives. In fact, increasingly, corporations are successfully coordinating product development and external development—often via joint ventures or strategic alliances.

In 1985, Pillsbury, entered into a joint venture with Suntory, Ltd. in Japan to introduce its newly acquired Häagen-Dazs there. Beyond licensing Häagen-Dazs trademarks and "know-how," product development teams adapted Häagen-Dazs to Japanese tastes and desired portion sizes. Ten years later, Häagen-Dazs Japan had grown from a $1 million (U.S.) initial capitalization to more than 250 million (U.S.) in revenues.

Business Extensions— Globalized

Worldwide joint ventures, partnerships, and acquisitions have been booming in the 90s. In the food products field, a few of the recent examples include General Mills, CPC International, PepsiCo, and Nestlé.

General Mills, which owns U.S. marketing rights for France-originated Yoplait yogurt, added to its import share of the category with its recent acquisition of Columbo yogurt, which holds strong share positions in the Northeast, complementing Yoplait's geographical strength in Central and Western markets.

Another growing international joint venture for General Mills is with PepsiCo Food International: Snack Ventures Europe.

Internationally, General Mills has a joint venture, known as Cereal Partners Worldwide (CPW), with Switzerland's giant Nestlé, which markets throughout western Europe, including France, Spain, Portugal, Italy, and Germany, as well as the United Kingdom, the ASEAN (Association of Southeast Asian Nations) countries, Mexico, and Chile. It also has expanded its operations to Poland, with the purchase of Torun-Pacific, which holds the leading cornflake market share in Poland. CPW's sales goal is $1 billion by the year 2000.

More recently, General Mills and CPC International established International Dessert Partners (IDP), a joint venture with the goal of developing a major baking and dessert mix business in Latin America, one of the fastest growing regions in the world.

The General Mills/CPC partnership is of special interest, inasmuch as it brings together two of the most successful new food products corporations—both with powerful globalization achievements.

CPC International is an especially interesting example of business extensions involving acquisitions, as well as new products internally developed by both its basic organization and its joint-venture partners.

Nearly every relationship is special. For example, in the case of Western brand salad dressings, CPC acquired the rights to the brand, no plant and no people. At one time CPC was a player in South Africa. Then it divested its business there in 1987. Then it reentered in the early 1990s. In Vietnam, a CPC-employed manager runs CPC's small office. It imports and promotes Knorr bouillon and other products formulated for Vietnamese eating habits. CPC sells through third-party distributors.

More recently, CPC acquired Lesieur brand mayonnaise and dressings in France, and established a Representative Office in Romania, where CPC markets soups, bouillons, and instant mashed potatoes. Also acquired was the Pot Noodle hot snacks business in the U.K.

CPC encourages internal new product development and (also) external business extensions. Some examples: Knorr Gemüseküche mealmakers were developed in one country and then extended to additional markets. CPC managers in Germany, seeing the rising levels of vegetable consumption, created mixes for preparing vegetable and potato dishes. CPC's Swiss affiliate built on that success and developed products that were even more convenient to use.

CPC's European division then identified this product category, which CPC created, as an opportunity for businesses throughout Europe. A task force of European managers, led by Germany and France and coordinated by CPC's European division, evaluated the expansion opportunity, and the products have been successfully launched in other markets. A fairly typical CPC action is using a task force to take a success from one country to others.

Other examples include Hellmann's Dijonnaise and High-Maltose Corn Syrup. Hellman's is a successful, unique product created in the United States that has been a solid success. CPC's managers in the United Kingdom decided that such a product could be a success in their market, where Hellmann's brand is already the market leader in mayonnaise. (In particular, note that the food scientist working at CPC's dressings center in Europe was a transplant from the United States, who had helped develop the original product. Another way that CPC leverages its strengths is by moving people and their expertise into new regions.)

The High-Maltose Corn Syrup example shows how CPC applies success from one region (North America) to another (Brazil and other Latin American markets). A big corn-refining competitor in North America, Cargill, moved to Brazil. CPC's North American managers were able to tip off its Brazilian businesses as to the products Cargill was likely to launch in Brazil, including syrup for the brewing business. This knowledge prompted CPC's Brazilian business to move first into this business, ahead of Cargill, using capabilities developed in North America, with successful results.

In late February 1997, CPC announced that it intends to spin off its corn-refining business to shareholders as a new independent, publicly owned company. The objective, says CPC's chairman and chief executive officer C. R. Shoemate, is "to give both CPC and the new corn-refining company the focus, flexibility, and resources they need for faster growth of sales, volumes, and profits." Following the spin-off, CPC International will continue as a global-branded packaged food company, with sales that increased 20 percent in 1996 compared to 1995. (Sales in 1996 were 9.8 billion.)

Table 5-2 provides an overall example of globalization of business extensions. It covers CPC's new business activities from 1992 through 1996. It identifies the key products, the extension method, and the strategic contributions made by the acquisitions, joint ventures, and new businesses launched in countries where CPC had not previously operated.*

---

* When this book went to press, CPC was planning to spin off its corn refining operations as part of its ongoing restructuring efforts.

Table 5-2 CPC International business extensions 1992–1996: acquisitions, new businesses, joint ventures (Partial List)

Country	Brand/Business Name	Key Products	Extension Method	Strategic Contribution
NORTH AMERICA				
United States	*LeGoût* brand	Soups, bouillons, gravies, entrées, desserts	Acquisition	Doubles CPC's food service business in U.S.; adds frozen food products.
United States	*Henri's* and *Western* brands	Pourable dressings	Acquisition	Adds to dressings capabilities; strong foothold in Midwestern markets.
United States	*Iberia* brand	Soups, bouillons, canned vegetables, oils	Acquisition	Builds Hispanic food lines; provides vehicle for introducing other CPC Hispanic products.
United States	*Entenmann's, Oroweat*, et al	Sweet baked goods, sliced bread, bread shells	Acquisition	Addition of four market-leading baked goods brands makes CPC the nation's No. 1 fresh premium baker.
EUROPE, AFRICA/MIDDLE EAST				
Bulgaria	Representative Office	Imported soups, bouillons, and mashed potatoes	New*	Coordinate distribution of CPC products in newly opened market.
Czech Republic	CPC Foods a.s.	Soups, bouillons, dressings	New/acquisition*	New business in newly opened market; dressings leader; exporting *Hellmann's* mayonnaise to new businesses in Central and Eastern Europe.
Germany	*Pfanni* brand	Convenience potato products	Acquisition	Leading extendable brand, compatible with the *Knorr* brand; also contributes to food service business.
Greece	Spitiko	Filo pastry dough	Acquisition	Adds to CPC's ethnic foods capabilities; products will be marketed under *Knorr* brand.
Hungary	CPC Hungary Rt.	Soups, bouillons, desserts, dressings	New/acquisition*	New business in newly opened market; soups and bouillons leader.
Poland	CPC Polska SP.zo.o	Soups, bouillons, desserts	New/acquisition*	New business in newly opened market; also currently providing soups, bouillons, and desserts for new business in Russia.
Russia	CPC Foods Company Ltd.	Soups, sauces, bouillons, dressings	New*	New business in newly opened market; first major international company to introduce soups, bouillons, and dressings.

Table 5-2 (Continued)

Country	Brand/Business Name	Key Products	Extension Method	Strategic Contribution
EUROPE, AFRICA/MIDDLE EAST *(continued)*				
France	*Lesieur* brand	Dressings	Acquisition	A leading dressings brand in critical European dressing market.
Jordan	Best Foods Jordan	Soups, bouillons, corn oil	New/joint venture*	CPC has majority share in a venture with local company in a new market.
Romania	Representative office	Soups, bouillons, and instant mashed potatoes (imported)	New*	Coordinated distribution by local companies to establish new business in newly opened market.
United Kingdom	*Pot Noodles*	Quick cook, hot, savory snacks	Acquisition	Strong leading market share and appeal among young consumers; excellent fit with CPC's *Knorr* brand; potential for geographic extension.
Israel	TAMI	Soups, bouillons, dressings, desserts, cereals	New/acquisition*	Leading brands and market positions in new market for CPC.
South Africa	Fine foods (food service)	Sauces, dressings, dry desserts	Acquisition	Strengthens CPC's food service business.
South Africa	CPC Tongaat Foods	Soups, sauces, oils, desserts, starches	New/joint venture*	Joint Venture reestablishes CPC in South Africa; platform for extension into sub-Saharan Africa.
Turkey	*Bozkurt* brand	Bread spreads, desserts	Acquisition	No. 2 brand for jams and helva desserts; a sales organization to support CPC's soups, bouillons, and desserts.
Turkey	*Capamarka* brand	Rice flour, edible starches, soups, wheat pilaf	Acquisition	Strong leading share in the rice flour and starch markets; adds to CPC's leading market share in soups.
LATIN AMERICA				
Regional	International Dessert Partners	Baking and dessert mixes	Joint venture	Joint venture combines CPC's organization and infrastructure with General Mills' expertise in dessert mixes.
Argentina	*AdeS* brand	Soya products	Acquisition	Unique, fast-growing nutritional beverages, with potential for geographic expansion.
Brazil	*Vitamilho* brand	Precooked corn flour to make dietary staple	Acquisition	Leader in huge northeast Brazil market; extends CPC's participation in starch/basic nutritious foods business.
Chile	*Juan Bas* brand	Sauces, mustards, mayonnaise	Acquisition	Strong market leader in chili sauces.

Table 5-2 (Continued)

Country	Brand/Business Name	Key Products	Extension Method	Strategic Contribution
LATIN AMERICA *(continued)*				
Costa Rica	*Don Luis & Maravilla* brands	Soups, bouillons, sauces, dressings, desserts	Acquisition	Adds to CPC's No. 1 mayonnaise and sauce business; provides entry into bouillon and desserts categories.
Mexico	Arancia CPC	Joint venture to produce corn refining products	Joint venture	Joint venture combines CPC's corn refining business with Arancia business to strengthen CPC's position in Mexico and in the NAFTA market.
Venezuela	*Ne-nerina, Polly* brands	Processed cereals	Acquisition	Market-leading products; well-established distribution network utilized to strengthen CPC's existing Venezuelan business.
ASIA				
China	CPC (Guangzhou) Foods Ltd.	Bouillons	New/joint venture	New business in newly opened south China market; first major international company to manufacture bouillons.
China	CPC Shanghai	Bouillons, soy sauce	Joint venture	New business in newly opened market in eastern China.
China	CPC (Beijing) Foods Ltd.	Bouillons, dressings	Joint venture	New business in newly opened north China market; first major international company in dressings business.
Hong Kong	*Torto* brand	Desserts, soups, cereal beverages, drink mixes	Acquisition	Strong leading market share in fast-growing "sweet soups" market, strengthening CPC's desserts leadership.
Indonesia	P.T. Knorr Indonesia	Soups, bouillons, corn oil	New*	New business in fast-growing market of 185 million people.
Sri Lanka	*Kist* brand	Sauces, jams	New/acquisition*	New business in fast-growing market; distribution for launch of CPC soups and bouillons.
Vietnam	CPC (Vietnam) Ltd.	Bouillons, soups, dressings, bread spreads (imported)	New*	Coordinating distribution by local companies to establish new business in newly opened market.

* Business established by CPC in country where it had not previously operated.

Section 1   Summary Afterword

New products and services, essential for any company's growth, may be defined as any product or service not now made or marketed by the company, or as any perceived as new by the consumer. Success is determined by goal achievement. Although no reliable overall success statistics exist, successful companies have high new product success ratios—that is, a high ratio of successful new products relative to those introduced.

There are many reasons for new product failures, most often related to faulty management and planning. New product information collection and its creative analysis, along with an involved top management, are key determinants of success.

New products are the key to a company's sales growth, both in products and services. This reliance is growing. Comprehensive growth programs utilize both internal and outside sources, and a multipronged organization is usually needed to fully address new product needs.

There are no reliable success vs. failure statistics on new products due to the use of variable definitions, survey designs, and evaluation techniques. A failure for one company may be a success for another—and thus not a result of concept failure. Many of the reasons for failure can be reasons for success under other circumstances.

Among the reasons for failure are:

- Poor planning
- Poor management
- Poor concept
- Poor research
- Poor technology
- Poor timing (often out of manufacturer's control)
- Poor distribution control
- Competitive moves, unanticipated changes not countered

Subsidiary reasons for failure include many that should have been anticipated prior to the program's development:

- Off strategy
- Insufficient technical expertise
- Insufficient distribution
- Insufficient margin, ROS, ROI
- Cost of entry
- Full line needed; only one or a few products entered
- Unfamiliar production
- Regulatory complication
- Patent, license infringement
- Inadequate market analysis
- Development program poorly planned

The hierarchy of new products progresses from the evolution of existing products through the expansion of a brand or product franchise to a new entry into an established category and finally the development of a new category or a new business.

Evolution of an existing product can include repositioning (to find a new audience), recycling (to introduce the product for a different use), appearance or form improvement, performance improvement, price/value change, or a combination of any of the preceding. Beyond that, the brand or product franchise can be expanded by adding line extensions and flankers, or by introducing the brand into a new category.

Another type of new product is a new entry into an established category. Factors to consider in this approach are the newness of the brand name, new positioning, appearance or form difference, performance difference, packaging difference, resource difference, price/value difference, and difference in distribution pattern.

On the other hand, an entirely new category may be created when a new solution is found to an old problem, when a solution is found to a new problem, or when a new need is discovered and filled. Sometimes the revival of an outmoded or dying category may also inspire new products. Other factors to consider in the creation of a new category are innovation and invention and discovery.

At the top of the new product hierarchy is the development of an entirely new business. This is the long-range portion of the plan. It does not replace other new product activities, but should operate in tandem with them.

Where do new products originate? Conventional sources for new products include internal development and R&D, adaptations of foreign developments, allied industry developments, new patents, and competitive knockoffs. What is needed is strong management leadership. Conventional approaches focus on gap analyses of industry and of consumer need fulfillment. The process that goes beyond this includes venture team structures—a means to look at information collection unconventionally. The inspirational, unsystematic process can also yield success.

Another path to new product is via acquisition and joint venture, which may follow an assessment of opportunity areas accessible through current corporate strengths vs. outside opportunities that are attainable through external growth.

There are pitfalls to avoid. Three guidelines to follow in acquisition are:

1. The acquiring company must contribute more than money to the acquired company.

2. The merged businesses must have a common core; this may be in markets or technology, or occasionally in production.

3. The acquiring company must respect the products, markets, and customers of the acquired company.

The acquisition process includes identification of prospects, courting, deal structuring and negotiation, the due diligence procedure and closing, and integration of the acquired company. The process should be controlled at senior management levels, through a centralized staff function.

Most of these guidelines also apply to joint ventures and partnerships, both opportunity areas increasingly initiated by corporations throughout developed countries, leading to product and brand globalization.

The advantages of diversification include the following:

1. Stimulates sales and earnings

2. Synergistically extends strengths to another business

3. Strategically balances the corporate business portfolio for risk and investment opportunities

5. Supports the retention and development of in-place management talent

Coordinated product development and acquisition generally takes two forms. The tactical approach complements existing product lines, management, and R&D for synergistic effects. The strategic approach, however, often requires new management, new sales systems, and new or extended R&D capabilities. It does not provide synergy or easy integration, but does offer opportunities for new markets and products. With all this, the strategic form of acquisition entails higher risk than the tactical approach.

Coordination is the key. New product development and external growth activities complement each other.

COMMITMENT

Section
2

6

Corporate Charter

Business needs new products just to survive.

While it is instructive to sort out the probable cause of new product failures, it's more important to learn from those high-achiever companies with a consistent new product track record. There appear to be common success characteristics. Among them are:

- Large, definable commitment in money and time—demonstrated by management style, priorities, professional organization, support services, caliber of outside consultants and suppliers, etc.

- Open communication of this commitment within the company and the industry, and to shareholders.

- Career progress of those entrepreneurial and conceptual spirits who are encouraged to stray from the routing paths of procedure into the more risky (and possibly more rewarding) world of new product development.

An environment that encourages commitment is needed at all levels.

Corporate Charter

In the strict legal sense, the corporate charter is an organization's basic starting document—a corporation's Articles of Incorporation, combined with the law, that gives the right to incorporate.

In the larger sense we invoke here, the corporate charter reflects the clearest possible strategic business focus. It is the basis for goal setting. Many corporations have not specifically defined themselves. Many entrepreneurial and founder-driven corporations depend on the leader's dreams and instincts to guide their growth patterns. Even in such cases, it is advisable that the charter be hammered out in writing—published as a management tool for use in the absence of the instinctual leaders. In all cases, the charter should be periodically revisited—and compared with the corporation's actual performance. One or the other may require revision.

When beginning a new product project, a fundamental question is: Does this fit the corporate charter? The mission's advisability depends on the answer.

Not a hymn to the eternal verities written by a babble of barristers, but a specific, refined—and periodically redefined—corporate charter sets the course. It recognizes the company's strengths and weaknesses in measurable performance comparisons within its industry and in the perceptions of the marketplace. Historically, firms with the most successful new product records stick closely to their areas of expertise and marketplace leverage.

The successful company must stay apace of its technology and customer needs. To be a leader, it must pioneer where both the risks and rewards are greatest (often concomitant).

The forces of change in demography, psychography, and technology require that an enterprise found its evolutionary base on its strongest capabilities. It is critical to recognize these—as well as identifying those areas where the endeavor may be at parity or worse. Nowhere is it written that an enterprise must be first in all things: first in financial leverage, first in science, first in production, first in marketing, first in management.

But *somewhere* it must be written—and posted on the door to corporate headquarters:

This is what we do.

And this is what we do best.

The corporate charter should be strategic. It should not only state, "This is what we are": it should also state, "This is what we are *not*." It should direct, "This is where we are *not* going."

Every important enterprise does something *best*—best among all the necessary skills, and clearly outstanding within its competitive field.

Bea Arthur, the Tony award-winning actress and a star of the NBC television series "Golden Girls," was asked by interviewer Dick Cavett: "Have you ever turned down a part that turned out to be something absolutely great?"

Replied Bea, "I'll tell you what I really feel. Even if you turn down something, whether it's as a director or an actor or whatever and it suddenly becomes an enormous commercial success, it still doesn't mean that *you* should have done it, because if it didn't do something to you originally then you were wrong for it, you know."

Miss Arthur knows *her* corporate charter. She knows what *she* does best.

The shoemaker should stick to his last. That leaves plenty of room to exploit the entire market between galoshes and Guccis. It is rare that a company moves into an entirely new field with a self-generated new product success. A good rule is to proceed with caution into even closely related categories.

Business, a melting of many humans, machines, and processes, may be more complex than an individual actor like Bea Arthur. That's all the more reason why it should articulate—and practice—its corporate charter.

The usual example of what results from a failure to define a corporate charter is the defunct buggy whip company that didn't identify itself as being in the transportation business—and was consequently made obsolete by the automobile. A charter must be both tightly defined and broadly conceived, so as to identify correctly the competitive industry and to be compatible with its trends.

Today, obvious examples of companies with successful corporate charters are found among those members of the petroleum industry that have defined themselves as being in the energy business, rather than as oil refiners and distributors. Today they are already deeply dedicated to coal, nuclear, solar, sea, biological, and even wind-generated energy.

To understand the corporate charter, it is best sometimes to write it—then get management to ratify it. The writing forces the necessary thorough thinking, the necessary development of perspective, the necessary commitment. The stronger the commitment, the more certain it is that successful new products will emerge. The commitment is not only a personal career dedication, but involves support staffing, funding, and psychic investment by both the company and its support resources (e.g., banks, advertising agencies, etc.). The responsibility begins with functional goals. The authority develops for the new product executive through accomplishment.

Other times, there is an existing charter that clearly defines the role of new products in corporate development—anticipating volume increases and expansion targets.

To develop a corporate charter for new products, classify short-range and long-range objectives, and place a dollar priority on each of them. Set volume, gross margin, return on investment, and payback goals; trade needs; time frame considerations; as well as defining target markets and product characteristics. Fit those objectives into the life of the marketplace, anticipating your competitors' resources and probable objectives. (One helpful exercise is to define each of your competitors' corporate charters, based on available external evidence. This often reveals attractive opportunities for *your* company.) Define the tools of expansion—which new products will come through internal generation and which by other means.

State the company's or division's image of itself: Is it: "We make air conditioners"—or is it: "We sell comfortable building environments"? Is it: "We process shelf-stable food"—or is it: "We make food quicker and easier to eat [at a given profit]'"? The second definition has breadth— the company will consider any form of food and it will consider such functions as manufacturing kitchen equipment, operating restaurants, providing service on air transport, etc.—and a qualifier: convenience. It is consumer-oriented.

To this, add such other qualifiers as: "We will enter a market that generates this return on investment and \$xxx in profits, based on a margin goal of xx percent"; and/or "We must be the volume leader, with a share in excess of 00 percent"; or similar objectives.

Conversely: "We will *not* pioneer—but we will out-execute the pioneers in the following areas"; or "We will enter only well-established [mature] market categories, where our captive distribution system provides an edge"; or "We will market only products with life cycles longer than xx years." Be specific.

A specific, refined—and periodically redefined—corporate charter sets the course for a company's commitment to new products. It recognizes the company's strengths and weaknesses within its industry and as perceived by the marketplace. As has been stated, historically companies with the most successful new product records stick closely to their areas of expertise and marketplace leverage; this, of course, with alertness to the changes in resource availability and market needs, as in the petroleum industry example.

Growth Program

Growth goals must be consistent with the corporate charter. Often they are not. Security analyst reports bear witness to the later spinoffs of whole companies as well as product lines that did not "fit" the corporate direction. In all candor, company spokesmen usually identify this as reason for divestiture.

It can be demonstrated that a large percentage of all new product failures were predictable, where the failure relates to the company marketing the product rather than to the validity of the concept. In other words, where the corporate charter is violated (including a violation of the financial guidelines), the risk multiplies. A balanced, well-funded new product growth program nurtures the business by constantly proliferating and upgrading product offerings in value, variety appropriateness, and availability.

There is also an important portion of the growth program beyond those market maintenance tactics. This critical area of development has the greatest risks, but also the potential of greatest rewards. This is the challenge to build a large, new business base. It requires long lead time, large infusions of money, and a steady hand on the corporate ship to steer an often frustrating course through the shoals of the financial press, shifting government regulations, and the queries of perplexed shareholders.

Table 6-1 illustrates such a total, balanced, growth program—one that looks at proprietary, industry, and breakthrough opportunities. This schematic represents one approach to managing and monitoring new product programs in line with corporate charter strategic needs. A typical company divides the new product budget between maintenance product changes and development of current markets vs. entrance into new businesses, and determines the optional advantages of contracted R&D, suppliers, joint ventures, licensing, and acquisitions. The company assigns appropriate numerical time and dollar guidelines for return on investment, cost of goods sold, sustaining profits, share of market, rank in category, etc. This approach is a useful discipline for any maker and marketer of goods and services with growth goals beyond those of efficient use of captive resources to increase baseline volume and profits.

Table 6-1 New products possible growth model

Expertise	*Proprietary*	*Proprietary + industry*	*New to industry*
Strategy	**IMPROVE** Maintain and build franchise	**INNOVATE** New franchise in familiar trade	**INVENT** New business base
Tactics	Appearance/form Performance Package Price/value Distribution Line extensions Flankers New category to brand	New brand New entry, old category New category New solution, old problem New problem solution Creation of new need Revive dying category Revive dying solution	
Sales goal	From hold volume to major increases	Major increases	Largest volume, major corporate impact
Life cycle	Continual process needed to stay viable	Continual process needed to stay a leader or establish it	Long life required to justify program, payout
Capital	Funded from existing product revenue base	Short-term added investment	Large, new money
Technology (inc. mfg.)	At hand	Available outside, e.g., contract suppliers, joint ventures, etc.	New knowledge, skills, staff professionals
Development time	Short	Short to medium	Long
The bottom line: Corporate commitment	Routine, within budgets	Normal approvals	Heavy, long range

Business Disciplines

Perspective is key. This is particularly true for the long-term, major investment ventures. The successful ones are well-conceived at the beginning, thoroughly planned, then professionally executed in a cohesive program. Changing policy guidelines may have other corporate benefits, but they are usually not conducive to the realization of major new business development goals nor are they characteristic of companies with impressive new product success records.

It takes more than a corporate charter and a growth program to succeed. Companies with impressive new product successes benefit most from well-organized new product policies and procedures—the disciplines of the business.

Opportunity identification, conceptualization, and prototype modeling are the areas where talent, inspiration, insight, and pragmatism count most. Often, too, these are areas where programs run aground. If this is to be, it is less expensive at this stage than later, when plant and marketing commitments escalate costs.

As preventive medicine, use a new products checklist denoting just about every major predictable factor that should be audited at every phase of development—in R&D (or R&E), production, finance, legal, distribution, communications. A useful example is included in Appendix 2A. It lists more than 120 chronologically phased operational considerations—where things can go wrong, as well as right.

Most disastrous is to *not know* when a program is foundering—and to plunge ahead, evading the obvious. It is the obvious (on hindsight) that is usually the cause of failure and—just as often—it is the obvious that is the single most important ingredient of success. *Never overlook the obvious.*

7

Goals—Deciding Where to Go

Now that the corporate charter is understood, it must be executed in strategic new product growth goals to provide direction to managers, impetus to the system, and a trigger to the process.

The corporate charter sheds some light; it tells you where you are; it tells you in general where you want to go. It doesn't take you there, nor prescribe the route.

For this, directional goals must be established.

Product Portfolio Assessment

In an article written for the January–February 1981 issue of the *Harvard Business Review*, Yoram Wind and Vijay Mahajan described how to design a product and business portfolio:

> Since its emergence in the early 1970s, the portfolio technique—along with related concepts like the Strategic Business Unit and the experience curve—has become the framework for strategic planning in many diversified companies. Now the art has advanced enough to give a diversified company a variety of approaches when it is considering installing such a system or substituting one that evidently meets its needs better than the current portfolio.

97

Conceptually, we think, the tailor-made approaches are superior because they:

- Permit inclusion of the conceptually desirable dimensions of risk and return, plus any other idiosyncratic elements viewed by management as important.

- Stimulate creativity by forcing management's involvement in developing strategic options.

- Help to gain an advantage over competitors, who are ignorant of the company's portfolio framework and so cannot "read" it with the aim of anticipating the company's strategic moves.

- Can offer explicit guidelines for resource allocation among the portfolio items.

But a tailormade system costs more, mainly in data requirements and management time. Even if top management decides not to implement an idiosyncratic approach (based on cost-benefit analysis), an evaluation of currently used portfolio models . . . should add to the value of the portfolio analysis and the quality of the strategies designed to build a new portfolio.

There are many approaches that can be taken in assessing a company's strategy for new products and its compatibility with the needs, resources, and objectives of the organization. *The Harvard Business Review* article describes nine product profile models that merit study, if only to identify the many variables that must be considered and the need for management to assign (largely judgmental) weights to each element of any model's equation. The nine portfolio models are classified according to degree of adaptability, allocation rules, and dimensions, with appropriate comments. They are:

1. Growth/share matrix

2. Business assessment array

3. Business profile matrix

4. Directional policy matrix

5. Product performance matrix

6. Conjoint analysis-based approach

7. Analytic hierarchy process

8. Risk/return model

9. Stochastic dominance

These models are designed to assess corporate strategies for ongoing businesses as well as to help determine whether the company should add new businesses, and whether these new businesses will be compatible with the needs, resources, and objectives of the organization. Each new product line requires an investment designed to yield a certain return. Top management's role is to determine the products or businesses that will comprise the portfolio and to allot funds to them on some rational basis.

It is clear, in evaluating the various approaches to setting business enterprise development goals, that subjective judgment is the most important aspect in determining success. After all, any and every company presumably can plug into the various business portfolio models. Also, presumably, most of the fact sources will be similar. Therefore, the critical difference in determining the course of action is management judgment.

Because weighing the facts calls for subjective judgment, it is management's responsibility to decide who the evaluators will be and how conflict among them will be resolved. These decisions cannot be left to staff members involved in the construction or implementation of the new product or enterprise development programs.

Establish a New Front

Management must decide where to compete, how to compete, and when to compete. Management must decide whether to follow the generally acceptable strategies of business, or to try to change the rules of the game to obtain a major advantage.

A new front may hit competition where it is strategically weak, it may outflank the field, and it may be the theater in which new weaponry is introduced. Certainly, it gives a timing advantage not available when joining the already identified battle, with its fortresses, entrenchments, and deep logistics. Besides surprise and control of one's own destiny, this approach also often offers the added advantage of creating new entries that are not readily available to the entrenched competition. Among the flanking actions not available to competition are new product standards and tactics, which if adopted by them would recognize obsolescence or improvement of their presumable parity or better lines, new technology that requires costly replacement of existing models, new sources of supplies not adaptable to present manufacture and assembly, and new forms of distribution, which if adopted would negatively affect support from present distribution factors.

Once essence of success in this approach is to upset the static equilibrium in a mature industry. In new, emerging industries still in flux, this approach gives the innovator who has committed a full front advance the ability to establish the rules for the category.

Find a "Sitting Duck"

Where management has the luxury of selecting points of attack, selective evaluation of the practices (and successes) of entrenched competition often reveals a "sitting duck" for new product invasion. In many large, mature fields, the leaders maintain position for historic reasons, and have built up capital-intensive manufacturing with large (often obsolete) plant commitments, unfavorable labor contracts, and dependence on (often captive) sources of raw material or parts supply.

Under such conditions, which are prevalent, the manufacturer can hardly be marketing intensive. The production and transport drain takes up funding that might otherwise go to plant sophistication, R&D, and marketing. Sales operations are likely to be trade intensive, because moving the plant product at optimum capacity is the first order.

An extreme example of this is the meat packing industry, where it is logistically detrimental to hold large quantities of raw material, or, on the other hand, to be undersupplied. No wonder the priorities are clearly spelled out in the motto: "Sell it or smell it." The leaders in this field, incidentally, have deemphasized their fresh meat operations in favor of further-processed products, with raw material needs beyond minimum supplies provided by *other* meat sources. In other words, they are not locked into under-capacity slaughterhouses.

Quick indications of vulnerability are industries where leadership positions have been stable, with little market share change; one-product companies and industries; industries with a high percentage of contract packing; and industries and leader companies that have not adapted to new and more cost-efficient processes utilized by similar makers, and do not use new, cost-saving materials or distribution techniques that will benefit major customers. Opportunistic goals are suggested by protracted price-war battles among industry leaders, which will sap their financial resources and divert their perspectives. Other opportunities are suggested by conservative, entrenched management and by well-investigated changes in ownership and in management.

Framework for Business Planning

Management, then, provides the leadership for risk taking. Its attitudes will set the tone for the corporation and will largely determine whether the company will be in the forefront of new enterprise development or merely an adequate follower of industry new product practice.

Gil Amelio, chairman and CEO of Apple Computer Inc. and formerly in the same position at National Semiconductor Corp., has based much of his success on new products. His 1996 book *Profit from Experience* (co-written with William L. Simon) states:

> The need for management comes about when the organization must create new products and market them. That's what management energy most needs to be devoted to— managing change . . . When you want to increase the rate of change, you need more management energy injected into the system. But no company today can afford to have an army of managers waiting in the winds to be assigned.
>
> One powerful way of enabling the corporation to create rapid change is to enroll the aid of consultants. At times of the greatest need for change, I enhance the capabilities of the corporate team by calling on the talents of a carefully selected group of consultants—people screened by our experience with them or information about their back-

Figure 7-1 The strategic game board

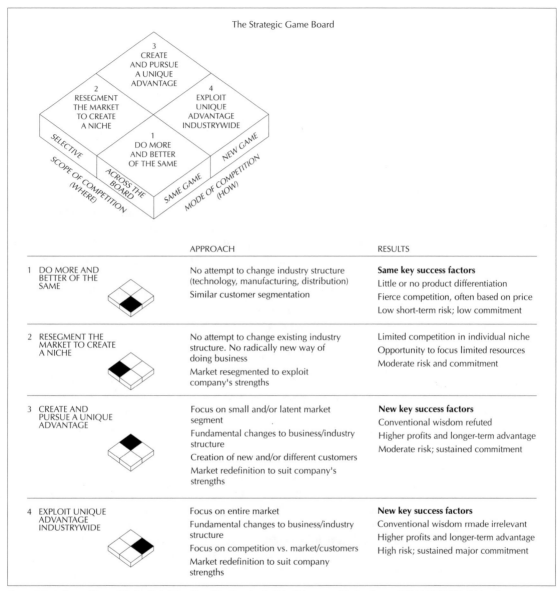

Source: Roberto Buaron, "How to Win the Market Share Game? Try Changing the Rules," Management Review, January 1981 (c) AMACOM, division of American Management Association.

ground, and chosen for their specific talent to help aug-
ment the existing management teams. . . .

The best consultants have the spirit of the teacher imbedded in their style and help people learn in the way we all
know is best: by doing and discovering for themselves.
There's a clear difference between the contractor brought
in to do a specific task, and the consultant who works
with your company over an extended period. It's important not to confuse the two by measuring their performance against the same set of criteria.

As much as we wish business to be a science, chance forces often
prevent this. In fact, Nobel Laureate scientist Sir Francis Crick says:
"Chance is the only source of true novelty." True, but there *is* a scientific
method—and the investigational and experimental elements of it have
been adapted by business, to enhance the odds for success. Professional
do better at games of chance than do amateurs.

Perhaps chance is the reason Roberto Buaron, writing in *Management Review*, refers to his market-entry strategic planning model (Figure
7-1) as "The Strategic Game board." The moves are a choice, highly reactive to the competitive set:

1. Do more and better of the same

2. Resegment the market to create a niche

3. Create and pursue a unique advantage

4. Exploit unique advantage industrywide

The scope and mode of competition affects the strategic approach and
results.

Before entering any game of chance, however, the possible missions
should be reviewed—and the goals established. At this planning stage,
management is in control of events. In Figure 7-2, "A framework for business planning," SRI International defines the first step in business as
"Formulating the Task." This is management's obligation in setting goals.

SRI defines components of this goal setting as:

1. Define the scope of the task

2. Identify the reasons it is being undertaken

3. Define characteristics of the answers sought

4. Consider alternative methods of procuring answers

5. Select a method of solution based on cost-value analysis and
   resource availability

6. List the information required for solution

7. Specify the action required to develop the information needed

This is followed by development of the inputs from available sources, evaluation of the alternatives along a continuum of possible-to-feasible-to-desirable—to arrive at the consequential goals.

This generative phase completed, management translates the decision(s) into statements of:

1. Why the action is required

2. Action and resources involved; consequences expected and when

3. Controls for interim measurement of progress, by

   a.   Identifying critical forecasts and conditions to be monitored

   b.   Prescribing necessary performance standards

   c.   Prescribing the performance schedule to be met

   d.   Prescribing the budget requirements to be met

For further study by its subscribers, SRI International's Business Intelligence Program, formerly Long Range Planning Service, details this approach in Long Range Planning Service Report No. 162.

Less Risk, More Control

Although entrepreneurial risk-taking in internal development of new products has been emphasized in much that has been written about the subject, the application of narrowly disciplined controls also provides incentives.

Some companies recognize that they are not particularly good at product innovation—but that they are superior at cultivating and harvesting. This logically leads to an emphasis on brand development—and an acquisition strategy. The goal is to acquire well-managed, high-performing companies that are compatible to headquarter controls and ability to provide growth financing for the new subsidiaries.

H. J. Heinz Company is a good example.

Heinz has acquired Ore-Ida, Foodways National, Star Kist, Weight Watchers International, Cardio-Fitness, The Fitness Institute, Pestritto Foods, Pro Bakers, Shady Maple Farm, W. P. Foods, Hubinger, Jerky Treats, Skippy Premium dog food, Recipe dog food, Bavarian Specialty Foods, Tasty Frozen Products, Les Boulangeries Maison Bakeries, and Celestial Farms, as well as a host of companies all over the world, including Canada, Venezuela, England, Italy, Belgium, Netherlands, Germany, France, Portugal, Australia, Botswana, Zimbabwe, Japan, China, India, New Zealand, South Korea, Thailand, and American Samoa.

As reported in *The New York Times*: "Heinz's new products have come mainly through such acquisitions—of small companies with few, although highly successful products—rather than internal development. 'The record of large companies in new product development is chilling,'

Figure 7-2 A framework for business planning

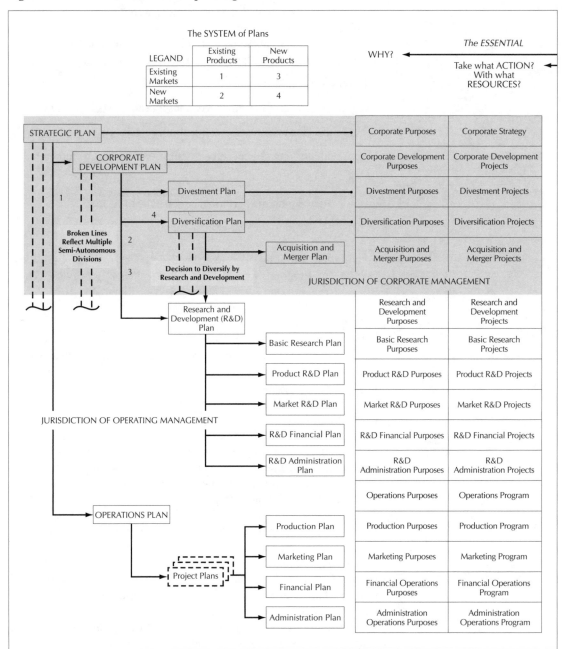

Source: From *Long Range Planning Service Report No. 162, SRI International's Business Intelligence Report*, SRI International, Menlo Park, California.

Figure 7-2 (Continued)

ELEMENTS of Each Plan

The PROCESS of Creating a Plan

To ACCOMPLISH what? when?

What CONDITIONS must be met?

Corporate Goals	Forecasts Policy Decision Guidelines
Corporate Development Goals	Forecasts Policy Schedules and Budget
Divestment Goals	Goal Feasibility Criteria for Decision
Diversification Goals	Forecasts Criteria for Decision
Acquisition and Merger Goals	Availability of Candidates Criteria for Decision
Research and Development Goals	Policy Decision Guidelines Schedules and Budgets
Basic Research Goals	Goal Feasibility Criteria for Decision
Product R&D Goals	Technical Feasibility Cost Feasibility Schedules and Budgets
Market R&D Goals	Forecasts Competition Schedules and Budgets
R&D Financial Goals	Technical Feasibility Market Forecasts Cost Performance
R&D Administration Goals	Business Feasibility Managerial Availability Other Resource Availability
Operations Goals	Business Forecasts Organization and Procedures Schedules and Budgets
Production Goals	Workload Forecasts Methods and Standards Schedules and Budgets
Marketing Goals	Sales Forecasts Competition Schedules and Budgets
Financial Operations Goals	Financial Performance Schedules and Budgets
Administration Operations Goals	Managerial Performance

FORMULATE THE TASK

Define its scope
Identify the reasons it is being undertaken
Define the characteristics of the answers sought
Consider alternative methods of procuring answers
Select a method of solution based on cost-value analysis and resource availability
List the information required for solution
Specify the action required to develop the information needed

DEVELOP THE INPUTS

Assemble the facts
Forecast or postulate the uncertainties
Develop the alternatives to be considered

Note: Information can be developed by assembling what is known by search and discovery and by creative thought. It is in the development of alternatives for consideration that creativity exerts the greatest influence on the planning process.

EVALUATE THE ALTERNATIVE COURSES OF ACTION

Convert alternatives to terms that can be compared
Establish criteria for making a selection
Compare alternatives

Note: Refine the alternatives from the possible to the feasible to the desirable if the evaluation is complex.

DECIDE

TRANSLATE THE DECISIONS INTO STATEMENTS OF

Why the action is required

Action and resources involved

Consequences expected and when

Controls for interim measurement of progress by
Identifying critical forecasts and conditions to be monitored
Prescribing necessary performance standards
Prescribing the performance schedule to be met
Prescribing the budget requirements to be met

noted Anthony J. F. O'Reilly, chief executive of Heinz. 'We've experimented and find that we're not as good at it as the entrepreneur.'

Within its existing product range, Heinz has concentrated mainly on line extensions."

Commenting in *The Journal of Business Strategy*, Heinz's former vice president of corporate planning, Walter G. Schmid, said:

> "Acquisition has become a popular way for companies to grow over the past decade. Yet all acquisitions are not alike. To be successful, acquisition must be regarded as a tactic that contributes to a larger corporate strategy. Companies that absorb other businesses without considering compatibility of markets, products, or management do so at their peril.
>
> Our company has taken this philosophy to heart. We have developed an acquisition strategy that complements our goals for growth by exploiting opportunities in niche markets related to our core business.
>
> At Heinz, our growth equation is the sum of both internal initiatives and acquisitions. Our low-cost operator programs, marketing of big brands, and development of new products fuel our internal development. Acquisitions constitute the primary source of growth for new market niches and geographic expansion. It is an important tool for extending our network of worldwide brands. . . .
>
> So what is the Heinz acquisition equation? Basically, it is this: persistence + vision + discipline + courage + patience = success in acquisitions."

The strategy seems to be working, propelling Heinz into the ranks of the top performing food-processing companies.

Different strokes for different folks. General Mills, another top performer (with nearly all sales from consumer products), has successfully advanced on many fronts: flankers and line extensions from its strong stable of brands; new brands, new lines; licensing-in and licensing-out; acquisitions; innovative, internally developed technology; and new enterprises. This is an example of a large, multidivisional corporation whose management has been able to engender entrepreneurial flair in its goal setting.

Managements, then, are seen to set goals that include an acceptable percentage of failures and limited successes, in order to instill the dynamism necessary to assure both the short-term and long-term future. The "acceptable percentage" differs widely, or course—but no company can expect to be in the product battle without a willingness to risk failure. The phased programming of each venture, tightly budgeted in advance, provides the controls.

The optimum goal may be to achieve a balanced portfolio of growth opportunities, both from within markets currently represented with company entries and from markets new to the company. Within that framework, sales, return on investment, and life cycle are calculated. The smaller the risk (close-in opportunities), the lower the sales and ROI required, with development time and cost at a minimum. At the other end of the scale are developmental needs for new technology and a heavy, extended infusion of capital. Here sales goals and ROI must be high and be sustainable over a lengthy life cycle.

Such goals can be spelled out in measurable terms for the future, and used to audit present and past performance.

Attached to these directions can be some broad goals, such as:

1. Build the basis for a *new brand franchise* with a specific dimension new to the company

2. Build the basis for a *new distribution system*, whether it be through conventional means and staff or one newly employed or contracted

3. Build the basis for *new outlets or store section* penetration

4. Build the basis for a *new preemptive product technology*

5. Build the basis for a *new manufacturing process* that fits the company's present marketing system or the systems employed by the previously stated goals.

8

Top Management Support

The surest motivation for new product success is the attention of top management, not only to the strategic goals but to the evolving details of the business. This requires that management send clear signals of career advancement potential to those entrepreneurial spirits who have the instincts as well as skills to pioneer.

The entire organization must be turned on by the opportunity.

For example, L. W. Lehr, former chairman of the board and chief executive officer, 3M Company, writes:

> Nothing is more important to 3M Company's continued success than its ability to efficiently develop and market new products which are acceptable to society and profitable to the company. . . . A basic 3M philosophy is to encourage all employees of whatever special discipline to participate in the creation of new, profitable products, and for the company to provide an unstructured climate in which to do so. . . . While not necessarily part of the prerequisite for a successful new product, an orderly process helps to insure that our new or modified products are compatible with both 3M's profit objectives and the ever-growing demands of society.

The 3M Company's "Guidelines for Planned Product Responsibility" describe the functions of the technical, marketing, manufacturing, and specialized staff services that assist in the successful introduction of new or modified products. The guidelines not only cover the standard developmental phase procedures, but also provide guidance in the areas of product assurance, product safety, and the product's environmental impact. They are detailed in Appendix 2B.

Encouraging Participation

3M is one company that provides broad direction, specific aids, and, most importantly, the atmosphere of management encouragement of brand participation in new product ventures.

In order to innovate, it is up to management to break the mold of tradition, industry cliché, and standard ways of doing business. Most new enterprises follow the guideposts of the industry in which they compete. This follows logically from the industry's public information sources, whether audits of sales or trade channel inputs, and the standard definition of "markets" common to the industry. New divisions of the market drawn along different patterns are conceptually more challenging, but often not as objectively supportable. For these reasons, the rare risk-taking that occurs frequently does not have the opportunity to yield the greater results that the "follow-the-leader" approach routinely sets as objectives.

Gadfly and Catalyst

In a January 1981 article in *Management Review*, published by AMA-COM, a division of the American Management Association, Robert Buaron wrote:

> It is not surprising, then, that successful new-game strategies are rare. To upset the competitive balance and rewrite the rules of the game of an industry calls not only for exceptionally imaginative entrepreneurial thinking but for uncommonly strong and sustained commitment. Inevitably, both must start with a strong lead from the top.

> In the interest of fostering a no-holds-barred approach to strategic thinking, the chief executive will need to get involved early in the planning process as gadfly and catalyst, probing conventional assumptions and proposing novel alternatives to begin breaking down planners' mental barriers to radical change.

Many major companies have delegated the gadfly/catalyst roles to outside consultants, who speak with the internally well-publicized knowledge and support of management—but do not have line authority. This allows an experienced perspective to intercede without inordinate time demands on the chief executive, who has an easy-access, informal, off-the-record dialog with his consultant. Such an outside influence, of course, must be chosen with extreme care by the chief executive, because the consultant will also serve as an alter ego and trusted confidant.

Buaron continues:

> To support the necessary level of organizational commitment, the chief executive should take particular care that he is personally sending the right signals to the organization. This means, above all, visibly concentrating his own time and attention on key strategic functions (such as R&D, marketing) and activities (competitor analysis, for example). It also means encouraging open communication and, in most cases, downplaying rank and protocol by giving special recognition to bright junior executives.
>
> Finally, and by no means least important, he can and should, if necessary, reshape the corporate reward and value system to bring it into line with the desired strategic orientation. Tunnel vision is unavoidable in companies where managers' pay and prospects are consistently tied to short-term earnings growth. Strategic thinking can only flourish in organizations where successful risk-takers and innovators, rather than "solid citizens" who are best at avoiding conspicuous mistakes, are seen to reap the kudos and financial rewards.

Providing Directional Spark—and Support

So, whether a company is in its entrepreneurial phase, or is a highly disciplined, well-established one competing in a mature industry, it is up to management to provide the directional spark—and support—that will yield points-of-entry for new enterprises.

Management must hold high the standards, must flaunt its support for the innovators—to motivate others as well as these essential contributors. Successful top executives who have built companies on outstanding new product track records will never be satisfied with anything short of superiority. Their statements, their actions, their rewards systems recognize this. As Somerset Maugham wrote: "It's a funny thing about life, if you refuse to accept anything but the best, you very often get it."

To demand a lot requires giving a lot. To learn, to teach, to make a difference is the role of a leader in the conception of new enterprises.

Management should know the business and human resources of the company, and the technology and practices of the industry. Management should not know as much or more than the supervisors responsible for each aspect. Sufficient knowledge is needed to give a clear direction that can be acted upon: what to do, not how to do it. Not what cannot be done, but what goals and challenges to offer.

Management should know enough—but not too much.

A Few Examples

EMI Music

When James Fifield arrived at U.K.–based Thorn EMI PLC's big music division, EMI Music, in 1988, the new president brought with him experience as head of CBS/Fox Video, the nation's largest video company, plus 20 years of General Mills management experience ranging from consumer package goods to toys.

Forbes magazine reports: "Fifield. . . found a sleepy highly centralized company" with sales of $1.1 billion, but earnings of just $50 million.

"Fifield took a year to check out EMI Music's businesses in 37 countries, including its largest label, money-losing Capitol Records in Los Angeles. Fifield gave Capitol-EMI Music President Joe Smith authority to streamline operations. Smith cut more than 50 percent of overhead, and Capitol is now profitable.

"Fifield then set out to expand EMI's product line through acquisition." By the end of May 1990, EMI labels "had the top four albums and eight of the top 20. Music's sales were up to $1.7 billion, and earnings had tripled to $155 million," reports *Forbes'* Peter Newcomb.

And the growth is still on a roll. By the end of March 1995, sales had grown to $3.5 billion, earnings to $478 million. In the five years since 1990, profits have nearly tripled, growing at a compound annual rate of 28 percent.

What's CEO Fifield's secret? Here's what he says:

"To manage a business that requires a strong element of intuition and risk taking, you have to give people the freedom to fail. You can't make local decisions on an international scale. You've got to leave it to the person on the spot. . . . I can't second-guess what we're doing in Malaysia. I just know we need to sign acts there."

Looking to the future, Fifield says EMI Music will continue to build and improve upon its strong artistic and financial record; to invest in the development of outstanding talent across all genres and markets—and continue its innovative marketing efforts, continue to be in the forefront of new technologies.

"And, we will continue to develop an entrepreneurial, creative, winning culture internally. We will have fun doing it—because, after all, it's only rock and roll."

(In late February 1996, Thorn EMI PLC announced that it would split into two publicly listed companies: Thorn PLC, the consumer-durables rental and rent-to-purchase business, and EMI Group PLC. James Fifield will continue as president and chief executive officer of Thorn EMI Group PLC.)

Crown Zellerbach[*]

When Harold Reed left the packaged food products industry in the early 1970s to join the great West Coast wood products company, Crown Zellerbach, as head of its Consumer Products Business Unit, he set about learning just enough about the conversion of trees into products, spending time with R&D, with quality control, with every plant superintendent. He learned enough—but not too much.

*Since acquired by James River Co.

As a consequence, he was able to suggest direction and challenges. If met with reasons why something might not work, he knew just enough to be able to say: "Perhaps you're right—but why not try to do it another way?" The managers responded with remarkable technical breakthroughs, receiving great self-satisfaction in proving their expertise while improving the company's new product superiorities.

Today, Reed heads the RE-MARKETING SERVICES company.

Support for Risk Taking

The record bears out that the highest percentage of new product successes are made by those companies who emphasize renewal management—repeating the success pattern over and over. There is nothing wrong with support for "doing what you do best—but doing it better." You need the old pro approach to less risk, albeit quicker but likely less return. The renewal process and the diversification process are more easily quantifiable, because they are based on track record and industry example.

Nonetheless, dynamic leadership also encourages and supports diversification and innovation. Because of the risks involved in innovation, the overall corporate performance from year to year is more likely to affect a consistent commitment to innovation. Net: New products are a need—and therefore a cost—of doing business.

The strongest signal management can send to staff regarding innovation is the development of a new products organization structure that has both high status and high visibility outside the company, as well as internally. This means that forward progress can be made with management blessing and support, but that the organization also has its own independent explanatory budget and charter.

However, the major thrust of the operation must involve top management, to understand its direction, to merit its support—and to gain by the contributions made by responsible executives who have a broad perspective, but are usually not involved in new product disciplines on a day-to-day basis.

Management is looking at the long run. Management is looking for consistent success at a predictable level. Management is also looking for major, breakthrough successes that can carry the company well ahead of planned growth patterns. For this, management will run risks.

A personal aside, to provide an example:

Very early in my career I was exposed to two types of innovative risk-takers, both in the same company. There were the entrepreneurial Harris brothers, who sold their Toni company[1] to Gillette; and there was Joseph Spang, chairman of the parent company. Mr. Spang made a visit of state to our division, to see how his newly acquired hair care company was integrating with his hair removal company. He was reviewing his troops.

---

[1] Now Gillette Personal Care division

Toni's management arrayed their newly minted brand managers around the boardroom table. Each gave his report in turn. Each had glowing words. Everything we did was a success. Every nationally distributed product was increasing share, we were beating back P&G, Lever, and Colgate at every turn. Every new product being introduced was exceeding test market performance. Every product in test was ahead of program.

We (rather smugly, as I look back at it) completed our reports.

Mr. Spang, dark-serge–vested proper Bostonian, said: "You gentlemen are to be complimented. It appears that everything you are doing is going very well." He paused, "However, I must confess to being disappointed. You see, when everything is going right, it means to me that everything you could be trying isn't being done."

That management support (and attitude) led Gillette into entirely new areas of growth, beyond the logical line extensions and "fighting brands" (to counter competitive new products) that had formerly been the hallmark of the company's success.

What this all means is that top managers must support new product ventures, encourage risk taking, and find means to cultivate entrepreneurial approaches uncommon to standard business practice—if the company is to be a consistent leader. This encouragement includes financial rewards and, perhaps even more importantly, the psychic reward of recognition that the new product area is most important to the growth of the company.

That spirit carries on to this day. Long after the Harris brothers and Joe Spang retired, Gillette kept pushing ahead—even as it fought off no fewer than four takeover attempts in the late 1980s.

Gillette's March 1996 annual report proves that the 90+-year-old Boston-based company continues to outperform its class, through new products, globalization, and effective marketing.

More than three-fourths of sales came from product categories in which Gillette holds the worldwide leadership position, a proportion that has risen 20 percent in the last five years.

New product activity is at an all-time high, with more than 20 products launched in 1995, along with the geographical rollout of major products such as SensorExcel. In the last five years, more than 45 percent of sales came from new products.

Globalization continues to increase success. In 1995, 70 percent of operating profits were generated outside the United States, up from two-thirds sales and profits in 1990.

9

Organizing for New Products

"The selection and development of new products must, in the final analysis, be the responsibility of top management. . . . Of course, top management cannot carry out such a responsibility by itself. The question is how to go about organizing for it."

—SAMUEL C. JOHNSON AND CONRAD JONES[1]

Just how does one go about organizing for new product development?

The answer is: It depends.

It depends on the nature of the corporation and its goals. It depends on the existing structural order of things. It depends on the corporation's management style. It depends on the caliber, motivations, and growth potential of the staff in place at the time of installing the new products organization. It depends on past (historic) performance by organizations charged with the responsibility. It depends on the orientation of the corporation, if this is not to change. (Are the present strengths or weaknesses centered in certain areas?)

It depends on patience.

Often, the first structure is not the enduring one. Of all areas, that of new products should be susceptible to new organizations—whether they be flanker organizations (to a new or existing new products department, but charged with a different order of new product innovation), or quite separately conceived organizations, with different reporting paths and budgets, maybe charged with acquisitions identification, or with development of entries into industries new to the corporation—or, perhaps, ad hoc committees and venture groups with limited time assignments. Sometimes, a corporation will "test" various organizational approaches to find the suitable setup for its specific needs.

[1] Samuel C. Johnson and Conrad Jones, "How to Organize for New Products," *Harvard Business Review*, May–June 1957. Mr. Johnson is chairman of S. C. Johnson & Son, Inc. Mr. Jones is a former group vice president of Booz Allen & Hamilton, Inc.

It depends on geography.

Some corporations set up their new product organizations in separate quarters from the day-to-day operations. Some locate the new product leaders near the department most important to early development—e.g., if the new product leader is a marketing person, he may have an office near R&D, and vice versa. Some companies do not change the geography, but create liaison staff positions to integrate one key function with another. For example, a businessperson might be attached to the laboratories with no lab functions other than to act as facilitator between the lab staff and the new product marketing development department.

Whether accomplished through rearrangement of geography, assignment of a coordinator, or frequently scheduled meetings (including informal ones), it is essential that the marketer and the scientist learn each other's language. When addressing new enterprises where outside expertise is needed, it is critical for the inside scientists as well as the marketers to "go to school" on the communications of the new technology and the new marketing disciplines. Many companies sponsor sufficiently lengthy seminars between parties so that personal rapport as well as a common language is established.

And, it depends on timing.

Proactive and reactive needs are different. For the second need, a strike force with no other priority is an acceptable ad hoc organization. For the first, a venture team is a sometimes solution.

No one type of organization, therefore, is an ideal or even highly practicable organization for any one industry, let alone more than a few companies. Each company will seek its own structure, relying on both its needs and its talent pool.

Defining Goals by New Product Functions

To find the proper new products structure means defining the goals of the organization along lines that can define the functions of such a new products structure.

As an example, let's look at S. C. Johnson & Son, Inc. In setting up its new products department, S. C. Johnson described its needs along the continuums of *increasing technological newness and of increasing market newness*. (See Figure 9-1.) The divisions of technology range from "no change" to "improved technology" to "new technology." The divisions of marketing range from "no market change" to "strengthened market" to "new market." Working out the grid shows what type of new product activity is appropriate.

In S. C. Johnson & Son's case, the new products department reports to a top management officer, in order to provide the stature and independence necessary for coordinating interdepartmental programs. The department's director has the staff and freedom to participate in the broad affairs of the top planning committees of the company. The department draws on the various company departments to support its functions: administrative, marketing, technical, and negotiating (external).

Figure 9-1 Relationship of new product responsibilities by department

PRODUCT EFFECT	NO TECHNOLOGICAL CHANGE	IMPROVED TECHNOLOGY	NEW TECHNOLOGY
NO MARKET CHANGE		REFORMULATION	REPLACEMENT
STRENGTHENED MARKET	REMERCHANDISING	IMPROVED PRODUCT	PRODUCT LINE EXTENSION
NEW MARKET	NEW USE	MARKET EXTENSION	DIVERSIFICATION

KEY

☐ R&D   ▦ Marketing   ▪ Joint Responsibility

Source: Adaptation from Exhibit II. "How to Organize for New Products" by Samuel C. Johnson and Conrad Jones, *Harvard Business Review*, 35 (May–June 1957). © by the President and Fellows of Harvard College.

Several task forces report to the new products director: sponsor groups and product committees.

As defined by S. C. Johnson:

> Sponsor groups formulate a proposal and guide its development. Each group is formally charged, after the screening phase, with responsibility for successful development into a realistic product . . . Marketing, R&D, and the new products department are always represented: in addition, there may be one or two individuals drawn from other departments. (This) device discharges its responsibilities in the proposal and development phases. It provides minimum interference with the established departments and maximum reliance on their existing personnel and services.

> Product committees are formally organized with regular meetings and agenda, and have a large membership drawn from many departments—but the nucleus of each committee is the sponsor group that developed the product. The product committee is responsible for carrying a product, once developed, through to full-scale commercialization.

The benefits of this organizational approach for S. C. Johnson & Son read like the goals for most companies' new product departments. To summarize, they are:

1. Total product strategy is clarified and scheduled to fit long-range plans.

2. The staff is motivated by the knowledge that the product will be developed and that management knows who worked on it.

3. Sponsor groups and product committees develop broader management skills in participants.

4. Group efforts stimulate more creative ideas.

5. Project profit potential is enhanced by upgraded, controlled selection standards that maximize available resources.

6. A reduction of lost effort and lower product mortality relieves staffing pressures and minimizes personal disappointment.

7. Top management has a complete overview in condensed business terms. Prompt decisions can be made based on complete information.

8. Management is relieved of much supervision and coordination, leaving more time for analysis and judgment.

9. Long-considered as well as new ideas are quickly moved to conclusion, with more new products than before (this approach was applied) moving to market.

10. Ideas are commercialized faster by group anticipation of problems, with solutions devised in advance.

11. Sales features are designed into the product by team thinking before full-scale development, yielding enhanced market success.

Means to Fit the Needs

It is generally wise to consider segregating new product efforts for on-going revenue divisions from the activities of the long-range planning, corporate growth, and new enterprise development functions. An established division or subsidiary or brand franchise or customer segment organization should be responsible for all new product developments that it funds to enhance achievement of its measurable goals. It provides the budget. It must have the responsibility. Under these terms, all appropriate line extensions and flankers belong there.

Not infrequently, a concept is developed by a revenue division that does not automatically fit. In this instance, it can become the basis for that division's redefinition (expansion), can be assigned to another more appropriate channel (another division or an independent new products department), can be sold off to another company—or it can become "lost." To protect against the latter, a company must have an information system among departments and divisions that allows exploration of all activities for "fit," because it may be likely (especially in large companies) that divisions are not fully aware of each other's needs, goals, and plans. Where division charters are exceedingly well defined, they may be so tight that they allow large gaps between divisions, making it ordinarily impossible for the new concept to find a "home," even if it is highly appealing and within the company's expertise to execute. In this instance, a management review of all projects should spot the opportunity and assign it or profitably dispose of it.

As a company moves from the close-in to the far-out opportunities, it has a number of organizational structures to review. The first priority should be to define the *needs*. Then the means may be devised.

No set of boxes and dotted lines will help.

People are Paramount

A revealing evaluation of the business best-seller, *In Search of Excellence: Lessons from America's Best-Run Companies*, appeared in the *Los Angeles Times* on August 28, 1983. Written by Paul W. MacAvoy, professor of economics and dean of the University of Rochester's graduate school of management, the article states:

> [The authors] do not seem to get closer to knowledge when they find that their exemplary companies practice "almost radical decentralizations and autonomy" in setting up small organizations within the firm, the division, and even the plant within the division. This decentralization is not enough to produce better results alone. There has to be present a product manager able to sustain creative development of new products and services. The Peters-Waterman excellent companies reward the "champion" (project manager), do not strongly penalize the losers, and extend remarkably "complete support systems for champions."
>
> Although this incentive system is found to a degree in other companies as well, this is still a very important insight. The large organizations that make up manufacturing in this country become more efficient and innovative by reproducing within themselves an extremely numerous set of small organizations. They also reproduce within the company the outside public market for progressive and venturesome managers. This involves paying much more to those in the division and even in the plant that are successful in making profit.

The S. C. Johnson & Son, Inc. approach drew all new products responsibilities together into one functional model. MacAvoy seems to be saying that, for other companies, it may be wise to break out new products according to different divisions of interest, investment, and payoff.

Long-Range Planning

This farthest-out planning role has no line responsibility. It provides a business perspective background for actable decision-making. It surveys and forecasts the effects of change in science, technology, economics, agriculture, legislation, politics, etc.

Two examples:

- If long-range planning had effectively signaled possible impacts of fuel supply changes, the emergence of more efficient new plants and labor practices by overseas competitors, and other changes related to OPEC and post–World War II reindustrialization, this may well have been translated into earlier new product strategies by the U.S. auto industry.

  On top of this, according to Peter Brown, editor *Automotive News,* commenting in late 1990: "The Big 3 were unprepared to compete with what is becoming known as the 'lean production' system, as led by Toyota and practiced by most of the Japanese. Better long-range planning would have helped a lot, of course. But the cumbersome Big 3 bureaucracies still need to be hit by a two-by-four to see that they had to change the way they were doing business. (Saturn Corp. is GM's best response so far.)"

- In the information technology field, the monolithic leader's long-range planning process correctly predicted the explosive growth of the market for small presonal and business computers. IBM made unusual strategic moves to quickly enter the market with machines utilizing components, programs, and distribution systems from outside sources—tactics formed and executed by a separate and unconventional division set up to achieve market leadership in segments of the business new to IBM.

  Specific examples of Big Blue's new product innovations include the IBM RISC System/6000, described as the "hottest box" in the industry; the PS/1, IBM's entry into the home computer marketplace, and System/390, regarded as IBM's most significant product announcement since 1964.

Growth and Development

Growth and development articulates the perspective of long-range planning by establishing corporate missions for new market entry areas, acquisition of new resources and technology, and other opportunities in character with the corporate charter. From these missions (or goals), growth and development established strategies and preliminary budgets categorized in logical, timely authorization phases.

This operation is responsible for the search, both within the company and outside, to determine the best way to proceed to meet the goals. It may be determined that building up certain internal resources is the best way to move or that, on the other hand, there are enough differences in the new market components to require arrangements for external generation of the new entry.

Proliferation

Proliferation is the extension of existing expertise and facilities along various continuums. For example:

Existing product lines may be extended with different types of the same products. Easy examples would be more automobile and truck types, body styles, carrying capacities, etc.

Existing brands may be extended with new models. Again using the auto industry, examples are the Chevrolet Cavalier, Corsica, Beretta, Camaro, Lumina, Caprice, and Corvette.

Existing markets that lend themselves to the expertise of the manufacturer may be reached by easy proliferation from a base of both factory and sales performance. Staying with the automotive model, Honda has broadened from automobiles to motorcycles to power equipment for lawn care—gasoline-driven, service-intensive, relatively high-ticket hard goods all leveraging the same corporate expertise.

While growth and development and separate proliferation activities, under certain circumstances, may fit together, it is often better for them to be separated, with different channels of funding and accountability. Certainly, in all but the very largest corporate environments, the different organizations will draw upon common staff services, thus preventing uneconomic duplication. Growth and development most likely is funded from the corporate treasury, while proliferation is usually funded from a division or brand's own revenue generation.

Example: Dun & Bradstreet Corporation

"Our goal is to be in a state of continuous transition so we can always accommodate the changing environment of our clients," insists Harrington "Duke" Drake, former chairman and chief executive of Dun & Bradstreet Corporation. "Instead of concentrating on new ways to package and sell information we happen to have on hand, we are beginning to look at the changing needs of the marketplace and to devise ways to fill those needs," he told *Business Week* in an interview published November 16, 1981.

D&B carved out many freestanding profit centers that encourage managers to be entrepreneurial in their operations. The company coupled its new market-oriented mission and its vast computerization program to provide the main tool for the new strategy. Drake brought managers together to develop interdisciplinary cooperation that led to new products. And he mobilized outside consultants, NCSS staffers, and D&B trainers to teach D&B's staff of 25,000 to view new electronic equipment as vehicles to help create those products. As he described it to *Business Week*:

> There is an influx of new talent throughout the company. Its once meager strategic planning staff is now second only to its financial department in size. Divisions once filled almost exclusively with salespeople and operating

specialists are now salted with computer experts and market researchers—some of whom are specially trained to debrief salespeople on customer comments that might indicate a new-product need.

Interdepartmental communications have become the driving force behind D&B's management approach since 1980. An example described by *Business Week*.

> For the first time in the company's history, 140 senior managers [met] to brainstorm about the company's new market thrust. Financial officers, data processing managers, and other functional specialists are pooling ideas at their own interdisciplinary meetings. "Most of the ideas you need to grow a business are in somebody's lower right-hand desk drawer," explains Charles W. Moritz, chairman and chief executive offers. "We didn't want to miss a new product because divisions can't get together."

> So far, D&B has avoided any backlash from managers who might miss the simpler life of the product-driven days. "The process of change has been revolutionary in its impact, but evolutionary in its development," Moritz explains.

Some Different Approaches

One approach commonly used is to have a new products department that is responsible for enhancement of a company's chief strengths through utilization of internal technology and production, and appropriate established outside sources. This department brings the company no new businesses. Rather, it has the task of keeping the company in the forefront of its industry through the conceptualization and development of easily commercialized new products, beyond those relatively routine line extensions and flankers launched by the revenue divisions. Within each revenue division, an executive (a new product manager) is assigned to supervise this latter task, utilizing the resources (and budget) of the division.

Separately funded, on a par organizationally with upper-middle management, and reporting directly to top management may be an additional entity assigned the task of diversification into allied new businesses (as opposed to entirely unrelated businesses, such as those making up conglomerates attracted primarily by financial leverage opportunities). These businesses probably are identified in the corporation's long-range growth plans as new enterprises appropriate for the company's future development. Common titles for this department are New Enterprises, New Business, or Growth and Development.

Beyond this, of course, are growth plans unrelated to new products, but rather related to improved efficiencies (vertical integration can be an example), broader distribution (made feasible by additional plant sites, warehouses), overseas expansion, licensing, etc.

The Human Equations

In earlier chapters, it has been stressed that new products must have highly visible, actual support from top management. There are other human equations necessary to the success of the staffing of a new products organization.

When a business is established and going along reasonably well it needs careful managing. There is plentiful information input available. Many of the business circumstances are controllable. The competitors become well known and, to a degree, predictable. The company knows how to buy parts and material, how to make and assemble, how to sell and distribute, how to advertise and promote, how to fund, and how to profit.

This takes a certain kind of professional manager. This person deals with many understood facts on which to base judgments. He or she has a training organization.

For new products, different situations exist.

A new products manager must have an entrepreneurial ability, be a risk taker, be flexible, be very open-minded—in addition to being a sound strategist, negotiator, and salesperson. Ideas are fragile. Well-nurtured, they become concepts. Dismissed out-of-hand, they die before they are rounded out for expert evaluation. A new products manager must be a protector of the ideation process and its product. The manager must encourage the innovators and inventors, serving as mentor, sponsor, and, when absolutely necessary, protector from the demands of the system or the uninvolved critics. The manager should champion the ideation process and its participants, then make judgments that bring the concept into the more objective screening process. In short, it takes a different kind of leadership to run a new products program.

The new products manager calls on help from within his department, usually built around R&D and marketing, and from within the company. He uses corporate staff services: advertising, promotion, market research, sales administration, finance, etc. And he forms teams, for overall direction and to deal with explicit problems.

He may get the corporation to underwrite a venture group, a free-standing adjunct to his charter, but with a separate budget and the entrepreneurial freedom to conduct broad creative exploration. After the group isolates and embellishes the new enterprise to a point where it is suitable for inclusion within the new products department activities, it goes on to other freewheeling new development assignments or is disbanded.

On an ongoing basis, the new products manager may establish a review committee that includes interested representatives from each staff department, as well as the sponsor member of the new products staff. Subcommittees are established for particularly complicated issues. The committee aids the manager in evaluating the various projects, in providing the direction to their staffs in development of the necessary information and support programming, and in reviewing the department's management clearance recommendations. The department itself, of course, is responsible for initiating action and for the direction of approved new product programs.

Use of Outside Resources

Often, a new products organization is not wholly self-contained and needs outside help beyond corporate resources.

Except for close-in new product evolutions, the use of outside resources enables an organization to job out product development to selected professionals who bring new expertise that does not fit the table of organization until after the company is on stream in the new enterprise. Outside resources make it possible to hire on a part-time basis experts otherwise unavailable within the company or, in some cases, in the employment market. Outside resources can often play a key role in new product development.

Types of Outside Resources

Outside resources are of different varieties.

Suppliers of processing and assembly machinery, original equipment, processed ingredients and parts, laboratory and engineering components, and materials, etc., often make available experts gratis or at a nominal charge, depending on the degree of involvement and commitment from the contracting company. Sometimes these suppliers have free-lance sources on a consultancy basis to whom they may refer.

Dennis Piper, product development manager of the Troxel Bicycle Products Group, San Diego, CA (subsidiary of the Troxel Company, Moscow, TN), offers an especially innovative example of use of outside resources for product development: university students.

Mr. Piper explains that during one point in its evolution, a small generic task vitally important to completion of a development effort had no available staff to assign. Rather than hire a temporary employee or contract with a professional designer for this straightforward job, the engineering liaison office at a local university was contacted—and an engineering student was paid for a few hours of off-school time. The task was completed in less-than-estimated man-hours and calendar time, with acceptable quality work.

Troxel was encouraged by the result, so when an opportunity arose for a more complete but simple product development project the following year, the university was again approached. This time, the more advanced assignment was directed to an engineering professor who taught a course for a select group of senior students, in which local industrial companies work with the students on engineering tasks. The companies define an engineering task, communicate it to the students, provide feedback during the term, and fund fabrication of a prototype or model of the developed concept. There are usually four to six students on each company team, in order to provide a cross-section of ideas for each project. The final exam consists of making a presentation to the sponsors and the professor of their prototype. If Troxel was willing to fund such a project, the professor volunteered to present it to his class and see if any one wanted to do it.

"We jumped at the chance," Mr. Piper says, adding:

> There is some risk to the sponsoring company, because there is no way to guarantee that the student group will be able to handle the transition from class work to practical design in such a short time, or that their ideas will be as workable as desired. On the other hand, it provides great potential to get a simple design accomplished at little expense in a predictable time—the prototype must be done by the end of the term.

> We defined two relatively small development projects and for each we presented a list of desired features to the students, as well as information about similar and competing products. They obtained samples of the similar products, evaluated them, and rewrote the features list into their version of specifications. Once we agreed on the specifications, they began conceptualizing designs and passing them by us for review. After only a couple of iterations, they had rough designs we liked, and they went on with detail design. As they were completing the design, they were also beginning the prototypes, so some parts of the design were modified in accordance with their findings from fabricating the prototype—similar to the reverse engineering that no one wants to admit, but which nearly everyone does. In a number of cases, we had to assist them in obtaining materials for the prototypes, as they had no experience in locating or purchasing many of the required components. The university gave them access to the school machine shop, so they gained some experience in steel tube bending and processing, with a little milling and other tasks thrown in.

> About two days before the final exam date, they had completed both functional prototypes, and spent the rest of the time writing reports and adding decorative touches to the products. Their presentation prototypes behaved when put through their paces—and we recommended them for high grades.

Troxel considered the process to be very beneficial, but offered these comments to others who may consider using students in this manner:

Benefits:
1. The students are tremendously motivated, and bring many fresh ideas that might be overlooked by professionals who are experienced in the industry. They almost need to be held back at times.

2. They are fast, as they have to be to complete the design and prototype within one school term.

3. They are extremely analytical, possibly because they are familiar and comfortable with analytical processes from their coursework.

4. They provide an inexpensive method for conducting feasibility studies or first shot designs. If the project is too big to complete in one term, they can perhaps complete the skeleton to which professionals can add the meat of the design.

5. For small projects, they can do the complete design and assist in preparation for production. In our case, we continued to "consult" with the group leader on an as-needed basis for a few months after the end of the term.

6. They feel a huge sense of accomplishment from completing the design, and their pride is immeasurable when they see a finished sample of their product on a retail store shelf.

Cautions:
1. They require precise definition of the project in order to have any chance to complete the task. If the concept is nebulous at the beginning, they tend to wallow in it until it takes shape, and that is unfair to both them and the company.

2. During the specification and design phases, they must be watched rather closely, requiring more supervision than professionals to keep focused on the correct goal.

3. In a large task, they may have to take shortcuts to complete the project in time for the final exam, bypassing or not completing some necessary steps.

4. Their documentation may not be in the expected format, and drawings done by different members of the group may not resemble each other.

5. They probably have no experience at all in product costing, so the sponsoring company may have to adjust their designs to keep costs inside the desired guidelines.

Overall, with proper definition and supervision, this type of applied coursework can be very beneficial for both the students and the sponsoring company.

The creative use of the engineering student is one example of the many rewarding ways to discover and use outside resources.

Developmental research firms exist in all disciplines, from far-out futurist specialists looking beyond basic research to close-in technologists. In-between are the bulk of large, well-established R&D expert firms. Beyond the technical development and production aspects, outside experts in packaging engineering and design, sales, distribution, marketing and communications research, and communications also abound. Specialist legal firms in the patent and copyright areas should also be available to the corporate staff and its outside law services. Rather than having them "go to school" as involved participants in the project, let them audit the practices of the experienced experts.

Where companies have very active new product programs or are thin in internal management staffing, using outside services to provide executional controls is also merited. There are specialist firms in this field, primarily concentrated in marketing-oriented product categories.

In the author's experience as a consultant, I have served as a hands-on developer in a variety of fields appropriate to the client companies' missions and distribution, but either low in R&D priority, inappropriate to existing manufacturing, or without assignable internal start-up management. This has put responsibility for all early Go/No Go phases in my hands—often through subcontracting technical development and start-up manufacturing. This has been true in a wide range of consumer product, some involving patentable innovations.

Additionally, there are some advertising agencies with exceptional expertise and success patterns in new product development programs. The use of such resources can help accomplish a number of objectives, including:

1. Acting as an extension of the company's existing new products department or division

2. Acting as an additional, long-range exploratory new products resource

3. Providing a coordinated new product creative resource on a continuing basis, without disturbing regular company operations/programming

4. Acting as a study group or task force in a specialized area on a limited time basis without requiring the addition of costly internal staffing

5. Acting as a partner with a company venture team

6. Acting to reduce internal resource loads

7. Acting to get more projects moving faster

One of the benefits of assigning one or more of these roles to a properly qualified advertising agency is that there is an ongoing established relationship and a familiarity with the general business style and its participants.

However, this can be a trap.

One of the advantages of an outside resource is its presumed lack of inhibitions. A long, close relationship with an outside source sometimes takes on the same set of inhibitions as the inside staff. Therefore, before assigning a major conceptual and developmental role to an established supplier, be certain that the new product relationship, ground rules, and contractual signals all support independence of thought and candor of comment.

Role of the Advertising Agency

Because a product or a service or a business or a corporation is a communication in itself, early involvement of the advertising agency is advisable. However, as with any other resource, management must be certain that the advertising agency is qualified in the new product consultancy and development role beyond the areas of paid advertising, where the agency is an expert professional that can be held accountable for its performance.

There is no artists and writers school for new product practitioners. Writing a television commercial or a sonnet is not the same as creating a new product idea. A copywriter may describe it better, and that is very important. Equally, the ability to visualize does not automatically carry with it a new product specialty—although it often can convey an idea faster, or reveal a flaw in a product concept. Likewise, an advanced degree in the management sciences may expedite the plotting of the critical path—but promises no special hope for what may start down that path.

Understanding this is important to the assessment of the role of your advertising agency in dealing with new products marketing development. It is a different field than advertising development—although many similar skills and tools are employed.

Often a special type of agency team—an agency venture team—is necessary to best fulfill the needs of a new product assignment. That same team will not necessarily carry through its successfully launched product.

But why should an advertising agency be considered for the assignment in the first place?

First and foremost, because of the increasing inseparability of the product from its image, no one communication alone moves the new product to success. The audience identification, the empathetic message, the appropriate package (for the audience, for the shelf, for the advertising medium and its message) all meld together to form either an integrated or fractionated personality. An important part of that personality building occurs at birth, heavily influenced by the parents—who are hopefully bright, contemporary, strong, mutually reinforcing, and (it helps a lot) successful.

Therefore, the early perspective of how the agency views the eventual communication of the product image should play a highly influential role in the shaping of the product itself. It is often easier for the product to succeed when the partners who conceived it also bring it to the world.

In a *Marketing News* interview by staff writer Chad Rubel (published March 25, 1996), this author/new product development consultant stated that he had "always encouraged interaction from various departments and . . . bringing in outsiders contributes to the creative process, because the barriers are eliminated. Built-in hierarchies in companies often limit discussions between workers and management."

The need for agency flexibility is extreme—inasmuch as the differences among client needs, as reflected in their facilities and staffing, tend to vary more widely in the new product area than in advertising services. The company's advertising policy is established, has an operational pattern, and a common trade language. This is less likely to be so with new product practices.

The advertising agency's role, then, is to mesh with client capability; to be a fellow explorer; to provide an outside objectivity and perspective; to act as an intermediary in negotiations; to provide a synergistic effect in the creative process beyond the provision of optional concepts; to mobilize its special resources for program advancement; and, of course, to develop communication of the new product concepts themselves as well as their advertising messages.

Because a casual oversight, misjudgment, or lack of long-view perspective can create irretrievably disastrous results in the development of new products, there is a special demand for hardy candor, finicky nitpicking, devil's advocacy, and educated skepticism. The most fundamental new products revolutions have come from hard taskmasters, enthusiastic perfectionists; the marketer and the agency must both provide such courageous members to the new products team.

Sometimes it is the role of the company's advertising agency to "sell" the team's program to the top management of the corporation. It is often most effective to communicate a new product concept to top management as it would be done to a customer. The corporate top management expects that before the new product team comes to them, all the proper steps have been taken. Management can always ask questions and dig into details. But first, the team must get this attention.

There is no surer way to do this than by portraying the new product concept in a realistic consumer communications form—both the advertising and the product itself. If it needs further explanation, then there is something missing in the prototype communication. Preparation of prototypical exhibits, especially in package goods, fits the resources of the advertising agency. (Incidentally, studies show that consumer products companies tend to overemphasize and industrial products companies tend to underemphasize the importance of customer communication.)

Selecting Outside Resources

It is perhaps more difficult to select a new product specialist source than almost any other type of supplier or consultant.

After a company is satisfied with the professional qualifications, then the key matters often boil down to:

1. *Communications*. Do they understand what I mean? Do I understand what they mean?

2. *Enthusiasm*. Do they not only understand the goal, but do they already have in mind an easily understood program to meet it—and, perhaps, some contributory inspirations that demonstrate both their understanding and enthusiasm?

3. *Rapport*. Do I respect them and do they respect me? Will they be easy to work with, wear well, and justify my respect?

4. *Leadership*. Will they provide leadership for the program, not be merely contributors?

5. *Track Record and Methods.* Do their accomplishments appear valid and are their methods rational and sophisticated? (Check references.)

6. *Compensation Arrangement.* Is it fair and equitable? (Do not base a decision on the amount quoted. Equal expertise earns equal dollars. Low prices generally provide insufficient service or later additional. High prices generally provide the supplier with insurance against the unpredictable and the financial freedom to do wide-ranging explorations. Find out if these factors are the explanation.)

   Establish accounting practices up front. Occasionally, some services are appealed to by incentive arrangements, working at cost or cost-plus with a later addition for success. Even royalty arrangements are made, on top of a fixed fee. (Appendices 2D and 2E cover these arrangements in more detail.)

No matter how comprehensive your company's new products organization structure is, by all means use outside services. We all need all the help we can get.

10

A Program to Address New Product Goals

The need for new business, for new products, has been established. The risks—and rewards—have been weighed. Your company has decided to hew to its charter or to break new ground (and, hence, revise the charter). An organized program of development is needed.

Before all of the elements of the critical path become event bubbles, a blueprint for action must be decided. It must proceed from the general to the specific, from an assortment of many options to a plan for introducing a few, from small financial commitment across an assortment of considerations to much larger commitments to major opportunities that have been identified in the development process.

The favored mode is to risk little in preliminary exploration, increasing the investment as knowledge is gained and the opportunity refined. Each stage in the development has a Go/No Go gate. Here it is decided to stop the program, retrace the route for further information and evaluation, or to proceed through the gate along the next path toward further refinement.

There are many acceptable structures for moving from the wide mouth of the exploration funnel to the narrow spout of new products output. The rest of the chapter outlines one that has well served many industries. Its general pattern will be the structure of succeeding sections of this book.

Phase 1: The Search for Opportunity— Compilation of Available Data

Market identification and opportunity targeting is the initiating phase necessary to determine whether a particular market area should be given major pursuit. Often, much of this determination has been made in the corporate charter and the goals it contains.

Knowing the industry, the sales volume and trends, the basic technology, the target consumer, the competition—all factors that help shape the development of a fact book and a plan—are necessary first steps. In some industry categories, there are readily obtainable information sources generally recognized as accurate by all participants. In others, original research, experienced judgments, and reasonable guesses may be required.

Recognizing this, the mission is to reduce the subjective factors and to assemble reasonably acceptable *facts*, on which the first cut at opportunity identification will depend. Because these are mostly quantifiable— whether by demographics, spending, plant utilization rates, etc.—the needed areas of investigation may be quickly listed.

Industry Analysis

All exploratory searches start with an analysis of the industry under consideration for a new product entry. Among the categories of information to consider are sales volume and trends, basic technology, the nature of the competition, and customer definition. These may be detailed as follows, and are explored at greater length in a later section:

Sales volume and trends

- By dollar volume and unit sales
- By specific manufacturer/marketer
- By specific product
- By geographic region
- By population density
- By economic index (per capita consumption, buying power, etc.)
- By media efficiency (if applicable)
- By customer use pattern (user defined by frequency of purchase, use occasion)
- By marketing expenditure as percent of sales, per prospect potential, etc.
- By sales, distribution, and pricing practice

Basic technology

- State of the art
- By component parts, raw materials, labor resources
- By process, assembly, packaging, etc., equipment and subcontract resources

- By patent barriers, opportunities
- By license opportunities
- By purchasing
- By transport

Competition

- By trade practices
- By product specifications
- By product reliability (including warranty practices, service, reputation)
- By product sales volume and trends, broken out from evaluations estimates, and projections above
- By advertising/promotion spending
- By media patterns
- By selling themes, major claims, image dimensions
- By share trends
- By share of marketing expenditures (and gross impressions) pattern
- By-end user and by trade channel marketing expenditure ratios
- By sales efficiency related to industry average, leading competitors, and trendlines

Customer definition

- By customer use pattern (by frequency of purchase, use occasion)
- By demographic characteristics
- By psychographic characteristics
- By awareness of category, competitive factors
- By attitude toward industry, competitive factors
- By alternative and substitute products (are products first choices, are brands first choices, is it an important decision, etc.?)
- By pricing effects (inelastic, elastic, responsive to small, large, frequent, etc., price adjustments)
- By regional and seasonal purchase, use patterns by individual products, marketers

Other factors, as available

- Outside affecting influences (foreign trade, regulatory restrictions, general consumption changes, ecological conditions, economic situation, etc.)
- Forecasts for the industry and its major elements (growth, diversification, replacement, various changes)

Opportunity Identification

After the industry analysis has been performed, appropriate opportunities can be identified. The process includes:

- Define targets
- Forecast rough volume and share
- Perform a risk-ratio analysis
- Conduct a preliminary feasibility study using secondary data and professional expert opinion—not prototypes or trial runs
- Study a war game assessment of competitive reactions, exclusivity, regulatory constraints or protection
- Look at exceptional technical hurdles
- Consider legal and policy issues

Decision

Proposal: Decide to abort, extend, or embellish Phase I investigation or to proceed to Phase 2.
(Go/No Go)

Phase 2: Conception

This phase translates market facts into product concepts and customer positioning communications, prior to extensive research and development. The objective is to create and to refine a variety of appropriate product concepts in the form of consumer communications, which may then be screened down to a workable number of the most appealing ones that may be carried forward into the prototype modeling phase.

Input Research

This is a background step, often required where "hands-on" experience, technical education, patent and literature review, as well as special consultant professionals, are needed for complete understanding of the opportunity area.

This input area also employs many diverse outside influences, from production equipment manufacturers to examination of foreign market trends, etc.

Ideation

Ideation is the generation of large quantities of unconstrained possibilities, utilizing a variety of stimulus techniques. Judgmental expert(s) screen concepts for technical viability. Some are also eliminated for legal, cost, or policy reasons.

Ideaforms

This is the shaping of concepts into single-minded, clear communications. Often a concept may be stated several discretely different ways to appeal to various market segments. As necessary, concepts are illustrated in semi-comprehensive form. The goal is a clear communication that neither goes beyond nor falls short of a real-world summary statement of each concept.

Prescreening Concepts

Broadbrush selection methods are applied to eliminate or improve concepts that are difficult to communicate or clearly off target in a very major sense. All others, some changed by this process, move into the next step.

Customer Communications

This is the preparation of customer communications of each concept, together with suitable representations of the product-in-use.

Screening Research

Using the above materials, an extensive face-to-face (or in some instances, a telephone or mail panel) consumer study evaluates the concepts on various dimensions. The techniques can rate many concepts rapidly—individually and in relationship to each other. Again, the aim is to improve the concept and its communications language and to eliminate from consideration only those that are grossly inadequate.

Decision

Proposal: Decide to abort, extend, or embellish Phase 2 investigation or to proceed to Phase 3.
(Go/No Go)

Phase 3: Modeling (Prototypes)

At this phase, preliminary concepts have survived several selection steps. Now it is necessary to bring the narrowed number of proposed new products closer to reality in the form of prototype products and prototype communications (sometimes called "protocepts"). When the laboratory or engineering department may have satisfactory experimental evidence—even blind test comparisons of bench models—the target customer prospect must see the concept "in the round," as closely as is timely and economically feasible. Modeling accomplishes the development of such stimulus materials.

Descriptors

This step involves classifying the product category and preliminary brand name development.

The category should be classified in the language of the prospect to communicate quickly and simply the product class, the product's difference from others in the class, and (if separate from that) its benefit.

Preliminary brand name development should include brand names that are already in-house as well as newly devised ones. The ideal is a brand name that is reinforced by a descriptor, is distinctive from the competition, has only one or a few words, has one or only a few syllables, and has a graphic appearance that is not generic and can be registered as a trademark. Unless the product is a line extension, a flanker, or it is otherwise necessarily appropriate to use a well-known house brand, hundreds of alternatives can be generated. These are given a preliminary trade name clearance search. Survivors are screened for suitability to all dimensions of the proposed brand franchise.

Prototypes

These cover all aspects of the product and its communications. Included are:

Product, service, system
This is rendered in quickly recognizable form—in appearance when that is sufficient, as a working model when necessary, or both when possible. The model should be suitably finished for photography, if not for actual use. Comprehensive art is rendered if necessary.

Package
This is rendered in true representational relative dimensions, colors, and graphics. Where the package plays an operational role in the product, the prototype should be able to represent this also (e.g., a childproof cap on a drug product).

Brand name and descriptor
One or several apparently final choices are depicted.

Communications themes development
Brief benefit descriptions in the context of a single major appeal are stated in separate communications themes, which differ by emphasis, nature, and the degree of the support statement, etc. These are screened by prospects for comprehension and to help devise a finally developed single communications selling theme.

Prototype of major communication
This is rendered in a semifinished state, encompassing product claims, representing product personality equity, and in a format that is reproducible in actual media (i.e., no more words nor

pictures than can be accommodated, legally supportable, within policy guidelines).

Prototype testing
The goal is to test the product prototype representation within the context of the communications prototype and among representative target prospects.

Decision

Proposal: Decide to abort, extend, or embellish Phase 3 investigation or to proceed to Phase 4.
(Go/No Go)

Phase 4: Research and Development

This phase of product development encompasses a number of different activities, including *in vitro/in vivo* trials, checking outside scientific resources, pilot plant production, analyzing the factors necessary to scale up from pilot plant production to full-scale commercialization, war game exercises, controlled tests, and feasibility studies.

In Vitro/In Vivo Trials

These are test-tube (*in vitro*) and real-world (*in vivo*) trials.

Outside Science

Study other disciplines to be certain nothing has been overlooked that might be employed to optimize the R&D project. Ordinarily, this results in a double check that sustains internal R&D direction. This step includes an outside patent search and process choices.

Pilot Plant

This involves a small-scale replication of mass production. It helps to debug the system and devise production controls, systems, and equipment design. It is basic to determining on-stream cost estimates.

Scaling Up (for Commercialization)

Before moving from pilot plant production to full-scale commercial manufacturing, it is necessary to carefully analyze the following factors.

- Manufacturing needs in resources—material, labor, factory location, procurement, capacity, parts production, assembly, integration
- Marketing factors—pricing, marketing budget (consumer, trade advertising, and promotion), sales force

- Distribution channels—inventory, warehousing, transport, integration
- Service—pricing, speed terms/warranty, factory-controlled or independent
- Financial
- Legal—any plant location regulations relative to pollution controls, sewage disposal, zoning, etc.

War Game Exercises

These are exercises to foretell possible consequences of competitive reactions, counterstrategies, etc. The variables are processed through computer models.

Controlled Tests

These are tightly controlled trial and retrial purchase tests to determine sales velocity, usage rate, cut-in on sales of competitive and house brands, promotional variations, etc. The manufacturer controls the distribution, so that the variables are in the product itself and its marketing communications.

Feasibility Studies

Now's the time to take another look at feasibility at a point where there is an abundance of research data, experience, and cost forecasts.

Decision

Proposal: Decide to abort, extend, or embellish Phase 4 investigation or to proceed to Phase 5.
(Go/No Go)

Phase 5:
Marketing Plan

The marketing plan should include the following elements:

- Prototype plan
- Test simulation and test market selection
- Sales and distribution trade practices and terms
- Creative strategy (communications of new products)
- Media plan
- Consumer promotion plan
- Trade promotion plan
- Merchandising plan
- Public relations plan

- Payout plan
- Start-up plan
- Test market tracking plan
- Assessment plan
- Expansion plan
- Finance and production plans

Decision

Proposal: Decide to abort, extend, or embellish Phase 5 development or to proceed to Phase 6.
(Go/No Go)

Phase 6: Market Testing

Market testing includes evaluation of the following factors:

- Test market execution
- Awareness, attitude, usage
- Sales, share
- Assessment
- Follow-up plan

Decision

Proposal: Decide to abort, extend, or embellish, repeat, readdress with major changes, or to proceed to Phase 7.
(Go/No Go)

Phase 7: Major Introduction

Finally comes the moment of truth—the major introduction. This is accompanied by a continual monitoring of the market environment, and adjusting the plan accordingly. Expanding from the original test market involves the following considerations:

- Trying additional test areas or an enlarged test area
- Expanding into regional distribution
- Using a phased rollout
- Completing expansion to the entire sales territory
- Continuing to track the original test area
- Planning to keep the product refreshed, continually "new"
- Close monitoring of performance vs. plan criteria
- Evaluating line extension and flanker opportunities
- Undertaking a remedial plan, if necessitated by the monitoring of performance

Program Summary

The program to address new products goals is simply an organized, step-by-step method that allows a company to take small risks in evaluating many alternatives in the early phases and take potentially larger, but better informed, risks in the later phases of development. Companies that have followed this process have a high record of failure in the early phases, as may be expected, and a very low record of failure in the later phases. The decision considerations that must be addressed after the new products of a business have been defined are:

1. Is there latent demand?

2. Can a product be made that will satisfy the market?

3. Can the company be competitive with the product and within the field?

4. Will the entry be profitable and satisfy the corporate charter, as well as other company objectives?

The author's simplified checklist is in Appendix 2A. His definitive, detailed checklist system is the book *New Product Development Checklists—Proven Checklists for Developing New Products from Mission to Market*, NTC Business Books, 1991.

Another brief and helpful perspective of decision considerations, prepared by Schrello Associates, Inc., of Long Beach, CA, appears in Appendix 2F.

Section 2

Summary Afterword

A well-articulated, specific corporate charter is the starting gate for an effective new products operation. It is the foundation for the strategic direction needed to accomplish the company's goals. Top management must take the lead in visibly recognizing the importance of the program, and in encouraging the entrepreneurial risk-taking. An organized approach to staffing and to the process is needed to establish accountability and program the decision points leading to predictable performance.

The corporate charter recognizes the company's strengths and weaknesses in measurable terms. It defines the corporation's purpose in a way that will provide growth goal direction, and thus yields both short- and long-range objectives. This, then, sets the stage for developing new products, new enterprises, and new business development programs.

The formalization of goals—of deciding where to go—sets the strategic direction of the company. The corporate portfolio is first evaluated to determine how to implement options that are compatible with and will enhance the corporate objectives. Next, various methods, or models, are discussed for the evaluation of a corporate new products strategy. Opportunistic competitive gaps within the industry are isolated in the search for exploitable vulnerabilities, and the company determines where, how, and when to compete—whether by upsetting equilibrium in a mature industry, setting the rules in a newly emerging industry, or searching out other opportunities.

The task of formulating a business plan may be defined to include:

- Outlining the scope of the plan
- Stating the reason for being
- Determining the characteristics of needed information
- Looking for alternative methods of obtaining answers
- Analyzing cost-value and resource availability
- Listing the information required for a solution
- Specifying the action needed to develop information

Such a plan should state why an action is required, what actions and resources are involved, what the expected consequences are and when, what controls are needed for an interim audit of progress, what performance standards are prescribed, and what the recommended schedule and budget are.

The company must determine whether it wants to achieve less risk and more control through downgrading innovation in favor of cultivating and harvesting current product lines; or whether it wants to proceed on many fronts, including internal and external development goals, licensing, acquisitions, or new technology. This is the risk ratio—to gain big success, there must be a willingness to accept failure, on a planned, projected basis.

It is also possible to attach other (implementary) goals to add new dimensions—e.g., by building a new brand franchise, building a new type of distribution system, building sales penetration in new trade categories, developing preemptive product technology, or developing a new production process.

Top management support is key. Top management not only directs strategy, but demonstrates the importance of the new products area by visible involvement. This is done by providing career advancement for entrepreneurial skills, encouraging broad employee participation, giving clear direction on what to do (*not* how to do it), and making a long-term, highly visible commitment to new products—thus encouraging risk.

There is no one way to organize for new products development. A needs assessment will help lead to the most appropriate organizational approach. Many corporate factors affect the new products organization, from corporate style to location, from history to timing. Among the factors that may be taken into consideration are:

- Correlating the degree of technological newness needed with the degree of marketing newness
- Studying the new products spin-off mode of a going business, in which a revenue division supports line extensions and flankers
- Determining what to do with misfit developments—those that do not easily fit into any existing revenue division
- Providing support for new product champions
- Motivating small organizations as part of a large one

The structure of new products organization is related to:

1. Long-range planning

2. Growth and development (strategy, search, internal/external generation)

3. Proliferation (existing expertise, facilities, product lines, brands, markets)

The new products operation may be organized in several different ways, including a new products department, new product activity under existing revenue divisions, or a new enterprise (or alternatively, a new business or growth and development) department.

The skills and interpersonal motivation characteristics required of new product management are different from those required for established product management. In addition, the new products manager requires assistance from both within and without the company. Internal aids include support services within the department, the ability to draw on company staff operations, the establishment of venture groups, review committees, and so forth. Outside resources can provide expertise not available within the company, but they must be carefully selected.

The following outlines a program to address new product goals:

I. Search for opportunity

    A. Industry analysis

        1. Sales volume and trends

        2. Basic technology

        3. Competition

        4. Customer definition

    B. Opportunity identification

        1. Targets

        2. Volume forecast

        3. Risk

        4. Feasibility study (preliminary)

        5. War game exercises

        6. Exceptional technological hurdles

        7. Legal and policy issues

II. Conception

    A. Input research

    B. Ideation

C. Prescreening concepts

D. Screening research

III. Modeling (prototypes)

A. Descriptors

B. Prototypes

IV. Research and development

A. Inside/outside science

B. Pilot plant

C. Scale up

D. Controlled testing

E. Feasibility

V. Marketing plan

VI. Market testing

A. Execution

B. Assessment

C. Follow-up

VII. Major introduction

A. Monitor environment

B. Adjust plan

C. Expand from test market

EXPLORATION

Section 3

11

The Search for Opportunity— Industry Analysis

The corporate charter, long-range plans, and strategic goals of the company set the stage for opportunity identification. Except where proliferation through the same trade channels and corporate resources is involved, new opportunity areas should begin with an investigation of the industry. Often, an opportunity looks appealing from without, when one is not acquainted with the complications from within. It is the obligation of the industry investigation to get *inside*.

An outside look is the first step. Maybe this will be sufficient either to abort the interest or to reveal some unexpected opportunities.

Sales

Sales volume, size, and trends are important. While your own sales figures are helpful, industry and leading competitor numbers may be even more useful. These are usually expressed in units or sales dollars, which can be translated into roughly comparable numbers to your own sales figures, using conventional trade margins, performance discounts, yielding an estimate of gross manufacturer sales or factory dollars.

If the industry is a relatively new one, then the growth figures may be difficult to project, especially if they do not relate to population trends, etc. A probability range will have to suffice. If there are only one

147

or two dominant factors in the industry, growth and seasonality may be determined by practices (or happenstances) peculiar to these companies.

The same figures should be evaluated in terms of the national, regional, and emerging (possibly geographically expanding) factors in the industry. If new entries are being test-marketed, these too should be tracked.

Because no company has similarly efficient performance everywhere at the same time, it is important to isolate the extremes as well as the norms. Why is it doing so well here—and so poorly there? Is it a consequence of geography, regional season length, population density, ethnic origin, economic index, media efficiency or media mix difference, special localized competitive forces, recent or long-established market penetration, abnormal media and/or promotional and merchandising spending patterns against the trade or prospect, special distribution situations and pricing practices, high or low purchase frequency of the category in particular areas, etc.? Or is it the result of a unique sales force performance, historic trade relations, particularly strong/weak local competition, etc.?

The answers to these questions will help determine your company's interest in the category, as well as isolate special circumstances, competitive vulnerabilities, etc. It may even be that there are clusters or competitive vulnerabilities, within a major factor, or within one or several analysis divisions and across several major factors.

For example, maybe the South is rising—but the big national competitors have been slow to recognize this, while entrenched regional manufacturers have continued their historic hold. This could represent a twofold opportunity. On the one hand, the big national companies don't do well in the South. On the other hand, the local factors have grown fat and complacent, satisfied with their profitable expansion carried along by the region's increasing prosperity. Interest in the category is enhanced by identification of this special regional situation. It will also have later effects on pretest operations and test market selection.

On yet another hand, it may be that the products marketed by the major competitors in the South are the same as they market everywhere else—yet Southern needs are different. That difference may be small enough to leave room for local businesses to market conventional products or may be necessarily addressed by the local marketers with product adaptations. Perhaps these special adaptations are not of interest to the opportunistic outsider.

Where you identify a sales performance difference that is peculiar to one market, you may find special trade circumstances, competitive activity, unidentified (till now) product performance failure, or an overlooked local holiday or habit of culture. If so, is the rest of the market still interesting, assuming the South is written off as not being of major importance to the category?

The numbers have to be looked at very closely. Sometimes each of the areas that are aberrations from the norm should be visited. Perhaps a seasonal influx of migrant workers is not accounted for, a new labor situation not reflected in last year's statistics, etc. Don't simply accept all differences as being necessary to make up an average—instead, investigate. Not everything is reported in secondary data, especially if the data are developed along standard norms or are part of surveys that are national in scope, with limited representation in each segment and/or subsegment of the sample.

If on-the-scene investigation indicates a different situation than the accepted data, either make a judgmental adjustment—or commission an expanded survey of the situation. In other words, for every major difference from the expected performance there should be an understandable reason. Discover this reason either from secondary data, observation, original research, or judgment. Where the difference may not be actable, then make a judgment. Where the difference may be actable, but the cost to determine the reasons is prohibitive at the investigation stage (although perhaps mandatory later), arrive at a consensus judgment through an experienced company team of involved associates from sales, market research, etc., as applicable.

Competition

Look hard at the competition, for they make the market you are considering entering.

Are the general trade practices compatible with your company's—from operational, philosophical, or even legal aspects?

Study the array of product specifications. Can you upgrade them? Are there too many adaptations in the leading lines—many models, for example, with but a few dominating the sales? By simplification and sophistication of specifications will you have an advantage both with the trade and with the customer? Perhaps by reducing the number of stocking units (SKUs) you will reduce your warehousing parts and assembly costs; increase sales emphasis on your most attractive items; and more clearly direct the consumer's attention to a more focused set of choices.

How reliable is the performance of the competitive products? Perhaps the industry is at an almost commodity stage, where parity products are the rule and positioning ploys and marketing muscle make the share differences. Here may be an opportunity to upgrade product reliability or performance, or both. Or, conversely, there may be an opportunity to slightly downgrade performance to achieve a major price/value advantage. This type of trade-off is difficult for an entrenched leader to follow, because it tends to undercut the established product franchise. Another tactic is to change the rules of the game, make a new and important component for a product in the category to carry, a certain feature that is inconsistent with the leader product's reason-for-being. The stronger and more well-developed the competition's customer franchise is, the more the competitor is locked into an easily identifiable product line position. Under this circumstance, the new entry company knows where the major competition is, and thus the gaps become more easily identifiable.

One example is the soft drink battles, where the leading cola brand was hesitant in meeting the assaults of its sugar-free and caffeine-free competition—because by responding under its most famous brand name with a like product change it both cannibalized its parent franchise and admitted to its frailties. On the other hand, the new-entry colas had little to lose, and much to gain.

Are there product servicing or warranty term vulnerabilities the new entry company can afford to exploit? For example, a new appliance company may market solely through service outlets—and thus can both promote them and underscore reliability with a speed of repair and/or length of warranty coverage claim, not deliverable by competitors selling through conventional channels.

But first, a clear understanding of the customer franchise of each major national, regional, and to the degree of important significance, local and emerging factor must be determined. A semantic differential study, a cluster analysis based on a factor survey, educated judgment, or secondary research can isolate this.

Various research methods may be employed, if published data do not exist. For example, a branded product can be assessed by customers and prospects in comparison to alternatives, on a feature-by-feature basis and in an overall sense related to occasion, time, and appropriateness of use. Various psychological probes are sometimes useful, soliciting reactions to various general descriptions on a scale ranging from very approving to highly disapproving. Sometimes, a list of personal characteristics is offered for selection after asking the question: "What kind of person would I be if I owned a (name of product)?"

Besides obtaining an understanding of the consumer perceptions of competitive entries, there are many additional dimensions of each established marketer that need to be identified and evaluated, such as the major selling theme (usually a user benefit expressed in memorable terms), as well as supporting claims.

Especially telling is the consistency over time of these aspects of communications. Is it a characteristic of the category for each leader to chase the other, changing its communications frequently? Is it a characteristic of some competitors to react quickly to competitive tactics and sales slumps with important copy changes, media adjustments up or down, different trade and consumer tactics? Is it the custom of the entrenched leaders to hew to the same line and style in their communications, dealing with competitive attacks with short-term tactics relating to media blitzes and price promotions, rather than adjusting image or major copy themes? How do advertising impressions and expenditures against the target market, as well as the total market, compare? What about the frequency of trade, consumer, and advertising delivery from period to period? How does this marketing spending compare with share-of-market performance? How do share-of-voice expenditures track with share-of-market? How does the marketing dollar divide among media, promotion against the trade, and prospect cultivation?

How does sales efficiency relate to the industry average, to leading competitors and trendlines? What does this tell the new-entry company about the differences in this new field—and how will it affect entry strategy?

Customers

In order to connect the variable performance of the industry and its major players from area to area, season to season, and over time, it is necessary to understand both the present and past state of the customer prospects. This will help project the future both for the industry and for the new entrant.

The prospects may be businesses and they may be people. In nearly every instance, they are both. People tend to influence businesses more than the other way around. Many whole industries have been sent foundering when not recognizing this.

Therefore, a look at the demographics of the prospects—how they have changed and are changing—helps direct thinking in the development of new opportunities.

Major population shifts provide major marketing challenges—and major new product opportunities. The post–WWII "baby boomers" are between 35 and 54 years of age, nearly one-third of the U.S. population. Changing immigration and birthrate patterns are creating an ever-more diverse population. With the surge of Latinos, African-Americans, Asians, Native Americans, and other ethnic groups, one in four Americans are of non-European origin.

Who one's parents are, where one has lived, been educated, when one was born, whether the prospect is a he or a she—all of the demographic facts of life join with many measurable, unmeasurable, and unexplained influences to help determine life-styles and personalities, intertwined to create one's psychographic makeup. The activities of the largest population segments affect the products and services offered, which in turn affect the life-styles of the other segments. These mainstreams provide further opportunities for emerging secondary markets, characterized by new fulfillment needs (designer jeans, expensive imported cars, macramé, and ferns all over the house) and segmented by location both in society and geographically, as well as style of living and value systems. Every change yields both problems and opportunities. The new entrant should be in the best position to capitalize not only on the prevalent mainstream, but to position the entry for adaptation by foreseeable waves of change.

The category and the industry may have a high level of recognition and respect. On the other hand, it may be out of sight for most prospects, or actually have attitudinal barriers to overcome. This must be discovered. How—and how well—are the industry, the category, and the various competing factors regarded by customers and potential prospects?

What is the awareness level? What are the attitudes? How loyal are customers to a category, to a product type, to a brand? Are there easy substitutes? Is it easy to forego the brand, product, or category? Which items tend to be first choices? What role do they fulfill? What, if anything, do they substitute for? If they were unavailable, what, if anything, would be the first substitute selection? How important to the prospect is the decision to select one vs. another offering within the category? What role does price play? Is it elastic or inelastic? Are there major differences in the answers to these questions in the demographic and psychographic breakouts? What is the customer-use pattern, frequency of purchase and use, and use occasion? What does this mean to the entry marketer?

Basic Technology

A thorough technology review precedes commitment to research and development (and engineering) of pilot prototypes and, in most instances, comes before concepts are developed for review by management and the hoped-for sales prospects. This is to determine manufacturing feasibility—how much ready technology is at hand, or must be acquired, and at what cost.

Although the product offerings of the category may have many characteristics similar to those your company now markets, the art and science of the field may be radically different from what you now do. The source and state of raw materials or parts may be affected by different processing, packaging, and assembly requirements. Different regulatory requirements, different types of transportation needs, different procurement practices and seasonal pricing, different patent and licensing restrictions may be present.

Assuming the technology is adaptable and applied rather than having to rely on basic research, there may be marginal or major opportunities presented simply because your company is a new entry into a mature category. This will allow you to use the most advanced plant application of the technology at the full commercialization phase. Although subcontractors may be utilized in the testing and early marketing phase, at short-term cost penalties, the long-term benefits of a utilized state-of-the-art process may be just enough to provide the new product with both a customer benefit competitive edge and a manufacturer cost benefit.

Early on, however, the company will need to adapt its own scientific resources to the new technology, either by buying expert staff additions or by buying outside consultant and bench-research services, or, most likely, all three.

Technology Review

Very important to many programs is the technology review, which not only assesses the industry and its resources within the planned making and marketing territory, but also thoroughly investigates foreign industry and technology resource developments. Frequently, there are advances here from less mature but more sophisticated technologies that can be easily adapted or moved into place.

In the light of the present economy and the shortage of long-term investment capital, Robert Rothberg, associate professor of marketing in the graduate school of business administration, Rutgers University, writes:

> Business will probably try to minimize the investment required to develop promising new products, and to seek greater assurance that acceptable levels of profit can be achieved. This would seem to imply two things: a heavier reliance on proprietary product technology and proven marketing strengths and a more deliberate pace through the process of product-market expansion.
>
> A greater reliance on proprietary technology and proven marketing strengths means that companies will tend to concentrate on what they do best and try to minimize their weaknesses by working more closely with and through other firms. Colgate-Palmolive, for example, considers itself to be a strong selling organization but recognizes its limitations insofar as the development of new product technology is concerned. This company has tried to maximize its strengths and minimize its weaknesses by entering into a variety of exclusive sales agreements with firms possessing complementary capabilities such as Wilkinson Sword (razor blades), Mobil Oil (Baggies), and Weetabix (Alpen cereal).
>
> Consider also Corning Glass Works. It is a leader in a variety of technologies, but it appreciates its weaknesses in the marketing area. It has long been willing to enter into licensing agreements and joint ventures of various kinds in order to obtain the marketing strengths it lacks.
>
> The point to be made here is that new products frequently require a sizable investment in new product technology or marketing capabilities. These investment requirements can be reduced by working with and through other firms with complementary strengths and weaknesses.

Patent Search

Part of the technology investigation is a patent search. Questions to consider include: Are there many significant patents that impede the development? Are there ways to improve on the technology by licensing patent rights or by working around the patents—or are there opportunities implied by the company's approach to the technology that will allow for its own patent protection? And should such patents be applied for—and when?

Importance of Patents

On this subject, R. Buckminster Fuller wrote:

> The worth of a patent, however, is not established by the merit of the invention but by the expertness with which its claims of invention are written . . . a patent that the great corporations' patent attorneys see no way of circumventing requires expensively expert professional services.

Where patents have had an important role in the career and reputation of Buckminster Fuller, for many corporations the view is different. Writing in *The Times (London)*, Clive Cookson says:

> Recent evidence suggests that patents may be losing the central role in technological progress which old-fashioned economic theory assigns to them. Companies are putting less reliance on patents as protection for their inventions.

> Particularly in industries where progress is most rapid, such as microelectronics and biotechnology, secrecy and a fast-moving research and development program seem more reliable defenses against would-be imitators.

> . . . Recent surveys in the United States suggest that if patent protection were suddenly abolished, the pace of innovation in most industries would not be affected all that much.

> Professor Edwin Mansfield of the University of Pennsylvania, who analyzed 48 inventions in several fields, found that the existence of patent added only 11 percent on average to a competitor's cost of copying the innovation. Some 60 percent of patents have been circumvented legally within four years and Professor Mansfield estimated that at least three-quarters of the patented inventions did not need patent protection . . . However, there is an exception to the general rule; the pharmaceutical industry. The development of drugs really does rely on patents. . . .

> Even companies that produce spectacular technological developments have had trouble defending their patents. A classic case is EMI, which had to spend more than $1 million in legal fees, asserting its patent for the CAT body scanner against infringement by American imitators. . . .

> Whatever the academic researchers may say about the overall irrelevance of patents for technological progress, there are too many clear cases of innovations, such as the Xerox photocopier, which have benefitted by the system.

> A satisfactory alternative to patents has never been proposed, and no one would want to establish secrecy as the only protection for innovation.

Sometimes secrecy is merited prior to commercialization, especially where there is a long development period. In the case of design patents (as opposed to the molecular structure patents involved in chemistry), which may be more easily circumscribed (with noteworthy exceptions such as Mr. Fuller's structural geometry), this is especially true. During this period, however, the innovator must keep constant track of all published applications, to intercept any potential encroachments.

Recent changes in the field of intellectual property protection can affect the manner in which management goes about developing new products. For this update, the author elicited the following input from his patent, trademark, and copyright counselor, Arthur A. Olson, Jr., of Leydig, Voit & Mayer, Ltd.:

> The importance of patents in today's management of a prosperous and progressive business has been greatly enhanced due to several recent court decisions,[1] some of which have piqued media attention, wherein substantial monetary damages and injunctive relief have been granted, and which have had a profound effect on the parties involved. Furthermore, since the establishment of the Court of Appeals for the Federal Circuit (CAFC) in the fall of 1982, the interpretation and implementation of the patent laws in the United States have been more consistent, and the attitude of the court appears to be more consistent with the constitutional underpinning, resulting in an increased respect for patents by both the patent owners and potential infringers—something an astute management does not ignore. One of the duties vested in the CAFC is to serve as the appellate tribunal for all appealed decisions rendered by the federal district courts and involving patent matters in some way.

> On July 1, 1990, the Code of Federal Regulations 37 *CFR* 1.1–1.825 relating to patents and 37 *CFR* 2.1–2.189 relating to trademarks was revised to incorporate numerous changes, some of which were to conform the U.S. practice to that followed by the member countries of the European Patent Community (EPC). While many of the changes made were of a technical or formal nature and not of particular interest to the layman, there were, however, some of which a layman as well as management personnel should be apprised. Included in this latter category is the increase in the number and amount of government fees (37 *CFR* 1.16–1.21) which are imposed at the time an application for patent is filed; while it is being prosecuted through the Patent and Trademark Office (PTO); and, after it matures into a patent, to maintain the patent for its full 17-year term. The amount of the government fees to be paid depends upon whether or not the ap-

---

[1] Polaroid v. Kodak (Oct. 1986); Kearns v. Ford Motor Co. (Nov. 27, 1989); J.M. Lemelson v. Mattel Inc. (Feb. 6, 1990).

plication and/or patent has been assigned to a business concern classified as either a "small entity" or "other than a small entity." Basically, one of the more important criteria of being "a small entity" is that it does not have more than 500 employees.

Because of budget restraints being imposed on various departments and agencies of the government, the PTO on November 5, 1990, increased, by 69 percent, many of its fees. Since then, there have been several upward adjustments, primarily reflecting inflationary trends. The effect of such increases in government fees likely will impact most severely on independent inventors and small businesses. (A schedule of most recent fees may be obtained from the PTO.)

The maintenance fee concept was derived from the more important foreign patent systems. While in most cases these foreign patent systems incorporate annual maintenance fees, which increase in amount on each anniversary date, the U.S. fee schedule only requires fees to be paid 3.5, 7.5, and 11.5 years after the issue date in order to maintain the patent for the full 17-year term. It should be noted that the government fees are exclusive of the cost of attorney services and drawing costs associated with the preparation and prosecution of the application, which are in many instances quite substantial.

To put some perspective on present government fees, note that effective October 1, 1994, the total of the *minimum* filing fee ($730), issue fee ($1,210), and three maintenance fees ($960, $1,930 and $2,900) for other than a small entity is $7,730. The minimum fees for a small entity would be half that amount, i.e., $3,865, not an insignificant amount. In addition, the attorney fees may substantially exceed the total of the government fees, sometimes manyfold.

During the prosecution of the application through the PTO, the proceedings involving the attorney for applicant(s) and the PTO personnel are confidential. Such is not the case, however, while an application is being prosecuted in most foreign countries. In most foreign countries, the pending foreign application is published 18 months after its effective filing date. While what constitutes the "effective filing date" might sometimes be a controversial issue, it is an important factor, nevertheless, to be considered particularly where the foreign patent application is derived from a co-pending U.S. application involving an important invention. In many instances, a competitor can gain an insight as to what is being claimed in the U.S. application as well as the filing date thereof by reviewing the corresponding published foreign application. With such knowledge, a competitor can make the necessary changes in its business strategy and future planning to meet the particular situation.

But there is another side to the issue of the early publication of an application. This is set forth in the following paragraph and has led to a concerted effort in recent years by a segment of the patent profession to harmonize the U.S. patent system with the foreign systems in regard to the 18-month publication feature.

One argument put forth for such harmonization is the recent appearance in the United States of so-called "submarine patents," which are deliberately kept pending as applications for extended periods, following which they would unexpectedly "surface" many years after the respective filing dates. Such "surfacing" is often prompted by the successful and costly commercialization of such subject matter by other parties having no knowledge of such pending applications and no way of obtaining such knowledge prior to making their costly commitment to make the technology available to the public. They suddenly find themselves unexpectedly exposed and liable as infringers despite initial due diligence in checking for potential infringement. The frustration is considered by some to be particularly egregious when it appears that the owner of the "submarine patent" never intended to commercialize the subject matter, but rather waited for someone else to take the commercial risk. The 18-month publication feature would provide a means for a party to minimize such potential future exposure or at least a basis for a party to make an informed decision.

Another important difference between the U.S. patent system and many foreign systems, particularly in those countries which constitute the EPC, is the absolute novelty requirement in the foreign systems wherein an application for patent *must be on file* in the particular country or treaty country prior to there being a public disclosure or sale of the claimed invention. By way of contrast, under the U.S. patent system the inventor is given a one-year grace period after there has been a public disclosure, a sale, or offer for sale within which to file a U.S. application. What constitutes such a public disclosure, sale, or offer for sale can become an involved legal issue beyond the scope of this review. The U.S. grace period is not recognized by most foreign countries and thus, an inventor(s) filing during the grace period does so at his peril, thereby prejudicing the right to file for a counterpart patent in most foreign countries.

The harmonization of other differences in patent systems is partially reflected in the North American Free Trade Agreement (NAFTA) reached by Canada, Mexico, and the United States, the real impact thereof being some years off. The GATT Agreement relating to tariffs and trade, if implemented, may well have a greater impact in enhancing harmonization.

For example, it is likely, as the result of the implementation of GATT, that instead of the 17-year term of a U.S. patent measured from the date of issuance (assuming all maintenance fees are paid) or variation thereof under NAFTA, a U.S. patent, like its foreign counterparts, will, upon issuance, have a term of protection expiring 20 years measured from its effective filing date. As another example, the patent interference proceedings in the United States to determine the first inventor are likely to change to make them more equitable and less prejudicial to foreign inventors. It is questionable, however, whether the United States will soon adopt the existing foreign concept of awarding a patent to the first applicant in contrast to the first inventor, a change espoused by some. Again, the full impact of GATT, if implemented, on these and other aspects of intellectual property will be some years off.

While there are many changes in the U.S. patent system, these are some of the factors which merit careful consideration before an individual or business concern embarks on an aggressive patent program.

With regard to trademarks, some important changes in trademark law have occurred since November 16, 1989. These changes include the term of a trademark registration being reduced from 20 years to 10 years. Secondly, one can apply for trademark registration without any prior use of the mark provided there is a "bonafide intention to use the mark in interstate commerce." In order to avoid the warehousing of unused marks, the statute requires that within six months after the notice of allowance of such application, a statement of use in interstate commerce must be filed in the PTO. The initial six-month period, however, may be extended for a like period provided the extension request is made prior to the expiration of the initial six-month period; an additional two-year extension may be obtained upon a showing of good cause and provided further that at six-month intervals during the additional two-year period, statements of continued bonafide intent to use are filed with the PTO.

These changes in the trademark laws as in the case of the patent laws are an effort to bring such laws into harmony with the laws of foreign countries, particularly those in the EPC and NAFTA countries.

In addition to the above critical patent, trademark, and copyright guidance, the following is an example of how limited copyright protection can be in today's business globalization, as reported by EMI

Music's President and CEO James G. Fifield in a University of Colorado presentation in March of 1995—(edited quotes from his report on the music business):

> New digital technologies should help build appreciation for music and help the business grow. However, they also pose significant copyright concerns: . . .
>
> The makers of U.S. copyright laws didn't contemplate the day when music was downloaded from a satellite to a disc. By the year 2000, you will undoubtedly be downloading the biggest hits through your computer, in a process known as digital transmission. . . .
>
> We and our artists need to have copyright laws updated to assure that digital transmission constitutes a "sale" . . . and to have our copyrights protected when this sale occurs. . . . Piracy is a major problem for the music industry worldwide, costing **more than $2 billion annually in lost revenue**. [Emphasis added.]

After providing many foreign country examples of CD and cassette tape piracies, Fifield stated:

"Fortunately, the U.S. has put the piracy of CDs, films, and movies at the top of its trade agenda with China. U.S. threats of trade sanctions resulted in a commitment from China to launch a crackdown. . . . U.S. policymakers recognize the importance of the entertainment business to our economy. It is, in fact, our second largest export business."

Other Factors

Other factors influence the industry analysis. They include foreign encroachment or vulnerability; general consumption changes; political, economic, or ecological influences on source labor, materials, and shipping; changes in the character of the industry and its leaders; and identifying growth sources whether from new demand, replacement, or diversification of offerings, whether they are important or negligible.

Sales, customer behavior patterns, demographics and psychographics, competition, technology, and other factors will help shape the company's interest in the marketing opportunity. If interested, how will the prospective entrant define the most profitable target?—That's the next question.

On the other hand, if the investigation of the industry and these other factors raise too many problems to confront as an alternative to other available opportunities, the company should elect either to give the situation further (perhaps deferred) study—or to drop the project. Then the investigative resources may be directed toward other areas of possibly greater potential interest.

However, sometimes it is wise to go ahead anyway. In fact, not getting a patent may provide protection. If the invention is very difficult to analyze and, therefore, difficult to duplicate, a patent's required detail could give away distinctive formulation to competition. Better to do what American Formulating and Manufacturing has done with its environmentally superior Safecoat paint. No patent. Difficult for competition to duplicate.

12

Targeting—Other Perspectives

The search for opportunity has taken us through an analysis of the industry, its competitive factors, its technology—and its consumers. That was the *traditional* outward look.

But this is not enough to identify and prioritize targets.

Most essential is the inward look.

Much is to be gained by a new product program that shores up a company's strongest segments, by leveraging corporate expertise. New products can correct real and predictable vulnerabilities to protect the mainline business—or to hedge it against future developments. The market is always changing—and new products are one consequence.

One example: For almost 70 years, Land O'Lakes has meant butter. It commands the leading share, ever increasing, with its premium-priced, premium-quality product—the only major advertised brand of butter. Land O'Lakes means butter. Only one problem—the market has changed radically over the years.

In the 1970s, while per capita consumption of fats and oils had remained fairly steady, butter share consistently fell and margarine share rose. Margarine's quality claim was that it tasted like butter. Who better to protect its franchise with a margarine entry than the leading butter brand? When Land O'Lakes says its margarine tastes like butter, there is no other authority to challenge. When Land O'Lakes introduces a new margarine, who has more to lose if its margarine is not of the highest quality? And which brand has the most concern about trading butter volume for margarine volume? Land O'Lakes, of course.

As a consequence, the giant farmer cooperative approached its margarine introduction with a very high R&D standard and a very sensitive marketing development program (see the case history in Appendix 1B).

The company's successful entry into the marketing-intensive field of margarine illustrates that the strong Land O'Lakes consumer franchise can be leveraged by continued dedication to the highest quality, effective positioning, and a consistent program of consumer communications.

The Inward Look

The inward look, as a dimension of new products targeting, should direct a company to rethink its approach to technology and to marketing. Are both of the activities advancing ahead of the industry? How can new product challenges meet the mutual goals of sales success and increased internal expertise sophistication?

Take marketing as an example. Innovative packaging, new distribution channels, new store fixtures, new sales and detailing operations were brought to the hosiery business when L'eggs brand hosiery was introduced (and later spawned a stream of imitators). This success was largely due to recognition of how a change in consumer shopping habits could be leveraged by a new marketing concept for their industry. (Their earlier contract manufacturing of hosiery for supermarket-controlled labels provided a lesson well learned.)

Looking inward, reevaluate the company's product mix and its sales emphasis. Look not only at financial contribution, but also analyze the mix as a reflection of present practices and for compatibility with coming change. Perhaps heretofore underachiever products and related categories should be readdressed in the light of regional population differences and shifts and demographic trends, as well as changing consumer habits and trade practices.

Perhaps a company's competitors have not met some potential needs. Perhaps one of the company's leading products still fails to make the desired market penetration. New products in these markets are important targets also.

An example of such an attempt is offered by a leader in the canned chili category. A new product opportunity was needed for further penetration—or to expand the size of the market. A new entrant was designed to attract those consumers not satisfied with canned chili. Consumer research indicated that 75 percent of all U.S. housewives make homemade chili for their families. Therefore, it was presumed that there was potentially a large, new market ready to be served.

In product tests, 74 percent of the women trying the prototype improved chili product like it "extremely" or "very much"; 57 percent preferred it "strongly" over the current brand; and 56 percent said they would "definitely" buy it. Based on these results, the new product, formulated with "homemade"-style ingredients, went through test markets successfully and began its market expansion—set both to enhance the marketer's share and to expand the market for canned chili.

In the beginning, a small number of chili aficionados were so impressed with the quality of the new chili that they bought it by the case. Unfortunately, too few were that enthusiastic. The marketer simply was not able to get enough of the upscale chili users interested in the canned product. Perhaps the image of the package form or the cooking habits of the target chili chefs were barriers to high-volume acceptance.

Nonetheless, an upscale version of the basic product or line is often an appropriate business-building strategy—as Campbell proved with its Home Cookin' Soups.

In doing a risk-ratio analysis of new product opportunities, give an edge to those ventures that shore up the going business, protect the corporate charter, and invade competitive territory to preempt logical flanker categories from pioneering competitive advances. In general, it is less expensive and more essential to reduce the risks on close-in, known areas than on far-out explorations. If those basic business elements are not protected; there will not be sufficient earnings available to underwrite the next generation of new business. The far-out exploration programs are planned developments with the expenses increasing with feasibility assurance, hence as the risks decrease.

The Outward Look

Simple matrix approaches reveal gaps that a company may advantageously address. Try this: Take population characteristics. Overlay present and predicted (time frame defined by industry development pace) grids with customer characteristics—now and as forecast.

You can make up any appropriate grid. For snacks, a grid could range from sweet to salty on one axis, from hard to soft on another, and from young to old on a third dimension. Each block in the grid would be filled in with mature and newly offered brands and dollar volume estimates. This would give a graphic view of whether emerging areas were being equally addressed, whether there were gaps, whether there were blocks filled only with old and perhaps tired offerings. This type of matrix is one quick way to possibly identify an opportunity.

There are many revealing questions that can point to opportunities:

- Is the company on the leading edge?

- How can a targeted new product program effect change to bring this about? This analysis can help target goals. In this way, the new product program is not only aimed at short-term business increments but also enhances future success.

- What is going on outside the business that may have inside effects? What is going on outside the business that will have inside effects *only if the company takes the lead?*

Some examples:

Architect Don Grieb decided that building the same way for centuries wasn't taking advantage of modern technology—which

Figure 12-1 Perfect House made of Macrotherm™ polystyrene foam-cement

Buildings were built the same way for centuries. Then architect Don Grieb brought modern technology to building, creating Macrotherm™, an extremely strong polystyrene building material, energy-efficient, so strong you can run a bulldozer into it and it won't break. Examples of it run from the cold north, to the warm south—including (above) the Scottsdale, AZ, home of its inventor.

could possibly speed up construction and be extremely energy-efficient at the same time. He invented Macrotherm™, a light-weight, extremely strong foam-cement, expanded polystyrene building material.

According to the Associated Press: " . . . it is strong enough to with-stand forces more powerful than the huff and puff of a wolf. . . . Inventor architect Grieb says: 'You can run a bulldozer into it and it won't break.'"

Although Grieb has a patent[1] on his system and contractors must be trained by representatives of his company to use it, building with lightweight expanded polystyrene blocks is easier than build-ing with "sticks and stones."

Macrotherm buildings are catching on fast—with Frank Lloyd Wright Foundation, in upscale areas of Florida and modest homes in Wisconsin, where the energy-efficiency kept one house so insu-lated in the dead of winter that the owner didn't know the furnace had been out for four days.

---

[1] U.S. Patent 4,774,794, Oct. 4, 1988

A laser engineer-inventor, observing the eating habits of Americans, envisions a niche market opportunity, somewhere between eating frozen foods and eating out. As *The Wall Street Journal* reported: "At the far fringes of innovation, you get RoboChef, an automated cooking device made by former Lockheed Corp. laser engineer Don Wong. . . . Using an eight-bit Motorola computer processor . . . a small gearbox, a memory card, a pot, and a hot plate, RoboChef will prepare an entire meal on its own . . . thus, the recipe for *coq au vin* looks something like this: HTO 10, TME 01 00, DSO, TME 0030, DSO, TME 00 05, STO and so on. (HTO stands for Heat Turn On, TME for Time, DSO for Dispense On, STO for Stir On)."[2]

A lawn sprinkler maker, capitalizing on the concern for water conservation, adapts technology from agribusiness and puts ground moisture sensor rods into its sprinklers—so they sprinkle only on a *need* basis, rather than by routine (whether automatically timed or not).

Financial service institutions redefine their businesses as retailing of financial product packages. Hence, the mergers, acquisitions, and conglomerations of banks with brokers with insurance underwriters with real estate sellers with credit card instruments, etc., to form money supermarkets.

New combinations of services make new products and new businesses. The new businesses, in turn, will spawn yet other new businesses, possibly to include many service packages now undertaken by government and transport agencies. The computer hookup of the retail service supermarket can direct the electronic satellite distribution system to sort and deliver mail, trigger warehouse withdrawals around the world, etc. The financial retailers tie universal product codes to the consumer's personal code card to coordinate financial transactions, prepare and validate tax returns, channel routine investments, etc. Technology and point-of-view make the difference. Adaptive marketing skills and consumer familiarity and trust determine the speed of acceptance.

More examples abound—but these are sufficient to the point.

As discussed in the preceding chapter, many targeting advantages lie in strategic reconstruction of the industry's trends, and of major competitors' corporate charters. Often, more is to be gained by imaginative interpretation of the industry's numerical reports than by merely following the forecasts that are projections of an established format. A company creates new hypotheses, establishing original formats—and hence new projections that may best serve the overall corporate goals. There is room for much intuition, much art in the translation of always meager information into major new product opportunities.

---

[2] By Joan E. Rigdon, staff reporter *The Wall Street Journal*, San Francisco Bureau, "Technology—The Smart Home" section, June 19, 1995

Section 3

Summary Afterword

Creative assembly and interpretation of data are the most important contributions a new products executive can make to the exploration of opportunities. This requires qualitative, subjective, and objective recasting of large quantities of information from the entire range of affecting influences, as well as from the standard category reports on the status quo. While the corporate charter defines general boundaries, and the long-range plans and strategic goals point to general direction, it is the mission of the exploration phase to both qualify and quantify specific targets.

In the exploration phase—the search for opportunity—the first step is the industry analysis. This includes analyzing sales, competition, customers, technology, and patents. Other factors to be investigated include foreign developments, the political and economic situation, consumption patterns, ecology implications, labor, materials, shipping, replacement, diversification, and the industry leaders.

In targeting new product opportunities, the analysis of industry opportunities can be used to determine whether to enhance, defend, or enlarge corporate strengths. Such an inward look directs the rethinking of technology and marketing for immediate and long-term new product success. Looking outward also provides clues about how change can be effected through new product development and marketing.

CONCEPTION

Section
4

13

Input Research

The creative process is based on a selective assembly of information. It's not a mere playback; its execution communicates something. In fine art, it may express the creator's own self. In the commercial world, it must express and fulfill a latent or at least a perceptually real desire.

It is based on knowledge.

The knowledge that leads to new products ideation comes from diverse sources. It is organized through reassembly, through simplification, through a penetrating grasp of the obvious—which has escaped the recorder.

Some examples:

- An office boy revolutionized the sewing machine industry by suggesting that the hole be placed at the point of the needle rather than at the opposite end.

- Celluloid was invented to make a better billiard ball—but it also made the movies possible (perhaps a more important use).

- In the beginning, Coca-Cola was only a soda fountain drink in which the syrup had to be mixed with carbonated water just before serving. Then someone suggested, "Bottle it."

- Years later, the wife of a very wealthy inventor inspired the packaging form which is revolutionizing shelf-stable retort packaging of food, the Tetra-Brik Pak, by observing that the objective could be accomplished by applying the principles she used in packing ground meat into sausage casing without trapping air. Today, beverages have another delivery form.

Problems Are Greatest Input Source

Problems are the greatest single source of new product input. Every problem is an opportunity. The new product solution results from a blend of the art and the science of problem solving. Problems may be real or perceived—it almost comes to the same—and may revolve around issues that are economically, biologically, demographically, psychographically, or ecologically important now and in the future.

The energies motivating problem solving are corporate charter commitments to growth areas, competitive pressures, unused production capacity, new and often proprietary R&D technology, the threat of technology, the threat of product obsolescence, government-agency technology, changes in regulations, synergistic corporate mergers, or new organizational structures. There are other outside influences—such as naturalism, consumerism, the energy crunch, the economy, a shutoff of raw materials due to foreign events, and changes in leading-edge products, services, and life-styles.

Such rapid changes explain why a high percentage of corporate growth is attributable to new products that were not marketed a few years ago. Identification of just such problems may be the most productive place for new products ideation to start.

Go for the easy one first. The most rapidly developing problems are the easiest to identify—and to solve.

As Buckminster Fuller said in an interview with the *Los Angeles Times*,

> In the world of electronics, where invisible electromagnetic waves move at 186,000 miles per second, there is only a two-year lag between invention and its industrial use. In aeronautics, where you move about 1,000 miles per hour, there is a five-year lag. . . . We can see the second hand on the clock moving, but we can't see the minute hand move. When you can't see something move, you don't get out of the way. The faster a thing moves, the more chances you have to see what is wrong. So we find that in a single-family dwelling, there is a least a 50-year lag because of the least visibility of motion.

Example—Waste By-Products

One fast-moving problem is industrial waste and its potential for pollution. Yet much of this waste may be salvageable if it is attacked as a new product opportunity. Examples: Garbage to alcohol. Monosodium glutamate residue used as a protein source. Cheesemakers' whey turned to a protein beverage, then to wine. Fat runoff from precooked meat used as an energy source to drive the oven. Paper sludge to charcoal briquets and cat litter. Must (the finely crushed grapes) from the winemaking process distilled into brandy, then the cellulose left behind made an important source of vegetable fiber.

These are cheap ingredients. The disposal problem is handled at a profit. And the resultant products fulfill genuine needs.

The Manufacturing Process

Sometimes there is something going on in manufacturing that no one at headquarters knows about, understands, or fully appreciates the significance of.

Get a lot of input from the factory.
Ask dumb questions.
Factory tours can yield dividends.

A "nonionic surfactant combined with a debonding agent" was being used in a facial tissue-making process to help line up the cellulose fibers for a smoother sheet. An advertising man asked about its chemical properties—and a familiar bell rang. By following up with the supplier, he learned that the identical compound was used for making skin conditioners—thereby suggesting an exclusive new product advantage *already* built into the product.

Trooping through a brand new margarine plant, several marketers noticed that fresh skimmed milk was being added. "Is that the way everyone else does it?" was asked. "No, we think it makes ours better," the plant superintendent answered. Another strong competitive claim to newness with a difference was born.

While visiting a small brewery on an informal tour, a writer was told: "Unless you want to see where we store the stuff, that's about it for the tour." Out of courtesy, the writer said he'd enjoy seeing the entire process—yes, let's see the storage bins. "Well, we age it over there in those limestone caves—they're naturally cool, so we save on refrigeration and, of course, we didn't have to build a warehouse." It doesn't take an Ernest Hemingway to know that there was a powerful, new, exclusive claim and an evocative image in that casual revelation.

No matter how the feet may hurt after that long tramp through the production lines—look for product ideas and inspiration right under your nose. They may be happening while no one knows it.

Manufacturing Innovation

Sometimes a refreshing point of view brings new product innovation to the factory.

Paul Hunter of Hunter Industries, Inc., San Marcos, California, maker and marketer of technologically advanced sprinkler systems, developed the initial concept of a carousel assembly line. (See Figure 13-1.)

"We wanted to devise a process that best met our goals," says Paul. "We knew that the traditional assembly process, where a person performs a single task or set of tasks repetitively, does not provide a rewarding experience for the people on the line. We wanted an approach that would allow a single person to complete an entire assembly."

Conventional assembly systems take a variety of forms, but all share one trait: the assemblies move and the people remain stationary. In the Hunter assembly carousel, both people and assemblies move, parts are supplied from overhead, and the completed assemblies are turned

Figure 13-1a Hunter Industries' assembly carousel

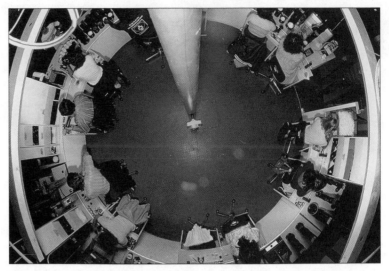

Hunter Industries' assembly carousel is one of the most unconventional and efficient systems in the world. In traditional assembly lines, work is usually completed by the last person in line. At the San Marcos, California, irrigation equipment manufacturing plant each person starts "from scratch" and builds a complete pop-up turf sprinkler with each minute and 55 seconds rotation of the carousel. Because the workers assemble independently, they are free to leave their stations anytime, without affecting the work of others.

Figure 13-1b

over to a lead person at a single point in the rotation. The benefits to this approach are numerous: it uses less space, allows easy access for service and maintenance, can be used by one person or by up to twelve, and, because wasted motion is minimized, it supports very rapid assembly.

Hunter Industries' principal concern as a manufacturer is for the people "working the line." "The most important difference," says Paul Hunter, "between this assembly carousel and the more standard types of assembly lines is the fact that this process was designed from the outset to serve the needs of the people working on the carousel. A single person completes an assembled part and is able to feel that satisfaction."

To maximize the potential for satisfaction, the Hunter assembly carousel incorporated the results of research in ergonomics (the study of how workplace design can address the physiological and psychological well-being of the worker). "The biggest challenge continues to be eliminating constant repetitive motions like the wrist-twisting associated with screwing motions," says Fred Danner, who manages daily carousel operations. "We discovered that certain constant movements, particularly the screwing motions, caused people to be prone to injury. We have developed machines that do that now."

By eliminating many repetitive motions through automation, Hunter's carousel has improved work life for the employee and helped increase efficiency and productivity. Says Fred, "Over time, improvements on the carousel have helped people increase their output tremendously. Eight years ago, 100 to 130 sprinklers per person was a typical day's output. Now they do 200 to 230."

The future for the carousel for Hunter?

Revis Hunter, who is in charge of maintaining and directing research improvements on the carousel, says: "We've found that changes we've made to improve the work environment for the assembler have also increased efficient production. Cutting down on repetitive movement is just one part of the work we're doing to improve the carousel. In a couple of years, the carousel as it exists today will be gone. Future carousels will be barrier-free (wheelchair accessible) and carry ten assemblers. All of the smaller parts people deal with today will be incorporated into sub-assemblies, which will be produced on automated equipment."

Hunter's commitment to ergonomics has paid off, providing them an efficient and reliable manufacturing capability within a quality, worker-conscious environment. And, by focusing on constant improvements to their assembly carousels, they're guaranteed not to be stuck on a production merry-go-round.

Contract Packers

Contract packers are manufacturing companies who will make products for any company under any brand. They'll make products to specification or make them to their own standard, with cosmetic differences for the contracting company.

There are other companies who are not in this business, but might be, if asked—or persuaded. They have good facilities, but they are not optimally occupied. Hook up with them and you might help both of your bottom lines.

In any event, you may well learn more about your new area of product interest.

Get to know them. Ask them: "What else can you make on this equipment? What else is this packaging line used for? How flexible is it?" Then suggest some opportunities. "Would it be a big deal if you made blankets instead of rugs on those looms? Can you extrude corn meal dough through those pasta dies?"

Sometimes, you can put a couple of packers together—or you can fabricate one part, while they make and assemble the rest. And so on. Do not overlook the input and idea-generation value of becoming familiar with what is going on in the factories.

Associated Trades

Your products may be designed to go directly to the consumer. Another division of your company—or even a competitor's—may make different formulations of similar products for different distribution classes or as sub-assemblies for further processing. Even more simply, they may pack out special versions for the service trades, such as restaurants or beauty shops. Often, these products can lead to mass-marketed consumer products.

Examples abound: Kraft's successful processed food spread Cheez-Wiz began as a food service item designed to speed up preparation of cheese-topped dishes. Gillette's Dippity-Do hair-setting gel was inspired by a beauty supply item used by hairdressers, and its Deep Magic line of skin care products by an expensive treatment line of cosmetics marketed by Max Factor.

Inventors and Patents

Patent searches can stimulate ideation. Furthermore, relatively inactive patents properly positioned may lead to new product breakthroughs—with a lot of protection from early competition.

Inventors can sometimes lead to new product opportunities, both with their own inventions—and through the original, outside viewpoints they bring to a project. Because of the legal sensitivities involved, a company should be wary of who reviews inventions (a designated party or department) and under what conditions. A tightly worded protective release must be signed before any invention may be reviewed. One of the outstanding new products companies is 3M. Their invention release process and format is shown in Appendix 2C.

Licensing

One crucial element of new product management is licensing, an effective means of exploiting technology. "Licensing agreements can open up new markets and new lines of business, and provide opportunities to increase corporate revenues," writes Linn Grieb in a professional report published by the University of Texas at Austin.

Licensing-in, where you license a product or name from another company, can be used to gain a faster start, to save internal development cost, and, in some instances, to also capture the stature of a licensor's reputation in trade and consumer marketing.

Licensing-out, where another company licenses a product from you, can help underwrite a company's own R&D costs, add volume to the manufacturing operation, help spread the reputation of a newly developed entity, spread the marketing cost across more items, and, in the case of consumer appeal items, increase the media reach and frequency behind an exclusive concept.

In certain circumstances, licensing out rights under specific terms may result in bringing the patent to the marketplace faster—and with more broad distribution—than the patent holder could achieve independently, particularly in instances where the developer has a broad appealing technology that addresses established prospect needs.

One dramatic example is Martek Biosciences Corporation, a small, publicly held, Maryland-based biotechnology company. Martek has recently used licensing of Formulaid®, its unusual vegetable-like oils, to the infant formula industry.

Martek's oils contain long chain-polyunsaturated fatty acids, rich in docosahexaenoic acid (DHA) and archidonic acid (ARA). DHA and ARA are found in human milk and have been associated with development of mental acuity in recent scientific studies. In the past, they have not been added to infant formula because of their unavailability in sufficient purity at an acceptable price.

To attain the largest coverage and quickest market entry for its DHA and ARA oils, Martek adopted a strategy of nonexclusive licensing of the use of its oils to infant formula companies. Martek's strategy was based on the hypothesis that competitive forces in the infant formula industry would cause the most rapid and universal acceptance of its oils in the marketplace. The result of this strategy yielded a speedy product development that may have been much slower under an exclusive license arrangement. Also, the company expects to obtain greater profits in the future by obtaining a "smaller piece of a much larger pie" using a nonexclusive approach.

Martek has licensed more than 40 percent of the world's infant formula manufacturers, and expects to expand this percentage in the future. Its current licensees include Wyeth-Ayerst, a subsidiary of American Home Products; Mead Johnson, a subsidiary of Bristol-Myers-Squibb; Sandoz Nutrition SA; Nutricia, a large Netherlands nutritional corporation; Maabarot, Ltd., an Israeli company; and others.

Figure 13-2 Multiple licensees

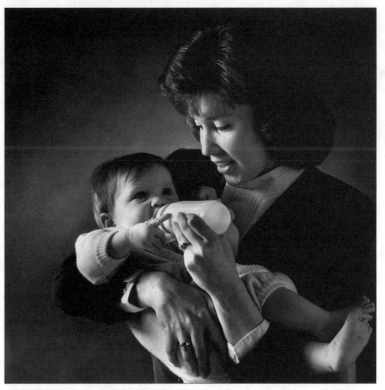

Martek Biosciences brought its patented Formulaid® ingredient to the infant formula market faster and with greater market share by granting multiple licensees to leading companies in the field, than would have been possible with one, exclusive licensee.

Source: Martek Biosciences Corporation

Many licensing experts claim that small companies often can make money by licensing concepts to foreign companies. Indeed, licensing may take off overseas even before the products or processes involved have established themselves in the United States.

In fact, it is quite possible to make more money from licensing know-how for a production or product control than from actually selling the finished product in a highly competitive market.

Or for patent rights—not necessarily the manufacturing knowledge, but rights to the end-product patent. Sometimes these rights may be limited to market areas outside the patent holder's interests.

Even so, licensing of all kinds seems on the upswing,

Reporting in the April 29, 1991, *Marketing News*, Cyndee Miller writes:

A growing number of companies are turning to corporate licensing to extend product lines without the usual financial commitment.

Some of America's best-known companies have taken that step, spawning such unique product hybrids as Jello-O toys, Louisville Slugger baseball shoes, and Caterpillar work-wear. Even the toy models of General Motors cars are products of a licensing agreement. . . . Licensed products with corporate trademarks racked up $21.6 billion in retail sales in 1990, representing 32.5 percent of the industry's sales compared to cartoon characters, which has $13 billion in sales and represented 19.5 percent of industry sales.

A unique example accompanying Miller's report: "For the sixtieth anniversary of Caterpillar's first diesel-powered tractor, one of the company's licensees is producing a $5,900 sterling silver replica embellished with 24-karat gold and a diamond radiator cap."

Getting Out and About

Men and Machines

There are always contract technologies and innovative new machinery. Make it a point to learn from these resources.

Some of the most advanced technologies suffer from want of cash to scale up, to do definitive testing, to fund the research protocol acceptable to governing agencies. Consider a technology joint-venture, or contract it. Buy in, if it looks promising. At any rate, investigate and learn. That's an important part of the input process.

The big trade fairs display the latest in machinery. All of the established companies already have machinery, but most of it is not state of the art. A company interested in a new area can gain an advantage through the acquisition of advanced machinery. With a big enough order, the company may be able to arrange for a significant lead time over incumbent competition. At the same time, learn as much as you can about more efficient factory layouts, materials handling, automation, etc. It's all part of the input. And may be a critical advantage.

Example: A visit to a trade fair exhibit by ex-Kitchens of Sara Lee executives Walter Friedman and David Tittle resulted in their being granted the U.S. franchise for Yoplait yogurt (since granted to General Mills, Inc.). Friedman brought the trademark and process to the United States from Sodima S.A., after seeing their exhibit at the S.I.A.L. biennial food fair in Paris. Yoplait has since become a major share brand in every U.S. market.

Trade Schools

Good trade schools look to the future. Audit a few classes related to your interest. Befriend the profs. Give a guest lecture, if they ask. Spot the top students. Ask a lot of questions. You're in school—so *learn*.

Other Trades

What is good for Peter may well be good for Paul.

But Paul may never have thought of it.

Find some parallel trades and see how they do it. Maybe you can exchange some ideas with the management. Cosmetics were bubble-packed before tools, but the techniques and benefits are the same.

One far afield example is borrowing chemistry from a wholly unrelated category, as with the Olin Mathieson zinc omadine fungicide marketed to orchard growers to treat peach blight. It was licensed to Vanderbuilt Chemical, which brought it to the attention of several toiletries manufacturers as a possible hair shampoo additive. One turned it down because of possible toxicology concerns. Another leading company, however, gave it more elaborate investigation, proved the ingredient acceptable to the Food and Drug Administration, and introduced a highly successful shampoo. This not only strengthened the marketer's dominance of the large business segment where it already had several successful entries, but also established an entire new category of home dermatological treatment for dandruff.

Other Places

It used to be that we were ahead of the world in almost everything—or thought we were. Today, neither is true. There's a lot to learn beyond our boundaries.

It depends on how you define boundaries.

For some companies, their boundaries are limited to the headquarters city; for others, to the area of distribution; for others, to the immediate competitive industry.

Determine what your boundaries are, and then look abroad. The smartest new products practitioners look to the most dynamic marketing areas in their field—whether they have distribution there or not. They look to the coasts, especially West, for consumer product trends. They look to Europe for new technologies and new packaging. They know which countries have the most liberal laws for authorizing the marketing of new products. They find a sugar-based product in Australia that prevents cavities. They find a carotene pill in France that gives the user a beautiful suntan. They find soft-sided plastic aerosol packages. They find shelf-stable food that tastes almost fresh. They discover single-lens-reflex photography (Pentax) in Japan. (See Figure 13-3.)

And they look into the most advanced marketing outlets for merchandise—and merchandising—trends. The sharpest retailers are bellwethers for their field. Listen to them; get input from the buyers and the merchandisers. Here, too, looking beyond the immediate geographic region of interest may pay dividends. The hypermarkets started in Europe. So did generics. Look and learn.

Figure 13-3 Photographing shelf setups in France

Seeing what competition and others in similar fields are doing may inspire helpful insights. Here a new products investigator is photographing shelf setups at Casino Supermarché in Cannes, France.

Have a system.

One company requires that all of its well-traveled executives allow time to make at least one store, or factory, or other learning-experience call on each trip made away from headquarters. The procedure is orchestrated by the company travel department. If the company or a competitor has a test market in the area, specific directions and information retrieval sheets are provided. If the area is a raw material source, factory, or trade association location for the industry—it is suggested that contacts be made here also. Trips are optimized to hype the learning curve.

Get Up off Your (er) Chair

Too many new product planners are tied to their computer consoles. All those teach is the product of a rapidly assembled feedback of data and assumptions fed by other armchair generals.

Get out into the field.

If all the forecasting programs worked so well, every company would have a market share in direct relationship to its investment in the programs and in its product marketing. Fortunately, it is not that simple.

The leaders not only cause change, they are alert to it. They not only read the numbers, but they buy the competitive products. While the laboratories are analyzing them, they try them—meticulously following the instructions. They have "hands on" experience. This sharpens their understanding of the research reports and deepens the questioning search for knowledge.

Research

Listen to Your Spouse

It is a standing joke around some offices that the boss has to check everything out with his or her spouse. Let him or her. Chances are the spouse has a good grasp of the business, its competitive set, and a deep interest in the product area . . . and is no security risk. There's also an about equal chance that the spouse is a shrewd businessperson in his or her own right. And more candid with the boss than most around. Occasionally, this is the best input of all. Don't miss a bet. (And don't forget the offspring, either.)

R&D and Marketing

These are among the most important inputs. Experiments. Simulations. Industry audits. Blind tests. Surveys. Monitoring systems. Panels. Stitch it all together in a cogent fact book that covers all the bases, from available sources, to syndicated, library, proprietary, and basic, fundamental research.

Then ask all the questions still unanswered. Then decide what it is worth to find out more answers. If the missing information is critical, do not spare the expense. Research "on the cheap" is not as trustworthy as the informed judgment of professionals in the chosen field of interest. Despite the cost, sometimes that is a quicker, more economical, and better choice.

Gurus and Geniuses

These are not necessarily the same. But neither is to be ignored. The former may symbolize a trend; the latter may presage the next important breakthrough. No matter how skeptically the professional societies may look upon these highly publicized mavericks, pay them heed. The gurus have affected the tide of civilization, as have the geniuses. The creative geniuses of science possess conceptual abilities far beyond entire graduating classes from the most prestigious universities. They may be ahead of their time. They may be pilloried and unfashionable. But listen to them.

The late Albert Szent-Györgyi, one of the world's most honored scientists, winner of the 1937 Nobel Prize for Physiology or Medicine (he discovered Vitamin C), told this story in a letter published in *Executive Health*:

> If Pasteur would rise from his grave and would want to work on cancer, he would have very little chance to get a grant. I can imagine him ringing the bell at the gates of the National Institute of Health, and the following conversation taking place:

Pasteur: I would like to work on cancer and need a grant.

NIH: You have only to write down what you will do and why.

Pasteur: Research is going out into the unknown and I don't know what I will find and do there.

NIH: How do you expect us to waste money on you if you do not know yourself what you will do? We are responsible for the taxpayers' money and have to know what will be done with it.

Pasteur: Thank you. I left my grave open and am going back.

General Observation

The world is changing rapidly. The population mix and its movement—the level of information being disseminated and absorbed—the meaning of special affinities unrelated to old demographic understandings—the tissue fabric of new fads obscuring strong strains of old ideals —all of this and more should be considered in new product planning, *any* new product planning that has less than an immediate payout and expects a reasonably long life in the marketplace.

There are new needs. There are opportunities for substitutions. There are new perceptions and new life-styles. Just as factories yield by-products, so do the changing patterns of trade and consumer behavior.

All of this, in the end, has to be synthesized into a workable body of knowledge, quickly grasped input that can initiate the ideation of new product concepts.

Force-fit a one-page summary—no matter how giant the appendix. This discipline requires the tough-minded thinking that produces clean direction.

Then, it is time to generate ideas to improve, to innovate, to invent.

14

Ideation

Albert Einstein had both of the essentials:

1. The ability to collect and to absorb positive knowledge

2. The gift of fantasy

That fairly sums up the ideation process.

How do we stimulate this process to yield the most productive results?

We discussed "input" in the preceding chapter. Now, *output* is the goal.

Ideation is based on many factors.

Between fantasy and routine solutions lie the beginning ideas for new product concepts. Both areas must be explored, for in apparently irrelevant wishes will be found seemingly impossible goals, while in precise possible solutions will be found the ways and means to the beginnings of innovation. When the dreamer and the scientist sit down together, wonders can and do happen. Schematically, the range of ideation application to new products is shown in Figure 14-1.

Lateral Thinking

Dr. Edward de Bono, a psychologist and professor of investigative medicine at Cambridge University, England, has assembled a set of simple skills for improving thinking. His system has been adopted by corporate executives, has been taught in schools, and has been studied by government officials from a score of nations.

Figure 14-1 Ideation

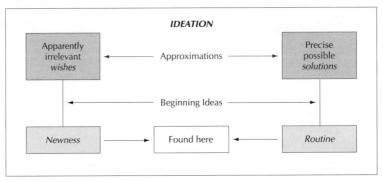

Dr. de Bono espouses a number of basic tools for better thinking, including broadmindedness; consideration of all factors; consideration of consequences and their sequels; assembly of aims, goals, and objectives; evaluation by setting top priorities; looking at all possible alternatives and choices; and turning to others for other points of view (the ideation sharing common to brainstorming).

As helpful as these approaches are to new product conceptualization, they are not new. De Bono himself asserts that yesterday's idioms don't work as well as they used to.

Today, he is advocating a notion he calls "lateral thinking," an unconventional way to think creatively.

Lateral thinking (an entry in the *Oxford English Dictionary*, as de Bono is quick to point out) is the opposite of vertical thinking. Quoted in *Forbes* magazine, he says that vertical thinking is a process by which one solves a problem by going from one logical step to the next, moving toward one correct solution. The lateral thinker essentially shuns the expected approach to a problem by playing games with the data he has to work with.

Thinking laterally involves scrambling the patterns into which your brain automatically arranges all received information. One type of lateral thinking is that in which a problem is posed and only outrageous solutions are suggested. From one of these a principle can be extracted and used to solve the original problem. An example he cites: How to invent a new advertising medium? Solution: Bring back the town crier. The working principle behind the idea is that the town crier is the ultimate advertising medium. He cannot be shut off.

Applied to reality, the principle yields the following possibility for an ad medium: a telephone booth in which local calls are made for free and paid for by an advertiser. Twenty seconds into each call the speaker at either end hears a recorded message that cannot be shut off.

The object of lateral thinking is not to arrive at workable solutions to problems each time at bat, but to train the mind to bring something extra to the raw facts of a situation to get more out of it.

Rearrangement of Information

Members of most industries look at their businesses according to trade styles, reporting-source categories, arbitrary research classifications, and government census and other statistical indices—in other words, convenient groupings of data that can be compared over time for trends and at any one time to assess share of market, share of mind, absolute volume, target audience, etc. Thus, there is yielded the "over 50 (years of age)" market, the A & B county market, the "under 500 employees" business target, the seasonal bulge, the geographic bias, etc.

But there is another way of looking at information.

Rearrange it. Look at it differently, to discover new opportunities. Some examples from the food industry:

1. One manufacturer used to base its products aimed at youngsters on the accepted premise that young people like bland food, and they don't like mixtures of ingredients. That had been the tradition—sometimes explained by the evolution from baby food, which had these characteristics (obviously built into them by adults!). Then it was pointed out that young people liked pizza, sloppy joes, hot dogs with mustard, etc. Interviews were conducted with school cafeteria supervisors and with youngsters—and it was found that they liked spicy food, but not strange or subtly spiced food; that they liked mixtures all right, just so that they could see each item in the mixtures—see the big chunks discretely identifiable, not all mushed together. This led the company down a new (and successful) new product path.

2. Still another food manufacturer used to classify its cost comparisons on a per-serving basis. When it was suggested that changing life-styles and smaller family units might yield an opportunity to market individual or two-pack serving sizes of their products, a logical barrier was confronted. Because of packaging and distribution costs, the cost per serving would rise dramatically—with an assumed loss of appeal. By rearranging the information, it was shown that the cost-per-leftover for users of the current product produced its own barrier to frequent and broad consumption. Research revealed that users would prefer to pay a per-serving premium in exchange for not "wasting" unconsumed food, eating too heartily, or eating warmed-over processed food. Thus a new product was born—a line extension that fit the changing needs of the consumer.

3. The industry called the category "all natural cereals," so (naturally!) that is what the first national brands called themselves. But consumers called them "granola" so that is what General Mills called its later (and successful) entry. It smartly preempted the generic descriptor and made it an identifiable brand: Nature Valley Granola Cereal.

But that was just the beginning. Looking at a production line differently can pay off also. Here's an example from one of the nation's leading new products companies, General Mills. Here's how F. Caleb Blodgett, former vice chairman of the board and chief financial and administrative officer, saw the obvious in 1974, as quoted in a January 1981 article in *Fortune*: "He watched as 6-by-300-foot sheets of granola came rolling out of an oven, only to be crumbled. 'Let's cut them into bars,' he said. A new product was born: Nature Valley Granola Bars," This helped spawn the most successful new dry grocery product line introduced in many years. Now, besides the cereal and bars, there are Nature Valley Granola Clusters, Light & Crunchy Snacks, Granola and Fruit Bars, Chewy Granola Bars, and more.

Mr. Blodgett's ability to see new products while viewing a production line calls to mind an illustrative aside. "Seeing differently" has been the inspiration of the world's greatest artistic creators from Leonardo to Picasso. In Vallauris, France (where this chapter was first drafted), Picasso saw a bullring crowd on the surface of a pitcher, a dove in a porringer, a goat in bicycle handlebars. So inventive was Picasso that he created whole new schools of art, each influenced by his "periods" of different directions in art and artifacts.

It is the genius of true creativity to see in the signals of everyday experience what later becomes obvious to the vicarious appreciators. The interpretation of the random assemblages of the invention process is crucial to selection of concepts for research sorting. Countless rearrangements are suggested by the array of life-style trends, industrial clichés, or manufacturing processes. I once participated in a problem-solving session that achieved a dramatic lowering of costs by changing the manufacturing technique for making nonwoven fabric garments. A production expert was on hand to explain the problem and the conventional techniques, but unencumbered amateurs were able to see original, nontraditional solutions. As a result, automated spray gluing on balloon forms was substituted for piece-work sewing on Union Special machines. Similarly, new recreational equipment for playgrounds was invented for Game Time Incorporated by outside imaginative minds, working with young children. Park board officials and school district experts were involved to explain the problems, safety regulations, etc.

Other rearrangements are suggested by the array of industry information. Wherever the industry has a pronounced seasonal skew—and *all* of the major brands participate in that skew—there is an implied opportunity for a contraseasonal new product.

The same is true of market size, geographic area, ethnic skew—there's usually an opportunity.

The same is true of a large, rapidly growing new market—one a company may be late in entering. There is usually a *better* opportunity offered by an understanding of the factors that have made the category take off, than by directly jumping into the fray of competitors with a late entry that has only a slight differential. Unfortunately the latter is too often the case.

On the other side of the coin, there may be opportunities in the so-called unattractive mature markets—those barely keeping up with population growth. Usually, these markets are characterized by having several major leaders who have held a stable share of market over a considerable period of time. One may assume that a lot of the dynamism has gone, that the trade style has become a cliché, and that reaction time is slow. The consumer is ripe for some excitement and it may be that rapid share gains are available to an aggressive new product line.

Similarly, the so-called parity/commodity categories that are so unattractive to most go-go marketers offer new product opportunities. These commodity producers tend to be manufacturing-oriented, not marketing-oriented. A sharp marketing company can often find ripe opportunity for slightly differentiated, but smartly marketed, new products.

Fisher Nut Company, for example, quickly latched onto the concern about salt intake and brought out salt-free peanuts, low-sodium peanuts (half the salt of ordinary salted peanuts), and other low-sodium snack nut lines. Consumer needs were met with smart line extensions that did not inhibit the established varieties, but did steal a march on the commodity snack nut competition.

Seeing the Category Differently

How do you get into a frame of mind to see the category differently?

Most products are based on old technologies. They improve by evolution, not revolution. But if a company is not beset with the old technology and the old state of mind—but *is* interested in the marketplace—it has conceptual advantages in thinking about product entries.

A company entering an established market could choose several perspectives:

1. How to make a better one

   This would result in optimizing the status quo. The incumbents are probably ahead here.

2. How to invent the first one

   This would result in applying all of the latest technologies, without the preconceived notions implied by the existing products. This process has yielded successes in many fields, from cameras to catamenial devices.

Thinking Outside-In

Another way to circumvent the evolutionary approach is to start thinking outside-in, instead of inside-out.

Most companies try to leverage their production engineering, or their distribution, or both. This is the inside-out point of view, and it is most prevalently, most successfully, employed in new product marketing development. However, there are many successes coming the other way, coming from the perspective of the end-user rather than that of the maker. A good example of the latter is the L'eggs recognition that supermarket distribution of panty hose would be a great time saver for consumers, and that inventory display maintenance provided both the problems and the opportunities. It was not the way L'eggs or its competitors marketed products via the inside-out tradition. Solving the new distribution channel problems (including the trade resistance) built a giant business for L'eggs, which has since been extended into additional profitable lines. Outside-in thinking—and action.

Another example comes from Jockey International. Long the leader in fitted, 100 percent cotton men's underwear, Jockey realized that the 100 percent cotton knitted underwear offered advantages for women as well. The absorbency of cotton, its breathability, its easy laundering, its form-fitting style, all offered benefits for female consumers. What's more, the vast majority of Jockey shorts for men were purchased for male family members by women. They were familiar with its excellent qualities. Hence, a line of fitted panties (from bikini to briefs), with a variety of colors and designs has been successfully introduced. Although inside-out thinking may have indicated that Jockey is for men only—a fresh perspective has created Jockey for Her.

Most product development lays out a program in phases from today to tomorrow, with optimization steps along the way. Instead, start with the end result—and build back from that, to arrive at the development program. This shift in point of view allows for greater scope in thinking.

That's a shift in time cycle perspective. Another shift is to think of making a new product, or an innovated product, or an improved products, differently also. The usual way is to *add* a feature, an extra function, an extra ingredient, an added appearance trim.

What happens if you think outside-in, think *subtraction*?

One company, Beech-Nut Nutrition Corporation, found that mothers had been avoiding or minimizing the use of prepared baby foods because of concern over additives. So, in 1977, it pioneered by removing all salt from all of its products and sugar from most (the exceptions being tart and/or acidic fruits). Beech-Nut ads featured such headlines as: "NEW Beech-Nut—131 baby foods with no added salt, preservatives, artificial flavors, or colors." Here's another: "In a recent national survey, 9 out of 10 pediatricians prefer baby foods with no sugar added." Two years later (in 1979), ads continued to stress the pediatrician preference, stressing, "Beech-Nut took over 5½ pounds of sugar and salt *out* of baby's first year." There are many, many other examples of positive subtraction, from stripped-down energy-efficient automobiles to the light (less calories) beer and wine (less alcohol).

Sometimes, as Ludwig Mies Van der Rohe said: "Less is more."

Peer Group

Gather together experts from different companies but related to the same area of interest. Tell them in advance that you are seeking their help in order to quickly get up to speed in an area of your interest, that they will not be asked to reveal any proprietary information, and that a transcript of the session(s) will be provided to each of them. (This is best arranged by a third-party consultant.)

The yield is a grouping of experienced professionals eager to share experiences and perceptions of the category with their peers—with much of this colored positively by their extensive work and research in the field. Inject into the discussion broad but specific areas of new product interest, to stimulate ideation. Usually, this will be practical, experiential ideation—not flights of fancy. However, if an excursion into fantasy seems appropriate to the group, it sometimes can be productive.

Delphi

Because grouping experts together can cause such side effects as status-jockeying and compromise instead of consensus decisions, the Rand Corporation devised the Delphi technique. In an article in the April 1976 issue of *Business Horizons*, Richard Tersine and Walter E. Riggs described it as follows:

> It is a method to systematically solicit, collect, evaluate, and tabulate independent opinion without group discussion. [It] replaces direct debate with a carefully designed program of individual interrogations, usually conducted by a series of questionnaires. The control of interaction among respondents is a deliberate attempt to avoid the disadvantages of the more conventional use of experts via round table discussions, committees, and conferences. The experts are not identified to each other in any way, and there is usually a greater flow of ideas, fuller participation, and increased evidence of problem closure.

Appropriate input questions can utilize Delphi as an ideation tool in new products invention. It also is a way of overcoming geographic and time availability problems that may prevent assembly of the experts.

Ideation Incentive Program

Dun & Bradstreet, Inc., reports in a 1981 AMACOM Management Review:

> Our ideas come from senior management, middle management, line management, salesmen, our credit reporters, and consultants. By encouraging the flow of ideas . . . we have been able to examine . . . more than 150 ideas in the last two years. We currently receive most of our new ideas from field personnel through our $5,000 Club—a new idea incentive program. Any eligible Dun & Bradstreet employee can receive $5,000 for suggesting an idea that reaches . . . nationwide introduction. Our CEO supports this program and ideas are sent *directly* [italics ours] to the director of product planning and research. This avoids any problems with the chain of command.

Consumer Mail

Many companies carefully classify and analyze customer complaints—and suggestions—as a means of tapping pent-up desires and direction from the marketplace. After all, if a customer makes the effort to applaud, castigate, or question, the subject must be an important one. Consumer mail and convenient special 800-number telephoning need to be promoted.

Brainstorming

Brainstorming is a step up from bull sessions. It involves getting a group together for an informal sharing of ideas, hoping to spark new ones as a result of the group dynamics, rapport, and a nonjudgmental context. It's often a very preliminary, unplanned project beginning. Although the yield may be high in conviviality, it may not be as focused as later developed embellishments may offer. It is sometimes also successfully employed as a follow-up technique to concept development or as an aid in communications developments (e.g., product descriptors, brand names, etc.).

Sometimes a "brainstorm" starts as an individual inspiration, then grows into a "creative jam session," which results in a totally innovative project.

One idea born from a challenging situation occurred when Gerald P. Hirshberg, vice president, Nissan Design International, Inc., San Diego, was returning home one summer night in 1988 after a particularly successful meeting in Los Angeles. But he remained uncomfortable about a recurring assumption that entry-level vehicles tended to be bland and conventional in design, and did not necessarily attract the upwardly mobile audience.

Figure 14-2 Result of a creative jam session

Nissan Design International's leader didn't believe that an entry-level vehicle's styling had to be bland, spartan, and uninteresting. His concept and a sketch launched an inspirational "creative jam session" at NDI, which led to the Gobi, a hybrid concept sport truck with a helicopter-style cockpit and cargo-carrying truck bed, fully loaded with innovations.

This was just the type of challenge the designer thrives on. By the end of his two-hour drive, he had mentally sketched a vehicle that combined highly distinctive design in a low-cost format.

The result is the Nissan Gobi, a hybrid concept sport truck with a helicopter-style cockpit and cargo-carrying truck bed, fully loaded with innovations. (See Figure 14-2.)

The Gobi got off the ground in what Nissan Design International calls a "creative jam" session. Hirshberg's initial "helicopter-truck" sketch was hung on a large design studio panel. The design team of Hirshberg, Bruce Campbell (Gobi's chief designer), Tom Semple, and Diane Taraskavage then added a number of related concepts and sketches. (The total NDI team had previously developed Nissan's Hardbody trucks, award-winning Pathfinder, and Pulsar NX.)

From the visual session came such ideas as a corrugated truck bed, auxiliary storage panels, and differentiated driver and passenger zones in the cabin. Scale clay models were quickly molded, then developed into a full-scale version. Simultaneously, chassis and component layouts were devised to accommodate emerging forms and concepts.

"We wanted to demonstrate it is possible to design an efficient, low-cost vehicle with a distinctive personality that would appeal to a wide market," said Hirshberg. "We explored a bold new design direction and developed a vehicle that has both high flair and functional applications."

"We developed the pod-shaped cab because its form naturally envelops and accommodates the human shape."

The Gobi demanded changes in the conventional design process. For example, the same designers developed the exterior and interior. The result is a "marriage" of design and practicability both inside and out.

"The interior is designed to flow with the exterior," said Bruce Campbell, "and in the same sense that the exterior is functional for cargo, the interior is functional for passengers."

"It was a highly stimulating project," Hirshberg said. "But the real reward is the end result with a vehicle that is not only visually striking, but also practical."

The Gobi made its public debut at the North American International Auto Show in Detroit, January 3, 1991. The Gobi also received the International Designers Society of America gold award.

Synectics

Another popular approach is "group think." One disciplined method, Synectics, pioneered by Synectics Inc., Cambridge, Mass., offers the benefit of stimulating uninhibited flights of fancy that can be brought down to earth and become practical concepts or problem solutions. They call it "dynamic group problem solving." It requires a role-playing client, a relatively uninvolved leader, and a small group of participants. (See Figure 14-3.) It is capable of generating large quantities of ideas in a short span of time—a matter of hours or, preferably, a few days. The best sessions often include appropriately expert participants, whether professionally expert or others briefed in advance on the general background and goals. This allows time for appropriate information "simmering."

The benefits of freewheeling ideation were summed up by E. M. Forster: "Think before you speak is criticism's motto; speak before you think, creation's."

Figure 14-3 Synectics

Synectics leader lists "what ifs" in session, where each participant builds on the ideas of others—no matter how fanciful. Such group dynamics can often help develop wild ideas into innovations.

Role-Playing

Assemble the participant group as a management body, charged with new product decision-making. Tell them that matters are moving rapidly, and that they will be expected to cope with each change as it is announced: competitive moves, government regulation, raw material shortages or cost rises, legal constraints, medical discoveries, etc. Brief them on the purpose of meeting: e.g., to build a better mousetrap than the General Mousetrap Corporation, if that's appropriate.

Shortly after the meeting begins, a news bulletin is delivered—it changes all of the briefing signals. The problem must be readdressed. A different new product than was originally being generated now begins to evolve. A long-distance telephone call comes from France, with the announcement that an international patent is being issued covering a critical area of the mechanism being considered. Furthermore, the international company already is beginning pilot plant manufacturing in several countries, including this one. Back to the drawing board. A new technology emerges. Then: a Senate committee staffer leaks word that they are going after the mousetrap industry in major hearings to be announced shortly.

The ground rules shift again, to make use of mousetrap technology for other purposes . . . the scenario goes on, to seek out, to inform, to create an atmosphere where new kinds of ideas are developed.

Roll Playing

Note the spelling. This is different.

Everyone can draw. Some can draw better than they can articulate verbally. Roll playing is named after the use of lengthy rolls of blank paper. Participants group around a small table and draw concepts—adding on to and embellishing each other's sketches. This works particularly well for hard goods conceptualization. (See Figure 14-4.)

Roll playing helps in surface design and structure invention. Many are familiar with the first phases of designing that "dream house." Shift the rooms around, alter the views, decide on the type of roof, etc. Much of this is helpful (and more economical than waiting until later) when the architect is finally selected. The preliminary thinking, the mandatory elements, and the rejected elements have been established.

Much the same process takes place in designing dimensional products. Verbal descriptions simply do not communicate as well. A sketch, no matter how crude, is concrete; others can add to it, redraw it, change it in ways that enhance the creative realization and future direction.

When several persons work together to sketch a concept, a mutual dynamic can take place that will enhance the idea. Often, too, one person's idea may have a problem that another person's insight (and drawing pen) may solve. Roll playing is working together with pictures and conversation, not just with words.

Figure 14-4 Roll Playing

"Roll Playing" author, left, and free-lance designer Paul Kemp ideate nonelectric housewares concepts, building on each other's construction sketches on a continuous roll of paper.

Ivory Tower

Not everyone performs best in a group. Some assimilate and ideate best as loners. Thinking time to generate ideas is provided at the participant's chosen place of solitude.

Some of the best ideation is done all alone—or by small teams. The designer Gabrielle "Coco" Chanel said: "Those who create are rare; those who cannot are numerous. Therefore, the latter are stronger." Not to be discouraged, the former make the world go around, are remembered longest, and can be the key to the most productive ideation. Bernice FitzGibbons, the retail advertising whiz, said: "Creativity varies inversely with the number of cooks involved in the broth."

So don't hesitate to turn over a giant assignment to one or two individuals or teams, while the conventional processes proceed.

Competitive Set

Some highly motivated ideators perform best under the fire of competition. Seek these out, put them together—and get out of the way.

Personification

Know your target. Know your target's role model. Then ask the question: "What kind of [fill in product category] would [fill in name of clearly characterized famous person] use?"

For example:

What kind of razor would Arsenio Hall use?

What kind of candy would the 49ers eat?

What kind of car would Madonna drive?

Self-identification

What kind of person am I if I buy [insert new product category]?

Now, here's my problem. I have it in my power to provide the solution. What is it?

Milk has just become extremely costly. What am I going to drink instead? Why?

Personalize the assignment in the most self-interested manner.

Ridiculous to the Sublime

Stretch out. Start by pushing yourself or the group out to the wildest possible fantasies. Locate the company on the planet Gorp, where any element is available just by invention, money is limitless, and there is a market for everything. Then take the tiniest aspects of the assignment and evolve the most elaborate, complicated optimization. Often, out of this comes a thought process that opens up new avenues of product exploration—ones that are really down to earth!

List Making

Start a list, add to a list, have associates add to the list—make it a game. (See Figure 14-5.) See how many ideas, in the form of topic sentences, challenges, names, etc., can be generated. Set a deadline. Give a prize (recognition) for the longest list (not the best, necessarily). Set a time limit. Have fun!

Finding an Equity

Many successful products stem from an equity that already exists. Easy examples are designer jeans, the equity being the fame of the designer's name; the Energizer batteries bunny; the partly borrowed and partly invented equities of children's cereals such as Undercover Bears, Teddy Grahams; the Muppet-spawned toys and games; the created equity, such as Garfield and Snoopy—or Michael Jackson.

Figure 14-5 List making

Ingredient	Drugs proprietary	Toiletries	Soap	Household	Food
Enzyme	•	•	•	•	•
Wine	•	•	•		•
Caffeine	•				•
Cocoa butter	•	•	•	•	•
Alcohol	•	•	•	•	•
Vitamins	•	•	•		•
Wheat germ	•				•
Aloevera	•	•	•		
Silica/S. gel	•	•	•		
Benzocaine	•	•			
Papain	•	•	•		
Anhydrous CO2	•	•	•		•
CO2	•	•			•
Nitrogen	•	•	•		
Glycerine	•	•	•	•	
Rose water		•	•		
Silicone		•	•	•	
Algae	•	•	•		•
Witch hazel	•	•	•		
Protein	•	•	•		•
Cactus		•	•		•
Optical brightener		•	•		
Lemon	•	•	•	•	•
Placenta		•	•		
Queen bee jel		•	•		
Hormones		•	•		
Iron	•				•
Avocado		•	•		•
Peach		•	•		•
Almond		•	•	•	•
Laurel (bay)		•	•		•
Mink oil		•	•		

Figure 14-5 (Continued)

Ingredient	Drugs proprietary	Toiletries	Soap	Household	Food
Cucumber		•	•		•
Honey	•	•			•
Mango		•	•		•
Milk	•	•	•		•
Papaya		•	•		•
Beer	•	•			•
Vinegar	•	•	•	•	•
Egg		•	•		•
Lanolin	•	•	•	•	
Rum	•	•	•		•
Germicide	•	•	•	•	
Insecticide		•		•	
Soil repellent		•	•	•	
Soil release		•	•	•	
Pine	•	•	•	•	
Ammonia	•			•	
Pumice		•	•	•	
Chlorophyll	•	•	•	•	•
Bran	•	•			•
Linoleic acid	•				•
Polypeptides	•	•	•		
Oatmeal		•	•		•
Menthol	•	•	•		
Beauty grains		•	•		
Bubble bath		•	•		
Baby oil		•	•		
Bath oil		•	•		
Baby lotion		•	•		
Coconut milk		•	•		•
Blusher		•	•		
Fruit fragrance		•	•		
Deep colors		•	•		

Figure 14-5 (Continued)

Ingredient	Drugs proprietary	Toiletries	Soap	Household	Food
Olive oil		•	•		•
Lecithin	•	•	•	•	•
Amino acids	•	•	•		
Casein		•	•		
APAP		•			
Histamine	•				
Sunscreen	•	•	•		
Ice melter				•	
Driers		•	•	•	
Stain resisters				•	
Spun soy					•
Avicell/CMC		•		•	•
Gel forms	•	•	•	•	•
Seaweed/kelp	•	•	•		
Linseed oil				•	
Iguana oil		•	•		
Myrrh	•	•	•		
FPC					•
Frankincense		•	•		
Mercaptan				•	

List making leads to clusters of ideas. Shown here are 92 ingredients spun out in an actual list-making session, which yielded 246 opportunities in the five areas of a company's interest. Lab technicians participated in the free-flowing session, which stimulated the concept for a successful new beauty soap.

Start the ideation process by identifying equities. Ones existing and not yet applied to your subject category. Ones existing and not yet applied to any category. Old ones, now in the public domain. New ones, which must be licensed. Really new ones, which are invented to suit the subject.

A noteworthy example: Designer Robin Roberts' Clarence House, the created equity that is responsible for selling $20 million in bed gear for Cannon Mills. Fifteen to 20 percent of bed gear carry such designer names as Yves St. Laurent, Calvin Klein, Oscar de la Renta, etc. Underscoring the importance that a bed sheet, like any other product, is a complete communication, Mr. Roberts keeps his designs simple, so that they will reproduce well in catalogs, the source of most sales.

What or Where

Start with a brand—possibly a mythical one; possibly it will become a real one. The brand says "what" you are striving for (to look thin in a bathing suit, hence: Skinny Dip). Or—it may say "where" you are coming from (a carefree uninhibited state, hence: Footloose).

Such words start to shape the new product concept, and get the ideators off and running.

No Holds Barred

It is a rule, in the beginning, that anything that is not immoral or illegal goes. Then, some practical constraints enter. An idea must be conceptually credible to the end-user, even if the scientists don't know how to make it work.

Then, it is an assignment to make the credible practicable.

Then, it is an assignment to make the practicable communicable in some format that may be used to convey the idea to a respondent.

You must know (and understand) what you have wrought. And so must the consumer. Don't be like Mickey Rooney in the burlesque musical "Sugar Babies." He plays a mad inventor of the light bulb. He displays it proudly. Then holds it to the side of his head and tries to place a telephone call.

That's okay in the ideation process, if it gets pointed in the right direction. At that time, the process for visionizing is even more important than the process for analyzing the visions and acting on the analysis.

Sometimes, trying everything at once produces exceptional results. Some years ago, with a goal of conceiving and executing in finished stimulus presentation format literally dozens of new products in the personal care field, ten bright, aware, young members of an advertising agency were assembled and given this challenge:

> Think about your personal care problems. What is there about your appearance, your bodily functions, outside effects on your comfort that some kind of product might improve? Bring back your ideas. Experts will tell you which ones are feasible. Then, we'll make prototypes. You will name them. You will put them into any type of presentation form you wish, just so it is simple and demonstrates the product and its benefit.

Individual members of the team, sometimes in groups and sometimes alone, arrived at the ideas by looking into mirrors, talking to boy and girl friends, consulting physicians, synecticizing, baring their souls before the group, dreaming, etc. As I reported in an *Advertising Age* article published Nov. 20, 1972, hundreds of ideas were generated, from very serious, clinically supportable, preventive medical regimens to hair deodorizers to costume jewelry insect repellents to a suntan gel that won't wash off[1] in fresh or salt water (except with soap) to a complete beauty spa home treatment line,[2] to a bikini leg line depilatory,[3] to a special breath mint Kiss Kiss (one for him, one for her)[4] to a spray toothpick,[5] etc.

All kinds of events stimulate innovation.

More than 30 years ago, a mutual friend of a major food corporation's R&D chief and of the author had a heart attack—and a consequent highly revised diet was prescribed. From this came many ideas, including *Happy Heart* salad dressing and *Yankee Doodles*—The *Low-Fat Snack for Happier Americans*.

But it was too early then. Since, heartwise marketers have addressed the problem.

Personal experiences can inspire innovation. Examples abound:

- A relative of Lois Claypool became handicapped and wheelchair-bound. It was difficult to dress. This inspired *Claypool Classics, Inc.*, of Lake Forest, IL, which markets sleepwear, bed jackets, and robes, as well as styles for casual or office environments. As *Paraplegic News* reports: "Many styles are reversible and have back or front openings for easier access."

- *Globie-Jam* is another example, based on personal experience. Some time ago, when Barbara Engberg was in Italy, she went to a store hoping to buy her daughter a toy that would teach her something about Italian culture. To her dismay, she found that all the products were American toys. That is when the thought first crossed her mind that there was a need for a multicultural toy that would teach children about the world around them.

  The concept starts with four wooden "Travel Friends" and their personal guide to adventure. A colorful, personalized travel case with more than 30 magnetic play pieces transforms itself into a complete world of play reflecting the sights, products, recreation, food, and sport of different countries around the globe. *Globie-Jam* travel sets are available representing the United States, France, Japan, and Kenya, with sets under development for Australia, Brazil, China, England, India, and Mexico.

  The world will open up to a child who plays with *Globie-Jam*, according to the company's brochure, which states that "when your children and Globie-Jam travel to Kenya, they'll beat on drums while observing jungle animals playing at a nearby hole;

---

[1] Similar product concept introduced seven years later in 1979 by 3M Company as Mmm—What a Tan.
[2] Similar product concept introduced three years later in 1975 as La Costa, by La Costa Resort Hotel & Spa.
[3] Similar product introduced in early 1980s as Bikini Bare.
[4] Similar product introduced in France in 1988 as Kiss Cool.
[5] More than 20 years later, AquaFloss introduced a similar concept.

Figure 14-6 Entrepreneurial success

Sandra Brue leveraged her love of animals and her sculpturing ability into a multimillion-dollar business—including statues celebrating the 1994 Disney movie *The Lion King*. (She was recently named the Woman Entrepreneur of the Year by the San Diego chapter of the National Association of Women Business Owners.)

in France, they'll eat a croissant while watching a bicycle racer pedal past the Eiffel Tower; and they'll practice martial arts in Japan, before leading a parade in a brightly colored mask." The toy offers the opportunity for kids to learn about travel . . . by touching and thinking while they play.

- *Sandicast, Inc.* is another entrepreneurial example which developed into a multimillion-dollar business. Like *Globie-Jam*, it was started in Rancho Santa Fe, CA, and inspired by children. (See Figure 14-6.) Founder/owner/artist Sandra Brue started her business 16 years ago as she dragged her four kids to watch animals in pet shops, and returned to her garage to sculpt. Her realistic animal sculptures are an international success—so many have been produced that there are thousands of members in the *Sandicast Collectors Guild*. Of course, the garage was long ago deserted for a 40,000-square-foot–facility and a staff of more than 200.

The chief points of these examples are:

- If the idea seems to have potential, even if evidently not a timely one, hang in, keep reviewing past notions. Times—and perceived and/or real needs—change.

- Leaving no stone unturned in the creative process is often rewarding. Although a high percentage of the ideas will be discarded, just having one that survives is worth the stimulating exercise of developing hundreds and hundreds.

A few gentle prods along those lines come from Peter J. Jessen of the International Policy Institute, who concurs with the stress on unencumbered inspirational ideation. In a May 21, 1981, seminar Jessen advocated

> turning to dreams and visions, not gurus and oracles; innovating the new, not repeating and duplicating the old; exciting possibilities explored, not tunnel-vision foreclosures; strategic planning and long-term views, not repetitive planning and short-term view; innovating the unthought of, not model building from extrapolations; creative dreaming, not equivocating predictions and prophecies; creative forecasting, not blindly accepting extrapolations.

These are challenges to meet, every one of them. And as new ideas are produced, the spirit and fulfillment of ideation starts all over again. The pipeline is filled with new opportunities—using all three aspects of the minds: thinking, willing, feeling.

15

Ideaforms

"*Great floods have flown from simple sources.*"

—**WILLIAM SHAKESPEARE**

All's Well That Ends Well
Act II, Scene I

The company charter is understood; the goals have been set, the opportunity areas have been defined; the ideation process has been productive. In order to sort out those ideas to be pursued, two elements are needed:

1. A clear communication of the idea
   a. In business terms
   b. In prospect communication terms

2. Methods of reducing the number of candidates for further development

This discussion deals with the *forms* in which ideas are expressed for evaluation.

Communicating the Idea

Business Term Description

A business term description will not spell out the customer benefits of the new product idea. Instead, it will look at the general attractiveness of the product in terms of financial goals (sales, margins, return on investment, cash flow, cost of money, etc.), expected growth potential (relates to maturity of the category and changing industry and population factors), competitive set, industry restructuring (required or ongoing), distribution of risk (related to other corporate activities and guidelines), energy, geography, ecology, regulations, etc. How will these elements perform over time?

Beyond this, you will ask how appropriate is this product to our business? Does it fit our capital structure, marketing strength, manufacturing, technology, raw material and component access, and other skills?

At this point, you can conduct a quick, broad screening of ideas based on their appropriateness to your business interests. Certain factors will immediately delete some ideas from further consideration, while raising the interest in others. Still, the choices are many and varied. To get at these in the rough screening process, assign a numerical value to each business element, on a scale ranging from 1 to 10, which will allow you to array your company strengths, financial considerations, supplier reliability, etc., across each appropriate consideration.

The usefulness of this approach is that it is largely objective, allows for the incorporation of internal expertise in the decision process (R&D, manufacturing, marketing—all participate in assigning values), and provides an early indication of the answers necessary to a "go" decision: What will it cost? How long will it take? What will the volume be?

On the flip side, it will also diagnose some of the idea's failings. This done, you may decide to remedy the failings, if they are few or not major. If they *are* major, but when/if solved the product shows great profit yield for the company over time, and may be protectable by proprietary technology or a special marketing edge, again it may be worthwhile to remedy the failings.

Even with this approach, there may be disagreement over the values assigned to certain business elements. Recast the numbers with the dissenter's figures. If this does not change the total picture, then the process is completed. If recasting the numbers alters the picture significantly you have the option of going to a higher (management) court or (if there are enough other positive elements) moving the idea into the next phase of ideaform development and assessment.

One company uses the in-house expert evaluation format shown in Figure 15-1. Here, as in the 1 to 10 ranking system described above, internal expertise is tapped early in the decision process, prior to any testing, prototype development, etc. Specific questions are posed for comparative purposes and decision weighting. Additional essay-type commentary is encouraged to cover areas that may have been overlooked in the questionnaire design.

Figure 15-1 In-house evaluation scoresheet

IN-HOUSE EXPERT EVALUATION

Information to be completed by MARKETING expert | Product Concept # _____ |

1. What do you think the *total* potential market is for this product?

    MOST LIKELY _____ units   LOW _____ units   HIGH _____ units

2. At each of the following points in the first fifteen years of the product's life, what level of annual unit sales do you forecast?

	MOST LIKELY	LOW	HIGH
1 year	_____ units	_____ units	_____ units
5 years	_____ units	_____ units	_____ units
10 years	_____ units	_____ units	_____ units

3. What market share do you expect for this product at the following points in its life cycle?

	MOST LIKELY	LOW	HIGH
1 year	_____ %	_____ %	_____ %
5 years	_____ %	_____ %	_____ %
10 years	_____ %	_____ %	_____ %

4. What do you see as the price for the product at the following points in its life cycle? (excluding inflation)

	MOST LIKELY	LOW	HIGH
1 year	$ _____	$ _____	$ _____
5 years	$ _____	$ _____	$ _____
10 years	$ _____	$ _____	$ _____

5. What level of *introductory* advertising and promotion will be required for this product?

    MOST LIKELY $ _____   LOW $ _____   HIGH $ _____

6. What level of advertising and promotion, as a percentage of sales, will be required to support this product once it is on the market?

    MOST LIKELY _____ %   LOW _____ %   HIGH _____ %

7. What test market costs would be required for this product?

    MOST LIKELY $ _____   LOW $ _____   HIGH $ _____

8. What level of selling costs (sales force's commissions, dealer support, displays; excluding advertising and promotion), as a percentage of sales, are required for this product?

    MOST LIKELY _____ %   LOW _____ %   HIGH _____ %

Figure 15-1 In-house evaluation scoresheet (Continued)

IN-HOUSE EXPERT EVALUATION

Information to be completed by RESEARCH & DEVELOPMENT expert

1. How many hours of R&D personnel time do you estimate is required to draw up the plans for this concept?

   MOST LIKELY _____ hours   LOW _____ hours   HIGH _____ hours

2. What rate (per hour) applies to R&D personnel? (including mix of management and engineering personnel)

   MOST LIKELY $ _____   LOW $ _____   HIGH $ _____

3. What costs are required to develop a protype model of this product concept?

   MOST LIKELY $ _____   LOW $ _____   HIGH $ _____

Information to be completed by PRODUCTION EXPERT,
by FINANCIAL EXPERT,
etc.

Prospect Communications

Prospect communications identify the target and describe the benefit (need fulfillment). If there is more than one benefit, the galaxy of advantages is arrayed and stressed in order of importance.

Here's an example:

> Automobile owners double their mileage when they add one pint of this new discovery to every tankful of gasoline.

The statement may go on to elaborate:

> Approved by Society of Automobile Engineers and all major automobile makers. Nonpoisonous, noncorrosive, made from a by-product of the plastics industry, costs no more than a gallon of gasoline—yet cuts your cost of gasoline almost in half.

The subparagraph of elaboration supports the claim, answers the obvious questions, and provides authoritative endorsement. It also adds credibility to the proposition.

Statements such as these, which describe easily measurable performance and do not have any special visual appeal, may be used in sorting and screening research results, whether they be obtained by mail, telephone, intercept, group, or intensive one-on-one discussions.

An illustration probably would add only a marginal enhancement—and may divert the respondents into the evaluation of (in this case) relatively low-priority considerations such as: packaging convenience, handling, material, disposal, etc. Further, an illustration could divert discussion from the chosen generic descriptor to that of the arbitrarily selected (for illustration purposes) container. For these reasons, no brand name or descriptor has been used in the stimulus communication. The attempt is to find out about the idea—*not* about its execution. That will come later.

In other situations, an illustration—no matter how schematic—may be necessary. In others, a very comprehensive illustration is necessary. Where relative size, visible texture, color, graphics, or mechanics are necessary to understanding, illustrations should be employed. Where the end effect has visual impact, as with decorative items and the appetite appeal essential to certain food and beverage items, supportive illustrations should be used in the concept stimulation material. While anyone can visualize a sugar-frosted cornflake, few are likely to be able to accurately imagine how a French-fried spaghetti snack would look. The first needn't be illustrated; the other should be.

For this reason, the selection of a research technique should be based on appropriate stimulus material—rather than stimulus material being developed to fit a predetermined research technique.

At this state in ideaform development, communications embellishment is to be eschewed. Just state the facts, arranged as a clear communication. You don't need personality, image, enhancing surroundings, or hyperbolic puffery at this point. The ideaform is not the advertising prototype. It is a bare, essential distillation of the concept. Because it is a bare essential, it allows the respondent to feed in information that may become part of the marketing communications blueprint. It seeks to describe a product in such a way as to make is understandable, leaving room for the respondent to embellish it with his or her own experience and language. It is hoped that the respondent will place the product into perspective as to its importance and the place it may play in the routine of the prospect's life or business.

The nature of the idea also helps determine the ideaform communication.

An idea may be able to go in multiple directions, yet one direction must (at least, initially) be selected or rejected prior to prototype development. In choosing among alternatives, a number of ideaform concept statements are prepared and studied. This is not *positioning* selection. That, too, comes later. At this point, you are trying to define the idea in each of the various ways it may be developed as a product, as an options guide to later R&D and/or prototype development.

Writing the Concept Statement

As already established, new products are essential to a company's successful growth. For this reason, top professional skills should be applied at every step of the way. This includes the preparation of ideaforms—the concept stimulus materials.

Unfortunately, the concept statement is often written by persons with professional skills in other fields—business management, marketing, engineering, medicine, pharmacy, research—but not in communications. Yet any of these same experts would not think of entrusting finished communications, which will be addressed to the prospect, to any but the finest communicators. The concept champions (especially!) will want the best possible communications to help introduce *their* new product. But often these champions become highly proprietary at the ideaform stage, rather than turning this critical task over to communications experts. Policy should require that professional communicators write the concept statements within prescribed research guidelines. If the research guidelines get in the way, revisit the purpose of the research and the rationale for the guidelines—and revise them if possible and necessary.

The clearest approach to writing a concept statement is to be knowledgeable about the new product and its market environment. Then, state in one clear sentence what you would tell an uninitiated friend about the product, so that he or she would immediately understand and possibly be infected by your enthusiasm. The best guidepost to this kind of writing is journalism—the who, what, when, where, why, and how formula, captured in a headline and lead sentence. Still the best text, for even the most complicated concept communication, is Rudolph Fleisch's *The Art of Plain Talk* (Macmillan, 1962).

(A highly paid professional communicator once told me that his first job was to write repair manuals for complicated data processing machines. "Me, who has never looked under the hood of a car—and can't drive a nail straight!" Undaunted, he set about interviewing the experts—and rigidly followed Rudolph Fleisch's directions. His manuals were so well received that their format, style, and relevant content are still in use to this day. "You know, I never repaired a single machine, I just watched, asked question, took notes, and wrote the manuals. Even with my excellent instructions, I'd still be afraid to approach those mysterious electronics, tools in hand.")

Concept Statement Preparation

A good communicator must be able to describe a complicated concept so that anyone can understand it—and understand it *accurately*. The first thing the professional does is to make the complicated simple. The second thing is to make the now-simple concept understandably relevant to the needs of the prospect. A well-written concept statement should embrace all of the following factors:

Differentiate

Give a reason to buy—a single one is best, just a few at most. A concept that is all things to all people usually interests none. The ideal concept appeals to selfish interests. It promises more convenience; it is cheaper; it is quicker; etc. A "preventive" concept (such as a vitamin compound) also must be differentiated from similar concepts in terms of form, use routine, accessibility, etc.

Some "Sell," But Not an Ad

Skip the hyperbole, but write the concept with a sale in mind. Position the concept so that the respondent can immediately place it in his or her world or company's world—can see a possible place where it may be applicable. Make clear who it is for, when and where and how it should be used—and what it may replace (another product, wasted time, wasted space, etc.).

The Pricing Issue

Do not include the price unless it is really relevant. If the product category is a known one and if the price of the concept product is within the expected range, do not include it. The respondent will either assume this or (possibly) say: "I'd expect to pay a bit more for this because . . . " or "I'd buy it if it didn't cost more than my regular brand" or "This would have to cost a lot less than X—because it seems less convenient." Lead the consumer into the pricing issue, if it is relevant; if it is not, lead the consumer into the value issue. An example: One of the truths in portable food product concept studies is that if the consumer says "It would be great for camping," you know that this expresses a search to place it somewhere positively—but that there is obviously no broad appeal.

Sometimes, however, the pricing issue is an essential. Sometimes, to price low in a price-sensitive market means a trade-off. In this case, where low price is a virtue but a sacrifice is made to achieve it, it is well to state the trade-off, minimizing the importance of the minor change. If the price is higher, justify the importance of the additional feature(s). Good examples abound in the home entertainment category, where the bells and whistles can be few or many—and usually relate to price points. Nonetheless, unless the only virtue of the new product is price, insert this issue separately in the respondent discussion process.

Other Factors

Accuracy of statement prevents misleading feedback from respondents. Too often, inaccurate statements creep into ideaforms because the author does not have a real-world, hands-on affinity for the use category. The result then becomes "factory talk"—description of the concept from the point of view of the maker, rather than its relevance to the use.

Another temptation to resist is telling more than the prospect needs (or *wants*) to know. It is better to err on the side of a well-stated main appeal with minimal support, than on the side of a fully rounded statement of everything you always wanted to know, but were afraid to ask.

The first approach allows the respondent to understand enough to stimulate questions and comments—which will provide clues to other important elements for consideration. The second approach may lead to unproductive comments and/or misunderstanding. (In the earlier example of the gasoline additive statement, a preliminary office screening of uninvolved respondents revealed that it was necessary to somehow describe the substance and its origin, but not in chemical terms. The industrial by-product allusion provided just enough information to close that information gap, and was added before the statement went into screening.)

The uninvolved office or factory screen should not be overlooked. It can save millions of dollars—and help make millions more.

An example: Years ago, a paper company developed a way to bond fibers together with water-soluble starch. One product suggestion was a sanitary napkin covering that would allow the cellulose fibers to be easily dispersed in the toilet and hence make the napkin readily flushable. The male conceptualizers had been confronted with many office and hotel signs warning against flushing sanitary napkins—and had invented a new product that had overcome the problem. Prototypes were made before any women were involved in concept statement studies. Products were placed in homes for use tests. Meanwhile, the outside new products consultant firm did a small sample office study (100 respondents) and found out a few simple facts that were ignored in a costly development program—but later proved to be correct. The majority of the 100 female respondents said: "I don't worry too much about what I flush down toilets in public office buildings . . . BUT I wouldn't flush *any* sanitary napkin down my *own* toilet. Besides, if the covering will dissolve in the toilet, won't it be a problem for me too?" Despite this, the product was introduced in test-market—and failed. This study illustrates the relevance of use-related concept evaluators as early as possible, even if informally involved.

Know the Language Territory

Obviously it is useful to try out feasible concepts on small samples of potential users very early in the process. This informal feedback can be conducted on a conversationally casual basis among possible prospects. Often, it will lead to concept refinement—or raise issues not well addressed or even anticipated. There may be a gap between the inventors and the intended recipients of the innovation.

This may be a language gap, not a gap between the product delivery and the respondent need. Knowing the language of the marketplace can help you sharpen the understandability of the concept refinement statement. What works in the lab may not work in the real world. This is why *in vitro* (test tube) experiments do not necessarily predict *in vivo* (real

Figure 15-2 Concept illustrations

These are representative illustrations of new products extensions in the canned meats field, all of which utilize existing production technology and minor capital investment. Packaged product drawings were used to stimulate discussion among manufacturers. Several items from the presentation have since been marketed.

world) results. It is important that concept statements be clear communications to the customer. The product or conception must be understood. The idea must inoculate a compatible culture. Words alone may not be enough to enliven the prospect's petri dish.

Concept Illustrations

Sometimes a picture or a graph is worth more than a thousand words. It may open a clearer path to understanding when you depict a complicated process with a flow chart, or show a multistage or many-featured product with schematic drawings of each component. The aim is understanding—not gloss or embellishment.

Sometimes a concept may be packaged in several alternative formats—although the resultant end-benefit does not change. The benefit

Figure 15-3 Concept illustrations—same product, different messages

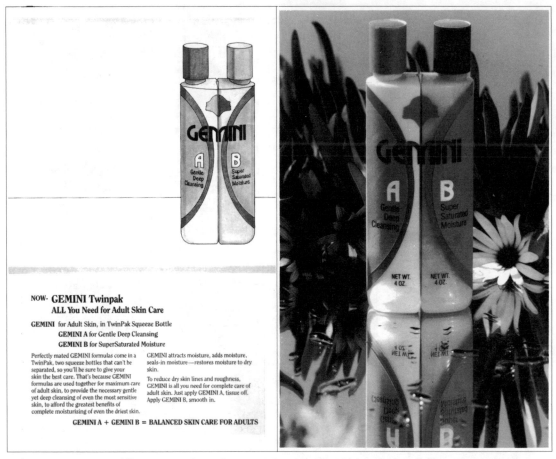

In this experiment, two different types of stimulus material were used, with matched audiences. The personal care product concepts received entirely different reactions. The detailed, explanatory poster received a logical, question-stimulated reaction. The full-color, atmospheric photo evoked emotional reactions and few questions about ingredients or basis for any claims.

Source: New Product Development, NTC Business Videos, 1989

description alone, then, is insufficient to promote understanding of the concept in alternative forms. Only an illustration will do the job well. Examples of such illustrations are shown in Figures 15-2, 15-3, 15-4, and 15-5.

Evidence of the ability of a simple illustration to change comprehension and interest in a concept is exhibited by many studies where the illustration was revealed after full discussion of the verbal description. The evaluation of written descriptions can change dramatically after visualizations are added.

Figure 15-4 Concept illustrations—buttery tasting

Buttery-tasting vegetable oil in a push-button dispenser was readily feasible, but a quick check to determine appeal and use-occasion frequency was handled with comprehensive drawings and descriptive copy before any major lab or communications development were committed. Here are two of the stimulus posters; on left, product is positioned primarily as a spread substitute, on right primarily as an ingredient.

Reducing the Candidates: Preresearch Screening

In the early stages, a typical interest area may yield hundreds of concepts, each with the possibility of various positionings, styling, packaging, trade names, features, and even various methods of sales and distribution. By this time in the developing process, the major technical feasibility and manufacturing issues should have been addressed. Broad costing guidelines are understood. Yet—the project team must screen down to a workable (and affordable) set of concepts for preliminary screening research. Following are some ways they might do this.

Identifying the Organizing Concept

Is there a single organizing concept—or is the concept statement a string of features, no one of which will justify the concept as a whole? A simple checklist and rating scale should help determine this. Alternatively, a single statement of the single element of innovation must stand up to

Figure 15-5   Concept illustrations—humidifier and bubble bath

NEW INVISIBLE SPACE-SAVER ROOM HUMIDIFIER

Now there's a wall-mounted room humidifier which takes no floor space. It's mounted between the wall studs -- and can be painted or papered to fit any decor. Completely automatic on-off cycle. Easily installed near any standard electrical outlet. Complete installation instructions and template included. Room humidifier helps guard against colds, protects wood furniture from drying and cracking, provides comfortable atmosphere with less heating energy. Space-Saver Room Humidifier costs no more than bulky similar-capacity free-standing floor models.

NEW PUSH-BUTTON BUBBLE BATH

Just attach to the faucet of your tub, turn on the hot water and push the button once. Tub floods with giant bubbles that soften and condition the skin. 100 relaxing bubble baths in each refillable container. (Fits most faucets.)

judgmental evaluation by the team. No "yes, buts" allowed. If a concept falls down on this basis, it should be dropped from further consideration.

For each case, make a listing of important considerations, then weight them in order of importance. The most promising concepts, then, will be those that focus on the single elements that are determined to be perceived as yielding the greatest benefit to the user. Using such a scale, you can rank the concepts. (In some instances, negative considerations are also listed, creating penalties to consider in the concept evaluation. For example: something may be terrific, but the cost will not justify the benefit.)

The best, the strongest single-statement stoppers say it all in a few words. When the talkies were young, this was enough: "Garbo talks!" Other examples: "How do you spell relief? . . . R-O-L-A-I-D-S." "M&Ms melt in your mouth, not in your hand." "Visine gets the red out." The "Excedrin Headache," which came out of retirement in 1991.

If the concept is a novel use of a key technique or ingredient that is hoped to be the star across a range of choices, then the importance or exclusivity of performance of that factor must be weighed. How long will it be important and exclusive? Are its costs elastic or inelastic? Can the company lock up its source? Is it protectable (and for how long) through proprietary processing or patents? If it is a short-range, unprotectable factor, then will it be a fast-moving, high-margin fad opportunity? Is it quickly communicated—or is prospect education needed? Is it better— or only *apparently* better?

Judgment Grid

Sometimes all of the key judgment factors can be laid out in such a way that each concept in a set can be quite easily screened.

Here's an example. For a food products assignment, a tic-tac-toe grid (Figure 15-6) was erected as a quick way to sort out concepts that have a variety of differences, but no single revolutionary improvement. Usually the category under study will allow assignment of predetermined weights to certain factors.

Figure 15-6 Concept sorting

Package	Portion	Components
Occasion	User	Convenience
Value	Substitution	Preparation

In this example, after poor scorers were eliminated, new weights were assigned to the *other* important characteristics, and the survivor concepts were regrouped. This method quickly screened several hundreds of concepts down to 40, then to 20 that went into consumer concept research.

A similar evaluation method is to determine the principal attributes of the interest category. Then rank these attributes according to the performance of the entrenched competition. Then do it for the concepts under question. First, this isolates whether the concept really addresses a need or a gap. Second, it helps answer whether its promise is in an area of significant interest.

As an example, for hair shampoo, the attribute ranking in order of importance might be:

1. Quick, large, and copious suds

2. Quick conditioning effects

3. Easy rinsing

4. Fragrance/lack of fragrance

5. Cleansing ability

As this list shows, a concept for a superior conditioning shampoo that, however, did not suds well might have outstanding efficacy—but still fail. A concept that offered cleaner hair than any other shampoo would provide a marginal benefit and might create a fear of stripping and drying the hair.

Gap Analysis

A frequently used approach in evaluating new product concepts is *gap analysis*. Such factors as brand identity, attributes, differentiation, reward, and payoff are arrayed across a horizontal plane. On the vertical axis are listed the concept categories to be evaluated, such as those five cited in the shampoo example above. For each competing brand, the relevant information is entered in the boxes created by the intersecting horizontal and vertical lines. This matrix tends to isolate the gaps in the competitive market. If the concept under consideration fills the gaps, it may have a competitive edge.

Outsiders Who Are Insiders

Probably every concept in the preliminary set has a sponsor. The initial cut can be made by the coach—based on experience and ultimate responsibility for subsequent performance. Or it can be made by noninvolved insiders unaware of ego-attachments carried by the various concepts. A "ranking" approach, which tends to be impersonal, is asked of each. Sometimes a briefing (in writing) precedes. Clusters of top and bottom ranking emerge. Top ranks and those middle ranks with a few top scores survive. Others are cut, unless a fervent champion makes an extremely strong case for moving ahead with further investigation.

The Champion Screen

Throughout this book we champion the Champion—that individual who is willing to risk ridicule or a career for belief in an idea. To such a strong belief, heed should be paid—there are few enough champions in business, yet they are often the most important factors in the truly new.

Here's an example. A classic example of research versus instinct was well described by Bob Shanks in his book *The Cool Fire* (Vintage Books division of Random House, ©1976 by Comco Productions).

> The Ford Motor Company researched the introduction of a new automobile tirelessly and expensively and came up with the Edsel. A few years later, Lee Iacocca fought for his instinct that Americans wanted a hot car—and came up with the Mustang, Ford's single greatest success.

Incidentally, *after* the failure of the Edsel, I attended a seminar on new product development in Detroit, which featured a presentation by a Ford research director. His case history of a model meticulously managed research program was that done for the Edsel. No matter that the program provided misdirection—it was well planned and executed!

Figure 15-7 The Edsel vs. today's research

☑ **Definitely will buy**

Consumers are a pretty strange breed.
What they say they will do is not always what they wind up doing. A fact which some of us have learned the hard way.

That's why "intend to buy" research and "top box" scores don't necessarily give serious marketing people the kind of information they need to judge product performance in the real world. And that's what makes Yankelovich Clancy Shulman LITMUS™-based testing absolutely essential to the new generation of marketing professionals.

Simply put, the LITMUS™ model has taken marketing analysis into a new era. It provides more answers—more valuable answers to your real-world marketing questions.

Answers like trial, awareness, market share, sales…even *profitability.* Answers that project, month by month, the *optimal* marketing plan. The kind of answers that you just can't get anywhere else. And LITMUS™ does it with astonishing accuracy.

Whether you're introducing a new product, restaging an old one or looking at the competition, we would like to show you exactly how and why LITMUS™ works to provide you with consumer intelligence that translates into real consumer behavior.

Call our Senior Vice President of Marketing, Mr. Watts Wacker, at (203) 227-2700.

Because consumers are a strange breed.
And you don't have to learn that the hard way.

LITMUS™
The acid test. Worldwide.

Yankelovich Clancy Shulman
Eight Wright Street   Westport   Connecticut 06880

Concept research is used for new products, new services, new advertising themes, new movies, and new television shows. Still, creative judgment cannot be replaced by any standardized evaluation technique. As TV producer Bob Shanks says:

> Frequently, networks will themselves make up concepts for shows, test them, and, if certain ones do well, commission shows to be written and produced, based on these concepts. Again, this research is normally used prudently by network executives.

> Executives who are trained up through law, research, accounting, or sales generally rely more heavily on this so-called objective evidence; those who have come up through the creative ranks usually rely more on instinct, a sense of actually experiencing what audiences like by having exposed themselves to audiences.

The Experience Screen

Often, the best research is experimental. This comes only from hands-on observation in the field. Not from books. Not from case histories. Not from GIGO[1] computer programs—or any kind, even some that have been validated. After all, while every experience isn't exactly original, each one isn't exactly the same, either. Repeated observations and participatory experiences tend to cluster common themes, which become the basis for trained judgments.

One bad (or good) experience is apt to be misleading. How often have we heard something like this: "That may concept test well—but it will never sell. We tried a product just like that a few years ago and it flopped." Often, upon examination, you find that the referenced concept was not just exactly like that old flop—or that it had a different audience target, times have changed, etc.

Sometimes personal tastes (rather than observations of the behavior of others) unduly affect business judgments. One of the factors contributing to the failure of a frozen main-dish line was the absolute blandness of the products, achieved over the protests of the corporate kitchens and food technologists. The CEO just didn't like onions in anything—and that went for lots of other spices and seasonings, too.

What's Left Goes Forward

The mere writing of a clear concept statement can often reveal flaws in the offering—underneath the fancy dress may be a pale figure of an idea. If so, eliminate it from consideration.

As for others in the cut-down process, use experience, personal taste, pragmatic data-based judgments, field observations, etc. Set a tar-

---

[1] "Garbage In, Garbage Out," which means you only get as good as you give, from computers like anything else.

get: Only ten concepts can go into the research screening phase. This will force-fit the selection.

And now you move ahead, to develop rounded materials and more reliable screening methods. The costs are mounting but progress is being made. Research among true prospects will help determine the path ahead. It will be the basis for the next important commitment of the company's funds.

16

Screening Research

General investigation to seek knowledge at minimal cost is the first step in screening research. As the project progresses, the stimulus becomes more refined, the research technique more precise, and both the promise and the investment escalate.

This chapter is devoted to those research steps that help to refine the guidelines for prototype products and communications.

Sometimes, research is an overpromise. Remember, it can yield perspective on yesterday (depending on who writes the history), a snapshot of today (as accurate as the aim and focus, the speed of the film, and the truth of the colors), and the basis for a close-in tomorrow. Predictive research at its best can be no more accurate than its unpredictable subject: the marketplace.

In a paper presented at the 41st annual meeting of the Institute of Food Technologists (June 7–10, 1981, Atlanta, GA), David K. Hardin, then chairman of Market Facts, Inc., noted:

> Satisfaction with new product screening and product testing results is relatively low. Hardly anyone feels that his or her techniques provide a very good prediction of new product potentials. Two out of five believe that the techniques are not really very good.

Many experts agree. In a review contained in *Harvard Business Review on Management* (Harper & Row), an overview of qualitative methods, time series analysis and projection, and casual methods provided these ratings on seven applicable basic forecasting techniques. In paraphrase, these evaluations are:

A. Qualitative methods (forecasts of long-range and new product sales, forecasts of margins)

1. Delphi
   Accuracy: Fair to very good.
   Identification of turning points: Fair to good.

2. Market research (systematic, formal, and conscious procedure for evolving and testing hypotheses about real markets)
   Accuracy: Short-term (0–3 mos.): Excellent.
   Mid-term (3 mos.–2 yrs.): Good.
   Long-term (2 yrs. +): Fair to good.
   Identification of turning points: Fair to very good.
   Data required: At least two sets of reports over time, including a considerable collection of market data from questionnaires, surveys, and time series analyses of market variables.

3. Panel consensus (technique based on assumption that several experts can arrive at a better forecast than one. There is no secrecy—unlike Delphi—and communication is encouraged. The forecasts are sometimes influenced by social factors, and may not reflect a true consensus.)
   Accuracy: Short- and mid-term: Poor to fair.
   Long-term: Poor.
   Identification of turning points: Poor to fair.

4. Visionary forecast (prophecy using personal insights, judgments, and, when possible, facts about different scenarios of the future. It is characterized by subjective guesswork and imagination; in general, methods used are nonscientific.)
   Accuracy: Poor.
   Identification of turning points: Poor.

5. Historical analogy (comparative analysis of introduction and growth of similar new products, which bases the forecast on similarity patterns)
   Accuracy: Short-term: Poor.
   Mid- and long-term: Good to fair.
   Identification of turning points: Poor to fair.
   Data required: Several years' history of one or more products.

B. Time series analysis and projection

6. Trend projections (technique fits a trend line to a mathematical equation and then projects it into the future by means of this equation. There are several variations: the slope-characteristic

method, polynomials, logarithms, etc.)
Accuracy: Short-term: Very good.
          Mid- and long-term: Good.
Identification of turning points: Poor.
Data required: Varies with technique used. Good rule of thumb
is to use a minimum of five years' annual data to start.
Thereafter, the complete history.
Typical application: New product forecasts (particularly
intermediate and long-term).

C. Casual methods

7. Life-cycle analysis (analysis and forecasting of new product
    growth rates based on S-curves. The phases of product accep-
    tance by the various groups such as innovators, early adapters,
    early majority, late majority, and laggards are central to the
    analysis.)
    Accuracy: Short-term: Poor.
              Mid- to long-term: Poor to good.
    Identification of turning points: Poor to good.
    Typical application: Forecasts of new product sales.
    Data required: Minimally, annual sales of product being
    considered or of a similar product. Often necessary to
    do market surveys.

Learning (as Well as Testing)

One of the reasons for widespread dissatisfaction with new product research is that too much is expected. In reality, as opposed to research
that monitors ongoing experience, new product research is learning, as
much as it is testing.

Unfortunately, all too many researchers in new product areas opt to
design research instruments (questionnaires) that are highly structured:
lots of multiple choice, agree/disagree, and checklist types of questions
that, in most cases, facilitate "testing," but deter "learning." Such testing
does build up big numbers at a relatively low cost. Numbers tend to be
objective support for facts. And objectivity tends to carry more weight
in the decision process.

Closed-end or check-off questions are appealing because:

*   They're easy to administer.
*   They're easy to tabulate.
*   They're easy to compare with norms or pars from other tests.
*   They're less expensive both to administer and to tabulate.
*   They're easy to understand (require no thought).

Closed-end questions yield "scores," "norms," "pars," "means,"
and, if the sample is large and random, are readily susceptible to a vast
variety of statistical analyses.

In new product work, however, particularly in the early stages, highly structured, closed-end questions serve to gag and to straitjacket the respondent, rendering him/her the freedom to only nod or shake his/her head when presented with agreeable or disagreeable stimuli. These stimuli, unfortunately, are based on the assumption that we have learned all there is to know about a new product—and that all that is left for research to find out is what numbers of people feel this way or that.

Research Guidelines

Whether it be qualitative research to seek knowledge, projective techniques to make forecasts, or testing to evaluate scenarios, professional disciplines are necessary to assure comparability and validity within the scope of the test.

The Advertising Research Foundation has published guidelines for the public use of research. Although the purpose was to provide an aid to the evaluation of the validity and reliability of research results and of the weight to be given to them in public use, a relatively easy modification of these guidelines is useful when approaching new product screening. Thus, this excellent document has been adopted for the purposes of this chapter.

The approach is both realistic and pragmatic. According to ARF:

> Few absolute standards of quality ever apply to market and opinion research. Decisions about what to do and how many cases to study, and what words to use to communicate what meaning are often pragmatic and, on occasion, somewhat arbitrary. The realities of the field make compromise inevitable and perfection impossible. Nonetheless . . . it is essential that [research] be fairly and competently conducted and that it be honestly reported.

The ARF guidelines group the relevant factors into seven areas of evaluation:

- **Origin**—What is behind the research
- **Design**—The concept and the plan
- **Execution**—Collecting and handling the information
- **Stability**—Sample size and reliability
- **Applicability**—Generalizing the findings
- **Meaning**—Interpretations and conclusions
- **Candor**—Open reporting and disclosure

Although much of this is just common sense, it is surprising how often these disciplines are overlooked. Therefore, it is useful to emphasize that those who do the research and those who sponsor and design it should acknowledge responsibility for it and, when the research is reported, should say whether they concur with the findings presented.

Likewise, research should be designed to produce fair measurements and honest information. It should not try to mislead its users. It should not pretend to an objectivity or a significance it does not merit. In planning, the time, money, and skills to be invested in the research should be balanced against the impact of the expected information. Important decisions ought not to be based on poorly conceived and grossly inadequate studies, nor should great efforts be invested to product trivial data. After all, the integrity and value of research depend on the competence and honesty with which information is collected and processed. Care in performing these functions determines, in large measure, how good the data finally are.

Here, then, are the key questions and quality checkpoints essential to each step in new products screening (as adapted from the ARF work).

Origin—What is Behind the Research

Key Questions

Is there a statement of the purpose of the research that says clearly what it was meant to accomplish?

Are the suppliers or company departments/individuals identified as responsible for conducting the research?

Quality Checkpoints

Is there a statement by the sponsors acknowledging their acceptance of the research and its reported findings?

Is there a statement from the responsible researchers of their concurrence with the reported findings?

Are the problems to which the research is directed distinguished (in a clear statement) from other related or broader problems that the research was not designed to address?

Is the present use of research the use for which it was designed?

Design—the Concept and the Plan

Key Questions

Is there a full description, in nontechnical language, of the research design, including a definition of what is being measured and how the data are collected?

Is the design consistent with the stated purpose for which the research was conducted?

Is the design evenhanded, that is, is it free of leading questions and other bias; does it address questions of fact and opinion without inducing answers that unfairly benefit the study sponsors?

Have precautions been taken to avoid or to equalize patterns of sequence or timing or other factors that might prejudice or distort findings?

Does it ask questions that respondents are capable of answering?

Is there a precise statement of the universe or population the research is meant to research?

Does the sampling source or frame fairly represent the population under study?

Does the report specify the kind of sample used, and clearly describe the method of sample selection?

Does the report describe the plan for analysis of the data?

Are copies of all questionnaire forms, field and sampling instructions, and other study materials available to anyone with a legitimate interest in the research?

Quality Checkpoints

Does the study use a random sample—that is, one that gives every member of the sampling frame an equal or known chance of selection?

Does the research use procedures for the selection of respondents that are not subject to the orientation or convenience of interviewers?

If the research calls for continuing panels or repeated studies, are there unbiased ways to update or rotate the original sample?

In field use, would the questionnaire hold the interest and attention of the respondents and the interviewer?

Is the information requested limited to what people can supply and can reasonably be expected to give openly and accurately?

Are study or test conditions or responses relevant to the situation to which the findings are supposed to relate?

Where controls or other products are involved, are they the appropriate ones to be included?

Was the plan for analysis set up and agreed to before the data were collected?

Execution—Collecting and Handling the Information

Key Questions

Does the report specify the proportion of the designated sample from which information was collected and processed, or does it say the proportion cannot be determined?

Is there an objective report on the care with which the data were collected?

Were those who collected data kept free of clues to the study sponsorship or the expected response, or other leads or information that might condition or bias the information they obtained and recorded?

Quality Checkpoints

Are the coding rules and procedures available for review?

If the data are weighted, is the range of the weights reported?

Is the basis for the weights described and evaluated?

Is the effect of the weights on the reliability of the final estimates reported?

Were there persistent efforts, through carefully scheduled call-backs, to interview designated respondents?

Is the rate of sample completion calculated on the basis of the total designated sample (including all eligible respondents, whether or not a contact was made or attempted)?

Were objective tests made to determine how completing the balance of the sample would have changed the results?

Does the report discuss any substitutions made for any parts of the selected sample, either in the field or when the sample was designed and drawn, or state that there were no substitutions?

Are problems that were encountered in the course of the data collection reported?

Were the interviewers carefully selected, trained, supervised, and paid enough to ensure their positive attitude and cooperation?

Were the interviewers compensated on the basis of hours worked rather than on the basis of the amount of work completed?

If the research was part of a continuing design, was the identity of respondents, interviewers, and sampling locations protected to avoid possible manipulation of reported behavior or other contamination of future findings?

Was data gathering limited to what was reported firsthand by respondents or observed directly in the field?

Were there confidential validation checks of the field sampling and the data gathering by unbiased independent researchers with no financial stake in a positive validation?

Does the report give specific information on the result of the field validations?

Does the report give a full explanation of any unplanned or uncommon mathematical manipulation of the collected data?

To the extent that it can be checked, did the data processing preserve the meaning and integrity of the collected information?

Were the research operations opened to objective professional inspection, with full disclosure of the results of each inspection?

Stability—Sample Size and Reliability

Key Questions

Was the sample large enough to provide stable findings?

Are sampling error limits shown if they can be computed?

Are methods of calculating the sampling error described, or if the error cannot be computed, is this stated and explained?

Does the treatment of sampling error limits make clear that they do not cover nonsampling error?

For the major findings, are the reported error tolerances based on direct analysis of the variability of the collected data?

Quality Checkpoints

Is the sample's reliability discussed in language that can be clearly understood without a technical knowledge of statistics?

Is the unweighted sample size reported both for the sample as a whole and for each subgroup for which data are analyzed?

If findings are reported for small numbers of respondents, are appropriate restrictions brought to the attention of the users of the research?

In balancing disproportionate sampling, were reasonable limits placed on the weights assigned to individual cases?

Applicability—Generalizing the Findings

Key Questions

Does the report specify when the data were collected?

Does the report say clearly whether its findings do or do not apply beyond the direct source of the data?

Is it clear who is underrepresented by the research, or not represented at all?

If the research has limited application, is there a statement covering who or what it represents, and the times or conditions under which it applies?

Quality Checkpoints

If the information comes from sources that are easy to contact or specially interested in the subject, is it noted that this information may not be typical of other parts of the population?

Does the report comment on the presence or absence of any exceptional events that might be reflected in the reported data, noting, for example, any audience and circulation drives, brand deals, publicity and promotion, and other transient factors that could affect the results?

Meaning—Interpretations and Conclusions

Key Questions

Are the measurements described in simple and direct language?

Does it make logical sense to use such measurements for the purpose to which they are being put?

Are the actual findings clearly differentiated from the interpretation of the findings?

Has rigorous objectivity and sound judgment been exercised in interpreting research findings as evidence of causation or as predictive of future behavior?

Quality Checkpoints

Is there an effort to make explicit any important assumptions that must be made in drawing conclusions from the research?

Does the report treat realistically people's ability to give valid or unbiased or quantitative responses?

Does the report specifically qualify any data that depend on the respondents' memories over time or their ability to predict future behavior?

Are the effects of the data-gathering instruments and methods made clear?

Candor—Open Reporting and Disclosure

Key Questions

Is there full and forthright disclosure of how research was done?

Have all of the relevant findings been released, including any information potentially unfavorable to the sponsor or embarrassing to the responsible researcher?

Has the research been fairly presented?

Quality Checkpoints

Are all definitions, classification rules, coding procedures, weights, and terminology explained in clear and unambiguous language?

Are the records of the research preserved, and with proper safeguards to the privacy of respondents, and are they available to answer responsible inquiries about the collected data?

Is the presentation free of bias, exaggeration, and graphic or other distortions?

Is there a statement on the limitations of the research and possible misinterpretations of the findings?

Screening— and Beyond

The Market Facts Inc. study, "Practices, Trends and Expectations for Market Research Industry—1988/89," a report on outside custom research expenditures, shows gains in nine categories (1988 vs. 1983 expenditures):

Applications That Are Gaining in Share of Outside Custom Research Expenditures

	Percentage who said these applications are gaining in share of expenditures	
	Grocery, drug companies	Durables, service companies
New product/concept studies	43%	37%
Basic market strategy studies	30%	46%
Laboratory test marketing	38%	10%
Tracking studies	30%	41%
Advertising pretesting	28%	27%
Advertising campaign testing	11%	20%
Product testing	17%	7%
Product optimizing studies	19%	34%
In-store test marketing	9%	4%

Those are the gainers. Now, let's look at the overall picture. Brand attitude/usage tracking studies were the most widely employed, by 93 percent. Other research applications employed in the past year by more than four out of five companies included advertising copy tests (89 percent). (The study was based on a self-administered mail questionnaire provided corporate market research directors from 145 of the largest marketers of products and services to consumers, with a completion rate of 61 percent collected in September 1988.)

The use of traditional in-market marketing using corporately managed distribution facilities was reported by 42 percent of the packaged goods marketers. Just over half (53 percent) said they employed controlled store testing.

At least nine out of ten companies conducted custom studies through each of three methodologies in the past year: focus groups, centrally supervised WATS, and mall intercept. Controlled mail panels ranked fourth in usage, and were employed by 66 percent.

"Door-to-door" interviewing is trending back up from its drop to 39 percent in 1987 (61 percent was the 1978 high) and is reported as 47 percent, suggesting that there's been a resurgence in the use of this methodology.

In late 1990, Verne B. Churchill, chairman/CEO of Market Facts, said: "This would suggest there's been a resurgence in the use of this methodology, which is the case for some companies who have been frustrated by their experience in shopping malls for face-to-face surveys. Nonetheless, the most recent report also shows that only 3 percent named it as the technique accounting for the 'greatest proportion of outside, custom expenditures,' and it was the methodology named most often (23 percent) as the technique with a declining share of expenditures."

Over a ten-year period of comparable observations, the two most notable trends have been a consistent and significant increase in the share of expenditures accounted for by tracking studies, and a corresponding decline in advertising campaign evaluation studies.

Laboratory test markets (STMs) have grown to a level of broad-scale use by grocery and drug marketers. More than four out of five packaged goods marketers (81 percent) employed STMs in the past year, and 38 percent named STMs as an application that is gaining in share of outside expenditures, according to the Market Facts study. Fifty-seven percent named simulated test markets as a technique accounting for the greatest proportion of their test marketing investment.

Scanner panels have maintained their popularity with packaged goods marketers, of whom 49 percent said they employed such systems for test marketing *without* split cable capabilities, and 38 percent said they did so *with* cable options.

Concept Exploration

Qualitative research is most often employed to explore prospect/consumer reaction to concepts, consumer language, and identification of potential target market(s). Frequently, stimulus material takes the shape of concept cards or posters with rough art renderings of alternative product prototypes (developed prior to actual model making, in many cases). Focus groups and one-on-one interviews are usually employed. In certain areas of new product interest, so-called depth interviews plumb the implications and psychological triggers behind reactions.

In both types of interactive research, interview guides allow both a free-ranging exploration of respondent interest and a programmed coverage of specific sponsor queries.

As discussed in the preceding chapter on ideaforms, a verbal description may get one score, but its concrete further explication through an illustration may change the perceptions. An actual example is shown in Figure 16-1. This chart shows interest levels for nine of the many concepts studied. Concepts were screened through a series of monadic interviews, then the results were arranged according to the key issues in purchase and repeat use intent. Note how the perceptions changed in various instances after an illustration of the concept product was shown (bottom line)—overall initial interest went down in one instance (concept P) and up in others. Other evaluations also changed.

Concept Testing

Quantitative testing is used to rank each concept's potential against the others being considered and to provide a rough guideline volume estimate. Several systems generally in use by consumer package goods marketers include:

> **Mail panel of matched members,** who receive concept descriptions and drawings. Each respondent household receives only one concept. Measurement of intent to try the product and intended frequency of buying are the key data of the analysis. The sample size is determined by the dimension of the target market.

> **Mall or In-Store Intercept,** random interviews against predetermined cells. Comprehensive ad-like posters to convey the reality of the concepts are often used to stimulate more dependable reactions from respondents who are in a shopping mode and location. Wide-ranging concepts may be shown to individual respondents. Subtle-difference concepts are used monadically. The resulting intent to buy is scaled numerically.

Various research suppliers offer proprietary techniques to determine trial and repeat buying intentions from simple descriptions and

Figure 16-1 Concept screening

	High group			Medium group			Low group		
Composite rank	1	2	3	11	12	13	20	21	22
1. Concept	Q	A	D	B	T	P	O	U	M
2. Interest and involvement									
a. Overall initial interest	H	H	H	M	M	M	L	L	L
b. Immediacy of perceived purchase	H	H	H	M	M	L	L	L	L
3. Perceived user	F	C/W	C/G	C/G/W	F/G	F	C	C	C
4. Replacement of current product									
a. Current product replaced	PRODUCT R	PRODUCT F	PRODUCT Z	PRODUCT B	PRODUCT G	PRODUCT A	PRODUCT L	PRODUCT Y	PRODUCT U
b. Frequency of use of current	H	H	M	L	M	M	L	H	L
c. Quality of new vs. current	H	H	H	M	L	L	L	L	L
d. Frequency of replacement by new	H	H	H	M	M	L	L	L	L
e. Willingness to pay more than for current	H	M	H	M	L	H	L	L	L
5. Effect of picture	H	H	H	M	M	L	M	L	L

Code: F: Family, G: Gatekeeper (purchaser, but not user), C: Child, W: Woman. (All interviewees were female in this sample.) H: High, M: Medium, L: Low interest levels. Current Product Replaced Summary indicates most frequent product that would be replaced by concept product. (By permission, Pilot Products Incorporated)

drawings. Prominent among them are BASES, a pretest market volume estimate technique offered by Burke Marketing Research Inc., employing in-store intercept sampling, with measures on a five-point intent-to-buy scale. Another is E.S.P. (Estimating Sales Potential), offered by NPD Research and designed to project trial, repeat, and volume purchases of new products.

Positioning Testing

This is quantitative testing to help determine which positioning maximizes the impact of the concept. Depending on the nature of the product concept and the primary communications medium of the category, stimulus material may be a mock-up print ad or a live-action presenter or a voice-over still photo presentation on a videotape monitor. With the rapid development of interactive cable television, discrete cable channels, and interactive telephone interviewing, all recognizing the preconditioning of respondents to the medium, more testing is using techniques related to the pervasive electronic medium.

Matched samples of consumers with predetermined purchase patterns are sometimes used on the assumption that the interaction with the new concept-stimulus material represents a universal set; e.g., a 25-year-old middle-income homemaker mother of two children, married to a professional, and a loyal consumer of Twinkies, if geographically dispersed throughout the set, will be representative of similar Twinkie consumers in reaction to each concept position. The incidence of sample stimulus material exposure is equalized against each respondent segment.

Name Testing

Name testing—whether brand name or generic, but most often the former—is approached in different manners, depending on the category. A popular, yet somewhat superficial, method utilizes card sorting. The respondent simply goes through a series of card sorts until a rank order from most to least preferred evolves. An "appropriateness" scale is sometimes also used. Testing of alternative names is best done monadically among a competitive array to allow for measurement of interaction or confusion of the test name vis-à-vis competition.

Competitive Shelf Tests

Competitive shelf tests involve separate panels of respondents evaluating one name or packaging variable within the context of a competitive shelf display. For example, a new name for a Twinkie analog might be monadically tested in the context of a shelf display mock-up containing other current Twinkie analogs, as well as the best-known Twinkie competitors. Also employed in shelf testing are eye cameras and similar devices that measure attention and pupil dilation. This purports to document the attention dynamics of the package being tested and its ability to break through the cluttered in-store environment.

Theme Testing

Whereas a "position" is relative to something else (a position has a "location," in the competitive environment, life-style, and/or needs of the prospect), a "theme" is a simple, memorable, attention-getting expression of the new offering's appeal. Occasionally, theme testing is part of new product exploration at this early screening phase. It is most likely to be so in cases where the product differential is little or lacking and the positioning is highly preemptible. In such cases, the "theme" must carry a great burden in the decision to move forward with the new product concept. Techniques employed are similar to the concept sorting techniques, but more likely represent finished advertising language. Whenever possible, it is recommended that theme testing be delayed until a reasonably accurate and differentiating product prototype, with a preemptive position, has been determined.

A Step Forward

Every company works at establishing data norms or, at least, cutoff classifications. Often numbers without meaning in themselves take on credibility through history. By interpolation, X percent of interest in category Y is a better score than the same X percent in category Z, assuming market intelligence about each category is sufficient. According to Market Facts Inc., new product data norms for concept and product success are not universal. About one-fourth of the companies surveyed by Market Facts have established norms, and another one-half have partially established norms. There is obviously a strong need for continuing development in this area.

So far, the risks we have discussed have been within the constraints of a modest investigative budget. A few mistakes won't break the company. What we don't know perhaps won't hurt us—so the concepts that have fallen through the screen are still lying somewhere to be visited another day, possibly by the same company but with new champions or changing market dynamics such as demographics (baby boom) or economics (energy shortage/recession). Meanwhile, some concepts have survived the process—and they must be brought closer to reality.

Section 4

Summary Afterword

Conception is the inoculation of a germ of an idea, giving it sufficient shape to recognize its possible potential. To begin, input is required—something must come from something. With input, ideation is spawned. With ideas, forms become concrete. With concrete ideaforms, the selection process begins.

Matters are specific enough now that a decision can be made to carry forward—or to abandon. In new product generation, the abandonment step is as much a contribution to progress as a blind move forward with all entries. In fact, the act of abandonment liberates time and money to fund the future evaluation of the more promising concepts.

Input can come from many sources. Among them are the following:

- Problems (as input)
- By-products
- Manufacturing process
- Contract packers
- Associated trades
- Inventors and patents
- Licensing
- Men and machines
- Trade schools
- Other trades (parallel ones)
- Other places (beyond business boundaries)
- Getting away from headquarters
- Listening
- Research—R&D and marketing
- Gurus and geniuses

After you have the input, it is time to germinate the ideas. We have looked at a number of ways of doing this, including the following:

- Collecting, absorbing, fantasizing
- Lateral thinking
- Rearranging information
- Seeing the obvious
- Seeing the category differently
- Making the product better
- Making the first product of its kind
- Thinking outside-in
- Using peer groups
- Using the Delphi method
- Creating an ideation incentive program
- Learning from consumer mail
- Brainstorming
- Using the Synectics approach
- Role-playing
- Roll playing
- Trying the ivory tower approach
- Studying the competitive set
- Using personification
- Learning from self-identification
- Moving from the ridiculous to the sublime
- List making
- Finding an equity
- Determining what and where
- Deciding there will be no holds barred

As ideas become more concrete, we move into more specific idea-forms. Ideaforms have two basic parts: the business term description and prospect communications. Communicating the idea involves several factors. First is writing the ideaform. Then comes concept statement preparation. This must provide product differentiation, some sell (but no ads at this point), and a discussion of the pricing issue. You must know the language territory and be able to provide concept illustrations, if needed.

There are a number of ways to prescreen the idea, before the research state. They involve identifying the organizing concept, making use of a judgment grid or gap analysis, utilizing outsiders who are insiders (consultants), or depending on the "champion" or experience to do the screening.

Screening research gets more precise. Basic forecasting techniques include qualitative methods (Delphi, market research, panel consensus, visionary forecasting, historical analogy); time series analysis and projection (trend projections); and more casual methods (life-cycle analysis). The process involves learning as much as testing.

Research guidelines include the following:

- Origin
- Design
- Execution
- Stability
- Applicability
- Meaning
- Candor

Under each of these guidelines should be listed the key questions to be considered and quality checkpoints.

Preliminary screening steps include concept exploration, concept testing (through mail panels or mall or in-store intercepts), positioning testing, name testing, shelf testing of the package, and theme testing.

And then one is ready for the next step forward.

MODELING

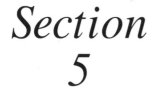

*Section
5*

17

The Product as Communication

"*Inventing is a combination of brains and materials. The more brains you use, the less materials you need.*"

—CHARLES F. KETTERING

"*A bad beginning makes a bad ending.*"

—EURIPIDES

Each product or service is a communication in itself. Although most evolve their personalities over time, some are predestined. Most do not deliver a clear image at the beginning—or ever. Some sharply stand for something from the day of birth—and are carefully nurtured throughout their histories.

The greatest successes know where they are going. Their creators had specific intentions—models—in mind. They worked to assure that the models fit their marketing motivations, that the finished products and their communications enforced those purposeful visions.

Although there are ephemeral categories—the beauty/fashion trades, games and toys, entertainment industry fads come to mind—the most successful of even these have an integral consistency of personality during their brief lifespans.

Model making is the key in the creating of new products. Just as certainly as a blueprint can be laid down for an office building or a libretto, so too can the guidelines for modeling.

Upfront thinking and planning; trial and error, experimentation and screening; user input—all are important to the process.

Family Model

Often a new product has a name before it is born. It is of the IBM or Revlon heritage. If it carries the family name, it must surely appear to be a legitimate progeny. A well-defined corporate or brand image helps set the modeling guidelines. Inappropriate, out-of-focus product dress may mask appropriate function, and lead to failed acceptance.

Most often, a new product is not pioneering a category. It is joining it, with a difference. Therefore, it must encompass the generic descriptor common to the category—but with a distinguishing difference, e.g., not cleansing creme, but deep cleansing lotion; not soap with cocoa butter, but bath soap with cocoa butter conditioners. Communicate the class, the difference from others in the class, and, where possible, the benefit. Leverage a powerful brand name when extending it to flankers. Upscale Arpege Parfum, a prestigious fragrance, is a good example. When it brought out its perfumed dusting powder it was called Arpege Dusting Powder. When it leveraged the Arpege image by changing its name and descriptor to Powdered Arpege for After Bath, sales soared.

Preliminary brand name development is a modeling step. Hundreds are generated for screening (including legal screening). Prospects may include in-house brands, as well as newly created brands. They should be appropriate to enforcing the generic descriptor, clearly set apart from competition, and stated in one or a few words, difficult to mispronounce—yet memorable. This distinction and an original graphic appearance will aid in securing the trademark.

Brand Name Bank

Many companies make it a practice to build a brand name bank of their own. Whenever a likely brand name is developed for a category of interest to the company—even if there is no current work underway in the category by the company—steps are taken to register the brand. Labels are printed and affixed to proper product classification lots of lab, pilot plant, or contract maker product. These are sold (in limited quantities) in interstate commerce—sometimes with a minimal direct response advertising support to assure retail transactions but usually simply by providing "guaranteed sale" merchandise at attractive prices to trade channels. Notice is given on the package (TM) that the trademark has been applied for—which is done, leading to a registration®, unless opposed. If opposed, attorneys often work out satisfactory arrangements with the contending party (who was not revealed in the preliminary trademark search). In categories where branding is an important aspect of communication success (package goods), the practice is helpful in protecting the future interests of the company—both offensively (for new products) and defensively (to block competition).

Category Model

Often an entry category sets the tone. Naturalistic product lines that leverage wholesome root values should not veer far from the path of tradition, whereas contemporary cool may be the only design for disc drive.

And, so, form before function—at least conceptually—is often the modeling creed on which a clear marketing communication personality is built.

Trial Parts

Modeling is necessary for function, as well.

Are the knobs big enough and far enough apart for the hands that will twist controls? Don't theorize. Model. Let those hands give them a whirl—*before* expensive working prototypes are built.

Model Instructions

Are the cooking instructions clear and easy to follow, and do they have a wide latitude of tolerance? Have the uninitiated try them out before putting the mix into the package and before printing the package. The results may require changes in the recipe formula or the instructions, or both. If a foreign manual translation is being used, is it rewritten in the colloquial of the sales area country?

Model in Use

Does the toy have play value that will keep youngsters occupied for sustained periods? Will is withstand constant usage punishment? Is it psychologically fitting? Observe a model in use by hidden camera or two-way mirror—and, if needed, with a child psychologist as an expert witness. The results will yield adjustments that may optimize success.

Manual and Model Matching

Does the owner manual match the machine? A model and its manual under use conditions may lead to better illustrations, more (or less) detailed instructions—or even a revision in the machine.

Scale Models

Often, the difference between a functional model and a bench prototype is small—and it is possible for pilot plants to reproduce sufficient quantities for user tests under varying conditions.

But not always.

Full-size models are often uneconomic in the developmental phases. A scale model may simulate the performance characteristics sufficiently well to project to the dimensions of the proposed working prototype. Sometimes, the need is only for cosmetic observation—do the angles balance, do the color breaks clearly relate to use progression or importance, does the overall appearance seem appropriate to the

Figure 17-1 Prototype models

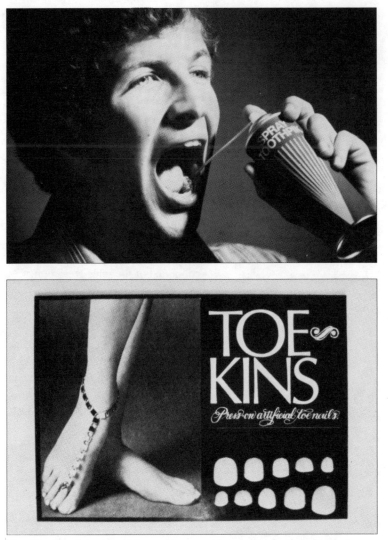

Very literal prototype models used in a sound-and-slide presentation that conveys brand, benefit, position, and package in finished format. Target prospect feedback from these exhibits provides direction for fine-tuning of well-accepted models.

tasks to be performed—or the promise to be delivered? Architectural models are common examples. A mural artist's sketch provides much the same effect. Another example is the wind-tunnel model used in the automotive field—where shape and not material is key, and where velocity of wind drag is computable to the dimension of the model. Figure 17-1 shows some very literal prototype models, and Figure 17-2 shows prototypes of a fruit syrup.

Figure 17-1 (Continued)

Competitive Environment

New products live or die by what makes them different. The fact that they are new isn't enough. If it's a me-too version of someone else's innovation, the developer shouldn't concentrate on improving on the competitor's model.

Figure 17-2 Fruit Syrup

Finished prototypes of a true fruit syrup dispensed from a push-button can were used for appeal study prior to home placement of the actual product.

So wrote Robert Cooper, associate dean, faculty of management, McGill University, in *Management Digest*, September 1981.

There are real differences and there are perceptual differences. If the real differences aren't perceived, they are handicapped. If minor, insignificant, or cosmetic differences are perceived as advantageous, they provide a competitive edge.

In either case, it is essential that the differences be perceived. Modeling provides a mode for observation—the means by which the new entity can be seen in its natural end-use environment and (if applicable) in its competitive environment.

In fact, sometimes to be new and different can be more critical than being new and better—if the "better" doesn't show. (In the early years of the foreign car craze, this was the lament of U.S. automakers.)

Modeling is also necessary to understand—and adapt to—the secondary communications, those visual and audio signals that are not product or service themselves: brochures, ads, packages; electronic sounds and visions carried by signage, video, and radio. A well-designed product that does not reproduce well in the pervasive media most common to its marketplace competes under a weighty handicap.

Figure 17-2 (Continued)

Modeling is necessary to gain a feel for the tactile and a sense of the visual psychology of the product. Certain textures and certain colors send certain signals—not always evident in the planning, blueprint, and elevation sketch phases. The heft and the "hand," the shape and the surround, the color and the contrast—all play a role in product perception—hence the importance of modeling.

Package Model

For many products, the package is the product symbol. It fights for attention on the shelf—in the store, at home in the cupboard, and (sometimes) on public display in the home, such as the perfume bottle, the fire extinguisher, the facial tissue box, the bathroom deodorizer, and the matchbook. Whether it is to make its statement in the store or in use, or both, its model evaluation is a critical early step. Often, the package plays an operational role as well, with a pour spout that readily pops out or a childproof cap or a push-up applicator stick or a spray-adjustable aerosol. These must be both visually and functionally tested in the modeling phase. Where possible, the modeling test should advance to the phase where final brand and descriptor candidates are in place on the model in the test—including all of the mandatory legal copy. Often, this affects the final choice. What appeared to be a preferred model in an unadorned state often fails as a final candidate when suitably decorated. Figure 17-3 shows different packaging options for an instant bacon product.

Communications Environment

As surely as the product is a communication, a communication is the product. They are inextricably part and parcel. To study one without the other is to ignore the gestalt of reality.

For this reason, not only must the product fit into the user's mode—it must also fit into the user's information system, the communications that alert and inform.

Whereas a "blind test" of purposely masked competitors may reveal the reality of performance differences, an open-eyed comparison will reveal *different realities*—realities more often true of the marketplace, despite what may be learned in the lab.

Model communication themes are developed and sorted within the context of the model product, with brief benefit descriptions in the context of single major appeals—the differences being a matter of emphasis, nature, and degree of support information. The goal is the development of major selling themes. (See Figure 17-4.)

For this reason, new product developers use communication models. To take the most complicated and expensive example, television, they use analogs of finished commercials to help sort out the most effective communications. (See Figure 17-5.) Sometimes these "commercials" do not include advertising themes, time constraints, or any of the conventions of promotion. The familiar format of television, with its third-party authority and cool separateness, is used to exhibit or to demonstrate the model and its promise. Often this is done in an episodic format, so that changeable modules can be inserted to determine changes in viewer-prospect reactions—and to help perfect the model, as well as provide a basis for advertising claims. Then, the models may be used in controlled tests of "model" commercials. The most primitive ones are drawn storyboards on videotape, with sound tracks (animatics). More advanced is still photography with tracks (photomatics). Beyond this are live-action sound on tape or film, but without sophistication special effects, full orchestration, etc.

Figure 17-3 New instant bacon prototype

New instant bacon could be packaged to reheat in a conventional or microwave oven, or on a range, or in a toaster. Prototype model photographs with descriptive copy helped sort out most appealing options. After successful test market, manufacturing difficulties aborted the project.

Figure 17-3 (Continued)

Manufacturing process to make the bacon "instant" removes the fat before packaging.

Figure 17-3 (Continued)

Bacon made easy, <u>any</u> way—bakes, broils or fries to crispness in less than three minutes. Here's lean, meaty bacon in a convenient cook-pak—new no mess, no grease, no spatter form. Just zip open new cook-pak and set in oven or broiler —or on top of the burner. In ⅓ the cooking time, crisp, crunchy sweet-smoked bacon's ready to serve. No pan to clean, no soiled oven or broiler. Saves you cooking time, clean-up time. Leaves just the eatin' for you.

(6 slices to a cook-pak, 3 cook-paks to a carton.)

With today's interest in low-fat foods, an *Instant Low-Fat Bacon* would have great appeal.

Figure 17-4 Hair color appeals

The growing senior demographics (and interest in youthful fitness) spawned a lot of interest in hair coloring for men. These four appeals in finished print advertising format, as well as those of competitors, were tested.

Similarly, tipped-in editorial features with model photographs are used as a stimulus. This presents the new product in the appropriate editorial environment. At another stage, when the model is perfected and the appeal tightly identified, comprehensive advertising layouts are tipped in—to help sort out those with the greatest executional appeal.

Model Result

Throughout this process, changes have been made in the models, both of the new product and of its secondary (media) communications. From this is obtained guidance for developing the prototypes that can confidently compete in the reality of the marketplace.

With modeling, the goal has been to develop both the product and the communication prototypes in a compatible system, hopefully synergistically superior within the competitive set in appealing to the target prospect.

Figure 17-4 (Continued)

Figure 17-5 Preparing a prototype commercial

Putting together a new product prototype commercial for use in on-air research. Internal production of all elements of new products research materials helps maintain critical confidentiality prior to in-market use. Top: Agency's food-service kitchen prepares finished product close-up shot. Bottom: Original music track recorded in agency studio.

Opposite Page
Top: Lighting rehearsal on location. Bottom: In-house final edit puts together all scenes, separately recorded tracks, optical effects for test of introductory television commercial.

Source: Campbell-Mithun, Inc.

Figure 17-5 *(continued)*

18

Research Guidelines

"*Numbers keep order.*"

— GEORGE KATONA

"*Order is a lovely thing.*"

— ANNA BRANCH

"*It takes two to speak the truth—one to speak and another to hear.*"

— THOREAU

"*Report to me and my cause aright.*"

— SHAKESPEARE

It seems so obvious, but it cannot be repeated too often: The research must fit the knowledge goal. Therefore, the stimulus and the method must yield actable results related to the true need. Unfortunately, the new product development success record is frequently marred by inappropriate research yielding misdirection. The life cycle, the usage pattern, the degree of consideration, the seasonal attractiveness—these are but a few of the factors that may influence the success of a product more importantly than those attention and performance measures characteristic of most syndicated and proprietary research dedicated to building supplier or corporate norms.

Each new product—even a simple line extension—presents a new problem for research. If it doesn't differ to that degree, then it is likely not justifiable as a market entrant.

Therefore, start with the question:

"What do we want to find out?"

Not

"What kind of research do we want to do?"

Nor necessarily with the decision:

"It is Phase I—so put this in our standard Phase I test."

Although there are many excellent syndicated proprietary techniques, it is often necessary to custom-design research to yield the specific knowledge you need. Often, critical research is demanded in the model development phase. The most valuable part of this step is defining the knowledge sought. Professional researchers then have little difficulty in recommending an existing program or devising a new design and procedure.

But beware—market researchers are discovering that if you ask a simple question these days, you might not get any answer at all. Randall Rothenberg, writing in the October 5, 1990, *New York Times*, states:

> Deluged by a growing number of telephone solicitations and increasingly jealous of their time, more and more Americans are refusing to participate in market-research surveys. . . . More than a third of all Americans routinely shut the door or hang up the phone on their questions. That leaves researchers confronting a new question: Is the ever-shrinking segment of consumers who will talk to them really representative of the population?

"Random samples are becoming impossible to obtain," said Don E. Schultz, a professor of advertising at Northwestern University's Medill School of Journalism. "With cooperation rates dropping like a rock, you may have large numbers of people who hold violently different views from those who are willing to talk."

"Everyone is fearful of self-selection and worried that the generalizations you make are based on cooperators only," said Verne B. Churchill, chairman and chief executive of Market Facts, one of the largest designers of custom market-research surveys. He said that rising refusal rates on telephone surveys had moved his company to depend more on mail surveys using large, fixed groups of people. "We get a high completion rate because they know we're legitimate questioners and we're not out to sell something," Mr. Churchill said. "But there's still fear that the panel is different from the rest of the population."

These are concerns worth considering both in the design and the interpretation of any result of any research.

Videotaped Demonstrations

When developing new products where the cost of the prototype is high and building several by hand for research purposes is prohibitive, the greatest boon to the research is videotape.

A high-ticket, mechanical new product prototype can be tested virtually anywhere among any target audience merely by videotaping the product demonstration. It's not hands-on—but it's next closest.

The Campbell-Mithun advertising agency did this for Gates Battery, Toro (articulated-frame riding mower), and the former toy division of General Mills (producing videotape demonstrations of 15 different toys ranging from slotless race car sets to board games).

When absolutely necessary, a nonoperative mock-up of the prototype can be made inexpensively to give respondents a more intimate feel for the size, proportions, design, and some of the features. (See Figure 18-1.)

Use-Trial Diary Panel

Where a new product requires some fairly concerted effort on the part of the user or where a slight oversight or mistake can cause user complaints, dissatisfaction, and disaster, there is a simple technique that can be used to avoid in-market failure.

An example: A consulting home economist for a food products company had developed what looked like a very complex bread recipe—one that eliminated the need to dissolve yeast in hot water before adding it to the other dry ingredients.

To confirm at-home success, several groups of novice breadmakers were recruited, given the recipes and $5 for ingredients—then turned loose in their own home kitchens. Each was also asked to complete a "diary" containing 25 questions to be answered at various points during the total baking experience. The diary invited them to jot down opinions, suggestions, points of confusion, and interpretation difficulties, as well as logistical information such as where the dough was placed in the kitchen to rise, total rising time, total kneading time, etc.

The homemakers then reconvened in groups, bringing their diaries *and* sample loaves of the end product. The recipe was discussed and comparisons made of the size, color, texture, and flavor of the baked bread.

From this, an absolutely fail-proof recipe was written, with several of the homemakers' suggestions incorporated.

The food manufacturer learned, in this case, that the consulting home economist's kitchen is one thing, but that the kitchens of America are something else—that oven temperatures are not always perfectly accurate, that the temperature of "hot tap water" varies from home to home, etc.

This type of "diary research" is relatively inexpensive and can help a new product marketer avoid what otherwise might be a tarnished new product introduction. The technique is applicable to any recipe, assembly instructions, installation directions, complex "mix" products, or designing electric or petroleum-powered products requiring periodic cleaning and/or maintenance.

Figure 18-1 Product development

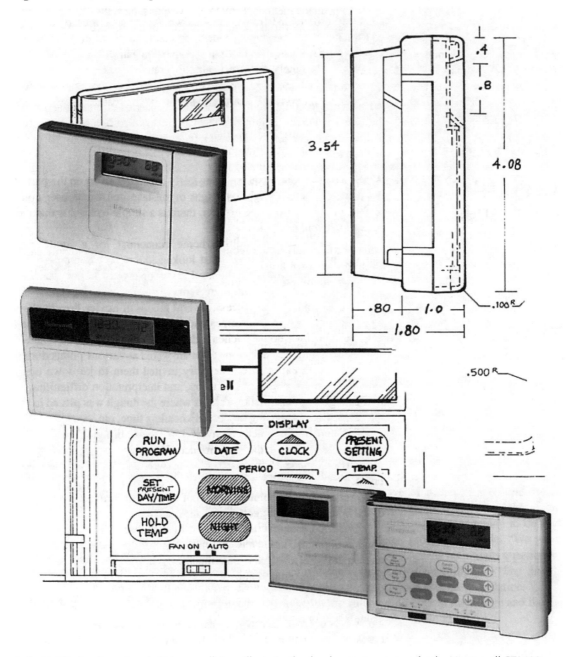

Industrial Design Department of Honeywell, Inc., illustrates the development sequence for the Honeywell CT3400 solid-state thermostat. Above photos of nonworking appearance models are superimposed on an example two-dimensional drawing prepared and reviewed with marketing and engineering. For the models, LCD images were simulated by using a photographic film positive prepared from a graphic layout and coating the background with a metallic paint representative of an LCD color. Design models on the upper left and lower right were ultimately chosen.

Figure 18-1 (Continued)

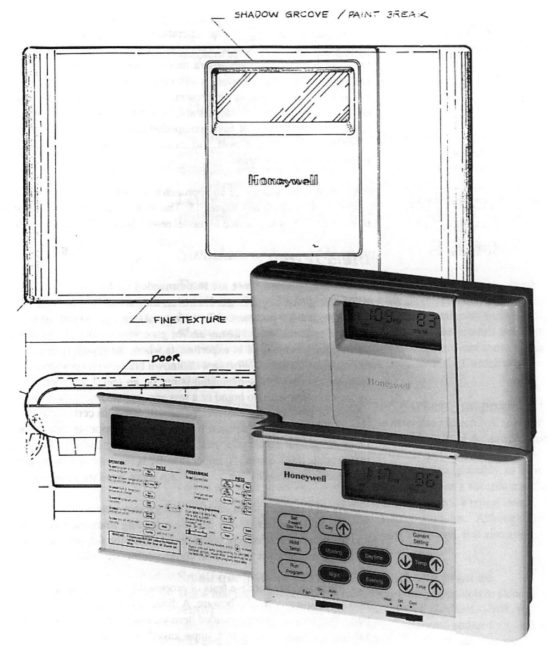

Final production device (above photos) is physically and graphically similar to the appearance model, which had been mocked up with a working door and simulated keyboard using a screened graphic layout on the back of a clear, matte-finish polycarbonate film. The backside (second surface) graphic treatment protects the screened ink from abrasion and creates a similar effect to the production process. Industrial design and model preparation were done by Ralph Pasquarette, Senior Designer, and Jim Odom, Senior Principal, of the Honeywell Residential Industrial Design Department.

Source: Honeywell, Inc.

Unobserved Observation

Conventional, Projectable Methods

Sometimes it is necessary to peek with permission.

An understanding of the operational aspects of a competitive game—or of the reactions to a personal care product—can be aided by two-way mirrors or videocamera monitor and/or taping. Respondents are told that expert professionals will observe their use and/or reactions, but will not participate or be present. Shortly after beginning, respondents drop playacting inhibitions and become involved in the subject at hand. The play value of toys, comprehension of computer-screen instructions, simple use of tools, and creative crafts, all have been evaluated effectively in this mode.

We looked at guidelines for an approach to conventional, numerical, and judgmental methods in Chapter 15. The Advertising Research Foundation's approach is applicable to model research as well as to ideaforms.

Blind Tests

As previously stated, these are recommended for laboratory (R&D) and engineering (R&E) guidance. However, they are not satisfactory for determining market preference. Even two unknown (invented for the purposes of research) brand names and/or generic descriptors can influence performance evaluation in experiments where the products have, in actuality, been identical. When a well-known brand with appropriate equity to the product being evaluated is put on an identical product to *test against* another with no brand or a less-appropriate brand name, the perception of performance characteristics will differ. In certain cases, such a test method may be devised to determine appropriate brand names. Does the peanut butter taste fresher, spread easier, and smell more like real peanuts if it's named A, rather than B? Is the taste sensation better if the generic is "crunchy" or "chunky"? A mere word may make a difference.

As an example, when identical margarines were compared in side-by-side, in-home usage, one bearing a leading margarine brand name and the other with a leading butter brand name, the famous butter branded margarine product won on all counts: color, spreadability, taste, frying, etc.

Although comparative tests of proposed product vs. target competition are frequently used—beware. A direct, identified side-by-side comparison of proposed new branded item vs. established leading brand will yield one result. A blind test, unpackaged, unbranded: another. A double-blind test, where the test supervisor doesn't even know the difference, may yield another. And a blindfold test, where the product cannot be seen—merely felt, smelled, tasted, for example—may yield yet another result. On top of all this, time of day, temperature (if a food), quantity, etc., will have effects. Furthermore, we know that an unidentified drug tested vs. a placebo will perform differently than an identified one, and that placebo vs. placebo, if therapy is indicated—or if the placebo carries a known drug brand name, may also perform well—and differently. The author has seen this demonstrated in such diverse areas as spaghetti sauces, colas, and analgesics.

The secret is to get as close as possible to the real situation.

Usage Tests

The further the model testing moves from controlled environments to reality, the more likely it is that the results will translate into market predictability, assuming unanticipated variables do not intervene.

In-home or in-office or in-factory usage tests are superior to central location trials. If a sales impulse can move the product into its usage environment, that is even better.

Simulating Sales Response

There are many systems and services that offer methods that simulate sales responses when products are in early developmental phases. Perhaps only a limited quantity of prototypical bench samples and a variety of sales appeal statements are available. Perhaps the product and communications model making is further advanced. Here are some typical approaches used in the packaged goods field, several of which are theoretically adaptable to other categories.

A prototype selling statement and package (no product)
Concepts are sorted on a relative basis to determine which will stimulate highest trial. Respondents are exposed to renderings of the proposition (a poster and a package, for example), which includes price. Each respondent is given the opportunity to buy the product (possibly, to be received at a later time—or, possibly, to be received as a substitute and a small gift for participating in the study) and to indicate a repeat intention or rate of purchase, based on the sketchy stimulus. Although this method is commonly employed in shopping situations, it is also applicable to interactive cable and mail techniques.

Small quantity of packaged product and print ad
The actual packaged product is sold against the proposition in a comprehensive print ad to help determine the rate of purchase—trial, repeat sales, and, subsequent to use, how the selling theme and/or formulation may be improved to increase product appeal. Occasionally, this approach is executed in shopping areas using videotape communications for stimulus, in a van or bus or mall location. The method is also applicable to cable, where viewers are given a telephone number to use in calling in orders or (on interactive cable) to punch up a home delivery order. Direct response techniques using the mail may also be employed; this is usually used when a broader geographic dispersion of specific psychographic characteristics, using extremely sophisticated sampling cells, is desired.

Pretest market sales

To answer the question, "Which presentation of my new product (or which new product) will produce more trial and repeat sales volume?" Frevert & Hall Research Associates Inc., Spring Park, MN, claims to offer the only pretest market service that measures both trial and repeat sales potential by actually selling a new product directly to a nationwide sample of shoppers. The service is called RSVP (*Relative Sales Volume Potential*). RSVP aims to provide direction in evaluating alternative presentations of a new product, i.e., communications or formulations, as well as providing inputs for projecting sales volume.

The procedure involves showing supermarket shoppers the new product's marketing communication, such as a print ad or a commercial. Shoppers are also shown a "New Products Introductions" offer letter with an order blank for the new product. If shoppers decide to buy, they pay the regular retail price for the product at the checkout counter. Triers are thereafter contacted by telephone and repeat orders are accepted throughout the sales period. Buyers also pay the regular retail price for all repeat purchases. (As an option, print advertising may be mailed to triers to further register the sales message throughout the repeat phase.)

The study yields regular reports on the percentage of buyers who repeat with each offer, cumulative repeaters, total repeat orders, repeat unit sales—and may also be expanded to determine the reasons underlying the purchase decisions, reactions to product attributes, and product usage information. This information is reported for buyers, repeaters, and nonrepeaters.

Store test

Another possibility is the controlled store test, utilizing only one or several stores. Here the packaged product is put into the appropriate store section, with a realistic share of shelf and display space. Depending on the information needed, various techniques are used. Introductory pricing flags on the package, frequent "store-cast" announcements over the supermarket's speaker system, shelf-talkers, etc., call attention to the product. An in-pack coupon offers a bonus for cooperating purchasers, allowing for callback interviews. For products in categories with high-volume repeat sales, observer/interviewers may intercept purchasers to ask for cooperation and complete the purchase impulse phase of the questioning.

One variation is to intercept recruits in shopping malls. After exposure to the ad, a respondent is led to a controlled store and given several items with incentive money provided, to obtain a purchase effectiveness score.

In other categories, such as home electronic entertainment products, store demonstrators and specially trained factory sales personnel intercept prospective purchasers and ask for relevant comments to obtain a measure of interest and understanding, with special emphasis on how the product is placed in the competitive set regarding features, price, brand, image, etc.

Mathematical Model Research

A number of developing mathematical model research programs have been devised to reduce the risk of new product introductions. Joseph D. Blackburn (Vanderbilt University) and Kevin J. Clancy (Boston University) presented such a concept at the Second ORSA/TIMS Conference on Market Measurement and Analysis (Austin, Texas, March 15, 1980). They stated:

> Some firms have turned to a combination of sophisticated test market research integrated with mathematical models of the new product introduction process. The objective is to provide more accurate forecasts of new product market performance and to discern how the product concept or marketing plan should be shaped to maximize the likelihood of success. Several mathematical models, which are designed to use test market data as input, have been developed in recent years. These include NEWS[1], Tracker[2], and Sprinter[3].

> Many firms have taken a different approach to this problem, choosing the alternative of relatively inexpensive simulated test markets, such as Yankelovich, Skelly and White Inc.'s Laboratory Test Market (or LTM).[4] Such simulations attempt to compress in time and dollars a test market experience. Some marketing managers use them as a low-risk step prior to a full-scale test market, while others have replaced traditional test markets with their simulated counterparts. Still other firms have adopted systems which combine the simulated test market with a mathematical model. Management Decision System's ASSESSOR[5] is a pioneering example of this approach. LITMUS, a new mathematical model developed in conjunction with Yankelovich's LTM, is another.

> LITMUS is an interactive stochastic [educated guess] model designed to forecast, diagnose, and improve the performance of alternative marketing strategies for new package goods either before or after test marketing.

[1] There have been numerous publications and presentations on the NEWS model, most published by BBDO Inc. and authored by Lewis Pringle, senior vice president of BBDO and director of research services. Among them are "BBDO Technical Report: The Theoretical Basis of NEWS" (1971) and "The News Model: A Technical Description" (No date).

[2] Blattberg, Robert, and John Golanty, "Tracker: An Early Test Market Forecasting and Diagnostic Model for New Product Planning," *Journal of Marketing Research*, May 1978, pp. 192–202.

[3] Urban, Glen L. "Sprinter Mod III: A Model for the Analysis of New Frequently Purchased Consumer Products," *Operations Research*, September–October 1970, pp. 805–853.

[4] This research was funded, in part, by Yankelovich, Skelly and White Inc., who also provided data for the model tests reported later.

[5] Silk, Alvin J., and Glen Urban, "Pretest Market Evaluation of New Packaged Goods: A Model and Measurement Methodology," *Journal of Marketing Research*, May 1978, pp. 171–191.

Using inputs derived from the new product's marketing plan, other empirical relationships, and Laboratory Test Market research, LITMUS forecasts brand awareness, trial, current usage, sales, and market share. The model's built-in sensitivity analysis then provides the planner with insights into the likely effects of changes in each strategic and tactical input on key measures of campaign effectiveness, notably sales and market share. In this manner, the reasons underlying the predicted success or failure of the new product launch can be quickly diagnosed and recommendations made which will improve the expected performance of the new product entry.

On the surface, LITMUS appears similar to its predecessors, especially NEWS, Tracker, and ASSESSOR, in terms of its objectives, easy-to-use conversational mode, input parameters, and published evidence of successful forecasting. However, surface similarities can be deceiving, for although LITMUS shares some of the strengths and weaknesses of other models, it has some distinctive features. Two such features are the large number of marketing mix variables and the extensive number of states of nature used to capture the richness and complexity of the new product introduction process.

The heart of LTM is the laboratory test. A cross section of 500 or more potential buyers are invited to a theater (30–35 at a time); the theaters are set up in markets throughout the United States. Following the completion of a brief, self-administered questionnaire (demographic information, as well as marketing), consumers are exposed to a television program in which a commercial for the new brand and competitive products are embedded. Afterwards, consumers are led in small groups to the "store," a store which stocks the brands advertised in the commercial and others which enjoy a significant market share in the testing area. Upon entering the "store" consumers are provided with a fixed amount of money to stimulate purchase. A fraction of the people go on to buy the "test" brand, others do not. This fraction, adjusted by LTM norms, experience, and marketing plan data, leads to an estimate of the probability of brand trial, given awareness.

Some time later (the lag dependent on the product category), consumers are reinterviewed by telephone to gauge their reactions to the product. These data, again adjusted by norms and experience, generate an estimate of first repeat purchase probability. Often, however, a sales wave or extended use test is incorporated in the research design and these data are used to estimate multiple repeat purchase probabilities. All of this information is then used to forecast brand sales and/or market share.

What LTM cannot do easily, however, is to evaluate many plans or assess the individual contribution of many variables in the marketing mix to market shares. As the more creative use of media flourishes, for example, there is a growing need by LTM management to forecast the effects of media variables, such as GRPs and advertising impact, on new product performance. Hence the interest in coupling the LTM output with a contextual model.

In its current state of development, LITMUS bases its projections on a given marketing plan [variables 1–10 and 19 in Figure 18-2]. However, as an interactive aid to the marketing manager, sensitivity analysis of the relationship between projected sales and specific components of the marketing plan can be carried out to indicate how to improve the plan. The program could be imbedded in an optimization model in which the marketing plan is characterized perhaps by a budget constraint. Then nonlinear search techniques could be employed to determine optimal (or near optimal) levels for each component in the marketing plan by purchase period. Future research will be directed toward this end.

LITMUS is a new product planning model, used in conjunction with LTM, designed to forecast, diagnose, and improve the performance of alternative marketing strategies and tactics for new packaged goods before or after test marketing. Though still in an exploratory stage of development, the model has shown evidence of the kind of construct and predictive validity that might be expected given its "genetic structure" through its "parents" LTM and NEWS.

Testing Communica- tions Models

Now that the product model has been optimized and the selling theme has been identified, advertising and promotion communications models become true prototypes—and methods must be selected to identify the most persuasive sales motivators.

Judgment is not to be cast aside at this critical step. The options for execution are so many and varied that judgment must, of necessity, be exercised. The cost of making test executions and of testing them is so great that further disciplines are needed in the selection of materials. Also, the cost of the media to deliver the messages is so high that a reasonably accurate means is needed to make a final selection. For some entrepreneurial marketers, personal subjective evaluations are sufficient—and successful. But as companies become publicly held, volume becomes larger and the organization more cumbersome; as the founding entrepreneurs give way to the professional managers, and the professional managers move up in the organization, partly based on performance adherence within company disciplines and procedures—the objectivity of research becomes the rule.

Figure 18-2 Model inputs

Type	Input	Source
MARKET CHARACTERISTICS	1. Size of potential market (in millions of buyers) 2. Number of units per case 3. Size of market (in millions of cases) 4. Estimated number of purchase cycles per year	
MARKETING PLAN CHARACTERISTICS	5. Average cost per 1,000 GRPs 6. Advertising dollars or GRPs per period 7. Average cost per sample dropped 8. Average cost per coupon 9. Percent of market couponed per period 10. Percent of market sampled per period	MARKETING PLAN
	11. Maximum likely brand awareness 12. Attention-getting power of advertising (1.0 = average) 13. Attention-getting power of media (1.0 = average)	COPY AND MEDIA RESEARCH
	14. Probability of remembering brand one period in the absence of additional exposures (1.0 = maximum)	MANAGEMENT JUDGMENT
	15. Probability of brand trial intention given awareness of advertising 16. Probability of brand trial given intention and distribution	LABORATORY TEST MARKET ESTIMATES
	17. Probability of brand trial given coupon 18. Probability of brand trial given sample	EMPIRICAL RELATIONSHIP OR CUSTOM RESEARCH
	19. Distribution per period 20. Trial purchase size (1.0 = average)	MARKETING PLAN
	21. Probability of first repeat purchase in period following trial 22. Probability of second repeat purchase in period following first repeat 23. Repeat purchase size (1.0 = average)	LABORATORY TEST MARKET ESTIMATES
	24. Price per standard unit (1.0 = average)	MARKETING PLAN

Source: Yankelovich, Skelly and White Inc., Laboratory Test Market (LTM).

Because creativity in commerce is hardly an art—but does possess aspects of art and its artifice, and not necessarily business—it assumes the halfway status of a craft. Whereas objective research could not forecast the market performance of a Mozart or a Van Gogh, it might well be properly used to measure interest in Nintendo or the Jolly Green Giant. Before determining the directions for creative strategy and selecting those executional roughs to go forward into testable format, it is necessary to determine guidelines for this subjective decision. Some tips follow later in Chapter 21, which stresses singleness of purpose and the shaping of a distinctive personality with sustained appeal.

Television Commercial Models

No two research techniques available to measure any aspect of communications are exactly alike, although many from respondents disguise the specific, commercial focus within a program and/or multiple commercial clutter. This makes it incumbent upon the new product research sponsor to have a clearly identifiable, ranked set of priorities to obtain the desired measurements. Most techniques measure one or more of the following attributes:

- Recall

- Attention (commercial intrusiveness)

- Impact (degree of reaction)

- Commercial holding power (sustained attention throughout message)

- Understanding

- Wear-out

- Persuasion (purchase intent)

- Actual purchase

In the majority of techniques, diagnostic research is additionally available to help understand the scores achieved. Most communicators agree that such direction is necessary to provide a basis for effective improvement or for entirely new communications.

An analysis of 25 selected syndicated television advertising research suppliers and techniques[6] using on-air central location (theater, van, enclosed mall) and direct response (mail and telephone) methods of forced or random viewing illustrates the necessity of understanding

---

[6] On-Air: ASI-Recall Plus Test, Burke-Marketing Research Inc., Gallup-Robinson Syndicated Subscription Service (TPT—Total Prime Time), Gallup-Robinson Custom Pretesting (In View), Gallup-Robinson (Custom Post Testing), Mapes and Ross, Sherman Buy[c] Test-Option Three, Westgate; Theater: ARS, ASI (Audience Studies Inc.), McCollum Spielman (AC-T Format); Forced Exposure: Harry Heller Corporation B/EST (Benefit Estimated Share Technique), Palshaw, Rabin Research (Search), Recap, Schrader Research & Rating Service, Schrader Copy Lab, Schrader Research & Rating Service Recall, Sherman Buy[c] Test—Option Two (clutter exposure), Telcom, Tele-Research, Video Storyboard Tests, Inc., VOPAN.

all of the most popular offerings before selecting those most appropriate to your new product introductory advertising task—or, alternatively, devising a proprietary technique to meet special needs. Most of the available services have developed norms in the most advertising-intensive categories.

If the new product commercial models fit these categories, then select a supplier whose service measures the most critical element of the message during its introductory phase (brand recall being most often paramount), and has the most reliable norms (recency and size of base are considerations).

Other considerations involve the phase of product development, and whether preliminary checks are needed of many very rough materials (e.g., chalk storyboards with small cast tracks) or of fewer, more comprehensive materials that are preliminary to finished production for on-air use. Although cost should not be the determining factor, it also enters into consideration. The trade-off for a low-cost test of more options that will yield limited, grossly directional information as opposed to a more reliable, sharply defined test at greater cost is judged in relationship to the phase of development, the willingness to make management decisions from broadly directional information, and the financial risks involved. If the next developmental phase is to be a controlled minimarket (a learning experience), the answer may be different than if the next step is a conventional test market, regional expansion, or major introduction.

Many central-location test methods necessarily reflect the demographic and life-style biases peculiar to the area. This is also true of mall intercepts (unless the sample is widely dispersed to represent the population), CATV viewer recruits, on-air tests of limited market scope, and other forced interview techniques. If a new product is targeted to a particular city size, region, program-content viewing habit, livelihood, discrete competitive set, etc., then it may be necessary to tailor the syndicated technique (several suppliers will do this at an extra charge) to the need—or to customize the technique exactly to the purpose, which likely obviates normative data. However, as earlier noted, the learning and direction correctness of the answers are often more important than the "score."

Radio Commercial Models

Radio commercial testing is done in similar fashion to television testing, except that on-air testing is rarely used, and telephone research is frequently used, inasmuch as the audio communication is what is to be evaluated. Because radio is less literal than two-dimensional television communication, the range of emotional responses is likely to be wide for dramatic and musical stimuli. Because radio production is much less expensive than television, it is less costly to do modular variations in a manner that helps to optimize final production.

One service, ERIS (Emotional Response Index System), performs a content analysis of the audio (including voice-over characteristics), sound effects, music, etc.) based on word and symbol response scores of a previously analyzed test group of 7,232 respondents. This system identifies and measures the elements in a commercial that will capture attention and create involvement with the message. The primary output of the system is the diagnostic information that specifies what makes a given commercial effective, or lessens the impact or memorability. The ERIS diagnostics further explain reasons for these findings, which enables improvement before final production and airing. In a review of ten popular syndicated radio commercial measurement techniques,[7] costs appeared to be similar to television studies, except that media costs are usually not involved and the production elements studied are apt to be far less costly.

Print Advertising Models

Natural in-home viewing and forced exposure are the prevalent environments for print advertising research.

In-home readers receive targeted publications with tipped-in model ads, usually with as near to fully comprehensive reproduction as possible. Telephone and in-person callbacks are common. Most services offer standard audience magazine norms, but will customize studies with special-interest books for an extra charge. In most instances, respondents know they are participating in a test; often, callback timing is unnatural for routine readership habits.

Forced-exposure readers are recruited at central locations (shopping malls or mobile units, most likely) or visited at homes or offices. Coupon-redemption techniques are available to help determine trial purchase. Special-analysis techniques (voice-analysis of respondent comments, eye-movement photography of view-scanning of an ad projected on a screen) can provide helpful additional insights about design and copy effects.

Most of the 14 syndicated services studied[8] reveal one very important characteristic of print research: editorial environment. This is rarely a factor in the broadcast advertising model studies. In broadcast cases, the editorial (program) environment is often used as a comparable common thread, with the advertising elements being the only differences. In most print research, the environment fits the target audience—hence is more directly segmented than other media surroundings. Additionally, it

---

[7] ASI, Burke, ERISCO Inc., McCollum/Spielman & Company, Inc., Radio Recall Research Inc., Schrader Research, Sherman Buy^c Test, Spencer Bruno Research Associates Inc., Telcom, Tele-Research Inc.

[8] In home-viewing: ASI, Burke, Gallup-Robinson, Mapes and Ross, Sherman BUT^c Test, Spencer-Bruno Research; Forced exposure: AHF Marketing Research (Competitive Environment Test), Palshaw, Perception Research, Print Animatic Tests Inc., Sherman BUY^c Test, Telcom, Tele-Research, Vopan.

is therefore more adaptable to special interest areas—merely by selection of the most appropriate publications and audiences. Except in the high-circulation general and women's service categories, there is likely to be a higher charge for this service and little or no current normative data. (Exceptions to these observations are those out-of-home techniques that use a standard "bogus" proprietary magazine to assure little or no editorial target bias, those that use print ads as individual posters, and those that project slides of print ads onto large screens.)

Ancillary Aspects

The critical elements of any communications are the impressions made by the visual and audio elements that represent the offerings. Although the gestalt—the total effect—must be integrated, involving, persuasive, and memorable, certain elements are more critical than others.

For new products, these include:

The brand—often unknown.

The generic descriptor—is it clear, appropriate?

The package—often unique; just as often, disguised by family resemblances, if a line extension or a flanker.

The product—does it quickly register?

The promise—does it fill a (possibly only latent) need?

The personality—is it distinctive, appropriate, attractive?

Additional probes and questions may often be added to the formats of syndicated research, to help in isolating these elements sufficiently for precise study. In the case of the brand, descriptor, and package elements, the commercial model studies may be the first instance of their being studied within the complex of a total selling message—even though they may have been "shelf-tested" and "use-tested" prior to their incorporation into model advertising. The interactions among these committed elements and between them and the newly added presentation elements must be optimized for maximum selling effectiveness.

For those new products that will spring forth on the world with a patron—whether it be a contrived character ("Mother Nature" or a dove flying through the window) or a real one (Bill Cosby, John Houseman, Orson Welles, The Osmonds, etc.) or an actor-authority (Mrs. Olson, Madge the Manicurist, Juan Valdez, etc.)—the patron must lend authority to the new product, but not be so powerful as to overwhelm the message or its meaning. Often, it is necessary to study such a persuasion element separately—prior to studying the complete communication—in order to understand as well as to screen likely candidates. Afterwards, the patron-in-place in the advertising may be testing by those techniques reviewed above.

Positioning–Advertising–Copy-Testing (PACT)

Overview guidelines on copy testing—no matter what the medium—were published in January 1982, in a consensus credo representing the views of leading members of the American Association of Advertising Agencies,[9] along with several committee participants who had formerly been advertisers and the then incumbent chairman of the Advertising Research Foundation. A brief review of their credo is useful in both planning and assessing model development for advertising research on new product communications. The following review refers *only* to those aspects that are particularly salient to introductory advertising. Here are the nine principles laid down in the PACT credo:

1. A good copy testing system provides measurements that are relevant to the objectives of the advertising.

For new products, this means:

- Reinforcing current perceptions, if they relate to a parent company or brand that has purchase influence and, possibly, providing greater saliency for a brand or company name.

- Encouraging trial of a product or service.

- Encouraging new uses of a product or service, especially where these new uses provide a point-of-difference for the new product.

- Changing perceptions and imagery and announcing new features and benefits if the mode of the new product is to make the parent brand more competitively contemporary.

2. A good copy testing system is one that requires agreement about how the results will be used *in advance* of each specific test.

Action standards should be set *before* testing, so that the evaluation of the results will be against such goals as:

- Improve (or achieve positive new perception) of brand perception, as measured by ___

- Achieve an attention level of ___ percent or better, as measured by ___

- Perform at least as well as (or ___ percent better than) (specify execution, which may be an ad norm, a previously tested model, etc.)

- Produce no more than ___ percent negative responses, as measured by ___

---

[9] Sponsors of PACT are N W Ayer,Inc.; Ted Bates Worldwide Inc.; Batten, Barton, Durstine & Osborn Inc.; Benton & Bowles Inc.; Campbell-Mithun Inc.; Cunningham & Walsh Inc; Dancer Fitzgerald Sample Inc.; D'Arcy-MacManus & Masius Inc.; Doyle Dane Bernbach Inc.; Grey Advertising Inc.; Kenyon & Eckhardt Inc.; KM&G International Inc.; Marschalk Campbell-Ewald Worldwide; Marsteller Inc.; McCaffrey and McCall Inc.; McCann-Erickson Inc.; Needham, Harper & Steers Inc.; Ogilvy & Mather Inc.; SSC&B Lintas Worldwide; J. Walter Thompson Company; Young & Rubicam.

3. A good copy testing system provides *multiple* measurements— because single measurements are generally inadequate to assess the performance of an advertisement.

Because there is no universally accepted single measurement that can serve as a surrogate for sales, determination should be made in advance of testing as to which method will be used to determine the measurement of how much the studied advertising will contribute to sales. Obviously, each measure will not be given equal weight—and, therefore, prior agreement is needed about the decision-influence of each finding.

4. A good copy testing system on a model of human response to communication— the *reception* of a stimulus, the *comprehension* of the stimulus and the *response* to the stimulus.

To succeed, advertising must have an effect on several levels: It must be received, it must be understood, and it must make an impression. Questions to consider:

- Did the advertising get through?
- Was it understood?
- Was the proposition accepted?
- Did the advertising affect attitudes toward the product/service/brand?
- Did it alter perceptions of competing brands?
- Did it cause response to direct action appeals?

5. A good copy testing system allows for consideration of whether the advertising stimulus should be exposed more than once.

In the light of experimental work, PACT agencies share the view that the issue of single versus multiple exposures should be carefully considered in each situation. There are situations in which a single exposure would be sufficient—given the objectives of the advertising and the nature of the test methodology. There are other situations where a single exposure could be inadequate—particularly for high-risk situations or for subtle or complex communications or for resolving questions about executional diagnostics.

6. A good copy testing system recognizes that the more finished a piece of copy is, the more soundly it can be evaluated and requires, as a minimum, that alternative executions be tested in the same degree of finish.

The judgment of the creators of the advertising should be given great weight regarding the degree of finish required to present the finished advertisement for test purposes. If there is reason to believe that alternative executions would be unequally penalized in preproduction form, then it is generally advisable to test them in a more finished form. (If alternatives are tested in different stages of finish within the same test, then it is not possible to ensure that the results are not biased.)

7. A good copy testing system provides controls to avoid the biasing effects of the exposure context.

Examples: Television commercials tested off-air versus on-air; in a clutter reel versus a program context; in a specific program context versus another specific program context. Each of these variables affect the perception of and response to the stimulus and must be carefully controlled to prevent comparative biases.

8. A good copy testing system is one that takes into account basic considerations of sample definition.

Testing should be conducted among a representative sample of the target audience. (Limited testing among the general population without provision for separate analysis of the target audience can be misleading.) Geographic differences, where critical, and sufficient sample size should allow for a confident decision based on the data obtained.

9. A good copy testing system is one that can demonstrate reliability and validity.

To be reliable, the system should yield the same results each time the same ad is tested. External variables always must be held constant.

To be valid, the system should yield results relevant to marketplace performance. This is a major and costly goal and requires industrywide participation. While some evidence of predictive validity is available, many systems are in use for which no evidence of validity is provided.

Now that the communications have been developed and the product prototypes sorted, the investment increases. However, the risks have been reduced by the thoroughness of the early phase, so the new product next moves confidently forward into scaled-up development toward commercialization.

Section
5

Summary Afterword

Because the new product is in itself a communication and because the carrying of that message off the catalog sheet, shelf, or television set is inextricably bound to the total selling personality—modeling of *both* the product and its marketing media must proceed down parallel courses. Each affects the other. In many instances, it is difficult, if not impossible, to determine which is more important. It is known, however, that an alteration of either element can affect the future success of the product. This explains the time and money premium placed on modeling.

Model making provides the blueprint for the further development of new products, offering the opportunity to experiment and screen ideas. The model may grow out of a family name and its heritage, or an entirely new brand can be developed. Many companies build a brand name bank, on which they can draw as new products evolve. Also influencing the model are the generic descriptor and the product category itself.

There are many different kinds of models. They include models for functional parts, instruction/direction models, and scale models. It is also useful to experiment with the model in use, and to evaluate it against its competitive environment. Questions to consider include: Is the model different, as well as being better? How does it feel, heft, and generally fit the surroundings? The package model acts as a symbol of the product, but it can also be functional, as with a pour spout.

Does the model fit the user information system? Communications modes, as well as the product, should also be modeled. One way of evaluating this is through blind testing. Or television (VTR) can simulate models in test modes. Television provides a third-party objectivity in evaluating communications models.

Every new product presents a new problem—hence, a new research or judgmental decision. The type of research undertaken must fit the knowledge goal. Videotaped demonstrations can simulate working models, as well as providing a method by which to perfect instructions.

Conventional, projectable research methods include blind tests, use tests, and the simulations of sales response. This last can be accomplished in several ways: with a prototype selling statement and package (without product); with a small quantity of the product plus a print ad/poster; through pretest market sales; or through store tests. Mathematical models include the use of a laboratory test market or an interactive aid to assess variables, such as LITMUS. The communications models can be tested in all forms of media, including television, radio, print, and ancillary aspects.

A system known as PACT (Positioning-Advertising-Copy-Testing) also can provide relevant measurements. There should be advance agreement on the use of results. PACT provides multiple measurements, including measures of reception, comprehension, and response to stimulus. It allows multiple-exposure testing, and testing of different messages in the same degree of comprehensive finish. It targets the sample and is generally regarded as reliable and valid. Controls are in order, however, to avoid bias in the exposure context.

MARKETING

Section
6

19

Plan, Simulation, Selection

The marketing plan begins with a "Fact Book" assembly of all of the relevant known data about the product category, as well as the new product introduction company. Never is there enough data. Where there are gaps in information, it is determined that:

1. The missing information is *not necessary* to the planning process, or

2. It *is necessary*—however, a consensus assumption is satisfactory to the process, or

3. It *is necessary*—and the data needs to be gathered and/or updated from syndicated sources that may be purchased, or generated from consultants in the field (or contract packers; trade groups; parts, materials, and ingredient suppliers), or requires an original research project that is justified on a cost-benefit basis.

Fact Book Planning Guide

A typical outline of a fact book may be as follows:

A. Executive summary

B. The industry

1. Total sales volume of industry (units and/or dollars)

2. Sales trends over 4–5 years

3. Consumer penetration of product/service by total industry

4. Major competitors—with unit and dollar shares

5. Estimated margins

6. Recent distribution trends in industry (overview only; details requested later)

7. Future industry outlook

8. Outside influences facing industry (government controls, shortages, etc.

9. Recent activities

10. Financial analysis of parent corporation of leading competitors

11. Reconstruction of corporate charter and style, based on performance history

C. The subject company(ies)

1. Brief history

2. Total sales/profit trends (all products) over 4–5 years

3. Sales/profit trends of *this* product/service over 4–5 years

4. Organization

D. The company's new product/service

1. Description (brand name, function, recent improvements)

2. Main user benefit(s)

3. Consumer profile

- Target prospect

- Target trade[1] factors

- Income category

- Ethnic factors

- Geographical influences

- Seasonal influences

- Psychological influences/factors

- Any differences from major competitors

---

[1] In many categories, the consumer—the end-user—is a trade factor. In other situations, the characteristic of the trade may be peculiar to the consumption patterns, e.g., although grocery outlets are thought of as the trade factor in pizza consumption, it may be a characteristic of the consumer profile that they buy pizzas not in restaurants and not at grocery stores, but at taverns, which are the "consumer" of conventional frozen pizzas also available in groceries.

4. Main selling points (packaging, pricing design, production, state-of-art advancement, prestige of manufacturing, etc.)

5. Secondary selling points

6. Exclusive selling points

7. Primary selling appeal(s)

8. Product/service prospect appeal barriers

- Price

- Lack of recognition

- Packaging

- Etc.

9. Foremost barrier

10. Frequency of purchase

11. Frequency of use

12. Type of guarantee or warranty; compared with competition

13. Quality control performance, reputation

14. Consumer awareness level

15. Resumé of other market research findings (indicate who conducted research)

E. Distribution/pricing

1. Chain of distribution (distributors, jobbers, brokers, direct, etc.)

2. Markups/commissions/other incentives

3. Weak links in distribution setup (e.g., inexperience, lack of training, apathy, low level of product knowledge, etc.)

4. Exceptional distribution and sales operation strengths

5. Distribution system compared with major competitors

- Structure

- Quality

- Number of dealers, outlets, etc.

6. Elements in subject company's distribution that handle competitive brands, if any

7. Available selling tool(s)

F. The current advertising/promotion program (for subject company and major competitor)

1. Media history, past 2–3 years, on intended new product/service area

- Total media investment

- Percent of total by media

- Media inhibitions peculiar to subject company or industry

2. Current selling appeals of leading competitors

3. Advertising effectiveness measures

4. Typical customer sales promotion material characteristic of category—including merchandising of advertising

5. Field acceptance/use of these materials

6. Use/value of trade shows, conventions, etc.

7. Use/value of sales development aids

- Couponing

- Sampling

- Loaders

- Tie-ins

- Etc.

8. Use/importance of publicity/public relations

9. Use/importance of direct mail

- Trade

  Size of list _____ Type of mailing _____

- Consumer

  Size of list _____ Type of mailing _____

- Assessment of value _____

  _____

  _____

G. Objectives for new product

1. Share of market

- Year 1 ___ percent

- Year 2 ___ percent

- 5-year goal ___ percent

2. Volume

	Units	*Dollars*
Year 1		
Year 2		
5-year goal (if known)		

3. Other objectives

H. Introductory communications and marketing strategy

I. Long-term brand personality goal

J. Vital missing information

Preparing the Executive Summary

One of the most useful steps in analyzing the "Fact Book" is the preparation of an executive summary. This forces separation of the critically salient information from the less important. It allows for a spotlighting of the atypical differences from the field demonstrated by the leaders, the growers, and the faltering factors in the category.

Finding Gaps

In nearly every marketing category there are uncovered opportunity areas. Analyze all of the market facts including the strength and weaknesses of the product/service offerings, distribution system, geographic and trade class coverage, media selection, target audience, historic developments, recent management structure and personnel changes, annual report analysis, stock performance, legal actions, union arrangements, location and modernity of manufacturing sources, shipping and warehousing, purchasing policies, etc. Array these factors against the new product entrant's strengths and weaknesses. This will show the gaps in the principal competition that can be attacked in the new product introductory plan—as well as illuminating the sponsoring company's own areas for improvement or, if the company is already especially strong in key attack areas, for major leveraging against the field and/or any strong competitor in the new product's target segment of the category.

A gap grid can be built for each area of analysis, with an assigned power number for each competitor and for the new product entry from the market planner company. This will provide a solid directional basis for the planning.

Information Sources

In those areas where the assessment of potential competitive activity is particularly critical, there are a number of perfectly legal secondary research approaches.

Competitive powerhouse International Business Machines Corporation has an elaborate intelligence-gathering apparatus that relies on published sources and detailed reports from its salespeople all over the world. Jim Waugh, who directs the Market Intelligence unit of IBM US Marketing Services, has a staff of about 60 persons to collect and analyze publicly available information about customers and other vendors to help determine which opportunities IBM should pursue in both hardware and software products.

While the name of this department conjures up an image of agents in trench coats, there's nothing mysterious about the group's activities. "Market research and vendor analysis have a wealth of tools to help find out why customers are making certain choices," says Waugh. "You take all the relevant information, target segments and try to understand clearly what it takes to succeed."

In the Summer 1990 issue of *IBM Directions*, a customer publication, Waugh describes how intelligence gathering helps shape a new product.

From the initial concept to the setting of prices, Market Intelligence worked with outside consultants and other IBM units on the design, development, and merchandising of IBM's RISC System/600™. About 18 months before the new workstation was announced in February 1990, Market Intelligence was trying to determine the key factors that prompt customers to buy such a machine. Is it the technology, the speed, the applications, the service support?

Focus groups of target audience representatives helped qualitatively assess customers' requirements. Quantitative information was then obtained through telephone interviews and a large study of end-user decision makers.

Using the statistical technique conjoint measurement, researchers asked participants to rank a series of attributes that might influence their buying decisions indicating which attributes were most important to potential customers. At the time of the new product announcement, quantitative work was done with the same groups to measure the initial impact.

"You want to be sure the product, when it's announced, is not only competitive but superior to the competition's," notes Waugh. That means studying other vendors' products, understanding the options they offer customers, and analyzing how customers will view them.

In the author's experience, salesmen for trade publication advertising space, who call on your competitors and often pick up clues and gossip, as well as suppliers of parts, ingredients, R&D, and production services who openly share their knowledge are additional information sources who can be the basis for further investigation and prospect response research. Trade meetings, scientific seminars, and professional junkets can also present opportunities for quick-witted technical people and executives to pick the brains of colleagues.

Intelligence Consulting

Other methods, used by other companies, as reported by the *Los Angeles Times*, include:

> For executives who want more than casual information, Washington Researchers, a consulting firm based in the nation's capital, offers a "company information seminar."

> A brochure advertising one seminar says the consultants will show participants how to use the public sources to find out, among other things, the nature of a competitor's marketing strategy or whether the competition is opening a new plant.

Reverse Engineering

And there's more, according to the article:

> Such major manufacturers as automobile makers rou-
> tinely examine their competitors' products as they appear
> on the market. Breaking down a rival's marketed products
> in this fashion is known as "reverse engineering," a tech-
> nique so common in industry that most courts find it ac-
> ceptable as a competitive practice. Reverse engineering is
> a particularly valued skill in such high-technology indus-
> tries as electronics, where it is often an important step to-
> ward duplicating or improving on a competing product.

Freedom of Information Act

Even the government helps. As the *LA Times* article points out:

> But perhaps the most important "legitimate" source of in-
> side information about competitors is the federal govern-
> ment, which for regulatory and contracting purposes re-
> quires public corporations and even private companies to
> make extensive disclosures about their products, fi-
> nances, and operations.
>
> Over the years, businessmen have become adept at using
> the federal Freedom of Information Act to extract some of
> this data. Although the 1966 law was tailored to help the
> press and public obtain information about the workings of
> government, in practice it has been more useful to busi-
> nesses looking for information about their rivals . . .
>
> According to a 1980 study by a University of Oregon pro-
> fessor, 37 percent of the freedom-of-information queries
> submitted to 29 federal agencies in 1978 (not including
> the FBI and CIA) were to the Food and Drug
> Administration. That agency is the repository of millions
> or even billions of dollars in proprietary formulas from
> cosmetics and pharmaceutical makers, among other
> companies.
>
> Other studies suggest that the vast majority of information
> requests to certain regulatory agencies comes from corpo-
> rate probers rather than from the general public or press.
> The Food and Drug Administration reported last year that
> of the 33,000 requests it answered in 1980, about 85 per-
> cent were from companies in the industries it regulates.

The Planning Process

All parties involved in the execution of the plan must play a part in the planning process. This means every player in the company in every affected division. Perhaps it seems unbelievable, but companies have had costly new enterprise failures in taken-for-granted areas for such reasons as unanticipated waste disposal regulations (the new product produced waste dissimilar to that with which the company had previous experience), misinterpretation of industry guidelines (for product and/or communications), lack of alternate sources (or source planning) for critical ingredients, incomplete cost-of-goods-sold build-up, off-target (inefficient) media planning, inappropriate product-sizing assortment to address regional differences (lines were limited to the industry's best-selling variations only, based on national averages—failing to take into consideration that the best sellers differed from region to region—so that the *average* leaders represented necessary coverage in only a few markets), etc.

Over the years, important changes have taken place in the procedures for preparing plans. A recent study by The Conference Board bears this out. (See Figure 19-1.)

Use of Specialist Experts

Failure to use specialists when entering a new field has also led to more expensive failures than the cost of employing these experts in the planning phase. Too often companies believe that because they can make the product competitively, can handle sales and distribution competitively, and will communicate competitively, there is no reason to employ the specialist in the new field. After all, these experts may be expected to provide the industry cliches of the competition—while the very opportunity for the new entry is a new approach to the market. Nonetheless, informed experts can save time and money, provide valuable input, and tell a company what competitive reactions are likely to be when the new entrant takes its original noncliche approach to the marketplace. The new product manager can decide whether to rely on the expert's advice and, if so, how to use it, if at all.

There are expert generalists, and there are expert specialists in every major industrial category. Both can be helpful to procurement and manufacturing, sales and distribution, legal and finance, staff recruitment, etc.

Elements of the Plan

All of the up-front work has been completed.

Now you must obtain management approval.

In seeking management approval for a full-scale go-ahead, it is necessary to review the highlights of the entire development program in an executive overview. Marketing, finance, legal, production (including

Figure 19-1 Most important changes in procedures for preparing plans

Question: Compared with, say, five years ago, what are the most important changes in your procedures for preparing marketing plans?

Manufacturers of	Industrial products	Consumer products	Service firms
More input from other groups	28%	24%	16%
More integration with company strategy	19	21	26
More formal, standardized	17	24	13
More focus on competitiveness	15	5	10
More focus on customers/markets	15	8	10
Plan is longer/more complex	9	8	10
Didn't have formal marketing plan in past	9	10	13
More emphasis on execution	9	11	3
More use of computers	7	6	3
Plan is shorter/less complex	6	11	-
More focus on short term	6	3	-
Responsibilities better defined	4	8	3
More focus on long term	1	11	3
Planning more decentralized	2	3	13
Objectives better defined	-	2	16
Planning more centralized	-	2	10
No change	5	3	-
Other (e.g., more lead time, better information, used to rely on consultants)	13	8	10
Number of respondents	96	63	31

Source: The Conference Board: *The Marketing Plan* in the 1990s

manufacturing, supply, shipping), technical (including R&D, engineering, medical, etc.) all participate in the combined recommendation of the new products team.

The elements of the recommended plan may include:

1. **Situation analysis** (including market potential and competitive analysis, e.g., product, sales, pricing, etc.)

2. **Business objectives** (volume for Year 1 and after in units and dollars, cost of goods sold, gross and net margins, etc.)

3. **Product strategy**

4. **Development review** (whether internal, acquisition, joint-venture, or outside supplier made, assembled, and/or packed)

- Includes findings of concept and prototype screening.
- Includes all physical (or operational service) elements, e.g., product, packaging structure, but not graphics; shipping cartons; on-site final assembly and/or service, etc.

5. **Detailed financial analysis of market's present entries**

6. **Price perception study results** (field entries plus new product)

7. **Benefits and claims study results** (present competitors and recommended new product entry)

8. **Marketing strategy**

9. **Communications strategy** (includes advertising, customer and trade promotion, sales incentives, media plan, etc.)

10. **Legal review** (includes product, price, communications, patents, etc.)

11. **National theoretical plan, all elements** (for stimulation)

12. **Financial review** (includes timing and capital risks)

13. **Test market simulation** (or otherwise) plan or (alternatively) major launch with other test methods

Upon receiving executive clearance, the normal course of events finds the new product team coordinating its efforts along these lines:

Code: M = Marketing, T = Technical, P = Production, F = Finance, L = Legal

- Finalize creative (M)
- Finalize package structure (T/P) and graphics (M)
- Obtain patent, labeling, and other package copy, and distribution policy clearances (L)
- Conduct dealer impressions study (M)
- Conduct final advertising creative execution tests and produce advertising elements (M)
- Conduct factory-production user trial tests prior to release of selling samples (M, T, P)
- Conduct final manufacturing feasibility measures (T, P)
- Scale up for production and shipping (P)
- Begin manufacturing (P)
- Conduct benchmark awareness study in test markets (M)
- Sell-in to trade (M)
- Set shelf detailing and displays (M)
- Start advertising (M)
- Follow-up test market awareness study (M)

- Conduct distribution and price audit (M)

- Develop buyer profile study (M)

- Develop repeat awareness, audit, and sales measures (M)

- Project test market performance against plan (M)

- Make management recommendation to expand, abort, or revise plan (M, with new product team consensus)

Being First

The most wonderful new product and the best possible marketing plan avail little against a competitor who beats the innovator to the market with a similar new product. The "new" has been taken away. The trade that has taken on the first entrant isn't going to enthusiastically add another "me-too" item until it is demonstrated that the new product will build or enlarge a category sufficiently to leave room for variations.

Predictive field surveillance of the category, and of the likely competitors, must be intensively continued throughout the marketing planning phase. Where certain categories have pronounced regional skews, these areas should be surveyed with care. If the competitors have foreign marketing operations, they should be monitored also. If there are major foreign competitors, then their activities in their home countries should be monitored. Frequently, the products are tried at home before being exported.

Beyond this, in those categories where test marketing is common, all of the syndicated test market cities plus those cities most commonly used for conventional test markets should be surveyed to see if new product tests are underway. If so, tests should be audited because the marketing planning needs to take into consideration the test activity. For example, it may be decided to "read" the competitor's test while readying the new enterprise company's product for a regional or national launch—forgoing the originally planned test market to beat the competitor to the broad-scale marketplace.

Even so, doing it right is more important than doing it first—if doing it first means shortchanging the optimization of the product or key elements of its launch. The risks should be carefully weighed. Where the test market is part of the plan because of prudence and fine-tuning, rather than a real need for important learning, then, if the downside trade-off for a preemptive strike prior to competitive moves is not great, skipping the test market may be justified. Other alternatives present themselves also.

Test While Launching

Go ahead with the test exactly as planned, but make the major launch at the same time. This will enable the test market laboratories, with all of their built-in controls, to provide detailed information not available from the operation of the free-market, large-area introduction. With test-market information at hand, adjustments of the broader rollout area can be based on a quicker, more detailed (hence, less risky) reading of the situation than available from the board, uncontrolled market situation.

Another alternative is available for certain merchandise categories. For low-ticket, frequently purchased package goods, it is possible to put together a sales test among a limited number of high-volume, geographically dispersed, controlled-test stores to measure shelf movement, assuming that a reasonable simulation of advertising communication is available. The best use of this technique is where differences are being measured in terms of price, packaging, brand, or sales theme emphasis, and store panels are well matched.

Contingency Planning

What we covered above are some of the downside issues. There are upside issues also. On occasion, new products are far more successful than anticipated. this means rapid step-up of manufacturing or a slower roll-out than planned or product allocation or fewer trade-category channels than planned or a cutback in promotion—or a combination of all of these. Lost sales are sales never made. Because initial trial is so important—especially if they are to be gained during the heaviest introductory advertising/promotional period—an ideal marketing plan considers contingency activity under all circumstances, including:

1. Everything goes according to plan. How to optimize.

2. Outside events intervene, affecting success. How to meet and control events, or take advantage of them.

3. Product acceptance is less than anticipated. How to take remedial action—or to cut losses.

4. Product is more successful than anticipated. How to leverage this opportunity and/or how to deal with the problems (supply, out-of-stocks, media commitments, etc.)

In other words, war game strategies and tactics are employed. The games can be played in the marketing planning phase, in order to anticipate all possible contingency planning needs, make financial allowances, and predetermine actions that will be triggered by various circumstances. In this way, little time is lost and funding provisions are both predictable and manageable.

Simulation

Presuming that the marketing plan calls for a test simulation, then the guidelines for the simulation need to be laid out prior to selection of the test areas.

To do this, the universe must be defined.

In very few instances is the test universe defined as contiguous-state U.S.A. Even for those new products that are expected to be on sale nationally after a successful test, this is true. And, where it will truly be a nationally distributed brand, state and regional differences—often legal (local regulations), more often developmental or psychographic—need to be considered. Average markets and average marketing approaches exist only in statistics and, unfortunately, in far too many marketing plans. How do you avoid this?

Because any simulation in several or more geographic market areas will represent the true picture throughout the intended major marketing area in only the most gross sense, this should be recognized early—in both the market selection and in the guidelines for performance analysis.

It is probably true that in nearly every new product category, success *must* be obtained in certain markets or market-types because performance in other areas will not make up for poor performance in these key areas. If this is true, then you will want to simulate those distinctive characteristics that have major influences in these critical key markets, with weighted allowances used to project results to the entire universe of eventual sales.

County size, population concentration, industrial vs. rural, all play roles in marketing reception. Sometimes, for presumed cost savings, relatively small, lightly industrialized test markets are selected to simulate marketing performance for a new product that must have its leading successes in large, heavily populated urban areas with an industrial and/or business service base. If this is the case, the cost savings are illusionary, because the misdirection thus supplied may result in faulty projections.

After all of the (updated) demographics and psychographics have been analyzed—but before you make any further commitment to the choices—the projected test markets should be visited in person by those responsible for market selection. Oftentimes, what is on the scene is different from what is on paper. Circumstances change rapidly and affect prospect behavior—whereas statistics and Chamber of Commerce descriptions tend to have mostly historical significance. Unless you carefully check local conditions and incorporate them in the plan, the phasing of the test pattern may not take into account consumption biases and such influences as an influx of migratory workers, illegal aliens, or across-state-line shoppers (where there are influential tax variances or legal marketing restrictions, such as controlled liquor stores, price advertising of professional products and services, etc.).

If possible, arrange to have some of the early consumer research panels set up in intended test market candidates—and ask questions about more than the product area. Find out who are the most credible spokespeople in the media, which are the "innovator" bell-cow store outlets (if they are not the big chains, their importance won't show up except in an apparently unimportant statistic), reputations of *local* competitive companies, and brand franchises, etc. Weigh all of this. Is it relatively representative? Will it affect your simulation marketing plan, media balance, etc.?

Although the simulation will represent the marketing plan quantitatively, how are *local qualitative decisions* made? If, for example, the national plan calls for use of network personalities, shouldn't the local plan do more than merely represent the gross rating points? Shouldn't it also use any available appropriately credible local personalities? Does a weighting adjustment need to be made for network ratings as simulated by local spots—or national print space as simulated by local print or regional editions? More pertinent to the plan to be simulated, should all major media be bought on a national scale?

If the new product will have (at least initially) biases by area size or location, perhaps the national plan should be highly regionalized in design. In this way, each area should be given the expected weight in sales potential and respective marketing spending. The simulation translation will be merely an execution of the plan for that particular area. In this way, the sales projection will be against its predetermined importance to the total marketing plan—a big difference compared with its unweighted arithmetical proportion of the national goal.

Not only does the plan require simulation of the proposed national product, package, pricing share-of-shelf, and share-of-mind—it should also simulate the minimum trade acceptance and distribution level. If this is not achieved, then the test should be delayed or aborted in the market before media are unavoidably committed and heavy shipments are made—or continue. The "start-up" must be simulated properly. If it is not, then this most critical aspect of the plan cannot be projected.

Too often, it is assumed that what is being tested is the prospect's acceptance of the new product. While this is usually true, many times what is being tested is the quality of the sales force, the reputation of the service organization, and the relations with the specific trade factors represented in the test markets.

Be certain to identify these issues before simulation plan guidance is given to the selection of test markets. It is possible that the new product requires a different type of sales organization or a different style of buyer persuasion than that which has been successful for the company in other areas. It's best to learn this in test market. If such factors contribute to unacceptable new product performance, but customer satisfaction is high among those few who did purchase, then this indicates that there are elements that can be corrected either in an expanded effort or in a retest (perhaps, and probably, in another "nonpolluted" area).

Test Market Selection

Under ideal circumstances, test markets are definable, projectable entities, which differ from the goal universe only in scale. Naturally, this objective is not achievable.

Because no one market or set of markets can replicate an entire population, the key decision in market selection is to set priorities regarding the information needed. This done, markets are selected that best represent opportunities to yield the most accurate measures, at least concerning cost.

Selection Considerations

Essential considerations in selecting a test market include:

1. Availability of in-place syndicated market measurement resources
   This often provides historic performance information within the category of interest. Because it is in place, it is less costly than the building of a proprietary service.

2. Establishment of a proprietary resource
   Some companies have continual performance audit markets that measure sales trends in all categories of corporate entry and contingent interests. Others establish fresh test markets to meet measurement goals in new categories of interest, if neither existing syndicated nor proprietary resources are available or appropriate.

3. Prospect demographic/psychographic mix
   Except for mass appeal, broad consumption products, most products are targeted at markets more refined than a national cross section. In such cases, care should be taken to identify over- or underrepresentation of the target audience in test markets. This means using care in selection and care in projection. During unsettled economic periods, the unemployment index (by type) is also apt to be a key factor in selection.

   One way to sharpen the test market selection for highly defined entries, those which may be classified by prospect behavior habits, is to adopt a cluster system, such as the Claritas PRIZM (Potential Rating Index by ZIP Markets).

   These computer-generated market research categories arrange the USA's 250,000 neighborhoods into 40 to 48 widely varying life-styles, based on the latest census and special behavior research. Although PRIZM's most frequent use by marketers is to predict buying preferences and purchasing patterns, the same input can be used to help in pinpointing high-yield test areas typical of market development picks should the test succeed. For example, if direct marketing is to be used, high-response–rate areas may be predicted; if life-style is important to a planned fast-food expansion, high repeater areas may be predictable.

4. Trade penetration mix
   Equal care is devoted to the trade mix, often a reflection of economics, ethnicity, age of the control city, maturity of local brands, recovery of competitive introductions, dominance or lack of it by individual trade factors, local price wars, coupon misredemption aberrations, etc.

5. Media mix
   Consideration should be given to the number of competitive TV and radio stations; local aberrations in viewing or listening; the strength of dailies, weeklies, and suburban shopper newspapers;

the strength and character of city magazines, etc. All types of media planned for the national introduction should be represented in the test markets.

6. Pricing of media
There is a pricing penalty in simulating the national plan on a local scale. All else being equal, select the lower cost-per-thousand media market. Media spill-in/spill-out should be at minimum levels. Further, the cost of media within each market is of primary consideration. Also, network TV affiliations and the possibility of regional local magazine translations should be investigated.

7. Location
When several test markets are selected, they should be in different regions, representing parts of a projectable whole—not looked at individually. Where shipping costs will be critical to profit margins after expansion (large, bulky items from a central plant), nearby key markets of sufficient size for profitability are needed. Performance *must* make it where there is no added shipping burden. Minimize transshipments to other geographic areas so as not to blur the assessment of sales performance readings.

8. Seasonal effects
Nearly every seasonally related new product should be tested in areas where seasonal influences represent the average peak timing and length of the planned rollout marketing area.

9. Competitive set
Consider the competitive industry mix—where competitive shares by *type* of product (e.g., sports cars vs. sedans) are either representative of the whole, representative of the target, or are measured for an otherwise identifiable reason. Look at the competitive brand share mix. Competition should be typical of the planned expansion market area.

10. Recent, accurate information
This should be obtained by on-the-scene investigation by local and regional services, not limited to published economic and societal data, but including the business, editorial, and news press, trade management, in-place company sales representatives, applicable professional groups, etc.

11. Retail pricing
This should be typical of the rest of the planned expansion area.

12. Sales force
The proficiency of the company's sales force in the test area should be typical of its performance throughout the rest of its entire trading area.

13. Projectability

The test market(s) must be statistically projectable. Most experts feel 3 percent of U.S. households is the minimum test market size for consumer package goods. Often, marketers go as small as 1 percent of the U.S., however, with care to see that the per capita consumption index does not vary more than 10 percent. Use of more than one market is recommended, to hedge market readings against unpredictable influences, such as layoffs, strikes, atypical weather conditions, etc.

The importance of selection, measurement, and performance interpretation in testmarketing cannot be overstressed. According to International Multifoods, in their study of package goods test marketing, the research of a test market costs three times as much as the production of the product itself. (See Figure 19-2.)

The Actual Markets

Now that all those factors that match the national plan have been laid down for the simulation guide, the actual test markets must be selected.

There are likely many more candidates than are called for by the needs of the test—perhaps two to four, unless matched sets are being used to test price, media weight, or communications strategy differences.

Choosing the Candidate(s)

These are further cut down on the basis of geographic dispersion and, possibly, by such logistical considerations as factory location, best air connections for headquarters staff, freight tariffs, special competitive biases, etc. Also to be considered is test wear-out. Some more or less representative areas have been used so many times that they are product cluttered. Others may currently be the scene of above average detailing or special promotional efforts by the company's own sales force—or competition.

Competition may be testing products in a similar competitive arena. In this case, it may be decided to monitor one or several without a face-off, to get a "pure" early reading—while, perhaps, facing competitors directly in others, to determine their reactions. In most instances of the latter scenario, if the second entry goes in with a reasonably projectable plan, a sophisticated competitor will stick to its plan—to see what happens in what could become reality in larger areas. Unfortunately, sometimes a war ensues—and marketing spending becomes out of line with anything that could be feasibly spent on a broad scale. In this instance, the only winner is the customer. The warring new products haven't been submitted to a true test.

Where sales are being projected from sales audits, it is sometimes found that the promising initial success occurred because of sales made to competitors picking up sample products for analysis. At least one

Figure 19-2 The test market dollar

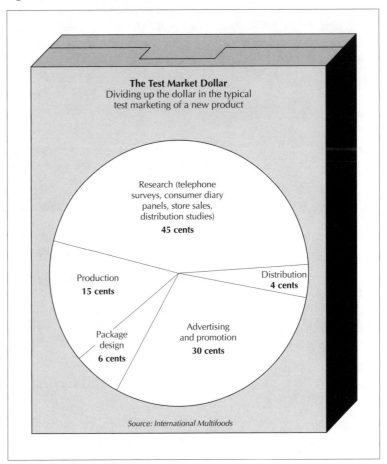

Source: *New York Times*, April 11, 1982.

wise national package goods supplier always sends a case of its new products to its competitors as it ships to the trade, with a letter that says:

> Our new X product is on its way to you for analysis. We'd be interested in your comments. Meanwhile, you'll be spared the trouble and the expense of picking up the product and hence, your reading of our sales performance will be more accurate.
>
> If you'd like another case of X product, just let us know. Catalog sheet enclosed.

Simulating Simulations

There are, of course, methods whereby conventional test markets may be themselves simulated. Where "control"—rather than unfettered reality—is needed, isolated minimarkets with managed controls are often used. These are especially useful in measuring variables between matched pairs, e.g., store or shelf position, price, promotions, sales activities, marketing spending, etc. On occasion, controlled markets are used in pairs against conventional markets. Where, for example, distribution and shelf facings are controlled in the managed markets and subject to haphazard circumstances in the others, it is possible to get a relative measure of sales force effectiveness, or attractiveness of trade promotions, as an element in sales success, etc.

Show and Tell

Now that the marketing plan has been approved, the simulation guidelines laid down, and the test markets selected—it's time to put the communications together that will tell the world about the new product about to be born.

This communications development process has been moving along parallel with product development. The learning process has contributed modifications that now will come together in the marketplace.

20

New Product Communications

You're only young once, so make the most of it.

Like a new baby, a new product is born only once—without a name (although its birth certificate may identify parentage), neither given (brand) nor surname (generic descriptor).

This is the most opportune time to get this youngster started off right—to help assure its successful future.

There are so many decisions to make. How will it be dressed? With whom will it associate? How often will it be seen in public—and where? And, most important in its productive life, what will its personality be?

Many factors enter, most importantly:

- The product
- Its performance
- Its name
- Its package
- Its price
- Its display
- Its advertising

Unless the new baby is a product of genetically matched parents, even its complexion, structure, and style are subject to many design variations for the marketplace. Even if it's a clone, a line extension, or a cousin, a flanker—there are opportunities to send the powerful signal of newness.

After all, *new* is one of the most arresting and trial-persuasive words in the marketing lexicon. *New* cannot be said for long (in many cases, it is legally limited to six months in your advertising and promotion). So, during this brief period of letting the world find your new baby, say *new* powerfully, frequently, and with great audience reach.

That is why it is so critical to understand those elements that send the signal of communications "newness."

The Product Itself

You want a product that is equal to or better than the competition. In a true commodity category, you must move the merchandise at almost any cost, because it is too costly to store, is perishable, or is subject to frequent vagaries of Mother Nature or market speculation. In such a classification, you must move the tonnage and (often unfortunately true) hang the profit margin.

But most marketers are not moving commodities. They are making products to provide a range of new benefits. often these benefits relate to new life-styles and changing demographics.

Within the constraints of technology and legality, and of perception and actual fact, there are geometric combinations of new product performance possibilities. Most of these are based on known technologies, readily available skins, and quickly communicated benefits.

The architecture, engineering design, texture, color, and assembly of the product must set it apart from the competition, while at the same time associating it with the field sufficiently to make a quick communication. It should not appear, feel, or behave so differently that it is misperceived or overlooked as not belonging to its category.

As discussed earlier, your new product selection has the greatest opportunity for success when it fits a strength of your company. New products are not an end in themselves, they are a means of leveraging your company's strengths to increase volume and profit.

Make no mistake, the product selected is a communication in itself. Everything about it is a communication, including the outwardly manifest enthusiasm of the corporate new products group, from science to manufacturing to marketing. This initial commitment often sets the pace for later marketplace achievement.

Product Performance

A new product must be both different and better to be an outstanding hit in the marketplace.

Experience tells us that it should be only a little bit different. Users tend to understand, accept, and adopt that which is close to the familiar. The signals are clearer. The differences are easier to accept—and, hence, more apt to be believed.

There are countless examples of major improvements that sit in the laboratories, in patent application files, or in the heads of their inventors—but will not reach the marketplace for years. All of the know-how necessary to make these products exists today—but their concepts are too advanced to find ready acceptance. This is true in every culture. It is also true that what may succeed in another culture, although possibly superior to what we offer in this one, may fail here because of sociological, regulatory, or other reasons unrelated to the performance superiorities of the new product.

And, so, great breakthroughs are usually *not* the order of the day. Those few exceptions have mostly been entrepreneurial commitments that have built businesses, not products per se.

Most new product managers will work for established companies. Few will be founders or have the benefit (and constitution) to be a working part in the conceptional explosion of the genius of an Edison, a Disney, or a Land. Perhaps typical of a truly inventive attitude is that of Polaroid founder Dr. Edwin H. Land: "Any market already existing is inherently boring and dull." (Quoted in *Business Week*, March 2, 1981.) He stressed *invention*, rather than innovation or improvement.

Contrary to this view, the action for most industry is in responding to the marketplace: the user habits, evolving technologies, competitive actions, available capacities, and distribution opportunities.

That is reality for most new product managers. And that is the way of the free marketplace.

As for being *better* . . .

Experience tells us "a lot better" is desirable if we are not "a lot different" at the same time. However, in the laboratory, being a lot better often goes with being a lot different. That's the rub. History shows that tiny performance advances usually appear to have the greatest opportunities in the market *precisely because they are easy to communicate and do not require habit change.*

Because small performance differences are most easily achievable, opportunity plays into the hands of communicators. New product performance just a slight bit ahead of competition is easily communicated through comparison with past user experience or by direct comparison with attributes of competitive offerings.

That slight difference is the trouble, also.

If it is only slightly better and only slightly different, then it will ordinarily take only a slight amount of effort and a slight amount of time for competition to catch up. For these reasons, the product's performance must constantly improve during its life cycle—to allow its producer to constantly renew its benefit claims. At the same time, the product's positioning in the user's mind should remain distinctive and relevant, and its personality must be so strong as to be nonpreemptible.

Position & Personality

Often, even leaders in their fields create new brands to go with new positioning of new products.

One recent example is new brand development in the hosiery category by Sara Lee Personal Products line of business, which includes the leading brand in department stores, Hanes: with more than a 60 percent share. Even so, Hanes Hosiery sought to extend the Hanes megabrand with innovative new products presented in an exciting manner at retail.

After comprehensive product development R&D, creating figure-enhancing pantyhose, Hanes worked with identity consultants and designers Landor Associates, which was retained to create the brand name, packaging system, and merchandising presentation for a new line of figure-shaping hosiery.

The challenge was development of a new brand that would signal a contemporary product line, communicate its benefits, and work within the classic Hanes umbrella identity. Packaging structure had to reinforce the brand's distinctive "contouring" attributes, fit within traditional retail merchandising units, and conform to Hanes' manufacturing requirements without substantial additional cost. The merchandising system was to create a strong retail image to support the brand, provide easy-to-shop product information, and meet the structural configurations of a wide variety of store environments.

The solution was the creation of Smooth Illusions, a "total brand" based on the body-contouring positioning of the products. The name, package structure, graphic identity, and unique color coding work together to powerfully communicate a distinct brand personality that reinforces the Hanes identity. (See Figure 20-1.)

The Name

This is one of the most critical decisions a marketer must make. Prospective user research is essential. Often, in the case of line extensions (another size, another color, another flavor, another horsepower, etc.), circumstances dictate a strong family resemblance, with just enough difference to indicate another selection.

Sometimes what appears to be an appropriate name for a flanker or for a new item sends the wrong signals. For example, a famous brand name of women's hair coloring was used for its parent company's pioneering brand of men's hair coloring. The logic went: this is the leading brand of hair coloring. Therefore, it will say to the prospect that he can trust the product, because it is made by the leader. However, what the brand actually said was: This must be a feminine product, because that brand name is associated with beauty parlors and cosmetics. Because I am hesitant about trying a hair color, I certainly don't want to use something that will diminish my self-image of masculinity. A famous package goods company, the maker of leading toiletries, went into test market with a line of frozen foods. Because the company's most famous brand was its toothpaste, it branded the food products with that name—and failed. Consumers probably couldn't separate the prestigious brand name from its peppermint flavor, its cleansing usage.

Figure 20-1 Hanes: creating new brand, new positioning

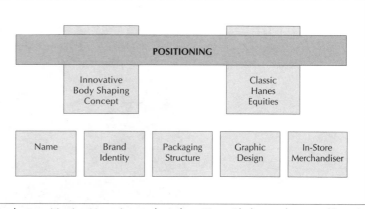

Product positioning Hanes's megabrand equities with the newly created brand Smooth Illusion's body-contouring pantyhose features required signaling a contemporary product line and leveraging the Hanes umbrella identity.

Every well-established brand has a meaning, a boundary. Often this establishes a capacious level of preliminary reception, as well as readily defined limits of extension for any new member carrying the family name. Johnson & Johnson found that its brand name meant "gentleness." Well-known and a leader in many fields, it learned that J&J's "gentle" meaning is nonetheless *not* appropriate to introduce a powerful germ fighter or its leading analgesic, Tylenol.

Betty Crocker is one of the best-known brands in the food business, yet General Mills has been careful to see that it is applied only to an appropriate range of new products. Studies have shown both the new areas that fit its image as well as those that are inappropriate.

Such studies are a requirement for every company with one or more strong brand names, or a corporate identity with a specific meaning. Usually, it will be found that the strong names carry great close-in opportunities and equally potent problems when entering new areas of consumer perception.

Example: Gerber's $20 million introduction in 7,200 eastern U.S. supermarkets[1] of its juice for adults "Juice & More" in September, 1990, underlines the point. The 72 percent share-dominating baby food maker didn't make it with adults, stopping production in July 1991.[2]

Often almost as important as the brand name itself is the generic description. Is the product "cosmetic beauty bar" or "Step 2—Nightly Skin Care System" or "solid beauty bath" or "toilet soap"? All of the above are essentially the same product, but with different generic de-

[1] *The Detroit News*, September 23, 1990

[2] *Advertising Age*, July, 1991

Figure 20-2 Form reflects function

A distinctive form can have two powerful attributes: It can set the product aside from others on the shelf—and send a promising message. Examples above appeal to aficionados of Pescevino wine (left) and Licor de Damiana. They can immediately spot their favorite beverages by their shape. The one on the left goes well with fish. The shapely one on the right implies an aphrodisiac.

scriptors. As you can see, this can make an important difference in the product's perceived personality, price point—and possibly even its distribution channels and advertising media selection.

The Package— Face, Form, Function

For some products, the face, form, and function of the package may be almost as important as its contents. This is certainly true in repeat-purchase package goods.

Adweek's Marketing Week, January 21, 1991: "The last five seconds of marketing—the supermarket aisle—is the hot media today. To make the most of their shelf impressions, brand managers are turning to designers to convert their packaging into permanent shelf ads." (See Figure 20-2.)

Function follows face and form for most packages, which are designed chiefly for display purposes, secondarily providing protection, a pedestal to rest upon, and space to readily identify the contents, provide printed directions, etc. Other packages are integral parts of the complete product appearance: the TV set cabinet (the set works perfectly well without it) and, at the other extreme, the cleansing tissue box. Both serve an appearance function as long as the product is in use—but play no critically necessary function in product performance. And both the packages—the cabinet and the cardboard box—send a message about the contents. Although the contents in each case may provide similar performance to other dissimilarly packaged products, the package appearance will affect how we perceive the product's newness, quality, and value.

Package form seems to be going in several directions. While, on the one hand, high-volume shelf goods are trying to fit as much product into as small a space as possible, on the other hand there are slow-moving specialty products that depend on offbeat shape to attract the prospect's preference.

Twenty-five years ago, in a talk for The Kroger Co. management, I made predictions that still haven't come true—but will. I said: "All product classes will come in standard sizes and shapes of packages—kilos and liters and .5 and .25 multiples. Packaging materials will either be made of recycled materials or be edible, in which case they will eventually be biologically recycled back into the cellulose and sugar compound that makes this milk carton so delicious.

"Products will be cubed. By that I mean, every measure will be modular, every package built around a cube, so that products will fit together like building blocks on home shelves." Shelf space is so precious that each linear and square foot must have optimum yield. DPP (direct product profitability) controls inventory and assesses profit performance.

This shelf management can reduce inventory spending more than 20 percent and increase profits per square foot as much as 75 percent, some studies show.

As retailers' databases become more accurate and sophisticated, the shape of packaging will be directly affected. The shape of packaging to come, especially in the slow-turnover category, will be rectangular, rather than round. (There'll always be exceptions, of course, as will be referred to later.)

You can shelve more than 27 percent more product in the same space, if the package is rectangular rather than cylindrical. It also reduces case cost, a cost/space saver in shipping and warehousing.

There are other ways to maximize space yield, including such innovative packaging as interlocking containers that can fit twice as much liquid into the same space as conventional bottles (Universal Symetrics Corp.'s Pack Mates, for example).

Concentrated versions of conventional products also save space, but reduce visual impact and implied quantity value. An educated adjustment must be made. Old habits change slowly. When they do, standardization will put competition on an even playing field.

On the flip side, of course, are the exceptions. Here are several described in my August 6, 1990, *Marketing News* column:

> Mrs. Butterworth's is a good example of instant ID, with her body-shaped pancake syrup bottle. There are also log cabins, orange shapes, etc.

Less common are the symbolic shapes in the liquor department: silver pendant-adorned voluptuous female torso shape of the reputed aphrodisiac Licor de Damiana of Guycura (made in Guadalajara, Mexico) and the fish-shaped bottle of Pescevino white table wine from Osimo, Italy, are two examples [Figure 20-2].

These are unique shapes that command attention, leaping out from the stock bottle competition, as well as conveying intended use and distinct personalities. If the contents live up to the sensory promise, then the DPP will be rewarding.

Environmentally sound packaging is a leading trend to be addressed in new product planning. Consumers are willing to pay more for this protection—recyclable and biodegradable packages—when they understand it.

Recycled paperboard and plastics in new packaging slow the landfill glut. Cellophane will make a comeback because it breaks down in soil just as leaves do. Plastic pouches and bag-in-the-box packaging add less volume to waste than the conventional rigid packaging they replace.

Vacuum-packed, bagged, and pouched products with extended shelf life for refrigerated specialties and meats will become more common. They've been in use in Europe for years, as has modified atmosphere packaging, which helps keep decay at bay in fresh produce.

Before this becomes common, a materials-combination breakthrough is needed to increase ease of recyclability.

Also to come on the agenda is conventional packaging which recognizes home-storage and appliance-shelving problems and makes certain packages reusable or multipurpose (that is, incorporating measurement markets, resealable lids, etc.).

Childproof caps will be given tamper indicators not requiring a grunt and a pair of pliers to remove. And color-code and descriptor printed cap sides on small container products such as branded and generic drugs, herbs and spices, etc., are on the way.

Better shelf accountability, customer-friendly packages, the greening of America—all have an impact on future packaging, no matter what the label.

But those packages, their look, feel, and usability must still shout from the shelves: "Buy me!"

Its Price

Price, of course, must reflect value. But it must also speak of the position and the personality of the product. Something that is priced at $1.99 is not the same as something priced at $2.00—what a difference that penny makes!

Years ago, a miniaturized reel-to-reel tape recorder was introduced by Webcor. At the same time, such items sold in the $79.05 to $129.95 range. Ads ran in hi-fi store retail newspaper space. Webcor's excellent performance, high-tech–styled machine was introduced as the Microcorder in *The Wall Street Journal* at $175. The price, the product name, the style of the package (the case), and the environment of the media all combined to set the product above its field in the minds of the consumers, the trade, and throughout the company itself—with sellout results.

Price communicates a message about how your company values its product and about how much a consumer might expect from its performance. Price tells a consumer how to value the product.

It is always possible to lower a price (in promotional periods or permanently). Except when the entire industry takes a price rise, it is often difficult to unilaterally price-up in a dynamic category.

Set a price that is appropriate to your personality, even if this does not reflect the price structure of the category or the minimum acceptable profit margin goal. If you cannot do this, then alter the factors: your product's cost, its committed marketing dollars, its profit goals, or its position in the competitive set. All elements of your communication should be integrated—consistent with your total personality. If that appears impossible, rethink the personality to fit the price. Be realistic. Rely on user research to help you establish a ceiling (as well as a basement) for a reasonable price range.

The Display

Most products and services are displayed somewhere—at a trade show, on a selling sheet or an ad, on a counter or a shelf, on a showroom floor, in a shopping cart or a shipping case, in an office, factory, or home.

And most are displayed more than one way at different times.

Establish the "look" of your new product from the very beginning. Send quick visual signals; symbols; clean, quick logotypes; proprietary color schemes and design elements; a style carried forward in typography, setting, and illustration—a fitting background for your products or services. Be pervasive with this in everything you do from the very beginning.

Do not leave any of this to chance. Do not assign it to uninvolved specialists. And do not look at display out of context.

Just as you look at and study your packages in their usage environments—look at your displays in their selling environments. Look at displays full of products and in the context of their trade use, such as next to the dissimilar and possibly similar displays.

See that your displays are functional. Do they do what you want? Are they single-minded? Do they lead the viewer to the focus or action you desire—without distraction or unnecessary additional elements? Are they compatible with various types of lighting and other display conditions? Are they easy to assemble quickly? Will they stay fresh-looking for their reasonable intended life—or are they easily refreshable?

And do they fit the personality that is being developed for the new product—not only fit it, but reinforce it? This is a must—to make the most of exhibiting the new offering under conditions the marketer controls.

The Advertising

Marketing communications must be based on a totally integrated, interactive, coordinated, supportive plan—usually most effectively leveraged by advertising—but utilizing closely coordinated product/service positioning, personality, promise, and appearance for the product/brand. The advertising strategy and its execution is critical to the development of the creative direction for all communications executions, in all media, by all sources, including paid media, direct marketing, sales promotion and other merchandising support, public relations, point-of-sale display, package design, structure and graphics, symbols, product descriptor, and brand name. Integrated Marketing Communications (IMC) to be most effective needs a market-focused management structure, in this world of infinite, fractionated multimedia choices—where a single creative direction is essential.

The creative execution is a tactical result directly flowing from the direction provided by written guidelines. In most cases, these guidelines are jointly developed by the advertiser (who will market the product) and the advertising agency (which will prepare the advertising). It is the advertiser's obligation to help develop and to approve guidelines that will be specific enough to form a basis for evaluation and for assessment of research results.

On the other hand, the direction should be general enough to allow for freedom in the creation of a variety of effective executions. Such executions should be consistent with the long-term strategy for the product throughout its marketing life. The executions should build one upon another over time, so that the introductory marketing investment will be leveraged after the brand has been well established and the mission of the advertising shifts from an informational to a reminder mode.

Although the execution is expected to persuade triers, buyers, and referrals, it must first attract attention before it can create desire. For this reason, awareness and recall measures are particularly critical in measuring introductory product advertising.

Advertising may be expected to help generate trial, and it may be expected to help remind initial triers to try *again*. However, it cannot be expected to generate retrial if the product does not deliver on the promised benefits. For this reason, it is mandatory that the advertising does not overpromise nor the product underdeliver. Overpromise can generate fast acceptance—and early rejection. Not infrequently, advertising has *underpromised*. The result is a slow buildup of consumer acceptance—rather than the fast take-off that may result from an accurate portrayal of product delivery. For this reason alone, it is essential that advertising execution communications be studied in conjunction with product appeal testing.

Advertising agencies and advertisers use different formats to provide creative direction. However, they generally include the following elements:

1. Business communications objective to be achieved by the advertising

2. Description of the target consumer in the category and, if different, for the new product entry (include attitudes toward category and product offering)

3. Single most important product benefit, stated as its strongest supportable (and demonstrable) claim. This tells what is different and better than the competition about the new product.

4. Image, equity, character, or personality to be established for the offering (and to be established and reflected by the advertising, as well as all other communications)

To this add various caveats (restrictions and mandatory requirements) affecting the range of possible media selections, trade style, brand registration, patent, trademark, and copyright notice, point of origin credit, code authority guidelines, etc. Backing this up, add a Fact Book that includes all of the essential information in summary form regarding the marketplace conditions, product composition, competitive activities (including their advertising executions), and relevant consumer research concept, product, and communications testing results.

The Organizing Communications Concept

Personality, as we have seen must be the organizing communications concept. All other elements are apt to become fugitive because of events beyond the maker's control, such as preemptive competitive activity.

As the pervasiveness and impact of communications increase, it takes more and more to stand out, to be recognized—and to be remembered.

In the old days of advertising, a simple claim, forcefully and repetitively presented, often sufficed: "Fights headaches 3 ways" ... "Contains Irium" ... "Contains chlorophyll" ... "Contains fluorides" ... "Biggest, best, tallest, cheapest, longest-lasting, cleans whiter, less tar, more vitamins," etc., etc.

Always necessary is the exclusive "reason for being"—the selling justification for selection of one product or service over another. A tangible, objective consumer benefit is needed for the newly introduced product. It is essential to find these benefits—whether naturally built-in or purposely engineered.

Today, however, this is simply not enough.

Why? Because most heavily advertised products are near-commodities, and they are subject to parity, or better, counterclaims. It takes more than an exclusive, differentiating consumer benefit claim to sustain the forward momentum and continuity of an introductory advertising campaign without changing the character of the product personality (often to be built over the years with millions of media dollars).

It is easy to understand the success of the Marlboro Man, the Green Giant, Tony the Tiger, California Raisin People, Garfield, etc. They all rely on the personality of the product offering—one that will be sustained no matter what the specific concrete consumer benefit offering may be. The personality is a benefit also. A favorite research technique is to ask: "What kind of person am I if I (buy, drink, use, etc.) Product X?" This reflects the personality signals of the communications—not the hard claims. It is often the most important factor in a successful product's life cycle.

Poppin Fresh, the Pillsbury Doughboy, is an excellent example of a personality that has the sustaining power to build brand equity over time.

While the business communications objective for Pillsbury Bakery products has evolved over the last 30+ years, the Doughboy's role as a helper and friend in the kitchen and spokesman for the hot, fresh-baked goodness of Pillsbury products has been maintained.

In 1965, Pillsbury was a good-sized business but it suffered low awareness. Consumers did not have much knowledge of refrigerated fresh dough—what it was or what it offered to them. While gaining in popularity, convenience foods were somewhat suspect at the time because they did not offer the quality or variety they do today. New, refrigerated dough needed both visibility and acceptance.

In getting to know the product, the creative team at Leo Burnett advertising agency was struck by how unique the product was. They summarized the consumer benefit as:

> the pleasure of fresh, hot home baking without the time-consuming effort of preparing baked goods from scratch.

In 1965, the opening instructions on the can read "crack on the black line" (it wasn't until the mid-1970s that the spoon opening can was introduced). Out of this "crack" popped the fresh dough and an idea. The dough seemed to grow, expand and even be alive . . . which was the beginning of Poppin Fresh, a small character made of dough. (The original sketch of the Doughboy is shown in Figure 20-3).

He was originally described as:

> " . . . warm, friendly, amusing, likable. He is a song and dance man, a friend to mothers and children. He is a salesman who can point up the features of fresh dough. . . .

> " . . . he can do anything that does not make him appear stupid or disagreeable, provided he does not overshadow the news inherent in the product we are advertising."

Figure 20-3 Poppin Fresh, the Pillsbury Doughboy

The original Poppin Fresh Pillsbury Doughboy as sketched in 1965 (left) and as the lively character of today. In 1990, he was rated number one in popularity among consumers.

Source: Leo Burnett Co.

The Doughboy personified the product. His friendly, unassuming demeanor and softness translated to product benefits—refrigerated dough was friendly/unintimidating to use, with a soft texture that consumers associated with freshness in baked goods.

The Doughboy was a three-dimensional figure (versus a cartoon character). It was felt that he would be most believable, memorable, and intrusive if he could interact with the preparer in the real world. A three-dimensional character was a new, innovative idea in consumer goods advertising in 1965.

The Doughboy clearly achieved the communications goals Pillsbury set out to accomplish. He was intrusive and memorable; 87 percent of Americans recognized him and associated him with Pillsbury after only three years; he was seen as "a secret friend who helps you bake what you otherwise might not be able to do." He was also associated with peak years of prepared dough volume and growth (+38 percent in 1965–70).

Thirty years later, the Doughboy continues to be an idea that has power of its own and a life of its own. He continues to capture the heart and imagination of consumers all over the country.

The Doughboy, in a 1990 "Q" survey, which measures the popularity of personalities among consumers, was rated number one:

"Q" Rating	April/May 1990 Score
The Pillsbury Doughboy	41
California Raisin People	35
Tony the Tiger	28
Domino's Pizza Noid	27
Charlie the Tuna	26

While his actions have been contemporized (he now sings "cinnamon roll rock n' roll" with an air guitar butter knife rather than dancing the "box step" with mom), he continues to stand for and communicate the same product benefit of "hot, fresh-baked goodness conveniently" to Pillsbury customers.

In all cases, the action/role of the Doughboy is to reinforce the strategy of the product. For example, to communicate that Pillsbury Soft Breadsticks go great with Italian meals, the Doughboy sings the praises of his product to the music of an Italian opera.

The Doughboy is incorporated into all elements of the marketing mix—on the package, in the advertising/promotions, in displays, etc. He continues to be used in fresh, engaging ways to convey the relevance and benefit in his products. His reintroduction in 1989 as a central spokesperson for Pillsbury Bakery Products has contributed to increasing the rate of annual growth for Pillsbury two-fold.

In summary:

- A new product should start out its communications life with an enduring personality that will sustain and build over time.

- To sell an idea, product or service, the most important communications equity is its personality.

- It must be distinctive, integrated, consistent, positive, and memorable.

- Nothing else is so important as a vivid personality.

  Competition may copy claims and product.

  It will not copy personality.

  Personality is nonpreemptible.

- It is a marketing obligation to discover and to build personality into new products communications.

- Personality builds sales over time.

21

Media/Promotion/
Payout

Now that the product people have produced this wonderful new product, somehow it has to be sold.

To be sold, the consumer has to know it exists.

For the consumer to know it exists, you—the marketer—have to communicate it. Better yet, you have to promote it.

To promote it effectively (and effectively means at a profit!), there is one clear challenge: Execute a program that satisfies everyone's selfish interests. That's the true test of a good sales program.

Everyone knows that a new product should satisfy a need—real, perceived, latent, or *basically* essential.

Not everyone knows that a successful new product introduction has to satisfy not only user needs—but seller needs. In other words, there has to be something in it for everyone.

Use the media to tell consumers about the product and about the trial purchase incentives—coupons, samples, trial sizes, etc. There's never enough to do everything, but with creativity and by phasing various elements so that the financial impact doesn't hit all at once, a lot may be accomplished. With a new product introduction, however, many of those costs do hit at once. That's why the introductory year (or two) is often an investment against future profit potential.

Serving Selfish Interests

Let's review those selfish interests that must be served in the introduction of a typical new package good.

Company Sales Force

The sales force is being asked to add an item. Maybe they're being asked to do this while maintaining the volume of all the other items out there. Maybe they are being asked to do it at the expense of one particular weak sister in a competitor's line—or in the company's own line.

The manufacturer is choosing—not the trade. Never mind the computer readouts, the sales force must sell the substitution headquarters recommends. They're being asked to put that item in a certain spot in the store, in a certain department, on a certain shelf, next to a certain other product. Maybe salespeople will get a little detailing muscle for assistance—but the sales force has to sell the program.

Or, maybe not. Maybe a broker organization will replace the sales force for this item. So? So they're losing an opportunity to add a new item to their line. Sure, the work is skipped—but the opportunity for gain is lost also.

No matter what the situation, there has to be something in it for the sales force—or else the new product isn't going to get all of the attention it rightfully deserves. Build in some incentive bonuses for performance: money, prizes, recognition—maybe all three. Do this first step thoroughly. If you miss on this one, much else that follows will have little effect.

Don't forget: on the average, 37 percent of all sales growth and 31 percent of profits for most marketers will come from new products in the next five years, according to a 1982 study by Booz Allen & Hamilton.

So doing this basic first step right is the foundation for all of the communications and promotions that overlay the field selling plan designed to get the introduction started off just right. Not only should there be the selfish-interest incentives, there should also be the tools of the trade to help serve that selfish interest. A full array of fact sheets, sales brochures, advertising media plans, and examples of the creative communications must be in the selling kit.

The Headquarters Distributor

Also in the selling kit must be something to appeal to the selfish interests of the chain headquarters and/or wholesaler.

The sales force is going to ask some very big businesses to change their assortment of merchandise. This means something has to move over to make room. The salesman has a suggestion, of course. Kick out that slow-moving competitor. However, he must have the facts to support this suggestion. Also, because the newly inventoried item means record-keeping changes for the merchandiser, sales must pay for this one-time cost. As an added incentive, the sales force will offer an introductory allowance to encourage a sufficiently large opening inventory to help the stores meet the predicted demand with plenty of merchandise at a "hot" feature price during the introductory advertising/promotion program. This allowance may also include add-on sweeteners to underwrite store advertising, support in-store and/or retailer ad couponing, pay for displays, and perhaps underwrite in-store sampling.

The Retail Level

But it's not that simple. Every store manager is his own boss. No matter what headquarters recommends, in most instances the store manager has the authority to elect whether or not to take on the item, in what assortment, and in what quantities. So—his selfish interest must be served also.

The new product may be a big deal at headquarters, but out at 2nd and Central, it's another matter. "My market isn't your average market. My customers are different. I am very careful about what I throw out, after all I picked that stuff in the first place—and my customers rely on us to carry it." And so a way must be found to squeeze in the new product—even if on a trial basis.

Right now, at introductory time, there may be a way for the local manager to benefit by a big consumer sweepstakes. If policy isn't against it, if the consumer winners are his customers, he can win the big award that goes to the retailer who cooperates by putting up the big sweepstakes display (which requires a lot of merchandise as well as those tear-off pads). Then there's the "mystery shopper" program—if the mystery shopper sees someone buy the item, the purchaser gets a prize, and so does the store!

That's the idea. A little cut of the pie for everyone. If the store is a big one and there are department managers, there should be something in it for them. After all, it's a big event—giving birth to a new product.

Marketing Interrelationships

The Quaker Oats Company, an active new products marketer, has collected much information on the related effects of various new products marketing forces. The following section, passed along to the author by Quaker's past president, Kenneth Mason, contains much information specifically interesting to the package goods industry—but also principles that cut across many new product marketing needs.

Figure 21-1 illustrates first-year retail sales for four ready-to-eat cereals from three leading manufacturers, each introduced in different years, but, considered together, representative of a typical cereal intro-

Figure 21-1 Four ready-to-eat cereals—retail sales

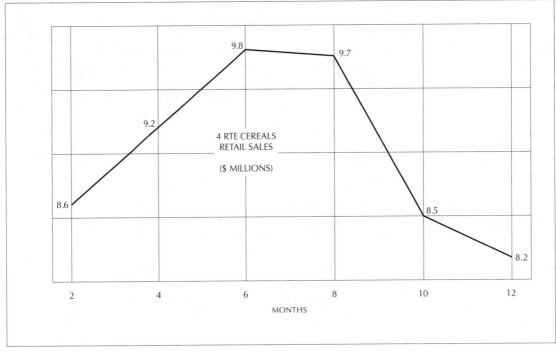

Source: A. C. Nielsen

duction pattern. The Quaker Oats report, "The New Item Problem," says:

> For the first A. C. Nielsen reporting period, the combined retail sales of the four cereals would have been $8,600,000 for the first two months; $9,200,000 for the second two months—with a general trend of from about $8,000,000 to $10,000,000, then back to about $8,000,000 where the trend levels off. This is the pattern of the industry.
>
> Why this particular pattern? Why do the sales of new products start at a certain level, rise to a peak, and then level off? Does the answer lie in advertising? As a new product is launched, advertising builds to a peak and sales follow. When advertising levels off, sales level off, creating this pattern. This sounds logical, but it isn't so.

As Figure 21-2 shows, advertising does not always start at a low level and then build up. In this example, media spending started at a

Figure 21-2 Four ready-to-eat cereals—advertising expenditures

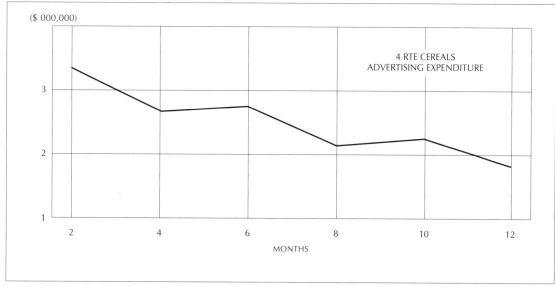

Source: A. C. Nielsen

very high level and then descended to a lower level: Advertising level and sales level are exactly contradictory!

> If it isn't advertising, then it must be consumer demand that causes our sales pattern. Demand builds up as the advertising becomes effective.

But Figure 21-3 shows that consumer demand starts at a peak and then levels off.

> Our illustration uses Nielsen figures showing sales per point of distribution. Our illustration shows that where these products were available, they moved almost twice as fast in the first period. Indexed at 100 percent, they show 189 percent the first two months. The products were moving off retail shelves at a rate almost twice as fast in the first two months as they did in the 12th. In other words, products were turning over faster *where they were stocked.*

> Consumer demand starts at a peak, advertising starts at a peak, then why do sales start low, rise, and then level off?

The only thing that correlates to the sales trend is effective distribution, as Figure 21-4 shows—"the gradual buildup of effective distribution from about 60 percent in the first two-month period to 88 percent at the end of the year."

Figure 21-3 Four ready-to-eat cereals—consumer demand

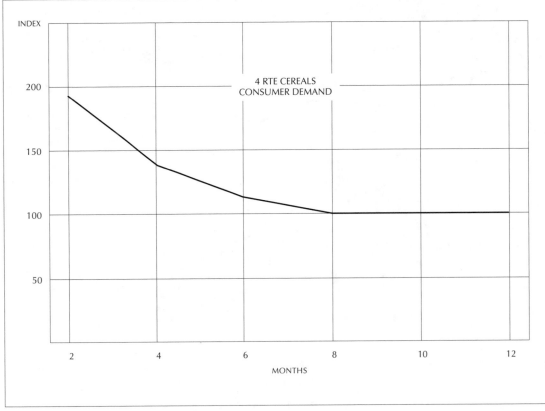

INDEX

4 RTE CEREALS
CONSUMER DEMAND

MONTHS

Source: A. C. Nielsen

Figure 21-5 suggests that:

We have produced a marketing model. As an industry, we are peaking advertising at the point where availability is lowest. We then let advertising—and demand—level off while availability rises. *In terms of profit, this model is very inefficient and really does not make sense.* [Author's italics]

What is needed is an improved model [see Figure 21-6], where availability is at its peak from the start. We don't mean 100 percent distribution—we are talking only about the distribution actually attained—in this specific case, 88 percent distribution at the end of the first year.

[Figure 21-7] shows the improved results. If we could alter the marketing model so that distribution/availability is at its peak from the beginning, a completely different sales picture emerges.

Figure 21-4 Four ready-to-eat cereals—effective distribution

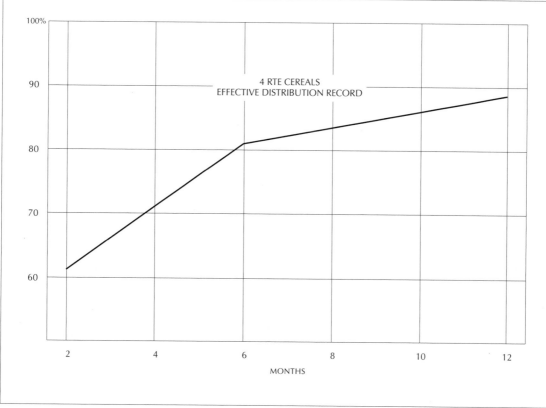

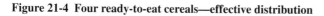

Source: A. C. Nielsen

The bottom line is the same line we showed in the first chart [Figure 21-1], the actual retail sales of the four ready-to-eat cereals. The top line shows what could have happened to those retail sales if distribution/availability was at its peak from the start. Actual sales were $54 million. Potential sales were $66 million . . . a difference of $12 million, or more than 20 percent. Filling this gap in sales required neither additional expenditure nor additional cost. The manufacturer has the same investment, the same sales costs, and the same advertising costs. The retailer has no increased distribution, except that stores that will ultimately carry the product have it when advertising breaks.

To test the hypothesis, Quaker Oats Company ran a similar tracking of six newly introduced semimoist dog foods from three major marketers, with the same general results.

Figure 21-5 Four ready-to-eat cereals—marketing model

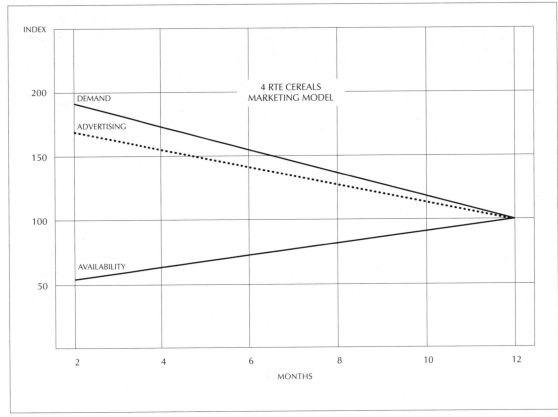

Source: A. C. Nielsen

The conclusion:

> These figures relate to consumer purchases and not man-
> ufacturers' shipments. The profits here relate more to the
> retailer than to the manufacturer because, in the new
> product explosion, a single manufacturer does not partic-
> ipate in the entire explosion. He participates only when
> he himself introduces a product and, for most manufac-
> turers, this is really quite seldom. A retailer, however, par-
> ticipates in all the new product introductions . . . in any
> given year, more than 10 percent of the business done in
> a retail store may be in new products.

Presumably, then, if the 20 percent loss of new product introduction
effectiveness is overcome, the 10 percent of business can produce a 2
percent increase in the total sales of the retailer.

Figure 21-6 Four ready-to-eat cereals—revised marketing model

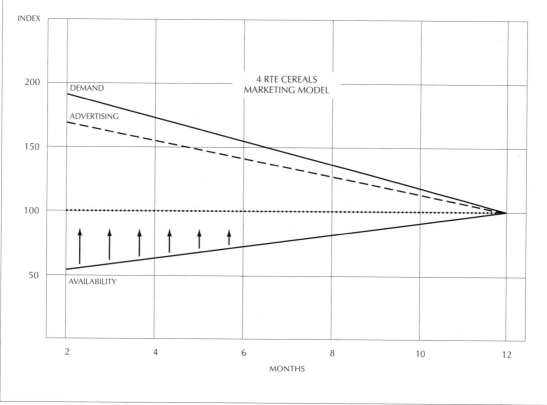

Source: A. C. Nielsen

The Quaker Oats Company concludes that by getting new products on the shelf at the height of introductory promotional efforts, both the manufacturer and the distributor can make more profits with the same investment.

To achieve this, the following is necessary, says Quaker:

1. A better job on the manufacturer's part in communicating with the retailer.

2. Coordinating new product introductions better and timing them so that the big advertising and promotional emphasis come when the retailer is ready with the product on his shelf—and . . .

3. A healthy respect on the part of the retailer for the tremendous extra profit potential that exists for him by working together and coordinating these new product introductions—to tie-in distribution with the manufacturer's efforts.

The Consumer

Even if all of this has been done right, nothing much will happen unless the ultimate consumer is served. The customer is always right—and serving that selfish interest is paramount.

To serve that consumer, the right assortment of merchandise has to be in the right place at the right time.

The advertising will direct the consumer's attention to the selfish interest the new product serves, whether it be reflected glory and status or a way to do a tough dirty job quicker, easier, and cleaner—or any of the many gradations between.

It will also tell the consumer about the special incentives being offered to encourage trial purchase. The deep price discounts, the high value coupons and bouncebacks, the free samples, the premium offers, and the contests will all be advertised and promoted.

The sales force, the trade headquarters, the retail store were all logistically easy to reach. They were fixed entities in known geographic locations with known sales potential. But the consumer—ah, that's different.

Figure 21-7 Four ready-to-eat cereals—retail sales projection

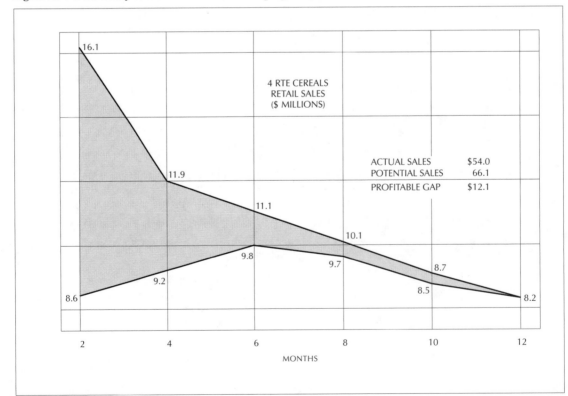

Source: A. C. Nielsen

Here's where skillful media and promotion planning can make or break the introduction. If the research backdrop for the launch has been done in terms that can be translated to the audience characteristics available in the census and zip codes, in media audits and guides, in the computer programs of the major advertising agencies—then efficient media planning can begin.

Media Planning Guidelines

Media planning involves targeting the audience, determining weight levels in terms of reach (coverage) and frequency, and timing. All of this translates into media efficiency: How well and at what cost is what percentage of the target reached at a goal frequency within a specified period?

The Numbers

All of that is programmable. If the target is numerically defined and located, media measures can be cranked in and the best use of any media daypart or combinations of dayparts can be computed and, given some fairly reliable assumptions, combinations of major media.

There are important qualitative considerations also, which are often overlooked.

Qualitative Considerations

During the birth of a new product—before it is known for itself alone—its close associates affect its perception. Therefore, editorial climate is important. This means that subjectivity enters into the selection of the specific publications and programs that will carry the advertising. In the case of spot broadcast advertising, program adjacencies are taken into consideration. Or, in the case of r.o.p. (run of press), newspaper section and editorial adjacencies are considered. In certain product categories, even the day of ad appearance becomes important (e.g., "best food day" for grocery products, aimed at the highest traffic periods, and weekends for major-ticket items where more than one member of the family may participate in the purchase decision).

The numbers are not the most important factor, although they are a reflection of the spending pattern.

Timing is critical. Heavy introductory weight designed to stimulate new product trial must not fall on deaf ears (wrong season, wrong day or daypart, wrong program or publication) or empty shelves (empty of the new product, because it either hasn't appeared yet or was understocked and is already sold out before the advertising begins).

There are space and time elements in media. How big should the ad be? How many colors? Should it have a pop-up coupon? Can we tell the story in 30 seconds? Does it need a full minute? Or is the budget so big and the product so sensational (yet easy to communicate) that 10-second announcements are needed also, to get into crowded time periods and to extend the frequency? What about cable and direct broadcast? Will they reach the target with greater efficiency?

Is continuity of media needed? Perhaps the new product has relatively flat seasonality and is frequently consumed. This may mean year-long advertising is necessary. After the big introductory blast, how much is left to carry that continuity? Can it be on an every day, every week, every month, every season basis? Are low levels spread across the calendar preferable to a flighted plan of clusters of advertising—or a blinking pattern of a week in and a week out? Will one time slot (or one type of publication) carry the target, or does the new product need several dayparts? Will a scatter plan across the board be most effective—or should roadblocks be used, to be certain that no matter what channel is turned on for the 6 o'clock news, the new product word will get across?

Targeting Directions

Media experts will know how to put the plan together. The new product marketing team, however, is responsible for precise targeting directions.

It is possible that one planning pattern is indicated for the introductory period—a media program that will reach all of the interested target segments—while a sustaining plan must of necessity concentrate only on those prime prospects in the center of the target. The introductory plan, in other words, reaches "Definitely" and "Probably" and "Might Buy." After the product is well established (perhaps a year or two later), the lower spending level sustaining pattern is best aimed at "Definitely," with media selections that will peripherally pick up bits of the wider target.

Sometimes a product has a dual audience. The user and the purchasing agent. Toys are an example. Toys for toddlers are advertised to mothers. Toys for older youngsters are advertised to user (purchase influencer), even though the purchaser may be a parent. Soft drinks, fast foods, and confections may be advertised across the board, with different creative approaches in different media and at different time periods aimed at different segments. A mammoth advertiser such as McDonald's, for example, has advertising creative and media tailored to kids, tweens, teens, and on up the segmentation of ages and life-styles. Sometimes there are shared experiences. All-family ready-to-eat cereals may be advertised to adults in one style and the same theme carried forward in another style in another time period to the high-volume kid consumer.

Bartered Media

Often, the heaviest investment in a product's life is at its inception—when it is not known how well it will perform against forecast. Entrepreneurs are especially eager to find media bargains while the cash flow is red, rather than black. Even huge marketers with awesome buying clout use barter. Some examples follow:

There are many ways to buy media beyond the negotiated deal. Barter buying is common. Barter means simply paying for media with merchandise (or services) instead of cash. There are four basic ways to use barter to buy media—all applicable to new product introductions.

1. Trade a new product directly to the media source you plan to use.

2. Trade out-of-date or discontinued products to purchase media to promote a new product.

3. Trade to acquire products or services that the media will accept in trade to promote a new product.

4. Purchase media at deep discounts from organizations who traded for media and want to liquidate it for cash.

To illustrate how barter is used to acquire media, with specific examples, Richard Rosenblatt was consulted. He founded the largest and oldest media barter company in the United States, Atwood Richard, the only media barter company ever listed on the New York Stock Exchange. Today, Rosenblatt heads the consulting firm, AdMedia International, Del Mar, CA 92014, which advises companies on how to introduce new products and services by trading for media.

Trading a new product directly for media is indicated when media will utilize the product itself or for audience-building promotions, and will not resell the bartered product back to the manufacturer's primary markets. The benefit of bartering for media with the new product, instead of purchasing it with money, is that the manufacturer lowers his cost for media to the difference between cost of goods and list price. Also, the product gains immediate publicity and gets distribution that speeds up market awareness without the added costs usually associated with a sampling campaign.

Example: When an imported newly developed sunbathing beauty aid line was acquired by makers of a leading upscale French perfume, a radio campaign was put together to introduce the new product. Stations needed large quantities of gifts to give away at Christmas. Holiday gift packets of the well-known fragrance and the sunbathing cream were traded in great quantity to stations across the country. The advertising time acquired was used the following spring to introduce the newly acquired sunbathing product.

Trading out-of-date or discontinued products to purchase media to promote a new product is advisable when a company has large inventories of good products no longer marketable through normal channels of distribution—yet the company doesn't wish to liquidate them at deep discount. The benefits of trading obsolete products for media to launch a new product into the market are decreased cost of advertising and less need to require restrictions and enforcement of disposition limitations on the media.

Example: Jeffrey Peterson, one of Rosenblatt's long-time associates and the managing director of AdMedia, tells of the time when the CD-ROM publishing division of a Fortune 500 media conglomerate approached him to find a way to get more than pennies on the dollar for the liquidation of discontinued and slow-moving titles. The CD-ROM inventory was evaluated and then separated into two categories: One group was traded to various barter exchanges throughout the United States that distributed the products to a closed membership base; the other group of products was traded to radio and television stations for advertising spots to be used for the promotion of the publisher's current product line. The CD-ROMs were used for joint-promotions with the station's cash advertisers and used as on-air giveaways to build station ratings.

The CD-ROM publisher and its parent company were able to utilize print and electronic advertising media; airline travel and hotel room nights; as well as packaging, printing, and warehousing services to satisfy line item expenses from their current-year budget. The inventory ultimately netted approximately 70 cents on the wholesale dollar.

Trading to acquire products or services that the media will accept in trade to promote a new product must be done when the product is not interesting to the media or when you don't want the product released except through normal channels. This two-step method of bartering develops more flexibility for the manufacturer.

Example: When two major Japanese automobile makers decided to introduce their cars to the U.S. market some years ago, Rosenblatt proposed that they pay for advertising media with the new cars. The problem was that they did not want the cars to show up in areas where they were arranging dealerships. Because they initially established dealership on the east and west coasts, he arranged a trade with a national car rental company that agreed to rent these cars only in the Midwest. The car rental credits were traded for media to advertise the cars on the east and west coasts.

Of course, barter isn't restricted to media trades only. An unsuccessful new product with a heavy inventory can be bartered for other services and merchandise. In fact, the largest players in the market are businesses trying to off-load surplus inventory, unproductive assets, or excess capacity, according to the International Reciprocal Trade Association, which reports in the November 16–17, 1996 *International Herald Tribune*: "Americans struck nearly $8.5 billion worth of deals in 1995 without a single dollar changing hands."

Television Syndication and Trading

Syndication in television involves programming traded or sold to local television stations in a number of markets or nationwide.

Syndication deals are constructed in many different ways, but three types are primarily of interest to new products marketers:

- Ad time in a syndicated program or series of programs can be purchased by the advertiser from the syndicator; i.e., wherever "Wheel of Fortune" runs across the country, the commercial would appear. If your product target fits well with specific program genre (talk or game shows, kids' programs, sports, etc.) this is an effective buying strategy, and may cost less than similar inventory purchased from one of the national networks.

- Syndication can involve combining cash and programming. A media buying agency can use traded programs in addition to an advertiser's budget to leverage additional commercial time for the advertiser. The cost of the programming is less than the value of the time, creating greater efficiency. (A leading media services group using this method is Cash Plus, Inc. of Minneapolis, MN.)

- An emerging strategy for marketers with larger introductory budgets is advertiser-produced programs traded in syndication. An advertiser, television producer, and media buyer/syndicator create a television program with content designed to enhance the selling context for the product. The program is then traded to stations, usually with an additional cash schedule, with the product commercials already in place. The marketer benefits by creating efficient media in an improved environment for its message. Cash Plus has very successfully executed this strategy for ConAgra's Healthy Choice brands, creating "A Healthy Challenge; The National Nutrition Test" for syndication on its client's behalf.

Syndication can involve greater lead times and less control of the geography and timing of the media, so these things should be discussed up-front. The benefits of efficiency and program environment can be quite significant.

The Role of Public Relations

You can only make a first impression once—often the most critical factor in success or failure.

For that reason, a higher priority must be given to marketing-integrated introductory public relations plans, execution, and tracking measurement.

PR gets high priority for damage control, as it should. More attention needs to be given to the role of positive PR at the inception of the life of a product, service, or program.

As Dr. A.J.F. O'Reilly, chairman, president, and CEO of H.J. Heinz, told the company's Global Communications Conference: "As part of the promotional mix of marketing, product PR has often suffered as the poor relation. Millions of dollars are spent on television advertising, but mere thousands are sometimes begrudged to PR."

Often it is the case during the introductory period that an especially innovative new product needs more communication than conventional paid media affords. Mere sound bites, 30-second interruptions, and page-dominating stoppers may not be enough to clarify the most important aspect of that first impression. PR can help a lot.

To help, it is necessary that PR practitioners play a part in planning the initial communications, defining the PR role, its timing, its link with all other communications themes, execution, media—the entire strategic execution.

Like advertising, PR can be pretested, at a much lower cost for stimulus materials in most instances. The information the PR message is to carry can also be predetermined, as can the key media elements: news releases, video demo-tapes, personal appearances by corporate executives (i.e., the auto company CEO), professionals (urologists explain the need for a highly personal need product, prior to network clearance of the advertising), expert practitioners (the cookbook author, the celebrity chef), the mass media entertainment personalities who endorse, etc. Local interview shows in test areas will happily turn their mikes and cameras on your product, if a *People* magazine personality has it in hand. They can give you their audience profiles in advance, so that you can do telephone checks on your message and its understanding, reception, and impact. Because this is a test, you can modify as you move along, market to market, prior to the total launch.

If your product is affiliated with a personality, a cartoon character, a publication feature, or a TV series, so much the better. Special arrangements may be made to localize these affiliations for testing, with captive audiences, as well as in local media only.

One aspect of PR is communications with influential bodies, such as government bureaucrats, as well as elected officials; with appropriate trade and professional associations; with any factors that may have a positive and/or negative influence on the reception of the new offering, whether it be an established lobbying group, a government body, the academic community, a nonprofit special-interest group, etc. This type of contact, this network of relations, this nonpaid media approach is often especially important when the new product requires different use patterns, components/ingredients not common to the category nor the trade class, a change in servicing needs, perhaps even a change in vocabulary.

As Dan Edelman, founder-chairman and CEO of Edelman Public Relations Worldwide, said in a speech to the Public Relations Institute of Australia in Sydney, there are many areas where PR may be more cost-efficient than advertising. His examples include:

1. There's a revolutionary, breakthrough type of product—one that can make news.

2. The company is new or small—there's little if any money available for advertising.

3. Television isn't available for regulatory reasons—for example, distilled spirits cannot advertise on U.S. television.

4. The environment is negative and has to be turned around quickly.

About cost-efficiency, Dan Edelman said: "We have to demonstrate measurability. We've made some progress in this area, but . . . we're going to do even better in this regard. We'll need more research before and after. We'll need to establish a scientific system that will be generally accepted that truly measures public relations results in marketing programs."

But don't wait.

Pump up your internal and outside-retained PR forces to be part of the new product marketing program, at the beginning—and as the product matures, with support for the total marketing program and its communications themes, with emphasis on nurturing the good image created at introduction, perhaps even allying it with a public-interest cause.

PR also can help pump in a continual aspect of newness over time, not only as improvements are made in the product, but in heralding new uses, new ways to use, and new combinations with other well-understood products and services.

Work on using PR to the benefit of new products at birth and throughout an ever-vital maturity. PR is an important part of the marketing arsenal—not only to make good first impressions, but to help ensure long-term loyalties with your users.

Effective Introductory Promotions

There are literally hundreds of promotion devices employed in the marketing life of any product. Generally, they are divisible into two areas—trade promotions and consumer promotions.

Trade Promotions

Trade promotions are designed to enlist trade cooperation in efforts to stimulate trial use of the new product. For consumer package goods products, off-invoice allowances and trade programs (displays, premiums, contests) are frequently employed.

The trade is often offered a per case payment for promotional support (e.g., display store ads, storecasts, hot feature pricing, etc.) for new orders placed during a specified period. These are used to sell-in the product, gain shelf facings, build inventory—to build trade support for an introductory consumer promotion.

- **Display allowances** pay for specific display performance only during the specified introductory period, generally while the new brand is being otherwise heavily promoted and advertised.

- **Buying allowances** grant a reduction in the list price of a product during the introductory period (within specified limitations). They are designed to obtain initial distribution, build trade inventories, and (if desired) reduce the inventory shelf price, increase trade support behind consumer promotion, and (occasionally) meet unexpected competitive threats.

Consumer Promotions

Immediate value promotions attract attention by lowering the price, adding value, or both. Examples of the former are "off-label packs" (with the cents-off offer flagged on the package); examples of the latter are in- or on-pack premiums (free FM tuner module with full-price cassette player). Established brands often use delayed value incentives that encourage the consumer to do something before being rewarded for purchasing the product. These are less effective (but less expensive) for an introduction seeking immediate trial impact.

A review of the most frequently used consumer promotion techniques indicates the following are most effective for new product introductions:

- **Off-label packs**
- **In- or on-pack premiums**
- **Coupon packs**

  Inexpensive distribution can be combined with an off-label pack to provide both trial and repeat incentive. There is little or no cost involved on either incentive until actual purchase.

- **Cross-ruffs**

  The established brand carries a sample and/or coupons for the new product; the new brand can reciprocate. Where targets are compatible and products noncompetitive, this can work well within a company's product array or with another company or industry association. For the established brand, it provides an additional incentive for retrial and early repeat; for the new product, it provides an accepted, established-value premium to loyal users of the established brand. It is workable both ways—or either way—to stimulate new product acceptance.

- **Mailed coupons**

  These packages can be zip-code targeted to the most susceptible prospects—thus cutting down waste distribution. The consumer makes the purchase decision at the mail receiving point (home/office) away from competitive influences. It is efficient in stimulating trial of new and low-share products. Costs are often spread among a number of noncompetitive participants in a single mailing. One drawback is that misredeemers and nonredeemers dilute the total effectiveness.

- **Product sampling**

  This technique is extremely expensive, difficult to police, and hard to control. It is best used for unique products, those with high repeat usage, or those in low unit-cost categories (example: street corner sampling of minipacks of new cigarette brands).

- **Media coupons**

Payout

There has been a tremendous expenditure to bring the new product this far. Now, it must pay off. How long will it be before it will pay out?

This differs in every case. It also differs by product category. In many consumer package goods categories, there are tried-and-nearly-always-true formulas. One is this: Year 1 New Product Introduction: Spend at *double* the Share Goal. In other words, if the year-end share goal or average Year 1 share is 20 percent of market, then media advertising spending should be 40 percent of the total media advertising in the category.

Here's how it works:

Market size:	$100,000,000	(factory dollars, not retail)
20% share goal:	20,000,000	
Total category Advertising Spending:	20,000,000	
Spend at 40% of total advertising:	8,000,000	

Assume Year 1 Sales:	$15,000,000	(reflecting retail movement)
	5,000,000	(year-end field inventory)

Total	$20,000,000	
Less:	8,000,000	for advertising
	4,000,000	for trade promotion
	6,000,000	for cost of goods
	1,000,000	for freight
	1,000,000	for advertising & promotion production, inventory

$20,000,000

This mythical Year 1 break-even, using the "double the category share-of-voice goal," is merely for illustration. Even for a product with 30 percent cost-of-goods, it is unlikely.

However, as can be seen in Figure 21-8, it is worth it—for a successful new product. The life-cycle concept, espoused by the management consultant firm of Booz Allen & Hamilton for 30 years, illustrates that new products are essential to the life of any marketer. It illustrates that like humans, products go through cycles—some with more revivals than others. Sales volume grows faster than profit margins, with absolute profits lagging behind the margins—but with an important dollar profit return growth during the maturity/saturation periods. This chart is based on the average of studies of 700 companies and 13,311 new product introductions. It recognizes the investment spending necessary to get a new product going, as well as the importance of doing that.

There is no absolute in approaching what must be invested, how fast it must pay out or what incremental volume it must add. It depends on many factors. Figure 21-8, it should be stated, represents new products of several definitions: Only 10 percent are new to the world, while 19 percent were new only to the organization. The remaining 71 percent were all changes within current product lines—much less costly to develop, introduce, and manage over time. These were additions to existing product lines, revisions or improvements, cost reductions, and repositionings. Their lesser cost helped pull down the total new products investment percentage per company. In other words, not only the mature products but the close-in line extension, flankers, and repositionings

Figure 21-8 Basic life cycle of products

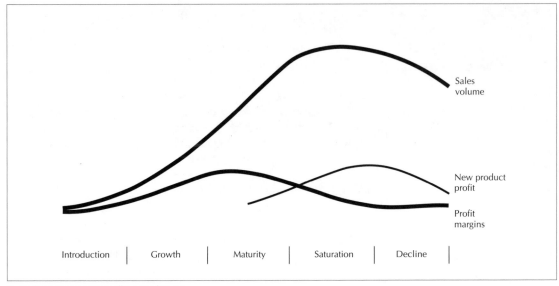

Source: By permission, (c) Booz Allen & Hamilton, Inc.

helped carry the company while it funded the investment in the dynamics of establishing truly new products.

This underlines the fact that every vital organization needs a program of new products, ranging from the easy-to-execute and none-too-risky line development items all across the board to innovations and inventions. It is this balance that will keep the new product flow going, at the same time making it all affordable by keeping the company profit dynamics in tune. Watch the individual payout, of course—but the payoff is at the corporate level, which benefits by the total effect of a skillfully managed new product development and marketing program.

Section 6

Summary Afterword

Once the product is ready, we enter upon the marketing phase. This involves planning, simulation, and selection of the test markets; determining the new product communications; and measuring the promotion payout.

Building a "Fact Book" is essential in planning. After determining the meaning of all the assembled facts, an executive summary should be prepared to provide needed perspective. This indicates where the opportunity gaps are to be found and what information sources might be used—intelligence consulting, reverse engineering, making use of the Freedom of Information Act.

Then comes the actual planning process. Here is where to consider the importance of being first, the possibility of testing while launching on a wide scale, and the importance of contingency planning.

In moving on to the actual selection of test markets, various candidates may be considered and rejected before lighting on the most suitable for the new product. There is also the possibility of simulating simulations by going into isolated and controlled micromarkets (extremely small test markets).

The product then is ready to move into test market. Now we must communicate its presence. Any number of factors enter into product communications, not the least of which is the product itself. Its personality should be established at birth, assuring newness and that the product is both better and different.

Then come all the other factors of communications: product performance; its names, both brand and generic; its package—the construction and graphics; the price—what it communicates about the product image; product display, both on the shelf and at home; and advertising.

The advertising, of course, is perhaps the most elaborate part of product communications. It is derived out of the business communication goal; the category target (and if different, the new product target); the communication of the product's most important benefit—both different and better; and the establishment of an image, equity, character, or personality that will be sustained over time in all communications.

Now you are ready to tell the world about your new baby. Keep in mind that this involves due regard to all the selfish interests involved—the company sales force, the headquarters distributor, the retailer, and the consumer.

Media planning guidelines should go beyond the numbers and include qualitative considerations. While the media experts can draw up the media specifics, it is up to the product manager to determine the targeting directions. Not to be overlooked are the possibilities of using bartered media and syndication trading.

Effective introductory promotions encompass both the trade and the consumer. Trade promotions include rewards for retail purchase performance, display allowances, and buying allowances. Major consumer promotion techniques include off-label packs, in- and on-pack premiums, coupon packs, cross ruffs, mailed coupons, product sampling, and media coupons. Introductory preview public relations programs aimed at both trade media and consumer-targeted and mass media enhance the impact of the paid media.

If all is handled right, the payout—and payoff—will extend over the product life cycle. The key is the development of a balanced new product program, taking into account the full range of risks.

MARKET TESTING

Section
7

22

Start and Monitor

The marketing plan has been approved.

The product is feasible. Scale-up tests confirm the costs. On-stream plant production yields the same product quality as laboratory or engineering prototypes and the pilot plant runs. Quality control guidelines are confirmed.

The test markets have been selected to simulate conditions of a successful later major launch.

The new product is about to be born. . . .

Born into the real world—not an incubator.

That controlled environment with extra-special attention is hard to resist. Everyone wants to do everything possible to see that the newborn is a success. The president flies into the markets and makes a few suggestions on how to improve matters. The general sales manager drops in at the district sales office to give an extra pep talk. Product managers swarm over the market, measuring, counting, photographing, computing. The advertising agency massages the local media—maybe even the program and editorial folks.

That's not how to give birth to a new product. If there's to be a silver spoon in its mouth, don't force-feed it in—let the prospect discover it.

Getting off the Ground

Certainly, the sales force should receive just as enthusiastic an introduction as will be made if the product successfully expands its marketing area.

If there is a national sales meeting planned prior to launch, then this should be simulated also—at headquarters if possible.

The more the sales force knows about the careful targeting, product benefits, and superiorities vs. competition, about forecasted sales success based on controlled test or simulated model projections, about share-of-voice vs. market share goals—the more the sales force knows, the better. It will help them communicate that enthusiasm to their customers.

But make it easy for them. Provide visual aids: catalog sheets, videotapes of commercials, ad proofs, advertising and promotion schedules, demonstration guides, selling samples, and whatever else is necessary to tell the story quickly and effectively. Be sure the salespeople know all about the total market, its progress, competitive moves and positions—literally everything a sharp prospect may know or question.

If there is a national press conference planned for the eventual expansion, then a mini–local press conference should be held in each test market. Invite the press, the trade, the sales force, and have a (quotable) headquarters executive make a few remarks and respond to questions.

Programmed Introductory Goals

Every plan should have market penetration goals. For mass-marketed retail-distributed products, this goal is usually a percent of distribution per size, per item—often with a shelf position and share of shelf target. There is trade acceptance, which is one positive level. There is actual appearance at retail, which is the more critical level. Products don't sell to consumers out of wholesale warehouses. They must be accessible.

Coping with the Slow Start

Where possible, advertising and promotion start dates should be keyed to the achievement of a certain percentage of availability to the consumer. If there is likely to be genuine difficulty in meeting the minimum distribution goal in time for the introduction, then the introduction should either be delayed or a plan to "feather" in a lead schedule of advertising/promotion before major weight is added should be prearranged with the trade and the media. Go for all of the flexibility possible on a national program. (Here the term "national" is used to represent the maximum expansion area, presumed to be significantly larger than the test market area.)

Coping with the Fast Start

Be certain there is adequate stock in the market—and in back of the initial shipments. It is very difficult to "read" the dimensions of a success if it is characterized by out-of-stock empty shelves. The business goes elsewhere. Important opportunities have been lost, at a time when the "newness" is most attractive.

It is even possible that if the new product appears to be a really hot item, the trade may jump the planned start date. One trade factor may hit the market long before your planned advertising introduction, possibly putting the product in the retailers' own ads at a "hot" feature price. This tips the competitive trade factors, who may follow suit.

This is the reason to have plenty of merchandise on hand to ship— or, better yet, in nearby warehouses. This is also the reason to have a flexible advertising plan, one that will allow for an earlier-than-planned introductory launch, with a shift of media scheduling at a moment's notice. The sales force should be alerted to these possibilities. Although an effort should be made to start everything off on the planned date, flexible programs to deal with early starts as well as slow starts should be in hand—and communicated to the sales force.

In those instances where a trade factor jumps the gun out of enthusiasm for the product, the trade deal, etc.—and many other trade factors are still hanging back—there is an opportunity for the sales force to use the renegade gate jumper as leverage to bring in the other slowly reacting factors fast. If they do, the sales department can promise earlier, stepped-up efforts—flexible devices such as an overlay of an early coupon drop on top of the introductory trade deal, a stepped-up cooperative payment for exceptional store advertising and mass displays.

Paired Market Sets

Often, test markets are paired—the combination being judged to provide a demographic mix more representative than either individually. Sometimes there are several pairs. One pairing of two-market sets may be designed to measure price differential, another pairing may be designed to measure spending level differentials, another to measure different creative strategies.

When part of a set behaves differently from the other part—such as one jumping the gun and another being laggard in gaining distribution—the difficulties in interpretation fall into the arena of subjective judgment, with a range of possible projections.

One such experience occurred with the test marketing of a famous beauty soap. The low-level spending market outperformed the high-level spending market. Distribution was gained much faster in the low-level market, although spending against thinning distribution was outshouting its competition at a greater clip.

Because test markets are leaning experiences, however, the manufacturer reasoned that if the product could sell so well at the lower level, it should perform even better at the higher level if factors were equalized. The product was left in both markets, the advertising adjusted up in one market and leveled-off in the original high-level market. Pragmatic reasoning rules. Projections were relative only to in-market performance. However, a pool of triers and repeaters was developed and studied thoroughly.

From these studies, the package design was revised, the color of the bar changed, the advertising execution refined (while maintaining the successful strategy). Then, the product rolled out to a successful national introduction. It was more of a risk than if the paired test had been one that behaved according to plan—but less of a risk than if the product was retested while competition gained the additional time. The many important areas of refinement made possible by the dislocated test market pairing had enhanced the new product's successful launch.

Premature Success

First, there is the excitement of commercialization and the test market launch. Then there is the "it's too early to read" period. Then the numbers start coming in. If they are right on target—or better—chances are conversation begins to suggest plans to abort the test early while the expansion commitments are advanced in time.

Another popular suggestion is an expansion from the test areas—to roll-out into divisions and regions from districts.

There's nothing wrong with enthusiasm.

But if the planning stage was handled correctly, these exigencies were anticipated. There is a plan in place that triggers action under the best and worst circumstances. Under most circumstances, it is advisable to move up the capital clearances in preparation for a rapid expansion—while remaining cautiously watchful until sufficient multiple repeat purchase has been measured—and competition comes out of the woods.

Early Failure

So, the numbers are not so good. The crepe begins to hang.

Now's the time to use a test market for all it is worth. Unless the failure can clearly be traced to bad product—the food turns rancid because of a poor package seal, the machine falters because of a poor component or an assembly goof—or unless the apparent failure is clearly caused by some other readily identifiable circumstances—find out why the flop.

This can require a great deal more searching study than originally planned. The start-up went according to plan—but the take-off never occurred. No need to be terribly concerned about giving the market a little extra attention now. Question every channel of the trade. Question more users in more depth more often and in both qualitative and quantifiable modes.

Often, it is a little thing—overlooked, perhaps. Sometimes the little thing is a last-minute "improvement." Sometimes the little thing is an adjustment made necessary when scaling-up from prototypes, an adjustment not thought significant at the time: a different closure on the package, a change in typeface to fit a slightly different dimension, a confusing promotion added to the package back, a change from a simple declarative description of the product to more esoteric or industrially sophisticated language. Tear down the differences between what is going on in the market and what was originally designed and planned. Do "reverse engineering" on the faltering new product entrant.

The inexplicable failure is very rare.

In the face of failure, there are many experts willing to point fingers. Listen. Test every reasonable hypothesis. When the fault or combination of faults is found, determine if it is worth fixing. If so, fix—and move ahead, to a new set of markets if the fixing or the faults indicate this. Then, erect fail-safe procedures to prevent recurrence of such events.

So-So Introduction

Well, it's not a barn burner—but it is still smoldering. It's not bad enough to abort—and it's not good enough to move ahead.

This is a much tougher decision point than the out-and-out flop or the runaway success.

Still, it is "only" the *introduction* of the new product that is a disappointment—not the test.

Patience—and some tinkering, perhaps—is required.

Go after it like the flop—but try to find the flickering spark that is giving it early life as well as the smothering factors that keep it from bursting into flame.

Sometimes the product is just fine. It is only that the proud parents were overly ambitious. A scaled-back program may still sustain the new product with sufficient velocity to justify its existence—and to sustain a profit within a reasonable payout period. Too much has gone into the development of the new product to give up too early.

And remember, this is only the beginning.

As the new product continues to live in various degrees of success, plans change. They're remade as a result of the test market introduction knowledge, now providing new insights to the monitoring of sales progress and expansion plans.

23

Assess and Expand

The higher you peak, the higher you level. That's been almost axiomatic in assessment of test market experience. That's why heavy promotional efforts, front-loaded media plans, and intensive sales training and motivation go into those early efforts. The communications assault means more when it is "new news" rather than the same old story.

Understand the Plan

Another old axiom is "plan your work, work your plan." Although there if often a temptation to improve on the plan, be careful. Sometimes the goal is achieved, and the input appears to indicate that the horizons might be even broader—so the expansion is modified based on a subjective interpretation of the implications of the findings (rather than the findings themselves).

Because a test market is a learning experience, modifications nearly always *should* be made in the expansion plan. However, care should be exercised to control those brilliant insights based on wishful thinking—rather than on tested performance.

As an example, some years ago, a major personal products company developed an extremely refreshing antiseptic toothpaste, with a flavor so powerful that it almost stung the tongue—and lingered on many minutes after rinsing. The hypothesis was that such a dentifrice would not only be hygienic—but the user would be able to "feel" the cleanliness. A realistic share-of-market goal was set for the aggressively flavored paste, which had proven to have an intense liking score among a hard core of triers prior to the market test.

The test was a success. The market share goal was achieved. Although the average repeat scores were relatively low, they were extremely high among a significant but small segment. The product quickly built up a very strong brand loyalty among users who could sustain the share goal on an ongoing basis.

Then, middle management changed.

The new marketing director read the findings differently than the planners and operators of the test. Whereas the premise had been to build a significant business on the special properties of the intense-tasting toothpaste, the newly assigned executive looked at the huge percentage of triers who had rejected the product because of the extremely aggressive flavor. "Yes, we have a success," he reasoned, "but look at how much more business we could have if we just reduced the flavor intensity to make it more broadly acceptable."

This was done. Advertising strategy was switched to "a pleasantly refreshing dentifrice"—away from the former "shockingly clean feeling" approach. An expanded regional market roll was begun, with higher share goals.

Of course, the result was a new product failure. Although more triers found the product acceptable, they did not find it sufficiently different from their regular brand to make a firmly committed repeat switch. The product was insufficiently differentiated and became just another new brand with generally parity proprieties.

"Don't fix it, if it ain't broke" is the lesson to be learned here.

Assessment Steps

Too often marketers read the numbers—but do not talk to the customers.

Of course, pre- and post-awareness checks should be made. Sufficiently large samples of telephone checks of either the target market or the general population, depending on the nature of the new product, should be executed. The premeasure gives a level of competitive product awareness (which can be related to their share-of-voice media spending and longevity in the market) and, surprisingly, sometimes finds a level of awareness for the as-yet-to-be-introduced brand—which relates to historic reasons (other similar names used in past) or other circumstances. At any rate, these levels of unaided and aided awareness of brand and generic classification become the basis for periodic postintroduction measures that will be tracked in relationship to marketing spending, competitive activity, and time.

Too often, the communications value of a sales presence is overlooked. In markets that are paired in all respects except retail shelf visibility, it is not surprising to find that awareness is higher in the market with strongest distribution and display. Marketers sometimes forget that there is the potential for huge numbers of impressions on the shelf—because it is the reach (coverage) and frequency of media and promotional devices that are usually related to sales performance.

Measuring Awareness

Experienced marketers have awareness goals to achieve at various stages in the development of the test market. As these are reached, exceeded, or underachieved, analysis of the causes may create the need for fine-tuning some aspect of the program. Such changes should always be projectable to the national plan's payout plan.

Meeting Competitive Moves

In some rare instances, of course, where special local competitive efforts are mounted, a marketer may decide to sacrifice the projectability of the test market in order to make abnormal counter moves to blunt the competitors' further interest and their ability to read their effect on the test.

The trade-off for this type of tactic is rarely advantageous in the long run. Better to find out how well the planned program can stand up to out-of-scale competitive moves, meanwhile measuring and projecting the competitive activity to determine if it is in fact a program that could be mounted against the new product on a major geographic scale.

Meaning of Awareness

Behind awareness are perceptions. A broad-scale telephone survey can ask how the brand is evaluated, based on awareness—and relate this to whether the awareness is unaided or aided, and whether the respondent is a trier, trier-rejector, trier-repeater, or considering trial. In each case, the rationale for the mode is reported. The ability to play back advertising is key. Is the playback related to the advertising's creative strategy, its central theme—or to something peripheral such as executional elements that may assume greater importance than the promise of the new product itself? This measure may be related to buyer attitude and trial.

Point-of-Sale Audits

While sales from the order sheets and withdrawals from the shipping department and warehouses are measured, actual shelf momentum (in retail goods terms) is the best indicator of whether stock backups or out-of-stocks are problems ahead. These shelf audits may be conducted on an actual count basis, using special detail services, syndicated research, service of some retail chains employing universal product code measures, etc. In fast-moving categories, even cursory but periodic visual checks of a sampling of key retailers can often spot the trends. The technique, in other words, should fit the circumstances. In any event, it is important to audit the activity at the point of final sale—not just at the point of factory sales.

Talking to the Customer

Until now, consumer reaction to the product has either been achieved in a controlled or laboratory situation during the early phases of product development—or has been the result of structured telephone (or, possibly, mail) interviews. In some instances, interactive cable television may have been employed.

During communications development, it is likely that focus groups and/or one-on-one intercept point-of-purchase interviews and/or carefully designed and guided individual interviews in depth had taken place and provided guidance.

Now, buying is taking place under real circumstances—off the shelf, in response to an offer made in person by a salesman, a commercial, an ad, or a mailer. Now is the time to again talk to a buyer, a user and—in many product categories—a potential repeat prospect.

As early as planned awareness has reached a substantial level, respondents should be sought for person-to-person discussion of the product reception and rejection, use-experience where applicable, elements of the paid (as applicable) editorial, and word-of-mouth characterizations. Depending on the product category, these may be conducted in the office, in the factory, in the home, through mall intercepts, or in central location groups.

Just as the point-of-purchase audit is an important indicator, so too is the prospect/consumer audit. Often, the predictability of the test progress is signalled at this juncture.

Talking to the Sales Channels

If the product moves through one or several channels before reaching the ultimate user—which is always the case except in certain direct response situations—then interviews should be conducted at each level in the process: sales force, wholesaler, distributor, broker, shelf detailer, chain buyer, merchandise manager, store manager, store department head, purchasing agent, etc., as applicable. Don't miss an element in the marketing chain!

Periodic Repeat Research

The factory-to-user research we have just described should be repeated at various points in the test market's development. Early wear-out of the message—or of the product's reception—can be spotted before either may be reflected in sales figures. Opportunity for modification of both, with clear direction, may result from the program of repeated research.

Occasionally, opportunities for product accessories, feature deletions or additions, line extension, flankers, and peripheral product opportunities are suggested as the new product gains market acceptance and user familiarity. This test market study process then may become a staging area for expansion of the opportunity as originally conceived.

This type of study has also led to revisions in pricing strategies, restructuring of trade deals, reengineering of package structure, resizing (size-ups, size-downs, multipacks, etc.), retiming of marketing spending, rebalancing of the media mix, etc.

The history of new product test markets is such that rarely is there a repeat opportunity to gather this information prior to major capital expenditure and market investment if the product achieves the test goals and is subsequently launched in a major way. Therefore, make the most of this one-time opportunity!

Market Checking

Make sure the travel department knows of every test market. When booking trips, the department can furnish a supply of appropriate store check questionnaires with a simple letter of instruction to each traveler. The request is simple:

> If you can find the time on your trip to (city names), please stop at as many (class of trade) stores as possible, and note the information needed in spaces provided. Route completed Store Check forms to the travel department for distribution. Thank you—you are helping us keep track of (name of category and key brands) progress.

The Fast Way

Ingenuity can sometimes save time, save money, and make a better record.

One time, the author had to cover three widely separated test markets in the same day. By commercial airline, it would have taken several overnight stays and hotel charges.

Solution: Charter a plan. Arrange in advance for each airport to have a rental car handy, complete with map and route list. Take along a camcorder. Start early in the morning, ring each city to hit suburban shopping centers, with one drive through the city center on the way back to the airport.

At each stop, photograph identifying locator—name of shopping mall on sign or, if not appropriate, street sign at crossing. Photograph signage over store entrance, photograph line-up of checkout counters (by counting the cash registers, you can estimate store volume), photograph appropriate store sections and displays. Zoom cameras in on price marking, special promotions, etc.

If the city is unfamiliar to business associates, take the opportunity to add highlight shots that provide a characteristic feeling of the neighborhoods surrounding the stores checked. When entering each store, be sure to tell the manager or assistant the purpose of your visit, so he will not become alarmed by on-scene photography. Secure his authorization.

Managing the Expansion

Early success indications have triggered activities back at the home office. Clearance has been obtained for scale-up to expansion, with various dates keyed for additional funding should indicated objectives be achieved according to program.

Although the expansion area has been predetermined prior to market testing, it should be reevaluated in light of the knowledge input from the test area. Whereas it was originally planned to expand into the area with the highest consumption of the product category, the test area results may indicate the opposite—that the best initial opportunity will be in areas where the category is not as well developed and where the new product offers a distinctiveness and advantages particularly appealing to category sub-par prospect groups. It may be learned that the major competitive thorn in the test area is a product line with unanticipated advantages in the planned rollout area. Regional economic factors may have changed since the major introductory plan was approved months or years earlier. Perhaps even the original assessment that the new product might "cannibalize" (steal sales) from similar products in the company's own line turns out to be just the opposite—if anything, it enhances the appeal of all elements of the line. This also can indicate a change in territorial expansion.

Outside Effects Affect the Plan

During the course of the test market, a major competitive new product may have been introduced nationally or into a major geographic area. This can alter plans, triggering a national launch rather than the rollout plans, a complementary regional pattern launch (filling in those areas of presumed rollout by the competitor), or a head-to-head launch in the competitive region.

The company's test market does not operate in a vacuum. The expansion plan should have been made with anticipatory directions understood given those happenstances that are possible to predict. Production planning and parts/material sourcing must be alerted as soon as any such changes become a possibility—even if the indicators come very late in the test program. The new product development team works closely together monitoring the environment—reassessing implications to the approved plan, securing alterations to the plan on an as-needed basis, but always with clear bottom-line performance objectives. Avoid the swashbuckling attitude: "We'll meet the situations as they come along, then adjust our payout after we ride out the rough waters." Success doesn't mean just to win, success means to win with a profit.

Merchandising the Expansion

The test market success should be packaged in a dramatic way, to turn on the enthusiasm of the sales force and the trade. Now there are hard facts—share of market, trial and repeat, profit performance for all distribution and sales channels, competitive steal, category expansion, realignment of the trade assortment, and space allocations. Quotas can be set for sales, with bonuses tied to achievement of goals clearly linked to realistic sales levels.

Trade advertising should feature the success as its major appeal—to encourage broad and deep product stocking while the deals are rich and while the introductory opportunity is most timely. Proven profit results, based on test performance, and the heavy consumer impressions plan, underscores that fact that the trade's opportunity is *now*.

Be liberal with trade samples, professional detailing, or demonstration trials (as applicable). For consumable products, consider sales seminars or introductory trade sessions and sample mailings or personal deliveries to the homes or offices of selling agents, whether they be retailers, service dealers, or any agent between company's sales force and the ultimate consumer. (First, be certain this is not in violation of any corporate, dealer body, or trade policy or custom.)

Here's an intriguing example. A major grocery chain has a policy forbidding its buyers to attend any vendor event where competitive chain buyers are present. One new product marketer complied by inviting the *wives* of every chain buyer—along with a guest of her choice in each instance—to a spectacular fashion showing and luncheon with a famous designer to help introduce its new personal care product. The invitation to the buyer's wife went to her home with a liberal assortment of samples of the product line, along with an autographed design from the famous guest she would meet at the chic hotel grand ballroom showings, which were conducted on a region-by-region basis. Being able to bring a friend along encouraged maximum attendance by the buyers' wives—100 percent of the trade factor wives were represented. Each received another gift favor at the upbeat, sophisticated luncheon, met the famous designer, and was introduced to the dramatic new product line—and shown how to use it for best results. Evidently, each went home to her buyer husband with a great deal of enthusiasm. There was 100 percent distribution acceptance.

Hard-to-Read Results

Successes and failures are usually easy to recognize.

It is the in-betweens that baffle and chew up corporate innards, fiscally and physically.

Here is where marketing research makes its greatest contribution. It isolates the reason for the so-so reception. Only usually it is reason*s*.

Therefore don't skimp on marketing research during any phase of development. Monitor everything. Talk to buyers, nonbuyers, repeaters, nonrepeaters, multiple-repeaters, single repeaters, heavy users, light users—and likewise to consumers of competitive products. Be aware that competitive products may not be in the industry category, same store section, or even the same store . . . or any store. If another product fills the same void, it is a competitor—even if you initially perceive it as not a part of your market. It competes against you for time, energy, and money—and it fulfills the same craving.

Don't skip the trade. Check the extent and time of distribution development. Check merchandisers, store managers, and, maybe most importantly, the stock clerks. Do store checks independently—not with the company salesman (clear this with the sales department). Have everyone use the same store check forms, dictating devices, or camera techniques. Do not alert store detailers in advance of your calls.

Don't skip the product. Buy a little here and there on each trip. Examine it. Try it. Record the code.

Be aware of special local situations—economic, social, weather, etc.

Sort all of this out. The answer is usually to be found, and often correctable. Sometimes it is so easily rectified that the company can expand the product from an apparent failure. Oftentimes, it is back to the drawing board for revisions and retesting. There must have been good reason to get this far, so there is often good reason to try to keep the project alive. If there is clearly no hope, the sooner the project is terminated, the better for all concerned.

Where Do You Go from Here?

The test market has measured the new product's vitality under actual market conditions, conducted to maximize economy while limiting risk and gaining knowledge. Usually several high-quality, geographically dispersed, all-media markets are used. The market performance is a measure of trade and customer acceptance.

Now the test has been analyzed and projected to success, perhaps with significant improvement modifications. Every aspect of the test has been examined, analyzed, and pumped into the process of perfecting the expansion plan.

Finally the new product is launched in its major marketing area. Big dollars, careers, and corporate fortunes are on the line.

Hopefully you've quickly rolled out with a success, filed a failure, or diagnosed an in-between. Summarize the knowledge gained for the record, and then move on to another project—so much the wiser.

Section 7 Summary Afterword

The marketing plan has been approved. The product is feasible. Scale-up confirms production costs. Plant production replicates the prototype quality. Quality control guidelines have been confirmed.

Market entry has been approved.

Caution: Don't overmanage.

While it is tempting to give the new entry every help possible, it is important that the market test mirror as much as possible the broad-scale rollout. While all potential selling tools—including sales meetings and press conferences—should be utilized, the national marketing plan should be translated as closely as possible to the test market.

The plan should incorporate contingency arrangements to deal with coping with a slow start, coping with a fast start, coping with competitive actions designed to confuse test results, what to do when paired market sets don't stay controlled pairs, premature success reaction, and early failures. Moreover, it should also make allowance for what to do in the case of a so-so introduction—when the product is neither an obvious success nor a failure.

The introductory period then leads to . . .

Assessment and expansion. Most important here is to know the plan and stick to it. This is where research comes into play, to distinguish facts from insights. Assessment steps include pre- and post-awareness checks, meeting competitive moves, point-of-sale audits, talking to the customer, and talking to the sales channels. And don't stop there. Periodic repeat research should be conducted throughout the life of the product to keep it fresh and on target.

The product is ready to go into full-scale expansion. Outside effects should be monitored to assess how they affect the plan. Then the expansion should be merchandised for all it is worth. Make the improvement modifications that are necessary—then go into the full-scale launch!

MAJOR
INTRODUCTION

Section
8

24

And Now What?

"*Some of the most significant new ideas in science involve the recognition of new problems.*"

—LINUS PAULING

In business, also, problems are among the best sources of opportunities.

So—now what?

Every new product encounters a stream of problems—and imparts a stream of knowledge that is capable of yielding both solutions and opportunities.

Comprehensive Marketing Plan

After the test marketing has been successfully completed and the major launch has been effectively executed, where do you go from here?

A comprehensive new product marketing plan looks beyond the introductory period.

1. **Revised P&L**

   The marketing plan should provide the expansion with a projectable P&L, realistically adjusted from the test simulation forecast to the pragmatic realities of change in operation at the actual time of broad-scale launch.

2. **Long-Range Communications Program**

   The plan nails down the communications platform on which to build the brand personality over time.

3. **Product and Resource Proliferation**

The plan recommends close-in product proliferation opportunities. As part of this, it should also suggest extensions of any new (to the company) technologies employed, both as applied to the new product and as a basis for other product improvements or new entries. The same goes for new distribution channels, sales force operations, warehouse locations, etc., added by the nature of the new product. Any one may become an important new avenue for a host of new sales opportunities.

There needs to be a continual program to feed a succession of adjacent new products into the system, be they resizing, repackaging, line extensions, flankers, new segmentation (upscale, downscale), new brands, etc.

Beyond this, there are other, perhaps less obvious, essentials to sound new products direction.

4. **The Refreshment Program**

A complete program includes a plan to keep the product offering forever new, a planned program of refreshment that (at the very least) will keep the product "newsy" or "newsworthy."

The aim is to avoid the typical bell curve of rising fortunes, maturity, and gradual demise. While countless new products do not live to a ripe old age, others evade the fortunes of the average and greet each new generation of prospective customers with a new face, a trusted, familiar, well-established name, and an integrated personality. Regular, programmed "face-lifts" help keep the offering fresh and appealing.

5. **Timely Changes**

On the other hand, it is likely that those most familiar with the product will tire of it first. That's what happens to many a manufacturer. All it takes to stir this up are a few soft sales periods.

Chances are the consumer is just beginning to become acquainted—or, having become acquainted, is just beginning to place the recently introduced new product in his or her repertoire of acceptable products.

How do you guard against premature refreshment—or, worse yet, destruction of a carefully crafted marketing communication concept?

In a large expansion region, a company cannot read the nuances of marketing dynamics as intensely as in test markets. Knowing this, resist the temptation (often, the standard operating procedure) to abort the test market measurements when the regional rollout is committed. Keep those test markets going. Already, they are months or years more mature than the introductory area. They have a history of product performance. They offer benchmarks.

While the new product is in Year 1 nationally, it is entering Year 2 in the test areas. Manage the test areas to simulate Year 2 as closely as possible. Modify the national marketing weight going into those areas as well as can be done, with network cut-ins and plate changes in publications—substitute other company products, promotions, etc.

If this is not practical or practicable, then make statistical adjustments. The worst that will happen is that the marketing effort will be overstated in test areas, if national Year 2 is planned as a step-down.

In that instance, test markets represent an exaggerated exposure to communications—and should flag early wear-out or (conversely) signal the important brand-building longevity of the creative executions that helped propel the successful test in the first place. Using test markets as a lead laboratory for the future of expansion areas will often save a marketer from hasty, less-well-researched changes that may bring the offering to an early demise— rather than position it for vital refreshment as it moves along a long life of achievement.

6. **Overall New Product Posture**

While particular new business entities are being nurtured, the company's overall program of development must be frequently assessed. This reevaluation looks at the long-range planning cycle and modes, at the definition of the corporate charter, and at all the other elements attendant to the business, regulatory, social, and scientific environmental changes.

7. **Process Surveillance**

Constant surveillance of the new product process, as appropriate to the company, staff, and organization, is also necessary—with appreciation of a possible need to change one or all of these components of the pattern.

Maintaining the Entrepreneurial Spirit

Commenting on the need for reexamination 16 years ago, management consultant John G. Main wrote in *Point of View*, published by Spencer Stuart & Associates:

> Innovation is a process in which flexibility, imagination, curiosity, intuition, and a large dash of freedom are essential. Managing that process calls for a creative interaction with those elements. And the highly structured, systems-oriented environments in many of today's large corporations are typically neither receptive to nor geared up for that kind of commitment.
>
> Fortunately, there are exceptions—a growing number of companies that are pursuing organizational options aimed at generating a flow of new ideas and new technologies.

Many experts hold that once a company has passed beyond its own entrepreneurial phase of development, it's next to impossible to encourage or to pursue innovation. Main writes:

> As a corporation grows larger, it tends to become more set in its ways, conservative in its fiscal thinking, and increasingly dependent on rigid systems and controls. All of this runs counter to the free-wheeling, entrepreneurial setting in which breakthroughs flourish.

Those companies that most effectively maintain the entrepreneurial spirit while leveraging the resources of the corporation employ one or more of the techniques covered in this book, including *Specially assigned new product managers*, who take over at an early stage; *internal entrepreneurial project teams; corporate venture groups; spin-offs*, which take products from one usage area into another; *cooperative agreements*, which combine the strengths of two companies, one perhaps technologically-intensive while another is marketing-intensive; *acquisition*, buying a new product opportunity; *contract entrepreneurs*, to manage the start-up phase so as to move the operation ahead without encountering the frustrations of the corporate organizational boundaries. Main adds another angle: "*Venture Capital Lending*—making selected portfolio investments in the ventures of other groups."

A change in the established way of doing business, of course, has its risks. However, the trade-offs may be necessary to effectuate a reasonably dynamic new products operation. Here is what Main has to say:

> Corporate management can take specific steps to provide an interface and environment that will facilitate implementation and promote full realization of the program's potential . . .
>
> The new activity should be managed continuously by one person or project team throughout its entire evolution—from inception, through research and planning, into an established operation with a structured organization.
>
> The CEO should prepare corporate management to accept and interact with the instinctive and intuitive forces at work in entrepreneurial management. Established views and practices may not be the appropriate response to a venture situation and, in some instances, may well prove counterproductive.
>
> At the same time, the CEO should be alert to individual sensitivities and fears that the new operation and top management's commitment to it may threaten existing positions within the corporate hierarchy. . . .
>
> Ultimately, the successful management of innovation in a large corporate environment will hinge on whether the leadership is willing to risk new challenges and explore new management cultures.

New product generation stimulates the entrepreneurial juices that nurture the future prosperity of the corporation—and, more likely than not, identify the successor leaders.

That is the pattern.

But—there is another element also.

New product programs do not always go so smoothly.

And now what?

Now—the program must be put back on track or aborted. It's time to discover just what has changed over which the marketer may have control—and to do something about it. Or—to discover the outside influences affecting the program and to determine whether something can affordably be done quickly enough to make the move the best long-term use of expensive capital and corporate energies.

A false start may not presage a poor finish, but a stumble once out of the gate is extremely difficult to overcome. Tenacity within reason, yea; stubbornness within blinders, nay.

New Product Lessons

New product managers learn lessons readily applicable to established businesses. They learn to break out of the mold of routine practice, to reap the attention and rewards accorded a new face on the block (even if it *is* an old face with new cosmetics, or a very close kin with something new to show or to proclaim). They know how to make a reintroduction of an old offering more exciting than a bigger trade allowance and a snappy new label. New product managers, the best ones, learn to be iconoclasts, to challenge the norms of today and yesterday so firmly entrenched in all but the most infant industries.

And they are not afraid to borrow from the successful tactics of (presumably) wholly unrelated industries. Nor to seek out consultation from across a wide range of disciplines, peer groups, and target prospects.

New product managers are selective sponges, soaking up everything—and retaining the important differences that leverage the meaning of "new."

New product managers are curious. They're anxious to discover, to turn over every rock, to challenge every cliché, to swim against the tide, and, thus, to create new channels and new tides.

Yet—new product managers know that the degree of change affects the degree of acceptance, most often in an inverse ratio. They know that too much gap jumping may represent true progress, but probably will be beyond the comprehension of the broad marketplace. They learn how much is enough—and how much is too much.

Since the fifties, when the author first saw the formal shaping of the new product process proven in practice, the lessons of this text have been validated. In those early years, the various steps were clearly identified—which my new products development company published in a slim proprietary volume widely shared within the field. Then, as now, that field embraced makers and marketers, advertising agencies, academia, and consultants, and the then newly emerging specialty field of new products development services.

Early coworkers in those vineyards soon spread out across many industries and applied the procedures.

The original go/no-go gates have changed little.

The process works. And it works everywhere—across oceans, across cultures, across real and imagined boundaries.

It is my hope that this book, built on the bedrock of experience in the trenches and biased by the lessons of reality, will be a lasting contribution to the art, science, craft, and gut instinct so important to the field.

This disciplined approach works because it is flexible to the demands of unanticipated events (problems and opportunities). The three outstanding case histories that follow are dazzling evidence of this.

CASE
HISTORIES

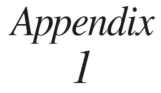

*Appendix
1*

Introduction

No text on new product marketing development would be complete without a few case histories that illustrate the principles and disciplines advocated therein.

These "real world" examples put it all together. Each is from a leading company in its field. Each was prepared expressly for this book in full cooperation with the companies' managements. The author is indebted to them for this. So, too, will the reader gain from a careful study of these case histories.

They illustrate:

- Knowledge of market characteristics

- Use of strategy as a management focus

- Management with stringent criteria

- Heavy up-front investment in the early development phases

- Extension of or refinement of the basic corporate charter as a new product directional focus

- Development of new products as either a basis for future proliferation of the line or as an actual extension of an existing brand franchise, or both

- Different organizational structures and different performance incentives employed by the case history subject companies

Each of the companies is continually learning, rethinking, and re-deploying its approach to new products. They are seeking ways in which to manage innovation, but also in which to encourage risk-taking entrepreneurship.

Each has a balanced program of new product development that focuses on various investment and longevity goals, so that there is a continuous flow of activity aimed at short-term opportunities, mid-term new business enterprises, and longer term innovations and inventions that require considerable investment in staff and capital equipment and a lengthy time frame. Both opportunistic and programmed acquisitions and joint ventures may play a role in the mid- and long-term programs, while licensing opportunities may be important to the short-term programs.

All are seeking a new product management approach that balances the orderly disciplines of an institutionalized publicly held business with the dynamic spirit of vital entrepreneurship. They appear to be succeeding.

The case histories are of the successful, technologically advanced Gillette Sensor shaving system and its extensions; of the leading butter maker Land O'Lakes' major entry into its competitive category, margarine; and of Toro's launch of a highly seasonal item, its Power Shovel snowthrower.

There are a number of common new product issues to be emphasized:

Name

- All three carry the same well-established, leadership corporate name as their brand.

- Gillette heavily invested in the belief that a superior shave at a higher price would have user appeal, in face of the disposable category (in which it also successfully competes).

- Land O'Lakes was concerned that naming a margarine after a butter brand would needlessly cannibalize its leading spread.

- Toro needed a generic "handle" for a lightweight snowthrower that would clearly differentiate it from the conventional machines aimed at a different prospect target.

Price

- Gillette's Sensor, Sensor for Women, and SensorExcel shaving systems would be at the very top of the price category. They had to deliver a clearly demonstrable, worthwhile quality performance difference.

- Land O'Lakes' brand reputation is appropriate to a premium-priced margarine. Although this is a smaller segment of the total market than the popular-priced segment, this could be an appropriate price point.

Seasonality

- Land O'Lakes margarine's introductory effort should avoid the peak holiday butter consumption period.
- Toro snowthrower sales respond to early significant snowfalls.

The consequences of the decisions made on each of these issues—and the behavior of Mother Nature in Toro's case—had major effects on the respective successes of each of the new product introductions.

A

Gillette Sensor Family of Wet Shaving Systems

In 1989, The Gillette Company launched the Sensor shaving system for men. It marked the second phase of a three-part strategy designed to redefine the shaving market and rebuild Gillette's technological leadership and value image worldwide after some years of share and image erosion caused by the growth of disposables. (A shaving *system*—in contrast to a disposable—consists of a permanent handle, or razor, and a replaceable blade cartridge.) Sensor proved extraordinarily successful, and Gillette soon began to build a family of Sensor shaving systems, launching Sensor for Women in 1992 and SensorExcel for men in 1993.

Informally, Gillette people define their mission in blades and razors by saying, "There is a better way to shave and we will find it." The original Sensor claimed 22 patents for a variety of technological and design features meant to deliver "a better shave." Sensor's successors, rather than acting as line extensions or flank products, introduced new features that further improved the quality of the shave, as proven by extensive testing with a broad sample of male and female wet shavers.

Sensor set Gillette on a new path—characterized by rapid product development, an emphasis on technological advantage, both in product design and manufacturing process, and the introduction of a far greater number of new products than ever before.

The Company

King C. Gillette—amateur inventor, entrepreneur, and utopian—introduced the safety razor with replaceable, double-edge blades in 1903. His invention delivered a safer and more comfortable shave than the traditional straight razor could provide and signaled the decline of the barbershop shave.

Gillette's safety razor took only a year to revolutionize the business of shaving. During the first year of production, Gillette sold 51 razors and 168 blades. The second year, sales rose to 90,884 razors and 123,648 blades—a one year increase of 180,000 percent. A decade later, Gillette was selling 41.4 million blades.

Gillette was an ardent internationalist, and soon took his burgeoning business overseas, opening facilities in the United Kingdom in 1904, in France in 1905, and in Berlin in 1909.

From the introduction of the first safety razor until the early 1970s, The Gillette Company built its business on the basic, double-edge safety razor design. The razor, or handle, was produced in a variety of styles and materials—including gold and silver—and was perceived by men around the world as a fine instrument and the center of their daily grooming ritual.

Early on, Gillette strove to build and enhance this image as a supplier of high-quality, superior-performing shaving instruments that possessed a deep understanding of and unique relationship with men. The company was an active marketer and early user of advertising. The first Gillette radio campaign aired in 1909, and the first television commercial ran in 1943, when TV was still an infant. After World War II, Gillette was a pioneer in corporate sports sponsorship, promoting and sponsoring a variety of sporting events that the company called Gillette Cavalcade of Sports. It included the Friday Night Fights in the United States and the World Cup Soccer Championships in Europe. Perhaps most extraordinary, Gillette was the sole commercial sponsor of the World Series from 1949 to 1962—the only advertiser on America's beloved sports event for more than a decade. It was during these events that the Gillette mascot and spokesperson, an animated parrot named Sharpie, became a familiar figure to men throughout America.

Starting in 1971, Gillette introduced a series of new product innovations. Trac II featured twin blades in a single cartridge, the first major technological advance in shaving systems since the first double-edge safety razor. Gillette introduced Atra in 1977, which featured twin-blades in a pivoting head. Men found that both products provided safer, smoother, more comfortable shaves and both systems became top sellers in worldwide markets, serving to reduce sales of double-edge razors and blades. In 1985, Gillette introduced Atra Plus with a lubricating strip mounted on the cartridge. The water-soluble, polyethylene-oxide strip exudes a coating that reduces the drag of the blades on the shaver's skin.

Situation Analysis

As Gillette improved the safety and performance of its signature shaving systems with these innovations, a competitive product appeared on the market that changed the wet shaving business dramatically. Bic had built a successful business with a variety of disposable products, first the ballpoint pen, then the cigarette lighter. In 1975 Bic introduced the disposable razor. The inexpensive, plastic, throwaway product was antithetical to the Gillette concept of a shaving device as a solid, high-quality, permanent instrument. What's more, entry into the disposables business was highly problematical for Gillette because every sale of a low-margin disposable potentially erodes the higher-margin systems business. Gillette did not wish to encourage disposable usage or build the disposables market, yet it could not cede a potentially huge market to arch-rival Bic. And, so, in 1976, Gillette responded with the Good News! disposable razor.

Disposables took off, proving especially popular with women and with men less than 30 years of age. Bic and Gillette found themselves in a heated battle for market share, and the key weapon was price. Year after year, Gillette committed greater resources to supporting promotions and special offers for disposables, while reducing advertising expenditures for its systems products. In fact, Gillette's advertising spending declined from a high of $61.4 million in 1975 (stated in 1987 constant dollars) to a low of $15.1 million in 1987.

By 1989, disposables had captured 53.2 percent of the wet shaving market in the United States, in comparison to a 34.1 percent share for shaving systems. Shaving instruments had become a commodity. Price, it seemed, was more important to the consumer than quality. The market had shifted.

To Gillette—a company that had built its business on product innovation and quality—the situation was no longer acceptable. In 1989, Gillette determined that a new strategy was required. The systems business offered far greater potential for growth than disposables, because Gillette enjoyed a strong technological advantage in systems. In addition, it believed that one of its greatest assets was the Gillette brand name, recognized around the world for quality and value—not for discount price and throwaway technology.

To formulate the new strategy, Gillette began by conducting extensive market research with hundreds of users and nonusers across the United States and Europe. The key findings:

- Gillette had an extremely positive image, linked almost entirely to shaving and shaving instruments and was seen as the quality leader.

- People assumed that any product made by Gillette would be made for men—not surprising considering the years of advertising and sponsorship aimed at men.

- There was a strong difference between the perceptions of men over the age of forty, and those younger. The older men felt strong associations with Gillette, the grooming ritual, and high-quality shaving instruments. Younger men thought of shaving as twin blades, plastic disposables, and blue color—the color of the Gillette Good News! disposable.

- Respondents believed that a systems product delivered a better shave than a disposable product could.

The overriding conclusion of the market research was that while Gillette was still seen as the undisputed world leader in shaving— known for innovation, quality, and tradition—the status of shaving products and even shaving itself had come into question.

The Strategic Plan

The Gillette Company's strategy for the 90s had three phases:

- Phase One. Rebuild the Gillette image and reestablish the company's relationship with male users. The primary method for achieving this goal would be advertising and lots of it. The *sole* focus of the advertising would be refillable systems. All advertising for disposables would cease.

- Phase Two. Revitalize and enhance the Gillette leadership position in shaving technology by bringing to market a breakthrough shaving system. The new products would convince the younger generation of the value of quality shaving instruments, and act as a lever to shift the market back toward refillable systems.

- Phase Three. Capitalize on the enhanced image and technology breakthrough to create a leadership position in a broader category, called male grooming, which includes blades and razors and such products as shave preparations, skin care products, and other toiletries.

To support this bold, three-phase strategy, Gillette made an equally bold move into global marketing. Since 1904, when Gillette first established operations in the United Kingdom, the company had operated as a multinational. By the mid-1980s, Gillette was conducting business in more than 200 countries and enjoyed a 50 percent share of the world shaving market. However, Gillette products were marketed under a variety of names. The Good News! disposable, for example, was known as Blue II in the U.K., Parat in Germany, Gillette in France and Spain, Radi e Getta (shave and throw) in Italy, Tandem in the Netherlands, and Handy in Switzerland. Sales and marketing activities were equally decentralized. Advertising, pricing, promotions, point-of-sale—all were determined by country staffs to meet local business conditions with little central coordination and little consistency from country to country.

Gillette knew that this decentralized organization, which had worked successfully for more than eight decades, would not be appropriate for the homogenous European market that would begin to emerge following the 1992 enactment of the single-market trade agreement. At the same time, its research and experience showed that shaving products were strong candidates for true global marketing—one product, one brand name, one package, one advertising approach across markets.

Accordingly, The Gillette Company reorganized its operations, creating the North Atlantic Group (NAG) comprising the United States, Canadian, and European markets. All marketing activities were centralized at headquarters in Boston, Massachusetts, and all suppliers of marketing materials (such as advertising and public relations) were required to build or make available their own global networks of personnel and services to support the Gillette global marketing strategy. This new structure also enabled Gillette to more efficiently manage manufacturing and distribution operations. "One factor, many locations" became the motto, meaning that Gillette manufacturing facilities are a single resource serving many markets.

With this organization in place, Gillette launched into Phase One of its global strategy.

Phase One: Image Building

For Gillette, advertising would be the primary method for rebuilding the corporate image. It set about to create a new advertising campaign that would touch men, involve them in shaving, reshape their perceptions of Gillette, and motivate them to try Gillette products. Further, because it would have to appeal to men in many markets, the advertising would have to focus on the similarities among men of different cultures, rather than their differences.

In collaboration with BBDO, their New York-based advertising agency, Gillette developed the theme line "The Best a Man Can Get." The line was based on the simple, core idea that had built the company: Gillette understands what it takes for a man to look and feel his best. It was not so different, in message, from the line that had accompanied Sharpie the parrot during the 1950s and 60s, "Look sharp, feel sharp, be sharp."

"The Best a Man Can Get" would serve as the creative platform for television and print advertising, but it was also intended as a strategic platform for all the shaving activities of The Gillette Company. The Gillette name stood for the very best shaving products that made a man feel his very best. (See Figure A-1.)

The new television commercials showed powerful vignettes of men in a variety of situations—as fathers, sons, athletes, husbands, lovers—and included the positive reactions of the women in their lives to their actions and appearance. The images were intended to be "aspirational," heroic and idealized, associating the best of man's achievements with Gillette products. The advertising ran throughout the North Atlantic markets with the theme line, The Best a Man Can Get, and with essentially the same images and vignettes. The only major variation from market to market was the voice-over narration, translated into the appropriate local

Figure A-1 Introductory Sensor TV commercial

V/O: Gillette announces a razor so revolutionary

it can sense the individual needs of your face.

Introducing the extraordinary Gillette Sensor Shaving System.

Song: Gillette. The Best a Man Can Get.

V/O: Sensor twin blades are

individually mounted on remarkably responsive springs.

They continuously sense and automatically adjust to

the individual curves and contours of your face.

Song: And we know how to make

the most of who you are.

V/O: The extraordinary Gillette Sensor.

Closer, smoother, safer than ever before.

To give you the best shave a man can get.

Song: Where the race is run, you're the champion. Gillette. The Best a Man Can Get.

V/O: New Gillette Sensor.

The Best a Man Can Get.

"The Best a Man Can Get" is the driving theme behind the introduction of the revolutionary new Gillette Sensor Shaving System, offering a closer, smoother, safer shave than ever before.

Source: BBDO, New York

language. And, true to strategy, Gillette committed significant resources to television advertising—climbing from the low of $15.1 million in 1985 to $50 million in 1995. At the same time, it ceased all advertising for disposables.

The campaign had immediate impact. By the end of 1989, sales of Gillette systems products had begun to increase. Growth in the disposable segment had begun to slow. And consumer research showed that the advertising was enhancing the Gillette image as a supplier of innovative, high-quality shaving products.

Phase Two: Technology Leadership

Gillette maintains research and development laboratories in Reading, England, and South Boston, Mass. At the Reading facility, the primary focus is on the development of new technologies. South Boston primarily concerns itself with incorporating new technologies into viable products, and developing manufacturing processes to bring them to market.

After the launch of the twin-blade Atra system in 1977, scientists and engineers at Reading had begun work on a new technology: moving blades. It took nearly ten years to perfect this new system, which incorporated two narrow blades, each mounted on two tiny springs, housed in a pivoting cartridge. The combination of spring-mounting and pivoting head enabled the blades to follow the contours of the face and skin more precisely than any existing shaving system and thus deliver a closer shave. The cartridge also included a skin guard—a thin, spring-mounted bar ahead of the blades—that stretched the skin for a more efficient shave. Because the new system could "sense" a man's face and immediately adapt to it, the new product would be called Sensor.

After the technology had been developed at the Reading facility, it was transferred to South Boston where it was further refined and modified for inclusion in the new product. The Boston team of designers, engineers, and manufacturing and marketing people were also responsible for the development of the razor and the packaging.

In keeping with the strategy, the team worked to create a masculine look and feel for Sensor. They chose stainless steel for the handle casing, reminiscent of the sturdy double-edge razors of Gillette's past. The handle was trimmed with black plastic, and was weighted and balanced to give the heft and feel of a high-quality instrument. Sensor offered a dramatic contrast to the lightweight plastic disposable razors on the market, and even stood apart from its predecessors Trac II and Atra.

A major challenge for any new Gillette product is developing a manufacturing process that will enable the company to produce billions of units to extremely high-quality standards and at the lowest possible cost. For Sensor, the manufacturing team adapted a welding system that employed lasers to attach the tiny blades to the tiny springs at extremely high speeds.

In all, the development of Sensor cost some $200 million. Gillette holds 22 U.S. patents on Sensor technologies and features, the greatest number of technological advances in any shaving system. And consumer-use testing of Sensor, conducted with 5,000 men prior to launch, showed that Sensor received higher marks for every shaving attribute than the best shaving system then on the market, the Gillette Atra Plus.

The Launch of Sensor

Gillette was convinced that Sensor would be a powerful tool for reaffirming the company as the technology leader in wet shaving, and further shifting the market away from disposables and back toward systems products. Gillette also believed it was a product that would appeal to men across boundaries and cultures. So, Gillette launched Sensor with a commitment and boldness that befitted its new strategy. It would be known as Sensor worldwide, and it would be launched with The Best a Man Can Get theme line and advertising treatment throughout the North Atlantic Group markets.

Before presenting Sensor to the consumer, however, Gillette needed to convince its own sales staff—and the press—of Sensor's potential. Accordingly, Gillette introduced Sensor to these audiences in an elaborate, multimedia extravaganza in September of 1989, three months prior to the introduction of the consumer advertising campaign. The event featured a 180-foot replica of Sensor and the audience entered the meeting space through the razor handle. For more than an hour, they were immersed in the Sensor story: its development, features, benefits, and launch plans—all translated into nine languages for non-English-speaking attendees. The product was revealed in a climax of theatrical smoke and laser light, serenaded by live singers and dancers.

Teaser ads for Sensor appeared on January 14, 1990, and the first three spots of the television campaign premiered during the Super Bowl on January 28. The $100 million launch campaign—including advertising, public relations, and promotional activities—created tremendous awareness for Sensor. Gillette estimates that media coverage created nearly 500 million "impressions" by summer. Sensor was featured in stories on national television news programs and hundreds of articles in trade and business publications. Simultaneous to the U.S. launch, Sensor was being introduced in 17 other countries on three continents. Demand for Sensor was so great that the product was placed on allocation and manufacturing capacity was increased well ahead of plan in both the South Boston and Berlin, Germany, plants.

David Shore, an analyst for Prudential-Bache Securities, called the launch of Sensor "the single most successful consumer nondurable product introduction in the history of the planet." By 1990, shipments of Sensor were 30 percent ahead of expectations. Twenty-seven million razors had been shipped since launch. In its first year, Sensor captured 42 percent of the razor market in North America and Europe and an 11 percent dollar share—the highest percentage ever for a new shaving system.

As of this writing, Sensor has continued to achieve phenomenal success. More than 50 million men shave with Sensor, worldwide, Sensor is the leader in virtually every one of the 72 markets where it is available. The Sensory business alone is bigger than the entire business of Gillette's key competitors—Bic and Schick. By the end of 1994, sales of Sensor razors totaled 175 million, and sales of Sensor cartridges reached 3.2 *billion* units. Twenty-five percent of the dollars spent in the North Atlantic wet shaving market went to Sensor.

And, equally as important as the impressive sales figures, Sensor helped Gillette achieve its strategic objectives. Sensor revitalized the systems category. By the end of 1990, the dollar value of the systems segment had increased 2.5 percentage points, while disposables showed a slight decline of 0.7 percent. By the end of 1994, systems accounted for 40 percent of the wet shaving market, disposables 57 percent.

Phase Three: Broaden the Category

Sensor also served to reinvigorate the Gillette brand name. Studies completed at the end of 1990 showed that consumers viewed Gillette as "the technological leader in its field" and as a company that "really understands men's grooming needs."

In addition, Sensor provided a strong platform for the third phase of the strategy, the push into the broader male grooming category. The Gillette Series line of male grooming products was launched in 1992, comprising shaving preparation, deodorants, and antiperspirants. The line, developed at a cost of $75 million, incorporated advances in chemistry, product forms, dispensing methods, and fragrances. Although the story is outside the scope of this article, the Gillette Series line has successfully broadened Gillette's presence in the male grooming category.

New Members of the Sensor Family

Sensor for Women

As the rollout of Sensor continued worldwide, Gillette prepared to bring Sensor technology to a potentially huge group of new systems customers: women. In the United States alone, 80 million women shave with a blade and razor, some 15 million more than men. However, because women tend to be "seasonal" shavers— shaving more often in the summer and less often in the winter—women, on average, use only one-third as many blades as do men.

Although Gillette offered its first female shaving product in 1915, a razor called Milady Décolleté—and has continued to develop new products for women through the years—these products, for the most part, were male products produced in supposedly feminine colors (usually pink) and repackaged to appeal to women. Although Gillette's female products found success in the market, the majority of female wet shavers chose to use a "male" brand of shaving product.

Through market research, Gillette set out to learn more about female shaving habits and what women need in a razor. The research revealed that women's habits and attitudes toward shaving are vastly different from those of men. The highlights:

- Most women shave in the bath or shower. In this wet, slippery,
  poorly lit environment they must bend and twist to see and to maneu-
  ver the blade across underarms and the backs of thighs and knees.

- Women shave up to nine times the surface area that a man does.

- Women are not interested in shaving and view it as a chore. Men
  view shaving as a skill and take pride in it.

- Women believe that the longer they use a blade, the less likely it
  is to irritate or nick them. Men believe the opposite.

- If a woman nicks or cuts herself while shaving, she tends to blame
  herself. If a man nicks or cuts himself, he blames the blade.

- Women believe that all shaving products are essentially alike, and
  therefore, choose the lowest-priced product. In fact, at the time of
  the research, some 73 percent shaved with a disposable rather
  than a systems product.

- In general, women were dissatisfied with all shaving products
  then on the market.

Clearly, the female wet shaving market represented a large opportunity
for Gillette, and they set about developing a product that would incorporate the Sensor blade technology into a razor designed specifically to
meet women's needs. The result was Sensor for Women.

Sensor for Women looks nothing like the conventional male razor.
The flat handle is designed so it won't roll in the hand—as a man's
round razor shaft will—so that the blade stays properly oriented even
when reaching areas the shaver can't see. The wave-shaped grooves
provide a sure grip in wet, soapy environments. And the modern, sleek
appearance is intended to encourage a woman to think of the razor as
part of the beauty regimen.

Sensor for Women was launched in the United States, Canada, and
the United Kingdom—the major female wet shaving markets—in 1992.
True to its global marketing philosophy, Gillette launched the product
under the same product name and with the same advertising theme line
"A Razor Worth Holding Onto." The line delivered two messages. First,
the handle design and the way it is meant to be held offers a unique advantage for the female wet shaver. Second, that Sensor for Women is a
high-quality, permanent product—not one you throw away.

The rollout of Sensor for Women continued through 1994, when it
was launched into Continental Europe. There, market research showed
that female shaving habits are strikingly different from those in the
United States, Canada, and the U.K. Women on the Continent think of
wet shaving as a male practice and favor alternative forms of hair removal such as waxes, creams, and epilators. As a result, Gillette pre-

ceded the product launch into France with a public relations effort designed to promote the advantages of wet shaving. And the product was launched as Sensor Pour Elle in France, demonstrating that even global products must sometimes be modified for local markets.

Sales of Sensor for Women have far exceeded expectations, both in Europe and in the United States. In France, for example, the product held a 37 percent share of the total razor market by August of 1994. In Holland, it captured an extraordinary 66 percent value share of the total razor market. In the United States, as of this writing, Sensor for Women has become the number one women's refillable shaving system with a 31 percent retail dollar share of the women's total wet shaving market and a 66 percent share of the women's refillable razor category.

SensorExcel

Gillette now faced a difficult challenge: how to improve on its own, market-leading Sensor system. In earlier days, it might have been content to sell Sensor in essentially the same form—with special editions, promotions, packaging variations—for many years. But the "new" Gillette was committed to being the technological leader in shaving, and that meant continuing to develop and bring to market a steady stream of product innovations that would deliver superior performance and could command premium prices. And, in particular, Gillette would continue its focus on shaving systems because they enjoy the greatest technology advantage in that category, and because systems provide higher margins than disposables.

And so, even as Sensor continued to conquer new markets around the world, Gillette management challenged the entire organization to develop the next-generation Sensor, a product that could improve on the world's best shaving system.

In the U.K. Research & Development Laboratory at Reading, scientists had been working on new skin guard technologies for some time. They had discovered that the skin guard played a major role in the quality of the shave, and had experimented with a number of different skin guard treatments and materials, including sponge, rubber, nylon fibers, even suede. Not long after the launch of Sensor, they began to focus on the use of a rubber-like material, called elastomer, configured in a series of flexible ridges—or "fins"—that would be affixed to the cartridge ahead of the blades. Laboratory testing proved that the fins dramatically improved the comfort and closeness of the shave for most men.

In South Boston, scientists and engineers had been experimenting with improvements to the lubricating strip, the blade housing, and a variety of other components. The most promising ideas from both laboratories were incorporated into a total of 12 product prototypes which, in September of 1990, were tested with thousands of male shavers. Two designs received high marks and were subsequently tested against the original Sensor. One of the designs—the one with the five elastomeric fins— was the clear favorite and was selected as the next-generation system.

Figure A-2 The SensorExcel revolutionary skin guard cartridge

The SensorExcel cartridge incorporates a revolutionary skin guard comprising five soft, flexible microfins that precede the individually spring-mounted twin blades and gently stretch the skin, causing beard hairs to spring upward so they can be cut more closely.

The product design team set to work developing the handle design, the color and surface treatments, and the packaging. The intention was to create a family resemblance to Sensor—with its masculine, high-quality, high-technology look—but with an unmistakable character of its own. A flexible, elastomeric material—similar to that of the fins—was chosen for the grips, because it provided improved maneuverability and control. From the dozens of finishes and coatings evaluated, a lustrous, silvery surface known as "pearlbrite" was selected. The final appearance is sleek, metallic, and modern.

Originally, the new Sensor system was conceived as a "flanker" product—a variant on the original that could sell at a slight premium. However, the results of consumer-use testing of the new system (handle and cartridge) were so decisive that Gillette was convinced this product should be the primary focus of marketing and sales efforts in the systems category. The consumer testing showed that men preferred the new system to Sensor on all the shaving attributes measured. Most important of these, the men tested said the new system delivered a closer, more comfortable shave than Sensor. It also reduced several of the negatives associated with shaving—it meant less irritation, less pulling and tugging, and even fewer nicks and cuts than Sensor. And the new system also won against Sensor on design and appearance characteristics, including holding comfort, maneuverability, and providing a sure grip. In short, the improved product improved on the Sensor shave in every way. Accordingly, Gillette chose to call it SensorExcel. (See Figure A-2.)

Figure A-3 SensorExcel launch ad

For the November 1994 launch of SensorExcel in the
United States, Gillette spent more than $40 million in
print and television advertising between Thanksgiving
and Christmas to increase awareness during the key
holiday selling season.

As with Sensor and disposables, Gillette made the decision to put
all its advertising expenditures behind SensorExcel and cease all advertising for Sensor. Its reasoning is that there is only one best way to
shave, and the entire communications effort must support that system.
Gillette chose to launch SensorExcel in Europe—the first Gillette product ever to be ushered into the world outside the United States—and
then roll it out through the United States, Canada, and the rest of the
world markets. The June 1993 launch in Monte Carlo kicked off a communications campaign even larger than that of Sensor. (See Figure A-3.)

Once again, results have exceeded expectations. As of this writing,
SensorExcel has achieved a 22 percent value share of razors in Europe
and a 21 percent share of razors in the United States. It continues to be
introduced to new markets worldwide.

The Future

For Gillette, the Sensor family (see Figure A-4) of shaving systems has not only been an unprecedented success in terms of sales and profits; Sensor has revitalized the wet shaving category, reenergized the company, enhanced the brand image, and set Gillette on a newly aggressive path of rapid product development and technology leadership. And Gillette believes that there is opportunity for substantial further growth in the wet shaving category—both male and female. Consider that only 30 percent of male shavers in the North Atlantic region have tried one of the Sensor products; the user base conceivably could grow to double or triple its current size. In addition, Sensor has provided a solid platform for the Gillette expansion into male toiletries.

The Sensor family also has substantially improved Gillette's dollar share of the North Atlantic wet shaving market. And Gillette will continue to encourage shavers to trade up from disposables and competitive systems to the shave that is "The Best a Man Can Get," and thus further improve the company's value share.

Sensor proved to the world and to Gillette itself the importance of new product development. The original Sensor took nearly ten years to develop. SensorExcel was developed in three. And, as of this writing, the next-generation wet shaving system—the one that will improve upon the SensorExcel shave—is already in the prototype testing phase in Gillette's R&D laboratories. It has become informal company policy that no new product be launched unless its successor is already at an advanced stage of development.

In the world of technologically advanced, high-performance shaving instruments, The Gillette Company has proven that its strategy and method of new product development can reap great rewards.

Figure A-4 Sensor family products

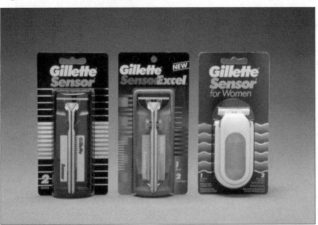

The Sensor family of Gillette Sensor, Gillette SensorExcel, and Gillette Sensor for Women. The world's most advanced shaving system incorporating proprietary manufacturing methods, ergonomic design, and spring-mounted twin blades to provide the closest, most comfortable shave available.

B

Land O Lakes Margarine

"*Land O'Lakes has redefined its business. Today, we are in the spread business, not the butter business alone. With our well-established leading brand of butter, our recent broad geographic expansion of our new margarine products and more spread products to follow, we expect to be Number One in spreads. There are few brands that carry the quality, wholesome, broad acceptance of Land O' Lakes. We intend to make the most of that fact.*"

—LAND O'LAKES, INC.

The Company

Land O'Lakes* 1995 sales were $3.0 billion. The company was organized as the Minnesota Cooperative Creameries Association Inc., in 1921, under the cooperative law of Minnesota, for the purpose of promoting, posturing, and securing improvements in:

1. Standardization and improvement of quality, through cream grading and proper methods of manufacture

2. Shipping and transportation of butter and dairy products through car-lot shipping

3. Service in the sale of products of Minnesota creameries through closer cooperation with present distributing agencies and wholesale market receivers

4. Cooperative purchase of supplies

5. Advertising of dairy products

Two years later, Land O Lakes brand was selected as an appropriate name for the company's sweet cream butter. Through a commitment to producing a consistent, high-quality product and building a consumer franchise through advertising, Land O Lakes became America's largest-selling butter, although it did not achieve national distribution until the

---

* As previously noted, Land O'Lakes (with apostrophe) is the company name; Land O Lakes (without apostrophe) is the brand name.

third quarter of 1983, when it added markets west of the Rocky Mountains. In 1933, its present advertising agency (Campbell-Mithun Inc., now Campbell Mithun Esty) was selected.

In a 1950 presentation, the agency pointed out that 30 companies (mostly meat packers) were making a large profit selling animal fat–based oleomargarine, while thousands of butter processors were operating on a very narrow margin. The packers had no qualms about selling both margarine and butter. The agency expressed the concern that the combined advertising weight of all those margarine producers would put margarine into all American homes and would eventually convince consumers that butter was uneconomical.

Situation Analysis

For the next 20 years, Land O'Lakes remained involved in food processing and marketing, as well as providing a limited supply of farm products and technical advice to its members.

In 1970, a farm supply and crop-processing cooperative named FELCO was merged into Land O'Lakes, adding soybeans and soy oil to its list of products. With this merger came the pressure from FELCO soybean farmers eager to become part of the growing margarine industry, which uses soybean oil in its production process.

Land O Lakes butter had enjoyed a phenomenal growth in the previous 20 years. However, margarine had overtaken and more than doubled the sale of all butter in the same period. Land O'Lakes took another look at margarine.

Margarine in 1970

Industry sales of margarine in 1970 were 1.8 billion pounds—87 percent of households used margarine in an average month; 35 percent of households used butter.

Per capita consumption of table spreads held steady at 16 to 17 pounds between 1950 and 1970. However, per capita consumption of margarine grew from 6 to 10.8 pounds, while butter slipped from 11 to 5.3 pounds. Lower retail price and perceived health benefits of vegetable fat over animal fat were the primary reasons for the shift. Research showed that *price* was by far the most important variable. (When oleomargarines, made from rendered animal fat, gave way to vegetable fat–based spreads, the shift had accelerated.)

Many homemakers used both margarine and butter. Land O'Lakes research showed margarine was used mainly for cooking and baking, while butter's chief use was as a table spread, topping for vegetables, and for special occasion recipes such as Christmas cookies. Land O Lakes butter users had a much higher brand loyalty than typical users and were less likely to accept substitutes.

Figure B-1 Margarine shares and prices—1970

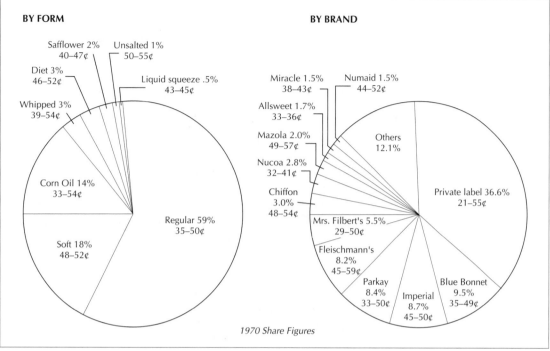

Source: A. C. Nielsen

Demographics

The heavy margarine user was female, 35 to 49 years of age, had children under 18 at home, had five or more in her household, had graduated from high school, and had a household income of $5,000 to 10,000.*

Margarine came in multiple forms marketed under many brands. In 1970, there were 14 national or important regional brands, plus private labels. The regular stick form accounted for 59 percent of business. Leading brands were Blue Bonnet (Standard Brands), Imperial (Lever Bros.), and Parkay (Dart & Kraft Inc.). Combined, they represented more than one-fourth of the market and 45 percent of the regular stick business. The category was (and is) categorized by very little brand loyalty, with the typical consumer buying within an orbit of two to three acceptable brands, and the decision primarily made on a price basis. There were also strong regional differences in terms of butter/margarine share, price points, and preferred forms. (See Figure B-1).

* In 1995, this translated to approximately $35,000–40,000.

Competitive Advertising

Advertising Claims/Positioning

At this time competitive advertising claims tended to concentrate in three areas:

Comparison with Butter

1. Blue Bonnet— "Everything's better with Blue Bonnet on it." (A comparison of similar dishes prepared with butter and with Blue Bonnet demonstrated that internationally known chefs could tell "no difference.")
2. Mrs. Filbert's— "Mrs. Filbert's fresh, sweet buttery flavor." (Not a heavily advertised brand.)
3. Chiffon— "Good enough to fool Mother Nature." "If you think it's butter but it's not, it's new Chiffon."
4. Mazola— "No matter how close you feel your margarine comes to butter flavor, Mazola margarine comes even closer."

Taste/Flavor

1. Imperial— "Tastes so good, it makes me feel like a king."
2. Parkay— "Country fresh flavor."
3. Allsweet— "Compare the sweet taste of Allsweet with any other margarine at any price."

Health

1. Fleischmann's— "It makes sensible eating delicious." (Emphasized "low cholesterol.")

Spending

Advertising spending was substantial, with the eight leaders spending approximately $500,000 per share point of media advertising. Adding non-advertising promotion, spending approached $1,000,000 per share point or more than $50,000,000. The leaders each spent about $4,000,000 to $5,000,000 in media, primarily television. (See Table B-1.)

Trade

Margarine was a better profit maker for the trade than butter (on a percentage basis). In the dairy case, it accounted for 9.9 percent of sales and 7.8 percent of profit, and returned a retail gross margin of 15.6 percent. Butter's comparable figures were 6.1 percent, 2.8 percent, and 9.1 percent. Margarine ranked third (behind milk and eggs) in the dairy case, and butter ranked ninth in departmental gross margin dollars.

On the other hand, butter generated more than twice the sales dollars per shelf foot, returned slightly more gross margin per shelf foot, and had a somewhat faster inventory turnover.

Margarine Potential for Land O'Lakes

Further processing the soybean oil of its new members into margarine would bring more consumer dollars to Land O'Lakes and to its members. But entering a large maturing market would not be easy, especially when the market was dominated by several well-managed companies who were aggressively marketing their margarine brands. Also, the success of a Land O Lakes branded margarine might jeopardize its successful Land O Lakes butter franchise.

Table B-1 Competitive ad spending—1970

Brand	Parent company	Nielsen Share ($)	(lbs)	Advertising expenditures*
Imperial	Lever Bros.	11.5%	8.7%	$ 5,393,796
Fleischmann's	Standard Brands	11.4	8.2	5,211,690
Blue Bonnet	Standard Brands	10.4	9.5	4,630,709
Parkay	Kraft	10.3	8.4	5,504,621
Mrs. Filbert's		6.6	5.5	105,700
Chiffon	Anderson Clayton	4.2	3.0	2,560,189
Mazola	CPC International	2.7	2.0	2,577,963
Allsweet	Swift	1.6	1.7	135,851
Miracle	Kraft	1.6	1.5	792,129
Private Label		33.0	36.6	

Source: LNA/Media Records

Research Projects

A number of related concerns were addressed by research projects with these objectives:

1. Estimate the impact Land O Lakes margarine would have on Land O Lakes butter sales.

2. Evaluate the total potential of a Land O Lakes branded margarine in terms of displacement of butter volume, total butter/margarine volume, and return to Land O Lakes members.

3. Determine likely acceptance of a margarine product under the Land O Lakes brand name, with product technology in line with that of the leading brands.

4. Determine consumer price/value expectations for a Land O Lakes branded margarine.

5. Provide a preliminary planning estimate of the potential for Land O Lakes margarine in a strong Land O' Lakes franchise market (e.g., Boston) vs. an average Land O' Lakes franchise market (e.g., Indianapolis).

A study was conducted in mid-1971 among a random sample of housewives in representative markets. Respondents saw simulated advertising of one of four brand positionings. (See Figure B-2.) Highly predisposed respondents received a sample product in labeled cartons carrying descriptive copy. Three to ten days later, 921 product evaluations were received from qualifying respondents. (Half the sample had received a leading national brand relabeled as Land O Lakes; the other half received a similar relabeled version of another leading national brand.)

Interpretation of Findings

Results of this test provided encouragement that Land O'Lakes could successfully position a new margarine product without jeopardizing its butter.

By developing a universe of all spread users, margarine-only users, butter-only users, users of both, with each cell broken out by brand, type, price point, demographics, and spread usage—it was possible to predict probable high and low ranges of acceptance and cannibalization. Against this backdrop, the concept of Land O Lakes branded margarine was tested in Boston and Indianapolis. The study made possible a very preliminary estimate of potential share performance, with both markets performing above goal—Boston projected to more than three times Indianapolis. This was attributed to Boston's historic high performance on Land O Lakes butter.

The study also allowed an estimate for the upper range of potential butter cut-in. This was derived by estimating the current volume of Land O Lakes butter among homemakers who would buy the new margarine. If *all* their butter purchases were converted to margarine, butter sales would decline 23 percent. But because most homemakers saw different uses for butter and margarine, the actual expected cut-in should be substantially less than 23 percent.

Respondents who received the sample product rated it highly (although, in fact, each panel was split between repackaged major national brands). The four copy approaches all were acceptable, with no particular positive or negative standout.

Figure B-2 Position posters for LOL margarine
NOW!
A NUMBER ONE MARGARINE
FROM THE NUMBER ONE BUTTER MAKER

New Land O Lakes margarine gives you the closest thing to butter there is. Natural-tasting flavor—rich creamy texture. Land O Lakes—best in butter—now best in margarine.

Source: Campbell Mithun Esty

Figure B-2 (Continued)
NOW!
A MARGARINE FOR ALL-AROUND USE

Now Land O Lakes margarine is a total spread for cooking, baking, frying, and table use. If hubby is finicky about your serving margarine, try him on this one—even he will like its rich creamy texture and natural flavor.

Source: Campbell Mithun Esty

Figure B-2 (Continued)
NOW!
A MARGARINE PERFECT FOR BAKING

This new margarine from Land O'Lakes is perfect for baking. Cookies don't run or burn. Cakes and pastries are moist and rich with no oily taste. The same high quality you expect from Land O'Lakes.

Source: Campbell Mithun Esty

Figure B-2 (Continued)
NOW!
A MARGARINE WITHOUT THE OILY TASTE

New Land O Lakes margarine has a rich creamy texture with no oily taste. Less greasy when frying and permits the natural taste of food to come through without the oily or artificial taste.

Source: Campbell Mithun Esty

Brand Name

Despite the positive findings, concern persisted about use of the best-known butter name on a margarine: Would it disproportionately affect butter sales?

Competitive margarine was repackaged as a Land O Lakes brand to test consumer reaction. Margarine users were monadically tested equally, using either a leading national product repackaged as Land O Lakes or a leading national with its correct brand name. Both the positive disposition and depth-of-interest scores for the Land O Lakes branded product exceeded the goal criteria. Consumers' predisposition was stronger for the Land O Lakes branded margarine, and the product was rated superior to any margarine any of the testers had previously tried.

This convinced Land O'Lakes that the flagship brand name was a major asset for margarine and clearly the brand name to use.

Key issues were the development of measurable marketing objectives including share, butter cut-in (of margarine to butter sales), consumer brand and advertising awareness, trial and repeat, and pricing strategies. This could only be done through testing that would include the actual Land O Lakes margarine product.

Product Development

R&D was directed to develop a top-quality product that could be duplicated in both soy and corn oil margarines. Six different forms had to be created: Soy regular stick, soft, and whipped, and corn oil base regular stick, unsalted stick, and soft.

Taste Tests

Dozens of central location consumer taste tests were conducted in the summer of 1972. The objective was for Land O'Lakes products to be preferred by as many (or more) margarine users as the leading Parkay and Imperial brands.

To qualify for the regular stick soy samples, respondents had to be current users of either stick or soft Blue Bonnet, Chiffon, Imperial, Miracle, or Parkay. To qualify for either of the corn oil test samples (stick or soft), respondents had to be current users of either stick or soft Fleischmann's, Mazola, Imperial Corn Oil, or Parkay Corn Oil.

Quotas were met for each comparison. Respondents tested an unidentified Land O'Lakes product vs. an unidentified competitor. Comparisons were on two pieces of bread and were alternated.

Research Findings

Regular Stick vs. Parkay. An equal number of women preferred each. More men preferred Land O Lakes.

Regular Stick vs. Imperial. A large majority of women preferred Land O Lakes. (No male panel.)

Corn Oil Stick vs. Parkay. The largest majority (all women) preferred Land O Lakes.

Corn Oil Soft vs. Parkay. A large majority of female panels preferred Land O Lakes.

Thus, all three taste-tested Land O Lakes margarine products met the objectives of equal or better performance than competition.

Product Quality

What contributed to this consumer blind test response?

Most margarines are similar in composition. One occasional difference is the level of skim milk content, if any. Some have none. Others use nonfat dry milk solids. Land O'Lakes uses only fresh skim milk. Taste tests indicated that the dairy flavor was positively discernible at the 10 to 17 percent level, the Land O'Lakes formulation range. This may have contributed to its recognition as the top-rated regular margarine by the Consumer's Union as reported in *Consumer Reports* magazine in February 1979.

> We established criteria for excellence for a product that resembles butter but isn't butter. Our sensory consultants independently evaluated each brand of margarine against the criteria. The experts tasted at least four samples of each brand. Their combined judgments formed the basis of our ratings.
>
> The top-rated product, regular Land O Lakes margarine, had no sensory defects. It had the appropriate pale yellow color and an even, solid texture. Its sweet dairy flavor and aroma had a slight vegetable-oil character. It was just a bit salty. And it melted rapidly and evenly. We rated Land O Lakes very good.

Product Manufacturing

Land O'Lakes used contract packer Miami Margarine of Cincinnati, Ohio, to make the product for controlled minimarkets and later test and expansion markets. (In 1976, Land O'Lakes completed its first margarine production facility in Hudson, Iowa. A second was added at Kent, Ohio, in 1983.)

Creative Exploration

Development of creative strategy for the product was conducted within this context:

1. Margarine is a low-interest category. Consumers are not waiting for new information about it.

2. At the time, there was a strong similarity among competitive claims. Almost every brand "tasted like butter." (Exception: corn oil margarine utilized health claims.)

3. Television was the principal medium.

4. Most competitors made frequent use of exaggerated visual devices: crown for Imperial, magically appearing countryside for Parkay, and "Mother Nature" for Chiffon.

5. Land O Lakes margarine advertising must avoid confusion with Land O Lakes butter.

Campbell-Mithun began creative development with an exploration of various strategies and positions.

Benefits and Claims Study

Previous testing already suggested that copy should borrow from the inherent appeal and heritage of Land O Lakes butter.

The next step was to examine the particular attributes within the margarine category that would be important to consumers and to evaluate a list of potential product claims and consumer benefits that would be used by Land O'Lakes in introducing the new margarine.

Personal in-home interviews were conducted among margarine users in February 1972, with 206 Atlanta housewives and 200 Indianapolis housewives. Each housewife rated alternative benefits and claims for margarine as to desirability, believability, exclusiveness, and appropriateness. The individual margarine claims were read by the respondents from flashcards. Each claim was rated on a scale of 1 to 10. Ratings of 8 or better were considered a positive response.

Here are the benefits studied:

- The margarine with the taste of butter . . .

- The margarine with no chemical additives . . .

- The completely natural margarine . . .

- The margarine from the farmer's own company—quality ingredients in all stages of processing . . .

- The margarine in reusable containers (coffee cups, flower pots, picnic dishes, etc.) . . .

- The number one margarine from the number one butter maker . . .

- The margarine in the biodegradable tub . . .

- The margarine for young, active families . . .

- The margarine made from natural soybean oil . . .

- An old-fashioned margarine . . .

- The margarine with a hint of lemon for cleaner, fresher, lighter flavor . . .

- The margarine with consistent high quality . . .
- The margarine that is high in nutrition . . .
- The margarine with the smooth creamy texture . . .
- The all-purpose margarine . . .
- The margarine that is lowest in saturated fats . . .
- The margarine best for health . . .
- The margarine that is "perfect for baking" . . .
- The margarine that is not greasy . . .
- The sunshine margarine—high in Vitamin D . . .
- The margarine with no aftertaste . . .
- The high-protein margarine . . .
- The margarine with country fresh flavor . . .
- The margarine with no oily taste . . .

The objective was to find a basic claim or theme for Land O Lakes margarine that a large proportion of margarine buyers felt embodied a very desirable promise not offered by existing brands. The findings of this study led to the development of a creative blueprint that would guide copy development.

Creative Blueprint

The next step was the creative direction—a blueprint to guide all communications execution:

What business goals must be accomplished?
Introduce a new line of margarine products from Land O'Lakes—with a share-of-market target of 3+ percent in the first year, while sustaining minimal loss in butter sales.

Initial markets will be in the central United States where the Land O'Lakes name is well known, but butter consumption is only moderate compared to margarine.

What kind of person must we sell?
Women who are looking for a margarine that comes as close as possible to a real butter taste with the economy of margarine. She probably uses both margarine and butter—and can still detect the difference. She reserves butter for certain uses such as "company," frying eggs, etc. The rest of the time she uses margarine. She probably also has an understanding that margarine is lower in cholesterol. She generally buys a premium-priced margarine—Imperial. She is 24 to 49 years old, has children at home, is medium upscale in income, and not a college graduate.

How does she now feel about us and competition?
She knows the Land O'Lakes name. Chances are she used Land O Lakes butter. She knows it is more expensive than competitive butters

and margarine. She also knows it is the freshest, highest-quality butter she can buy. She may also be aware that there are other Land O'Lakes dairy products in her store.

She buys one or two "acceptable" brands of margarine—usually switching for price reasons. Chances are she classes these two brands as "quality" brands—and is aware that there are other, cheaper ones on the market—but that they are further away from butter in taste.

What do we want her to feel and think and do?
To believe that Land O'Lakes has applied all its experience gained from developing the nation's best and most popular butter to develop a new margarine. That we recognize that she'll still want to use butter for some "special" occasions, but that now she can upgrade her margarine.

What key thought can we put into her mind to make her feel that way?
Land O'Lakes, the nation's number one butter maker, now makes a margarine that lives up to the Land O Lakes name. She can get a margarine with Land O Lakes quality.

What tone of voice will get her to hear and believe us?
Candid and newsy. One that presents this new margarine as something that is new and different in the margarine field. An approach that doesn't overimpose. One that makes a plausible case for a dairy products company developing a margarine.

To fulfill this blueprint, Campbell-Mithun pursued four approaches supported by the benefits and claims research. The concepts were based on:

1. Nutrition

2. America's number one butter maker

3. Consistent, high quality

4. No oily or greasy taste.

Success would be based on the ability to build product appeal with minimal Land O Lakes brand butter cut-in. An acceptable upper cut-in level was judgmentally felt to be 10 percent.

Execution Testing

Stimulus material for testing was developed in three 30-second TV commercial storyboards, which were converted into animatic form for the test in June 1972. They were:

1. Farmer's Own. Farmer talks about margarine, placing emphasis on "homegrown" aspect.

2. Sunshine Margarine. Emphasizes natural wholesomeness of sunshine and goodness and Land O'Lakes country.

3. From America's Number 1 butter maker. Features animated spokescow announcing that nation's favorite butter maker is now making margarine. (See Figure B-3.)

Figure B-3 Spokescow commercial

1. COW LEADER: Guess what, girls?

2. America's No. 1 butter maker has just introduced a margarine.

3. OTHER COWS: Gasp! Gasp! COW ONE: Oh, my! A Margarine?

4. COW TWO: They wouldn't.

5. COW LEADER: They did. New Land O Lakes Margarine is here.

6. COW ONE: But, why?

7. COW LEADER: Why? Because it takes a butter company like Land O' Lakes...

8. ...to give you the taste...

9. ...you really want in a margarine.

10. Here, try it.

11. COW ONE: M-m-m, delicious!

12. COW TWO: Oh! It's the cream of the margarines.

13. COW LEADER: New Land O Lakes Margarine is here.

14. All you other margarines...

15. ...mo-o-o-ve over!

Table B-2 Research on TV creative approaches

	Cows (50)	Sunshine (150)	Farmer (150)
Brand and product recall Correct (LOL margarine)	95%	95%	96%
Copy point recall Tastes like butter	34%	22%	—%
Tastes good	5	8	3
High quality	37	2	28
Buying Interest Requested coupon for product (first choice)	21%	13%	14%
Total coupon requests	67	56	63
Quality rating LOL margarine would be "better than all other margarines in overall quality"	21%	10%	17%
Average rating (5 pt. scale)	41	3.9	3.9
Reasons for quality rating Made by butter company	71%	57%	45%
Made to taste like butter	15	10	6

Source: Land O'Lakes, Inc.

The animatics were tested in Indianapolis, which was to be the initial test market.

Testing was monadic. Each respondent saw one of the test commercials in a cluttered environment of other test commercials. The "America's Number 1 butter maker" commercial featuring the spokescow was most effective on all counts. Of the three viewed by more than 450 persons, it was widely preferred over the other two. (See Table B-2.)

On the butter cut-in issue, only one respondent indicated a switch from Land O Lakes butter to its margarine, while almost 60 percent indicated a trial switch from the margarine brand presently used.

The spokescow approach dignified butter, borrowing from the strength of the established quality and sales leader—thus allowing the prospective consumer to make a similar inference about Land O Lakes margarine.

Packaging Graphics

The agency began working on packaging graphics with these design objectives:

1. To clearly identify the margarine as a Land O'Lakes product to capitalize on the brand's quality image.

2. To provide differentiation from the butter package, to prevent confusion or comparison.

Six designs were tested with users—and for eye appeal in the grocery dairy case.

Final design selection used the basic Land O'Lakes colors and Indian maiden logotype, with typography, background graphics, and cartoon construction providing the necessary differentiation from butter packages. (See Figures B-4 and B-5.)

Objectives and Strategies

The preliminary marketing and advertising strategies and objectives were refined from the comprehensive preparatory research to yield the following:

Marketing Objectives

Market share—Obtain a market poundage share of 3+ percent.

Cut-in (of margarine to butter sales) Hold to a maximum of 10 percent on a national basis. (A special study by Market Potential Inc. indicated that a cut-in of 10 percent could be expected.)

Distribution—Achieve a minimum 70 percent at the end of the first year.

Awareness—Achieve minimum 20 percent awareness of Land O Lakes brand margarine among margarine and butter/margarine users by the end of the first six months, 25 percent by the end of the first year.

Trial—Achieve minimum 25 percent sampling among all margarine users in the first year.

Image—Clearly establish a premium-quality image equal to or better than the premium margarine with the highest-quality image in the market (in areas where the Land O'Lakes name is already known). Also establish the idea of a "family" of margarines.

Pricing—Achieve a retail price equal to Imperial, the leading premium-priced brand.

Figure B-4 Forms of Land O Lakes margarine in the 1970s

Regular Stick, Soft, and Corn Oil—the three largest selling margarine categories.

Marketing Strategy

1. Build margarine identity on Land O'Lakes' strongly established reputation as the country's Number One butter.

2. Introduce Land O Lakes margarine at a first-year spending level of double the ongoing cost for market share point.

3. Concentrate first-year spending on current margarine consumers (rather than trade) to rapidly develop awareness in the first 16 weeks after advertising begins and to help achieve initial trade acceptance.

4. Use coupons to stimulate trial, generate rapid shelf movement, and aid in gaining initial placements and second-chance placements.

5. Increase spending efficiency after initial introduction weight by augmenting television with magazines, which perform better in top economic quintiles.

Advertising Objectives

1. Position Land O Lakes margarine as a high-quality, premium margarine.

2. Obtain minimum 20 percent consumer awareness of Land O Lakes margarine brand in the first six months.

3. Obtain 25 percent trial by all margarine users in the first year.

Figure B-5 Store planogram

Advertising Strategy

1. Help build a margarine identity on Land O Lakes' established reputation as the country's number one butter.

2. Use television as a key medium.

3. Concentrate the first-year budget on consumer advertising to "pull" the product.

4. Emphasize couponing to gain initial trial.

5. Use consumer-oriented promotions to add value to advertising and stimulate repeat purchases.

Media Objectives

1. Use the most efficient and effective media combination possible within the budget to reach the target audience.

2. Concentrate media weight against women 18 to 49 years of age with families who are premium margarine users.

3. Recognize that reach and trial will be of primary importance during the introductory period.

4. Provide effective continuity levels against the target audience during the sustaining period.

5. Keep the trade constantly aware of the media support.

Media Strategy

1. Use prime time network television as the basic medium to reach women 18 to 49.

2. Use daytime network television for additional low-cost efficient frequency among a target of women 18 to 49.

3. Use r.o.p. newspaper to stimulate more immediate consumer response (coupon ad). This will promote product sampling and be merchandisable with the grocery trade.

4. Use magazines to provide broad reach against the target and to reach the lower viewing TV quintiles.

5. Use direct mail to concentrate on the target while promoting more sampling and retrial by the consumer, serving as a vehicle to ensure that original distribution with the key trade is maintained and increased.

(See Figure B-6 for the resulting Media Planning Chart.)

National Theoretical Plans

National theoretical spending for Year One was estimated to require $12,000,000 to meet the 3+ percent share of market goal. This amount would be divided equally between advertising and sales promotion activities. (At the time, top national brands were spending $1,000,000 per share point on advertising and promotion to maintain share. Typically, new introductions in the category spent at least double this rate—possibly dividing the dollars 55 percent media and advertising production, 15 percent consumer promotion, 30 percent trade deals and other trade costs.)

Figure B-6 Media planning chart

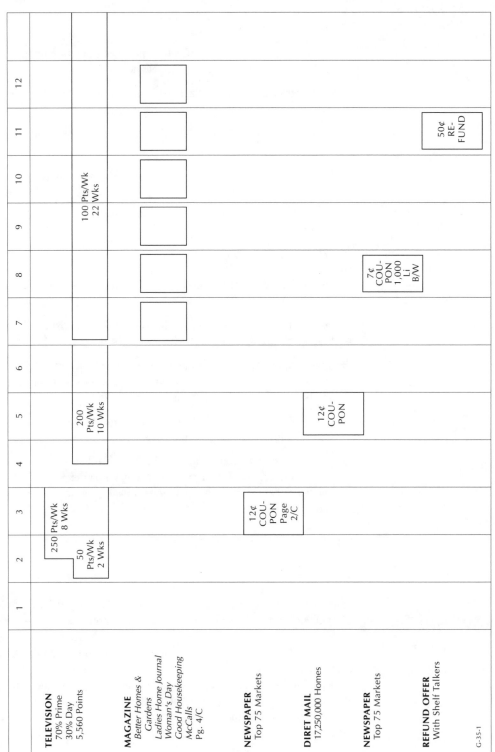

Test Market Planning

Normally, the next step would be preparation of test market simulation—selection of projectable markets and development of plans.

In this case, however, it was decided to take a tandem approach:

1. Institute minimarket testing, where all factors could be controlled

2. At nearly the same time, enter a single conventional test market situation

This approach provided a number of benefits for a marketer new to the category.

Minimarket Controlled Tests

Minimarkets would allow a measurement of performance under optimum conditions, measuring consumer acceptance unencumbered by distribution or pricing aberrations. Under these conditions, the butter cut-in effects could be precisely measured. Additionally, advertising timing would exactly match the broad availability of product. With this precision, two markets were selected—one, a highly developed margarine consumption market (Albany, GA); and another (Watertown, NY), more disposed to butter, and with a slightly older and lower-income population.

Benchmark studies prior to entry determined awareness and usage levels of various brands of both spread categories.

Conventional Test Markets

Indianapolis, IN, was the first of several conventionally operated and monitored test markets. It represented a medium development Land O Lakes butter market—and would be the first experience for the Land O' Lakes dairy products sales force in competing in the margarine section of the case. Until now, they had represented virtually the only well-advertised, broadly known butter brand—a premium product with a long and successful heritage with only modest marketing competition. Now, the sales force was up against shrewd package foods marketers with strong refrigerated case muscle.

The test markets began in the late fall 1972.

Test Market Performance—Controlled Markets

After six months, in May 1973, a survey of 200 women in each market showed that the controlled store markets were very close to their awareness and trial goals. (See Table B-3.)

After 24 weeks, actual share of market was 3.8 percent in Watertown, 2.3 percent in Albany. While this was not in excess of goal, it still demonstrated an ability to develop a successful franchise because share was building each month.

Table B-3 Awareness and usage (minimarkets)

	Albany %	Watertown %
Unaided awareness	18	19
Trial among margarine users	27	28
Repeat	20	17

Test Market Performance—Conventional Markets

After three months, distribution was building but still slowly. After six months, it peaked. (See Table B-4.) Retail store clerks revealed that the actual pricing was 2 to 3 cents higher than Imperial rather than a parity. After three months, market share hovered between 1.8 and 2.6 percent and was viewed as only a modest success. After three months of advertising, unaided awareness was 16 percent, trial among margarine users was 21 percent.

Table B-4 Retail distribution (conventional markets)

	3 month %	6 month %
Any LOL margarine	49	77
Regular	45	73
Soft	42	45
Corn oil	18	25

Source: Land O'Lakes, Inc.

Butter Cut-in

The telephone surveys in each market also focused on the butter cut-in issues. It was found that many of Land O Lakes margarine's repeat buyers were users of Land O Lakes butter. On the other hand, it was determined that those who had bought Land O Lakes margarine only once were not very heavy butter users (and of course, did not often use Land O Lakes butter). While the information obtained was not conclusive, it

Table B-5 Index of purchases

Other brands of margarine bought more than once	Bought LOL Margarine once	Bought LOL Margarine more than once	Total
Butter usage			
Indianapolis			
Bought butter in last 3 months	82	179	133
Bought LOL butter most recently	104	192	152
Bought LOL butter more than once	60	142	105
Albany			
Bought butter in last 3 months	105	142	132
Bought LOL most recently	117	178	165
Bought LOL more than once	90	163	143
Watertown			
Bought butter in last 3 months	101	107	104
Bought LOL most recently	83	123	106
Bought LOL more than once	100	114	108

Source: Land O' Lakes, Inc.

was taken as an indication that the Land O Lakes label on the margarine was doing what had been hoped—attracting Land O Lakes butter users to Land O Lakes margarine, without reducing their purchases of Land O Lake butter. (See Tables B-5 and B-6.)

This indication came from tracking Land O Lakes butter sales in Indianapolis. Through June 1973, sales were up to 10.3 percent versus the comparable period in 1972, while total U.S. sales of Land O Lakes butter were up less than 1 percent. This early indication provided encouragement to expand the test markets.

Rollout, Phase 1

Land O Lakes margarine had demonstrated preliminary consumer acceptance and the ability to hold distribution—and butter sales didn't appear to suffer. It was agreed Land O Lakes margarine should next be tested in areas with greater Land O Lakes butter acceptance and in areas of greater premium-priced margarine strength (e.g., higher shares for Imperial).

In September 1973, Land O'Lakes entered Syracuse, Buffalo/Rochester, Terre Haute, and St. Louis. Shares in these new markets showed significant improvement. Syracuse and Buffalo, traditionally strong Land O Lakes butter markets, averaged above 4.0 share and Rochester averaged over 7.0 share, once distribution was established. (See Table B-7.)

Table B-6 Competitive overview
Index of LOL Margarine's Market Strength

Other brands of margarine bought more than once	Bought LOL margarine once	Bought LOL Margarine more than once	Total
Indianapolis			
Blue Bonnet	120	132	126
Chiffon	120	223	177
Fleischmann's	135	151	144
Imperial	123	142	133
Mazola	214	177	195
Mrs. Filbert's	134	137	137
Parkay	124	112	118
Albany			
Blue Bonnet	99	119	114
Chiffon	168	115	130
Fleischmann's	114	146	137
Imperial	82	133	118
Mazola	127	148	139
Mrs. Filbert's	121	148	139
Parkay	128	97	105
Watertown			
Blue Bonnet	105	137	123
Chiffon	167	171	167
Fleischmann's	217	160	183
Imperial	107	160	136
Mazola	156	138	144
Mrs. Filbert's	110	107	110
Parkay	134	90	110

Source: Land O' Lakes, Inc.

The survey showed Land O Lakes margarine users were heavy users of every margarine. This further suggested that business would likely come from homemakers' other margarine purchases.

Land O' Lakes had now demonstrated the ability to successfully enter the margarine market.

Table B-7 LOL margarine market share (%)

| | 73/74 | | | | | | 74/75 | | Eff. | Adj.* |
	ON	DJ	FM	AM	JJ	AS	ON	DJ	Dist.	Share
Rochester Total	2.7	4.7	10.0	7.9	6.8	9.7	6.8	7.4	—	7.8
Soft	.7	1.6	2.7	2.0	1.7	2.2	1.6	2.3	74	2.5
Stick	1.8	2.9	6.8	5.5	4.6	5.2	4.1	3.9	88	3.9
Corn	.2	.2	.5	.4	.5	2.3	1.1	1.2	71	1.4
Syracuse Total	2.1	3.7	6.3	5.1	4.7	4.3	3.9	3.4	—	4.2
Soft	.4	.7	1.1	.6	.9	1.0	.7	.6	72	.7
Stick	1.6	2.5	4.3	3.5	3.1	2.5	2.4	2.1	94	2.1
Corn	.1	.5	.9	1.0	.7	.8	.8	.7	40	1.4
Buffalo Total	.5	3.6	6.9	4.9	4.7	4.9	3.8	3.9	—	6.0
Soft	.1	.6	1.5	1.0	0.7	1.1	.8	.7	58	1.0
Stick	.3	2.1	3.5	2.0	2.1	2.4	1.5	1.4	63	1.8
Corn	.1	.9	1.9	1.9	1.9	1.4	1.5	1.8	45	3.2
St. Louis Total	.8	2.7	3.7	2.9	3.1	3.1	3.1	2.5	—	12.5
Soft	.2	.6	1.4	1.0	1.0	1.1	1.1	.6	9	5.3
Stick	.6	2.0	2.2	1.9	2.1	2.0	1.9	1.8	32	4.5
Corn	—	.1	.1	—	—	—	.1	.1	3	2.7

*Adjusted for expected distribution goal of 80%.

Source: A.C. Nielsen Co.

1975–1995

A number of developments occurred over the years.

1. **Pricing.** In 1976, Land O'Lakes reduced its price to establish parity with Parkay and Blue Bonnet. Share of market increased by 0.7 percent almost immediately.

2. **Copy.** In 1980, the advertising campaign was replaced with a new high-scoring campaign that retained the "From America's Number One butter maker" theme but changed the focus away from the animated cows to real farm people.

3. **Volume/Share Projections.** A thorough analysis of current markets was done to determine if any variables might correlate to the

performance of Land O Lakes margarine in the marketplace—margarine consumption in pounds per capita, competition, advertising impact, and Land O Lakes butter sales per capita. The latter proved to be a good, consistent indicator. By applying the correlation between butter and margarine sales per capita in current markets to possible rollout markets, it was possible to project margarine volume in new markets. The system proved to be totally consistent, and led to more-accurate forecasting.

4. **Major Expansion.** In 1981, Land O Lakes margarine was introduced in 85 percent of the country with a strong acceptance. At the same time, a 40 percent butter/60 percent margarine, Land O Lakes brand Country Morning Blend, entered several major markets. Since 1981, Country Morning Blend has expanded to 85 percent of the U.S. (except the West Coast). In addition, a line extension product, Country Morning Blend Light, has been test marketed and expanded to 85 percent of the United States (Country Morning Blend Light is a 52 percent butter/corn oil blend).

In the mid-eighties, Land O'Lakes also test marketed Land O Lakes Spread with Sweet Cream (a spread product with 6 percent sweet cream added to a vegetable base). This was also successful and was expanded to 100 percent U.S. in 1991. At the same time, Land O'Lakes tested a light butter and rolled nationally with it in 1993 in stick and tub form. In 1995, Land O'Lakes introduced flavored butters into test market, with national distribution planned for 1996. (See also pages 39–41.)

Land O Lakes Butter's Future

Since the introduction of non-butter products to the Land O'Lakes line of butter products, the total butter category has been relatively stable. Some softness occurred in the late 1980s due to consumers' concerns about fat and cholesterol, but that softness has flattened out. The category experienced a modest growth in 1995. Land O Lakes butter's category share has still remained strong.

In fact, the Land O'Lakes share of the total table spread category has grown with the introduction of full-fat and low-fat products. Consumers are demanding both versions. Land O'Lakes has responded with quality products at both fat levels. Land O'Lakes recognizes that consumers have different spread needs and all can be met by using Land O'Lakes products.

Conclusions

The margarine experience for Land O'Lakes was a bold move with lasting effects on the corporation. It redefined its business from being "butter marketers" to becoming "spread marketers."

The margarine success helped provide today's Land O'Lakes management commitment and confidence in a more aggressive future program of new products development.

And this experience has demonstrated to Land O'Lakes the tremendous consumer franchise embodied in its brand name. This has caused the company not only to recognize the opportunities this represents, but also to place more stringent guidelines on the use of this valuable equity.

C

Toro Power Shovel

"As a leader, Toro places primacy not only on quality of product and a strong distribution and service network—but also on innovation, the creation of all new need-fulfillment products in the outdoor consumer and commercial maintenance fields."

—KENDRICK MELROSE
Chairman & CEO
The Toro Company

Background

The Toro Company began in the early 1900s as the Bull Tractor Company. The Toro Motor Company, a tractor engine subsidiary, was created in 1914.

Toro first turned away from its agricultural orientation in 1922 when the golf course superintendent of a Minneapolis, MN, country club suggested that the company design a tractor-towed gang mower unit for fairway maintenance. By 1925, Toro turf maintenance machines were in service on nearly every major golf course in the country and on parks and large estates as well.

Toro produced its first power mower for residential use in 1939, but it was not until 1945, when a group of World War II veterans took over the management of the company, that Toro began to move aggressively into the home lawn market.

Through a combination of acquisitions and innovative research and development, Toro began a program of expansion in 1948 that has served as the basic business strategy of the company for more than five decades.

Toro entered the snowthrower market in 1951. It was a major step in transforming the company from a seasonal business into a year-round one.

In the snowthrower market, Toro pioneered the development of compact, lightweight snowthrowers, first with the Snow Pup in 1964. The subject of this case history, the Toro Power Shovel, was introduced in 1979.

Toro has expanded the line further to include the outdoor power industry's widest selection of snow removal equipment, including eight gas-powered snowthrowers and three electric snowthrower models. In addition, the company pioneered the patented heavy-duty Toro Power Shift® system of two-stage machines.

Toro Today

Today, the Toro Company is the nation's leading independent manufacturer and marketer of equipment offering labor-saving, resource-conserving solutions to the problems of outdoor maintenance for both residential and commercial use. Toro is the leading independent producer of consumer lawn equipment, a category that includes walk power mowers, riding mowers, trimmers, and other lightweight appliance products.

Toro is also the worldwide leader in the snow removal equipment market, a category that includes a full line of products ranging in price from less than $100 for the Toro Power Shovel to more than $2,000 for heavy-duty, two-stage Power Shift Toro snowthrowers.

Toro is also a world leader in automatic underground irrigation systems and in professional turf equipment for the commercial and golf course markets.

Toro products are distributed through a network of distributors; approximately 40 in the United States and more than 50 in the rest of the world.

Toro sales exceeded $50,000,000 in 1959; $100,000,000 in 1973; $200,000,000 in 1978; and $400,000,000 in 1980. Due to two years of light snowfall, a downturn in the consumer economy, and inventory buildup throughout the distribution system, sales of $247,000,000 were reported in 1981.

By the fiscal year ending Oct. 31, 1995, Toro sales had rebounded to $919,427,000. Snowthrower sales for the winter of 1994–1995 were the third all-time highest, exceeded only by those two great snow years of 1979 and 1980. Record blizzards on the East Coast during the winter of 1995–1996 caused Toro to "sell out" of snowthrowers in the East. Toro responded by moving units from the West and Canada to the snow-ravaged East. Customers ordered snowthrowers on Toro's Internet page (www.Toro.com) and had them shipped by overnight express. Snowthrower sales now account for 6–10 percent of Toro's overall revenues. Toro's market share of the snowthrower market was a solid, market leading 24 percent.

Toro has supported its products and distribution partners with consistently high-quality marketing programs and advertising over the years. This, combined with a high-quality product offering, has made Toro the worldwide leader in the lawn and garden market.

Snowthrower Market

Toro entered the snowthrower market to gain a seasonal counterbalance to its growing summer yard care business. Toro's first products were two-stage* snowthrowers, then the mainstay of the industry. These machines were large, heavy, cumbersome to operate, and expensive. As a result, the market was limited to very heavy snow areas, primarily in the Northeast.

Toro completely changed the snowthrower market in 1964 when the company introduced the first single-stage* snowthrower. This machine, called the Snow Pup, was much lighter, more compact, easier to operate, and less expensive than the traditional two-stage snowthrower.

Following a successful test market effort, Toro launched a major marketing campaign behind its single-stage snowthrower, including heavy television advertising. The market responded and snowthrower sales took off.

Fueled by above-average snowfalls and a strong economy, the snowthrower market nearly doubled in size each year in the late 1970s. Homeowners in snowbelt markets found the Toro Snow Master, a later version of the Snow Pup, an irreplaceable partner in the battle against winter. The market expanded, sales outstripped production, and Toro firmly established itself as the market leader. Toro snowthrower sales jumped from $13,600,000 in 1975, to $30,400,000 in 1977, $122,700,000 in 1979, and $131,200,000 in 1980. Toro's third highest year of snowthrower sales occurred in 1995, $110,500,000. A typical snowthrower year is in the $60–65 million range.

Toro Power Shovel

It was in this period of sales growth and market expansion that the Toro Power Shovel was developed and prepared for market introduction. Since its introduction, a series of market factors, including two successive years of light snowfall and a sharp decline in the consumer economy, have resulted in sharp declines in the total snowthrower market.

Market Opportunity

The key to the tremendous growth of the snowthrower market in the late 1970s was above-average snowfalls and a product designed to meet consumer needs. Toro led the way in innovative product designs, shifting the market from big two-stage to compact, consumer-designed, single-stage machines.

By 1978, 72 percent of the industry volume was single-stage units, yet penetration was only 20 percent of the snowbelt households. Price was the primary buying deterrent. Toro saw this situation as an opportu-

---

*Two-stage snowthrowers employ an auger to meter the snow into the machine and a high-speed impeller to actually throw the snow. Single-stage snowthrowers utilize a single rotating mechanism to both lift and throw the snow in one continuous operation.

nity to further expand the market through the introduction of an even more compact, lower-cost unit—the Toro Power Shovel.

General consumer exploration of the snowthrower market had suggested the need for such a product. Many snowthrower prospects had a need for light snow removal—but many felt that even the smaller single-stage snowthrowers were too large and inappropriate for their snow removal problem.

Toro conceived the Power Shovel to fill this need. It was to be a smaller, lightweight, electric-powered unit that would work like a manual shovel except that the Power Shovel, not the shoveler, would lift and throw the snow.

First Product Concept

The Power Shovel marketing concept was transformed into a product concept. Additional consumer research was conducted. Respondents said that snow removal was a difficult chore, often undertaken in adverse conditions. They listed *bulk snow removal, snow directional control*, and *convenience* as important buying considerations for a snowthrower. *Price* was the reason most often cited for not owning a snowthrower.

Based on this research, the original Power Shovel product design was modified to enhance its actual and perceived performance. Directional vane controls were added to the unit along with a double bar handle and wheels.

The program moved rapidly through the remaining developmental stages, and in March 1978, a final prototype unit was presented to Toro management for approval. Concern was expressed that while the prototype presented looked excellent, it did not truly represent the original Power Shovel concept. As a result, two key decisions were made at this point:

1. Introduce this unit as a more compact, lightweight, modestly priced electric *snowthrower*. It was to become known as the "S-120."

2. Continue to pursue product development of a true Power Shovel.

The Toro S-120 was introduced in 1979 as the most compact, easiest to use, and easiest to afford snowthrower on the market. The unit was positioned as an extension of the Toro single-stage line and retailed for $129 to $149. It was sold primarily through Toro's two-step distribution system, but there was increased emphasis on expanding mass merchandiser outlets.

New, Refined Product Concept Development

To put the Power Shovel project back on track, a tight product concept statement was drafted. This "Reason for Being" concluded that the Power Shovel device "is offered for the prospect who currently removes snow with a snow shovel and is willing to pay as much as $75 to clear small areas of shallow snow with a minimum of strain and maximum of ease in less than 20 minutes."

Figure C-1 Toro snow removers

Toro expanded the consumer snowthrower market by innovating and introducing smaller, lighter, easier to use, and more affordable snow removal equipment. The progression of each new item reveals this development.

Source: The Toro Company

Power Shovel developmental efforts at Toro proceeded at an accelerated rate. Several outside consultant groups collaborated on the project. Booz Allen & Hamilton of Cleveland, OH, worked primarily in motor design and selection. BKM, Inc., of Bonita, CA, was charged with primary efforts in the rotor system. King Casey, of New Canaan, CT, was given responsibility for the final prototype development and styling efforts.

The product progressed through design development, including numerous design review meetings, cost reviews, and tooling releases. Manufacturing drawings and a final engineering release culminated in an Underwriters Laboratories' product listing. (The four pictures in Figure C-1 trace Toro's moves to develop a smaller, lightweight snow remover.)

Consumer research confirmed the appeal of the redesigned Toro Power Shovel. The unit was perceived as "easy to operate." Two-thirds of the target market felt it would meet their snow removal needs; more than a third indicated a high buying probability. Consumer estimates of the price were very close to the proposed $75 to $80.

Initial production began in October 1979 after late tool deliveries were overcome. By the end of January 1980, total units produced had reached 220,000.

Figure C-1   (Continued)

Market Plan

The Toro Power Shovel was recognized as an opportunity to create an entirely new snow market with tremendous growth potential. The product was believed appropriate for almost half the homeowners in the snowbelt, or a segment of 7,000,000 households.

The basic introductory strategy was to position the product as an all-new household convenience item, not a snowthrower, and to generate massive consumer impact through heavy advertising.

The Power Shovel was introduced in 1979 throughout the entire snowbelt. The objective was to achieve major first-year sales volume and establish a strong position in this new category before lower-priced competitive entries could be introduced.

Product Description

The Toro Power Shovel is a highly engineered snow removal product incorporating advanced technology in rotor, drive system, and electrical design. The versatility and performance of the unit makes it suitable for a wide range of applications, almost anywhere a manual shovel can be used.

Weighing only 11 pounds, the Power Shovel is operated basically like a push snow shovel. (See Figure C-2.) The operator slides the unit along any hard surface on its polyethylene scraper blade. Snow is pushed into the unit and thrown out at a rate of up to a hundred pounds a minute.

Figure C-2 Toro Power Shovel

The new Toro Power Shovel was unique, weighing less than 12 pounds, while throwing snow up to 20 feet.

Source: The Toro Company

Directional control of the snow being thrown is achieved by simply angling the Power Shovel to one side or the other as it's pushed forward.

The Power Shovel was introduced with a full one-year limited warranty, with a Toro option of over-the-counter exchange or repair. Toro also provided additional discounts for service distributors and dealers to encourage development of a service network and responsive consumer service.

Pricing

Toro's pricing objectives were to provide the trade with a standard 40 percent gross margin and a discount structure to support a volume sell-in. At the same time, Toro set its price to generate sufficient internal funds to afford a heavy marketing investment in the product.

The objectives were accomplished through the combination of premium price points with long discounts to encourage retail promotional activity. Toro also utilized a multiple discount structure based on functions performed and a strong early order incentive to gain fast distribution.

With a suggested manufacturer's retail price of $89.99, the Power Shovel was significantly less expensive than any snowthrower on the market. This low price point would encourage impulse buying and gift purchasing.

Figure C-3 Ad positioning test

Posterboards, used as stimulus material in appeal testing, focused on labor saving, time saving, and price. The poster on the left had preferred appeal. Indications from this led to successful print and television executions featuring the best-scoring appeals.

Source: Campbell Mithun Esty

Product Position Development

In the spring of 1978, Toro and its advertising agency, Campbell-Mithun Inc. (now Campbell Mithun Esty), developed six positioning statements for the Power Shovel. Two of the positions keyed on labor saving, two on time saving, and two on price. (See Figure C-3.)

Consumer testing indicated that the labor-saving appeal was the strongest. The winning position statement was headlined, "For people who are tired of lifting snow" and showed a weary shoveler, snow shovel in hand.

As a result of this work, the Toro Power Shovel was positioned as an *all new product for people who don't like to shovel snow*. The position underscored two key elements:

1. The Toro Power Shovel is all new—an innovation from Toro.

2. The Toro Power Shovel is for anyone with appropriate snow conditions who doesn't like to shovel snow.

Figure C-3   (Continued)

New Product Category Created

The Toro Power Shovel was not positioned as a small snowthrower or an extension of the single-stage product line. Instead, the overall objective of the product introduction was to create, and become the market leader in, a whole new product category—the power shovel category.

The strategy was based on the need to appeal to consumers who had already determined that a snowthrower was not appropriate for their needs, because of insufficient snowfall, too small an area to clear, or price. Clearly differentiating the Power Shovel would also minimize cannibalization of the highly profitable Toro single-stage business and help Toro more clearly position the new product with the trade.

Product Name Decision

The Toro snowthrower marketing group and advertising agency explored many product name candidates before deciding on *Toro Power Shovel*. However, after this name was considered, it was felt to be so appropriate and the rationale for it so sound that the name was adopted without consumer research.

Figure C-3   (Continued)

Fast getaway to what you'd rather do this winter.

The new Power Snow Shovel makes quick work of snow removal. In just 10 minutes, it clears two inches of snow from a 3 ft. x 50 ft. sidewalk. And saves you time getting to the ski slopes, ice rink, snowmobile trail, winter camp, bobsled or pipe and slippers by the fire. Whatever you'd rather do with winter.

Introducing the snowthrower for people who think snowthrowers are too expensive.

At $70, the Power Snow Shovel costs less than half as much as any other snowthrower. Which makes it not so much of a luxury, but more of a plain old, practical, economical labor saver. And that, in turn, makes it all the more attractive. Right?

Some of the supporting points for use of the name Toro Power Shovel were:

1. The buying prospect is currently using a snow *shovel*.

2. The product to be replaced is the *shovel*.

3. The motion used with the product is like a push snow *shovel*.

4. The name is unique and memorable.

5. The name helps differentiate the product from Toro's single-stage line.

6. The name capitalizes on the strong Toro awareness and quality image and works to further build the Toro consumer brand franchise.

Distribution

Historically, Toro had sold its snow equipment through its distributors and network of outdoor power equipment and hardware store dealers. While these dealers provided strong sales and quality service, they had a limited ability to generate a high volume of consumer traffic.

The Toro Power Shovel required a strategic shift in this distribution pattern. This change was supported by consumer research. While only 13 percent of all Toro buyers purchased at mass merchandisers in

1977–78, 77 percent of the Power Shovel prospects indicated they would shop for this product at mass merchant outlets. Toro's historical snow distribution channel did not adequately cover the indicated shopping habits of the primary market.

Broad distribution through mass merchants, as well as traditional power equipment and hardware dealers, was required to achieve strong consumer impact and major first-year sales volume. It also provided Toro's distributors with an opportunity to develop a profitable relationship with mass merchants.

Toro supplemented the distributors' effort with a direct sales program. This national account program was designed for direct quantity sales from Toro to national accounts with distributor support on re-orders, stock fill-ins, parts and service, and merchandising assistance. The single most important account sold through this program was J.C. Penney.

By the end of the first season, the Toro Power Shovel was stocked in more than 3,500 outlets, including 2,100 traditional independent dealers, 600 discount, 400 department, and 400 home center stores.

Target Market

The primary target market for the Toro Power Shovel consisted of single-family households in areas averaging a 20- to 49-inch annual snowfall. A majority of the target market was concentrated in the large industrial centers in the central and lower snowbelt, such as New York, Chicago, Philadelphia, Detroit, Cleveland, and Boston. A secondary market was the fringe snowbelt area averaging 10 to 19 inches of snowfall.

Market research indicated a large potential demand for the Power Shovel. Using a screen of "high interest to buy," the prime Power Shovel market potential was calculated at more than two million households.

Compared to Toro snowthrower buyers, the Power Shovel prospects were younger, lower income, had sidewalks instead of driveways, and there was greater female interest in the product. (See Table C-1.)

Table C-1 Prospects for Power Shovel

	Power Shovel	Toro S-120	Toro Snowthrower
Age: Under 35	47%	24%	19%
Income: $10,000–20,000	56	47	31
No Driveway	74	8	3
Sex: Female	41	24	20

Source: The Toro Company

Consumer attitude was determined to be just as important as demographics. The Power Shovel attracted people who had a need for snow removal but did not consider a snowthrower appropriate. They appreciated not having to shovel but considered snowthrowers too big and expensive for their situation.

It was also determined that the Power Shovel was seen as an appropriate gift, particularly for an older person.

Advertising

The early positioning work on the Power Shovel revealed that buying prospects for this product tended not be very knowledgeable about snowthrower operation and pricing. This suggested the need for a strong creative concept and product demonstration to stimulate initial interest.

The advertising agency recommended that the introductory advertising be *highly impactful* for several other reasons:

1. The Power Shovel was a new concept, a new category. They didn't want prospects relating the Toro Power Shovel to snowthrowers.

2. Prospects needed to be jolted into recognizing the value of the Toro Power Shovel. They'd already determined they didn't want or couldn't afford a snowthrower. There was a need to break through this mind-set.

3. The Power Shovel faced a short selling season; there were just 12 weeks during which time it was necessary to gain high awareness and move the prospect toward a buying decision.

4. Mass merchandisers were to become an important retail outlet. Prospects were not accustomed to seeing and buying Toro products at these outlets.

It was also believed that the advertising needed to be action-oriented, show the product at work, and capitalize on the fun and enjoyment of operating the Toro Power Shovel. The advertising needed to build talk value for the product.

The introductory television execution utilized the manual snow shovel as a foil. The commercial opened with an on-camera presenter holding up a shovel, while asking the viewers if they still had one. The presenter then abruptly broke the shovel handle over this knee. This opening not only grabbed the viewers' attention, but created interest and talk value by relating directly to their feelings about shoveling and the snow shovel. The presenter then introduced and demonstrated the new Toro Power Shovel. The demonstration so intrigued his watchful neighbors that they broke their snow shovels in favor of the new Toro Power Shovel. (See Figure C-4.)

The commercial proved highly effective. Copy testing generated a recall score 70 percent above the category norm and a brand preference change 60 percent above the norm. More importantly, the commercial generated consumer awareness, store traffic, and consumer sales.

Figure C-4 Introductory TV commercial

1. MAN: Ever wanted to...
do this?...

2. (Sfx: snap!)...

3. ...

4. Go ahead.

5. ...Toro just invented the
Power Shovel. It's light...

6. ...(Sfx: shovel starts)...
easy to handle.

7. (Sfx: motor running)
If you don't like...

8. ...to shovel...

9. ...let the Power Shovel...
shovel.

10. The new Toro Power Shovel.

11. (Sfx: snap, snap, snap, snap!)

12. Hey, don't break your shovel,...

13. ...get a Toro Power Shovel.

14. (Man VO) Haven't you done
without a Toro long enough?

15. (Silent fadeout)

Dramatic opening of conventional snow shovel being broken immediately captures attention and symbolizes the analogy of the light new Toro Power Shovel benefits vs. back-breaking hand shoveling in this introductory commercial. (Dealer identification is superimposed on closing frame.)

Media

The basic objective of the Toro Power Shovel introductory media plan was to build fast awareness and communicate the product concept. This supported the trade sell-in program and was designed to ensure fast sell-through and minimum end-of-season inventory.

Toro made a major investment in consumer media. The company allocated and spent about $2,000,000 for advertising in 1979, or 18 percent of planned net sales.

The basic media strategy was concentration. The media mix was concentrated in television, with 90 percent of the budget going into this medium. Spending was concentrated in key market ADIs: 2,000 GRPs in markets representing the top 50 percent of potential and 1,500 GRPs in markets representing the next 30 percent of potential. Scheduling was concentrated in a 12-week period to create maximum impact during the early winter and pre-Christmas periods. Communication was concentrated in one strong introductory television commercial, with dealer and Christmas gift five-second tags.

Toro funded 100 percent of the television advertising. A 75/25 percent Toro-funded co-op advertising allowance was also provided to help stimulate strong retail promotion advertising.

Promotion

The Toro Power Shovel was not included in the traditional Toro Red Tag preseason dollars-off promotion for other items in the Toro snowthrower line. Instead, distributors participated in an extension cord promotion that encouraged retailer displays, promotion, and tie-in advertising. The suggested consumer offer consisted of a free cord with purchase of a Power Shovel.

National and direct accounts were given a 100 percent Toro-paid advertising/merchandising allowance to support their Power Shovel purchases.

Toro also supported the introduction with a complete Power Shovel point-of-sale kit. The primary fixture was a product display stand with a build-in Fairchild projector and a two-minute concept-sell point-of-sale film. The display unit picked up the broken snow shovel visual idea from the television commercial and carried the "Hate shoveling? Try the new Toro Power Shovel" proposition right to the store.

When early winter snow failed to develop, Toro continued to support the product with a "Mid-Winter Clean-Up" promotion. Geared to stimulate retail activity, the event was supported with spot TV, including a Super Bowl announcement, newspaper, and radio.

Results

The recommended build quantity for the introductory year was 175,000 pieces. This was based on 7 percent first-year penetration of the total estimated potential power shovel market. That market potential was calculated to be 2,846,000 households, or the percent of total snowbelt households that indicated a high buying interest in the product. The projections were based on the assumptions of distribution through direct and distributor sales, average snowfall, and moderate economic growth.

Toro sold 207,000 units and moved them into the distribution pipeline. However, by the end of the first season, only 110,000 units had been sold at retail.

Consumer sales were hampered by a delayed introduction due to late tooling and a mild winter. Following record-setting snowfalls the two preceding seasons, the winter of 1979–80 almost didn't happen. Many key Power Shovel markets strolled through the season with mild temperatures and without a trace of snow.

Toro did succeed in creating a unique and innovative product. The Toro Power Shovel proved to be an excellent performing unit that met the needs of a potentially large segment of the snow market. However, it also became apparent that accurately forecasting sales volumes for snow products, including the Toro Power Shovel, was almost as difficult as predicting the very snowfall on which those sales depended.

Even so, there's still optimism. Toro finds its snowthrowers sell best in pre-season, especially following a year of heavy snows.

Chad Kelly, Toro's marketing manager for consumer products, as quoted in January 21, 1991, *Adweek's Marketing Week*:

> "People remember that last year they got dumped on real bad . . . so they say, "I'm not going to shovel by hand this year.'" But Kelly says there's always a surge of Toro sales just after a snowfall, too.

> Like any good marketer these days, Kelly is a student of baby boomers. The romance of shoveling snow recedes with age, and Kelly expects snowthrower sales to grow as boomers mature.

> "We're seeing a dramatic increase in consumers calling snow-throwers a necessity rather than a luxury," says Kelly. "Shoveling snow is so stressful on the heart and back. Now people are saying, "I need a snowthrower.'"

Summing up the Toro success in 1995, Chairman and Chief Executive Officer Kendrick Melrose states: One thing that has made the Toro brand a standard of excellence is our dedication to developing innovative new products that consistently lead the industry. In fact, it's one of Toro's core competencies. We've invested heavily in the process of innovation, because we believe Toro does it better than our competition. This skill of innovation made the Toro brand great, and it will keep it great long into the future.

Toro's leadership philosophy drives our innovation. Our philosophy states, 'Market leadership and financial success at Toro will best result by unleashing the potential of our people.' That has certainly been demonstrated by the innovation and advancement of our snowthrower products over the years."

Appendix
2

A

New Products Checklist

Condensed summary checkpoints selected from 122-page New Product Development Checklists *by George Gruenwald, NTC Business Books, 1991*

Loosely chronological organization of new products operational considerations.

Broad areas of major functions as follows:

Research & Development

All product and consumer research except for that directly related to development and evaluation of communications. This category includes technical, engineering, styling, and market research.

Production

Purchasing, manufacturing, warehousing, shipping, quality control, labor

Finance

Budgeting, cost analysis, pricing, profitability

Legal

Distribution

Sales operations, trade practices, and policies

Communications

Advertising, promotion, merchandising, product publicity, advertising research

Whenever action is required by the major operational officer responsible for the company activity, an asterisk (*) is indicated.

New Products Checklist

	Research and Development	Finance	Production	Distribution	Legal	Communications
I. EXPLORATION						
*Statement of company objective	Policy Objective					
Initial exploratory and creative activities					X	
Statement of product idea	Originator					
Judgment evaluation of merit	New Product Committee					
*Plan to investigate approved	Operations Executive					
Profile of products known on the market	X					
Survey of product ingredients, design standards, general technology of the field	X					
Analysis of competitive product claims	X					X
Analysis of competitive media use						X
Analysis of competitive advertising expenditures						X
Areas of brand share/volume history	X					
Survey of trade information regarding CGS, wholesale discounts, distribution costs	X			X		X
Survey of traditional channels of distribution and other distribution opportunities	X			X		X
Survey of general selling practices, promotional allowances, buying standards				X		X

	Research and Development	Finance	Production	Distribution	Legal	Communications
Survey of specific federal and state legal problems in reference to ingredients, sales practices, controls				X	X	X
Survey to determine marketing opportunity area	X					
Cyclical, seasonal, and long-term marketing considerations	X					
Product class profile study	X					
Survey of potential consumer interest in new product	X					
Definition of the selected market	X					
Preliminary opportunity estimate	New Product Committee					
II. SCREENING						
*Appointment of project coordinating executive	X					
Estimation of period product exclusivity	X		X	X		X
Research of consumer satisfaction and use habits of current products	X					
Consumer motivation research in area of advertised brand claims, etc.	X					X
Product concept screening	X					X
Analysis of sizes, colors, shapes, textures, types required	X					
Isolation of CGS/price opportunities in distribution mix	X	X				
Investigation of additional sales outlets—government, export, institutional, premiums				X		

New Products Checklist

	Research and Development	Finance	Production	Distribution	Legal	Communications
Report of findings and indicated opportunities	X			X		X
III. PROPOSAL						
*Request for Planned Development Program, with estimated investment and timetable	New Product Committee					
Approval of research and development budget	Operations Executive					
Initial design/formulation of product	X		X			
Copyrights or patents	X				X	
Preparation of product platform	X			X	X	X
Securement of required government clearances					X	
Initial costing based on optimum manufacturing levels	X	X	X			
Determination of local tax, licensing, and other financial considerations		X			X	
Life and fatigue tests of materials and finishes	X		X			
Performance and efficiency tests	X		X			
*Independent labor/engineering analysis of prototypes	X					
Preparation of copy platform						X
Social science evaluation of consumers relative to the new product area	X					X
Panel evaluation of prototype product	X					

	Research and Development	Finance	Production	Distribution	Legal	Communications
Forecast of volume potential	X			X		X
Determination of plant capacity and facilities availability			X			
Consumer blind test comparison	X					
IV. DEVELOPMENT						
Large-scale research of prototype product	X					
Plant location and transportation considerations			X			
*Basics of appropriation		New Product Committee				
Development of national media plan						X
Decision on manufacturer association-identification on/with product	X			X		X
Creation of brand name possibilities						X
Creation of/or agreement on established generic descriptive name						X
Legal search of brand name possibilities					X	
Registration of trademark, copyright brand name					X	
Development of basic consumer selling theme						X
Test of consumer selling theme						X
Labeling requirements					X	
Initial packaging	X					X

New Products Checklist

	Research and Development	Finance	Production	Distribution	Legal	Communications
Packaging testing	X					
Approval of package design (and inserts)						X
Preparation of instructions/directions to conform					X	X
Adoption of media, philosophy, based on selling theme, budgetary consideration, coverage of prospects, and availability						X
Test of advertising execution (in form of basic media)						X
Creation of total national campaign concept						X
Determination of labor availability			X			
Study of labor or union regulations			X		X	
Determination of raw material commitments and availability			X			
Determination of special tooling and equipment			X			
Packaging and components commitments			X			
Prediction of competitive reaction to new product	X			X		
V. SALES TESTING						
Assignment of product manager to work with project executive	Operations Executive					
Setting of test sales goals—share, penetration, unit, and dollar volume	New Product Committee					

	Research and Development	Finance	Production	Distribution	Legal	Communications
Determination of introductory test area timing	X					X
Determination of service and repair problems and facilities				X		
*Sales representative recruitment		X		X		
Sales training				X		
*Manufacturing pilot run			X			
*Approval of test area production	Operations Executive		X			
Shipping, storage, and packing tests			X			
Definition of all aspects of available test areas, including demographic, media patterns, trade outlet patterns, and distribution centers	X					X
Plan to meet competitive reaction				X		X
Finalization of test area(s)	X					X
Forecast of test area units and dollar volume (goals)	X			X		
*Forecast of P/L limits of successful venture and of unsuccessful write-off	X	X		X		
Test area simulation of national campaign concept						X
Development of test area media plan (in line with expansion objectives)						X
*Determination of test area total appropriation	New Product Committee					
Approval of test area consumer advertising materials						X

New Products Checklist

	Research and Development	Finance	Production	Distribution	Legal	Communications
Approval of trade advertising materials				X		X
Determination of merchandising plan and appropriation				X		X
Preparation of media merchandising				X		X
Preparation of trade selling sheets				X		X
Determination of educational plan and appropriation						X
Preparation of consumer educational materials						X
Determination of publicity plan and appropriation						X
Preparation of introductory publicity materials						X
Determination of sales promotion plan and appropriation				X		X
Devising of consumer incentives, if required—premiums, contests, price offers, couponing, etc.				X		X
Consideration of multiple product tie-ins				X		X
Determination of cooperative advertising policies				X		X
Preparation of cooperative ads				X		X
Preparation of point of purchase materials				X		X
Preparation of product hang tags, boots, self-displays			X	X		X
Decision on trade sampling appropriation			X	X		X
Approval of test area commercial plan and insertion schedule						X

	Research and Development	Finance	Production	Distribution	Legal	Communications
Determination of product indemnity for field test					X	
Setting of sales quotas				X		
Establishment of sales force incentives, bonuses, premiums				X		
Establishment of trade incentives—buying allowances, contests				X		
Commission of product printed material			X			
Setting up of test area consumer sales audit panel	X			X		
Trade sales kickoff				X		
Pre-introductory measurement of brand name awareness in test area	X					X
Advertising kickoff						X
Survey of trade performance in test area				X		
Research on test area users	X					
Media coverage and intensity progress reports in test area—adjust to meet standards						X
Post-introduction measurements of brand name awareness in test area	X					X
Post-introductory new product profile study in test area	X					
Analysis of factory sales data from test area	X					
Program performance reports in test area—adjust to meet standards						X

New Products Checklist

	Research and Development	Finance	Production	Distribution	Legal	Communications
Competitive media trend report of test area						X
Evaluation of sales and advertising, via progress reports throughout area test timetable	X			X		X
Test area evaluation	X			X		X
*Definition of special line management attention or policy changes required in large scale marketing	X	X	X	X		X
*Recommendation for major expansion	New Product Committee					
VI. MARKETING						
Turn over to appropriate product manager and revenue division						

B

New Products Responsibility Checklist

By permission of 3M Company, from its internal policy publication "Guidelines for Planned Policy Responsibility."

1. NAME OF PRODUCT

   Brand name or trademark clearance with the secretary of the corporate trademark screening committee.

2. PRODUCT CHARACTERISTICS AND FUNCTION

   Summary of the general composition or design of the product.

   Identification of the customers who will use the product, and where and how they will use it.

3. PATENTS

   Patent clearances.

   Determination by patent counsel of the patentability of the product and its use by customers before any divulgation outside 3M.

   Filing of appropriate patent applications.

   Investigation of possible infringement of patents owned by others.

4. MARKETING

   Legal approval of merchandising plans (pricing, discounts, proportionately equal treatment, terms and conditions of sale, etc.).

   Instructions, technical, and product literature to delineate product purpose, intended use, use instructions, and caution as to serious health and/or property hazards from reasonably foreseeable misuse.

   Warranty statements in conformance with warranty disclosure requirements.

Labeling in conformance with corporate policy.

Labeling in conformance with federal, state, and local laws.

Advertising and promotional messages including press releases and commercials in conformance with corporate policy.

Information on product claims and limitations to sales force, agents, brokers, and distributors.

5. PRODUCT ASSURANCE

A. Reliability

Conformance to applicable government or industry standards.

If there is no government or industry standard, evaluation against a "guideline" standard or a similar product of proven reliability.

Product evaluation assessment considering, but not limited to, its description and performance under normal storage conditions as well as after extended storage life in the warehouse and within production facilities.

A periodic program to verify and document reliability procedures.

Tests with extremes of reasonably foreseeable customer use environment (i.e., temperature, humidity, altitude, input voltage, etc.).

B. Quality

Establishment of quality requirements as determined by the user.

Comparison of optional methods of achieving quality requirements.

Establishment of quality monitoring procedure.

Periodic analysis of results-progress toward goal.

C. Maintenance (where applicable)

Definition of training and skill requirements for maintenance personnel and procedures for service and efficient maintenance.

Replacement parts system.

Information program on warranties for sales, distribution, and maintenance.

6. PRODUCT SAFETY

A. Health hazard evaluation

Evaluation of any adverse effect on human health of any component under conditions of recommended use or reasonably foreseeable misuse in these situations:

(1) If swallowed, ingested, or inhaled.

(2) With single or repeated eye or skin contact, the occurrence of irritation, toxic absorption, or future sensitization.

B. Product chemical substance regulatory evaluation

If the product contains a "new 3M" chemical substance; and it is subject to Premanufacturing Notification (PMN), to be considered six months prior to planned manufacture.

C. Physical safety evaluation

Evaluation of the following under recommended conditions of use or reasonably foreseeable misuse:

(1) Flammability/explosivity
(2) Static electricity
(3) Other electrical effects
(4) Thermal extremes
(5) Mechanical failures
(6) Muscle injury because of weight or design
(7) Noise, color, odor, brightness, etc., effects
(8) Potential injury from sharp corners or edges or "pinching" fingers
(9) Potential injury from unprotected moving parts

Appropriate measures—warning labels, advisory literature—for risks.

D. General safety considerations

Government safety regulations, approvals, or certification requirements for:

(1) Special safety warning labeling
(2) Disclosure of the product's ingredients
(3) Specific handling instructions, safety data sheets, etc.
(4) Special instructions regarding packaging, transportation, and/or storage
(5) Language requirements

E. Evaluation of the product safety characteristics for insurability and claims exposure as follows:

(1) Availability of product insurance in corporate program
(2) Claims exposure level
(3) Cost of insurance in relation to normal coverage

7. ENVIRONMENTAL IMPACT ASSESSMENT

A. Evaluation of the reasonably foreseeable impact of the product and its package on the atmosphere and on the aquatic and terrestrial ecosystems for applicable regulations, including registration and labeling, in all areas where sale is contemplated.

B. Evaluation of the product or material resulting during and from its manufacture, use or disposal for effects on environment regarding:

(1) Effect on human, plant, and animal life
(2) Persistence in the environment and the effects of any degradation products

       (3) Effect on air quality

       (4) Effect on any aquatic ecosystem into which product or its wastes are discharged.

C. Efforts in products and packaging development to minimize waste and eliminate adverse environmental effects

D. Noise considerations; acceptable levels for noise in manufacture and/or use of product

E. Acceptable methods of treatment disposal to recommend to customers

F. Determination of resource recovery potential from this product

G. Acceptable cleanup and disposal procedure for accidental spills

8. INTERNATIONAL DISTRIBUTION
Outside United States requirements for product responsibility

C

Legal Clearance for Inventions

By permission, 3M Company

Introduction

We understand you have an idea that you think may be of interest to 3M.

At the outset, let us say that 3M is committed to growth, and much of our past growth can be traced to new ideas. We appreciate the fact that you thought of 3M when you had your idea.

However, you must understand that it is only on rare occasions that we actually utilize an idea submitted to us by a person outside of the company.

With this fact in mind, you may, if you choose to do so, submit your idea to us. However, it will have to be according to the procedures set out in the following pages.

Also you must understand that it is 3M's policy not to accept ideas from the outside on any kind of confidential basis. If you decide to submit your idea to 3M you must keep this policy in mind.

Markets 3M Serves

3M is a large and growing company whose success has been based on the development of new and useful products for the home and industry. The vast majority of these products are developed by our laboratories.

3M currently sells products in the following marketing areas:

- Health care
- Transportation equipment manufacturing and maintenance
- Electronics/electrical manufacturing
- Safety and security
- Voice, video, and data communications
- Office, training, and business
- Consumer
- Communication arts
- Industrial production
- Construction and maintenance

Even though 3M sells over 40 thousand products, our markets are confined primarily to the ten listed. Also, history indicates that while 3M receives many ideas, few are truly new. For these reasons and others, the chances of acceptance of an idea are low . . . usually because the idea does not fit with 3M's overall goals even though it may have apparent value.

This booklet will tell you the basis on which we can consider your idea.

If Your Idea Is Already Patented

We prefer to consider an idea after it has been described and claimed in a patent, since we are then in a position to know exactly what is considered new. If you already have an ISSUED PATENT covering your invention, just send a copy to us; nothing else is required.

On occasion patents have been ruled invalid by courts after being challenged. Invalidity usually results because an earlier publication of products were already in use that were not discovered until after the grant of the patent. There are many other reasons why a patent can be invalid, and 3M has had patents held invalid in the past. Thus any individual or company—including 3M—must retain the right to challenge a patent it considers invalid, and that right extends to any patent submitted for our consideration.

If You Have No Patent and Seek No Compensation for Your Idea

Just complete the Idea Submission Agreement, check the box adjacent to "3M may use my idea freely. I neither expect nor seek compensation," and send us the information requested.

If You Have No Patent but Hope to Be Paid for Your Idea

3M will consider your idea only under certain conditions.

Your idea must fall in one of the classes of subject matter which could lead to the development of a product. (It must not, for instance, be concerned with advertising, slogans, selling, or how to run a business.)

You must complete and return to us the original of the Idea Submission Agreement form which is part of this booklet. Make certain you check the box adjacent to "If 3M uses my idea, I hope to receive compensation." If you have already sent us a description about your idea, we will keep it sealed in a locked file unavailable to 3M employees for evaluation until the signed form is returned.

You must accompany the completed Idea Submission Agreement form with a detailed written description of your idea, illustrating it with drawings or photographs, if you can. If you have a patent application pending before the U.S. Patent & Trademark Office, a copy of the specification and drawings will be satisfactory. Please do not send bulky models: We'll ask for them if we need them.

You must agree to let us keep whatever materials you submit for our records. To be certain that our files correspond, be sure to keep a copy of everything you send us.

3M Requirements

If 3M considers your idea, we do so with the understanding that it may not be new to us. Please also understand that any disclosure of your idea to a 3M officer or employee cannot establish any obligation to you on behalf of 3M.

We can't assume any obligation to act in a consulting capacity in regard to the patentability of your idea, the desirability of a patent, the commercial possibilities of your idea, or your rights against others.

Nor can we consider any idea you submit unless you are its sole owner. If anyone else has any rights to your idea, you must tell us the name of each such person and the nature of his/her interest.

If you are not at least 18 years old, we must have the signature of your parent or guardian on the Idea Submission Agreement.

You may, of course, appoint an attorney or agent to submit your idea; if you do, however, he should also submit proof of his appointment.

If you are employed, we will need a release from your employer if your employer has any right or equity in your idea.

In Addition, Your Idea Must Pass Some Tests

3M will be interested in your idea only if it passes these tests:

1. It is concerned with a working device, product, process, or formula and is not a sales promotion idea.

2. It is an idea for a new product, process, working device, or formula which was not in existence when you thought of it. By "in existence" we mean:

   - shown or described in a patent, catalog, magazine, encyclopedia, or some other printed publication

     •commonly known to the public or trade

     •already known to 3M

3. 3M believes the idea has attractive possibilities of becoming a useful product.

4. It fits the markets 3M serves.

Your Idea May Warrant Legal Advice

Unless your invention is already patented or is the subject of a pending patent application, your agreement to the conditions set forth in this booklet may cause you to lose the opportunity to obtain a valid patent in many foreign countries. Consequently, before subscribing to the terms of the agreement set forth in this booklet, we strongly urge you to see a lawyer specializing in patents.

What 3M Will Do

After you have sent us either (1) a copy of your issued patent, or (2) the completed Idea Submission Agreement form accompanied by the information you have checked and noted on the form, here's what we'll do:

We will submit your idea to those people in 3M best able to evaluate it.

If we have an interest in your idea, we will notify you as soon as we can—but this will probably take more time than you would suppose because we may want to have your idea fairly evaluated by several divisions of 3M. We'll try to write you within six weeks; but some ideas require more time than this to evaluate.

Meanwhile, you are free to submit your idea to other companies should you desire to do so.

After Our Evaluation

If we are interested in your idea after our evaluation, we may wish to enter into a formal written agreement which may, among other things, grant patent rights to 3M and provide for compensation. We will not conduct any negotiations before we receive an issued patent or a signed Idea Submission Agreement. A meeting may be arranged after our evaluation of the idea, if both you and 3M are interested in pursuing the matter further.

Until we have evaluated your idea, we can assume no obligation to you whatsoever other than to tell you whether or not we are interested in it. Further, we are not obligated to tell you anything we previously knew or have discovered since you submitted your idea.

In Summary, Here Is What We've Tried to Say:

- Although 3M does not solicit ideas, we will consider your idea at your request provided it is submitted on the enclosed form.

- You must assure us that to the best of your knowledge you are the one who originated the idea, that you own the idea, and that you have the legal right to negotiate with 3M concerning it.

- By submitting your idea to 3M you are not giving us any rights under a patent you now have or may obtain in the future.

- By considering your idea, we are not necessarily admitting that it is new.

- No confidential relationship between us is established when you submit your idea. 3M does not promise to keep it secret.

- After we have studied your idea, we will tell you in writing whether we are interested in it. We assume no obligation to tell you anything we previously knew or have discovered since you submitted your idea.

- Until we have evaluated your idea, we can assume no obligation to you whatsoever. If the evaluation of the idea is promising, 3M may enter into a formal written agreement with you.

- We suggest that you consult with an attorney before proceeding with the submission of your idea.

- Remember, the odds are very low that any idea will be one which will qualify as a new product possibility in which 3M will invest.

It's Your Move

If the rules for submitting your idea sound harsh, it's only because we're trying not to mislead you. We congratulate you for your creativity and thank you again for associating 3M with new ideas.

Now with these conditions in mind—if you would like to have 3M consider your idea, please complete the Idea Submission Agreement which follows. Make sure you describe your idea on the top line of the agreement. A duplicate form is included for your records. Tear out the original and mail it to:

> Corporate Technical Planning and Coordination/3M
> 223-5S 02, 3M Center
> St. Paul, Minnesota 55144
> Attn: External Ideas Correspondent

If your idea is described and claimed in your issued patent, you do not need to complete the Idea Submission Agreement—just send a copy of the patent to us at the address mentioned.

If you have more than one idea, each must be accompanied by an Idea Submission Agreement. Please note that in signing the agreement, you agree that any related ideas you send us will be subject to the same conditions as the present idea.

IDEA SUBMISSION AGREEMENT

Minnesota Mining and Manufacturing Company

Idea Submission Agreement

3M

My idea relates to _____

_____

_____

Check all
appropriate boxes
and fill in all
pertinent blanks.

☐ I have sent to you   ☐ I am enclosing
☐ I am sending under separate cover information on this idea

This information is in the form of:

☐ Patent Application (include serial number and filing date)

☐ Other (specify) _____

☐ Written description

☐ Photographs, drawings, or sketches

Please indicate the number of pages of any of the above materials you send us
on this line

_____

☐ 3M may use my idea freely.
   I neither expect nor seek
   compensation.

☐ If 3M uses my idea I hope to
   receive compensation.

☐ I am less than 18 years old

☐ I am at least 18 years old

☐ I am keeping a copy of this
   agreement and the other
   information sent to you as
   indicated above

Name and address of present employer _____

_____

Name and address of employer when you first got the idea _____

_____

Does either of above employers have any right or equity in the idea?   ☐ Yes   ☐ No

List the names, addresses and interests of others
having any rights in this idea and ask them to sign
this agreement (if none, write "None").

_____

_____

_____

_____

I have read the 3M "ABOUT YOUR IDEA" booklet, and particularly the conditions set forth on Pages
12 and 13, immediately preceding this agreement. I agree to each of the conditions contained in the 3M
"ABOUT YOUR IDEA" booklet with regard to the presently submitted idea and all ideas I send 3M in
the future.

_____   _____   _____

Signature of submitter   Date   Name (please print)

_____   _____   _____

Signature of parent or guardian if submitter is not   Date   Address (please print)
at least 18 years old

_____   _____

                                                                           _____

                                                                           City, State and Zip (please print)

If this idea is submitted by an agent of the
originator, the agent should sign and submit
written proof of his authority.

_____   _____

Signature of agent   Date

D

Checklist for Written Agreements with New Products Services

By permission, American Association of Advertising Agencies

This checklist represents some of the many considerations that must be taken into account in new product assignments.

1. Agency service

   A. Scope of agency work, including research, package design, sampling, etc.

2. General provisions

   A. Mutually exclusive arrangement

   B. Mutual cooperation

   C. Approval of expenditures by client

   D. Care of client's property

   E. Cancellation of plans

3. Charges for agency service

   A. Method of compensation

   B. Amount of compensation (fee, retainer, etc.)

4. Charges for materials and services purchased (including handling of cash discount from suppliers)

Reproduced by permission from American Association of Advertising Agencies, New York, NY, from its private membership publication, "Agency Compensation and Written Agreements with Clients for New Products Assignments," October 1981.

5. Reimbursement for out-of-pocket costs

   A. Telephone and telegraph

   B. Shipping costs

6. Terms of payment

   A. Client agreement to pay

   B. Mailing date of agency's invoices

   C. Agency right to change terms if client's credit impaired

7. Termination of agreement

   A. Period of agreement

   B. Notice of termination

   C. Payment for materials purchased and work done

   D. Disposition of client's property

   E. Agency title to unused plans and ideas

8. Examination of records

9. Client's acceptance

E

Sample New Products Agreements with Advertising Agencies

By permission, American Association of Advertising Agencies

Reproduced by permission from American Association of Advertising Agencies, New York, NY, from its private membership publication, "Agency Compensation and Written Agreements with Clients for New Products Assignments," October 1981.

Agency-Client New Product Agreement
Sample "A"

(DATE)

(NAME OF CLIENT)

Gentlemen:

This letter represents an amendment to the basic agreement in existence between your company and the agency and is intended to outline the method of compensation which is to prevail in connection with <u>new product development assignments</u> which we may be requested to perform on your behalf from time to time.

These new product assignments may include such work as brand name and concept development, creative concept development, product and creative concept testing, package design development, introductory and prototype advertising campaign development and production.

It is agreed that over and above the compensation provided for in our basic contract, you will reimburse us for the services of all agency personnel devoted to these assignments at hourly rates which recover the basic salaries of these persons to include a factor for overhead and normal profit. These hourly rates and the overhead-profit factor are detailed later in this letter.

These charges will be based on the agency's computer cost-accounting. Time sheets are kept by all agency personnel on a daily basis by quarter-hour units. These time sheets, as well as job jackets and other cost information related to these assignments, are available for client examination.

To the extent that charges other than those mentioned above are incurred in connection with new product development assignments, including charges in connection with production and creation of advertising materials and the placement of same, research, travel and cable expenses, etc., the provisions of our basic agreement will apply.

Billing for these services will be rendered on a monthly basis including documentation of all charges. (See prototype invoice attached.) The hourly rates will be billed according to our standard hourly rate schedule (attached). Rates on this schedule are based on actual annual salary costs, including benefits, divided by _____ hours and multiplied by a factor for overhead and profit. This factor is _____ for personnel in the agency's U.S. offices; _____ for offices in other countries.

Hourly charges will be billed by the 10th of the month following from time sheets for the month and are payable ten days from the date of invoice.

This agreement will apply to each product as long as it continues in the development, test and introductory campaign stages. It will terminate for each product at such time as regular commissionable media billing is in effect for the product. Thereafter, when advertising developed by the agency is placed by the agency or one of its associated offices throughout the world, the agency will continue to service the advertising of the new product in accordance with the terms and conditions set forth in our basic agreement. However, in those cases where the advertising developed by the agency is placed by one or more of (Client's Name) other agencies, (Name of Agency) will be entitled to a commission of _____ percent of the gross billing of such advertising.

If advertising for the product developed by the agency is placed domestically in media in the U.S.A. through the agency, _____ percent of media commissions on such advertising will be credited against the original development fees, up to _____ percent of such fees.

You may, of course, discontinue the development of a new product and our assignment in connection with it at any time by notifying us to such effect on ninety days' written notice. Termination of a new product assignment for any one product will not affect other product assignments or our basic contract agreement.

If the above meets with your approval, please sign both copies of this letter, retain one for your files and return the other to us.

Cordially,

_____

_____

Approved

_____

By _____ Title _____

Date _____

Attachments: Hourly rate schedule
     Prototype invoice

COPY

Agency-Client New Product Agreement
Sample "A"
(Supplementary Letter)

(DATE)

(NAME OF CLIENT)

Dear _____:

Attached is our supplementary agreement letter outlining the terms under which we handle new product assignments. I think you will find it in order.

Specifically, for the handling of the new product assignment you outlined to us, we will, of course, assign an account group to the project. The group will include an account supervisor, account executive, a creative copy-art team under supervision of the agency creative director, a research supervisor, media supervisor and international estimator, plus the necessary secretarial, administrative and traffic personnel.

We estimate the time charges for this group for the project outlined will average approximately $ _____ per month over the period of the assignment. Advertising preparation and mechanical production costs, of course, are not included in this figure nor is research.

Research in the three markets, _____, _____, and _____ will cost approximately $_____ to $_____ plus travel for the basic creative concept testing. To this you must add about _____ per country for the advertising pre-testing, plus production of animatics. An outline of the research proposal is attached.

In total, our services on the project will include brand name and product concept development, creative concept development (both including basic package design), creative concept testing (including package concept) and advertising development and testing. Advertising testing would include preliminary concept and copy evaluation and communications effectiveness and response evaluation.

In addition, we will develop, prepare and place introductory advertising campaigns for the various markets involved.

We appreciate this assignment. It's an exciting and interesting opportunity.

Cordially,

<u>**COPY**</u>

<u>**Agency-Client New Product Agreement**</u>
<u>**Sample "B"**</u>

(DATE)

(NAME OF CLIENT)

AGREEMENT made between (Company) having an office at (address) (herein called the "Advertiser"), and (Agency), a _____ corporation having an office at _____ (herein called the "Agency").

<u>WITNESSETH:</u>

The parties have entered into an agreement dated (date) (herein referred to as "The Advertiser-Agency agreement) wherein the Advertiser has retained Agency in connection with the advertising of certain existing products of Advertiser, and the parties now desire to extend these arrangements to cover the terms and conditions under which Agency will service and develop advertising and marketing plans for (such) new product or products developed by Advertiser as may be assigned in writing by Advertiser to Agency (these new products that may be so assigned to Agency hereunder are hereinafter individually referred to as "new product"). Accordingly, the parties hereby agree as follows:

1. The Agency will bill Advertiser for Agency's services on each new product in the following manner:

    (a) Except for the preparation of copy and layout for collateral material, Agency will bill Advertiser monthly in a lump sum for the actual salaries paid to Agency personnel for the time which they have spent in the preparation of advertising and the development of advertising and marketing plans for the new product, plus _____ percent (_____%) to cover profit-sharing, vacations, social security, Christmas bonus and insurance, and _____ percent (_____%) of the above two amounts to cover secretarial costs. The basis for computing salary costs will be the time sheets of individuals who work on the new product. At Advertiser's request, this basis will be subject to review of an independent firm of Certified Public Accountants designated by Advertiser.

    (b) For the preparation of copy and layout for collateral material, Agency will bill Advertiser monthly in a lump sum, at Agency's then prevailing hourly rate, for the entire time spent by art and copy creative personnel of the agency.

(c) Costs incurred by Agency on Advertiser's behalf for materials and services purchased from outside vendors and other expenses incurred by Agency on Advertiser's behalf in connection with each new product, and Agency's commissions on the foregoing costs and expenses, will be charged in accordance with and to the extent authorized by the Advertiser-Agency agreement.

2. This agreement will terminate as to each new product at such time as regular commissionable media billing is in effect for such new product. Thereafter, Agency will continue to service the advertising of the new product in accordance with the terms and conditions set forth in the Advertiser-Agency agreement. This agreement will also terminate simultaneously with the termination of the Advertiser-Agency agreement.

IN WITNESS WHEREOF, the parties hereto, each duly authorized, have set their hands this _____ day of _____ 19

(ADVERTISER)

By

_____

Title:

(AGENCY)

By

_____

Title:

<u>**COPY**</u>

<u>**Agency-Client New Product Agreement**</u>
<u>**Sample "C"**</u>

(DATE)

(NAME OF AGENCY)

Gentlemen:

This letter states the arrangements under which your organization is to provide services to the _____ Company in connection with specific new product developmental work as described in Paragraph 1, below, and subject to the terms of the remaining numbered paragraphs in this letter:

1. <u>Assignment</u>

   You will provide us with consultation, advice, analysis, reports, general planning and work assistance as required to complete all work pertaining to defining and evaluating new product opportunities in the specific areas of _____

   _____

2. <u>Compensation</u>

   a. <u>Basis</u>

      For your work in connection with the foregoing specifications, we agree to pay you monthly fees as follows:

      1) Part I: $_____ per month. This will purchase a month total of "Y" hours of supervisory staff time;
         or "Z" hours of internal staff time.

   b. <u>Special Conditions</u>

      1) It is agreed that the monthly charge for _____ will be $_____ but that if analysis reveals considerably less than the scheduled amount of time charges scheduled above, the amount deemed excessive will be returned to the _____ Company.

         If considerably more than the scheduled man hours are incurred, you will bill us for this extra time at per man hour charges consistent with the above schedule.

      2) General travel expenses and out-of-pocket costs for special activities requested by the _____ Company will be reimbursed by the _____ Company upon submission of itemized statements. Such statements shall be independent of and in addition to monthly retainer fee statements.

   c. <u>Billing Procedure</u>

      Monthly service fees and all other approved expense submissions will be billed on the last working day of each month and will be payable not later than the tenth working day of the following month.

3. Protection

    a. Service Exclusivity

        During the period covered by this letter of agreement, you will not assist in the marketing of physically developed products that compete with products of ours to which we have assigned your services unless prior approval is granted by us.

4. Period of Agreement

    a. All work pertaining to this agreement described will be accomplished between _____ and _____.

    b. Option to Terminate Agreement

        Written notice from either party may terminate this agreement at the end of a calendar month, provided that such notice is given at least one hundred and twenty days (120) in advance of the effective date of termination.

If the above meets with your approval, please sign both copies, retain one copy for your files, and return the other copy to us.

The _____

Company

By _____

Title _____

Date _____

Accepted by _____

Date _____

COPY

Agency-Client New Product Agreement
Sample "D"

(DATE)

(NAME OF CLIENT)

Gentlemen:

Effective _____ your company and our Agency have entered into an agreement pursuant to which we are to serve as your advertising agency for _____.

The nature of this product assignment is such that during the initial period of our relationship our cost of handling your account will exceed the amount of the commissions we will be able to earn from media billings.

Accordingly, in addition to our receiving a _____ percent Media Commission and _____ percent commission on non-media costs, you have agreed to reimburse us for all of our Direct Payroll and other Direct Costs, plus _____ percent of our Overhead incurred in handling the _____ account from and after _____.
The combined total payroll and other direct costs are referred to in this letter as "Direct Costs." For this purpose, the Direct Costs include, but are not limited to, necessary travel, lodging and meals incurred in servicing your account, but do not include entertainment costs. In all other respects, the elements of reimbursable Direct Costs and Overhead will be in accordance with the standard (Agency Name) accounting procedures.

We will bill you monthly on an estimated basis for all Direct Costs and Overhead to be incurred in the month. One month after the end of each calendar quarter, we will adjust the estimated reimbursable costs to the actual Direct Costs and Overhead incurred within the quarter. Any Media Commissions earned will be applied against the Direct Costs and Overhead. However, commissions on non-media costs shall be retained by the Agency and will not be utilized for the purpose of crediting costs.

In addition, either party may terminate this arrangement at any time by giving the other party at least 90 days written notice of such termination.

If the foregoing accurately reflects the understanding and agreement between us, will you please sign and return to us the enclosed copy of this letter.

Very truly yours,

COPY

Agency-Client New Product Agreement
Sample "E"

(DATE)

(NAME OF CLIENT)

Gentlemen:

This will confirm our Agreement with you, pursuant to which Agreement you have appointed us, and we accepted such appointment, to act as your advertising agency for various "new products" of the _____ on the following terms and conditions:

1. You retain us and we agree to act as your advertising agency for all advertising you may do on designated "new products" in any type of media.

    Definition of "new products": A "new product" is any product not already in test market or general distribution that requires separate marketing and advertising plans. (This distinguishes it from products which vary in only minor respects from products now in general distribution.) You and we will agree in advance what products shall be treated as "new products."

2. You shall have the sole right to designate which "new products" shall be handled by us. Our Agreement shall in no way be interpreted as granting us the exclusive right to act as your advertising agency on all "new products."

3. No advertising is to be contracted for in your behalf by us nor are we to undertake work or order work or material chargeable to you, unless it has been authorized by you. You agree to pay promptly any bills rendered on account of advertising work or material.

4. This agreement may be terminated at any time by either party having given the other party no less than ninety (90) days' prior written notice of its intention to terminate. In the event of termination, you will reimburse us for any commitments or expenditures authorized by you and made by us prior to the effective date of such termination.

5. Our compensation for commissionable advertising will be determined as follows:

    a. On media that allow agency commission of _____ percent, we are to retain these commissions. On media that allow agency commission of less than _____ percent, we are to charge you the net amount, plus an amount which will yield the agency _____ percent of agency's total charge before cash discount.

        All cash discounts allowed by media are offered to you predicated on the understanding that your funds are in the hands of the agency at the time the agency is required to make payment. In cases where media allows rebates or lower contractual rates to us, the amount of such reductions in cost shall be allowed in turn to you. You agree to pay us for all short rate payments made on your behalf.

    b. We shall be entitled to a commission of _____ net cost on all other services and materials purchased by us for you, including but not limited to, art work, engraving and other production costs.

6. We will be reimbursed monthly for all work on new products, except at the management level, at the rate of _____ per hour. The _____ per hour fee will apply to only those "new products" which have not as yet been committed to entering a test market. You will not be charged for any work done at the account management level. We will also be reimbursed monthly for all out-of-pocket expenses at cost.

    We agree to forego the above mentioned _____ per hour fee on a new product, after the time you designate that a specific "new product" will enter one or more test markets. Compensation, if any, will be derived from normal commissions earned in the test market(s) and in future national programs if you decide to use us as your advertising agency for such new product.

    A letter will be sent by you to us each time a "new product" is designated and approved by you to enter a test market.

7. Any notices required or given hereunder shall be deemed adequately given if by Certified Mail, postage prepaid, and addressed as follows:

    TO

    (NAME AND ADDRESS OF AGENCY)

8. This Agreement and the rights and obligations of the parties hereunder shall be construed in accordance with the laws of the State of _____.

If this letter correctly states our understanding with regard to this matter, please sign the enclosed copy and return it to us.

(NAME OF AGENCY)

By _____

Date _____

Accepted:

By _____

Date _____

F

Decision
Considerations

By permission,
Schrello Associates

Decision Considerations

Decision Factors

Is It *Real?*	Is the *Market* Real	Is There a *Need/Want?*
		Can the Customer Buy?
		Will the Customer Buy?
	Is the *Product* Real?	Is There a *Product* Idea?
		Can It Be *Made?*
		Will It *Satisfy The Market?*
Can We *Win?*	Can *Our Product* Be Competitive?	On *Design/Performance* Features?
		On *Promotion?*
		Is the *Price* Right?
		Is the *Timing* Right?
	Can *Our Company* Be Competitive?	In *Engineering/Production?*
		In Sales/*Distribution?*
		In *Management?*
		In *Other Considerations?*
Is It *Worth* It?	Will It *Be Profitable?*	Can We *Afford It?*
		Is the *Return* Adequate?
		Is the *Risk* Acceptable?
	Does it Satisfy Other *Company Needs?*	Does It Support *Company Objectives?*
		Are *External Relations* Improved?
		Is There an *Overriding* Factor?

Considerations

[Developed and Specialized for Each Company, Product Area, and Market by Their Experts]

Kind of need/want; Timing of need/want; Alternate ways to define need/want
Structure of the market; Market size & potential; Availability of funds
Priority; Product awareness; Perceived benefits/risks; Future expectations; Price vs. benefits
Ways to satisfy identified market; Feasibility; Acceptability; State-of-the-art
Designed; Developed; Tested; Produced; Inspected; Distributed; Installed; Serviced
Design/Performance features; Cost; Unit cost vs. volume; Availability
Quality; Utility; Convenience; Reliability; Serviceability; Style; Color; Safety; Uniqueness
Customer & trade advertising; Packaging; Technical services; Sales promotion
Cost; Pricing policies; Terms & conditions; Competition; Other price considerations
Introduction; Design changes; Sales campaigns; Price changes; Competitor reaction
Experience; Capabilities; Plant locations; Processes/Patents; Unique Ideas
Relation to present customers; Distributor/Dealer network; New marketing techniques
Experience; Organization; Financial strength; New management approaches; Commitment
Past performance; General reputation; Present market position; Geopolitical
Cash flow; Investment & timing; Sales & timing; Net cash flow
Absolute profit; Relative return on investment; Compared to other investments
What can go wrong? How likely? How serious? What can be done? Uncertainties
Future business; Relation to present products/markets; Use of resources; Company desires
Distributors; Dealers; Customers; Local communities; General public; Governments
Labor; Legal; Political; Stockholders/Owners; Company image; Executive judgment

Source: Copyright © 1977 Schrello Associates, Inc. Reprinted by permission from Forum/Schrello, 555 E. Ocean Blvd., Long Beach, CA 90802

Bibliography

Amelio, Gil and William Simon, *Profit from Experience*. New York: Van Nostrand Reinhold, 1996.

Auletta, Ken. *Three Blind Mice*. New York: Random House, 1991.

Banning, Douglas. *Techniques for Marketing New Products*. New York: McGraw-Hill Book Company Inc., 1957.

Belasco, James A. *Teaching the Elephant to Dance*. New York: Crown Publishers, Inc., 1990.

Bernhardt, Kenneth L., and Thomas C. Kinnear. Cases in *Marketing Management*. Plano, TX: Business Publications, Inc., 1985.

Betts, Jim. *The Million Dollar Idea*. Point Pleasant, NJ: Point Publishing Company, Inc., 1985.

Clark, Charles H. *Idea Management: How to Motivate Creativity and Innovation*. New York: AMACOM, a division of American Marketing Association, 1980.

deBone, Edward. *Lateral Thinking*. New York: Harper Colophon Books, 1970.

Douglas, Gordon, Philip Kemp, and Gordon Cash. *Systematic New Product Development*. New York: John Wiley & Sons, Halstead Press, 1978.

Drucker, Peter F. *Innovation and Entrepreneurship—Practices and Principles*. New York: Harper & Row, 1975.

Drucker, Peter F. *Management, Tasks, Responsibilities, Practices*. New York: Harper & Row, 1973.

Drucker, Peter F. *Managing in Turbulent Times*. New York: Harper & Row, 1980.

Engel, James F., Roger D. Blackwell, and David T. Kollat. *Consumer Behavior*. Hinsdale, IL: The Dryden Press, 1978.

Frand, Erwin A. *Art of Product Development from Concept to Market*. Homewood, IL: Dow Jones-Irwin, 1989.

Fuller, R. Buckminster. *Critical Path*. New York: St. Martin's Press, 1981.

Goldman, Jordan. *Public Relations in the Marketing Mix.* Lincolnwood, IL: NTC Business Books, 1992.

Gregory, James, and Kevin Mulligan. *The Patent Book.* New York: A & W Publishers, Inc., 1979.

Gruenwald, George. *New Product Development—Responding to Market Demand.* Lincolnwood, IL: NTC Business Books, 1992.

Gruenwald, George. *New Product Development Checklists—Proven Checklists for Developing New Products from Mission to Market.* Lincolnwood, IL: NTC Business Books, 1991.

Gruenwald, George. *New Product Development Video Interview* (with Robert Chesney). Lincolnwood, IL: NTC Business Videos, 1989.

Gruenwald, George. *New Product Development—What Really Works.* Chicago, IL: Crain Books, 1985.

Hafer, W. Keith, and Gordon E. White. *Advertising Writing.* St. Paul, MN: West Publishing Co., 1982.

Hambidge, Jay. *The Elements of Dynamic Symmetry.* New York: Dover Publications, Inc., 1967.

Harvard Business Review, On Management. New York: Harper & Row, 1967.

Henry, Walter, Michael Menasco, and Hirokazu Takada. *New Product Development and Testing.* Lexington, MA: Lexington Books, 1989.

Hilton, Peter. *Handbook of New Product Development.* Englewood Cliffs, NJ: Prentice-Hall, Inc., 1961.

Hoo, David, ed. *How to Develop and Market New Products . . . Better and Faster.* New York: Association of National Advertisers, Inc., 1985.

Kepner, Charles, and Benjamin B. Tregoe. *The Rational Manager.* New York: McGraw-Hill Book Company, 1965.

Kinnear, Thomas C., and James R. Taylor. *Marketing Research—An Applied Approach.* New York: McGraw-Hill Book Company, 1979.

Kraushar, Peter M. *New Products and Diversification.* London: Business Books Limited, 1969.

Larson, Gustav E. *Developing and Selling New Products.* Washington, DC: U.S. Department of Commerce, 1955.

Lynn, Gary S. *From Concept to Market.* New York: John Wiley & Sons, Inc., 1989.

Marting, Elizabeth, ed. *New Products, New Profits.* New York: American Management Association, 1964.

Melrose, Ken. *Making the Grass Greener on Your Side.* San Francisco, CA: Berrett-Koehler Publishers, 1995.

Mitchell, Mark and Janina Jolley. *Research Design Explained.* New York: Holt, Rinehart and Winston, Inc., 1988.

National Society of Professional Engineers. *Engineering Stages of New Product Development.* Alexandria, VA: NSPE, 1990.

O'Dell, William F. *Effective Business Decision Making . . . and the Educated Guess.* Lincolnwood, IL: NTC Business Books, 1991.

Peters, Thomas J., and Robert H. Waterman, Jr. *In Search of Excellence.* New York: Harper & Row, 1982.

Peterson, Peter G. *Facing Up.* New York: Simon & Schuster, 1993.

Pinchott III, Gifford. *Intrapreneurship.* New York: Harper & Row, 1985.

Porter, Michael E. *Competitive Strategy.* New York: The Free Press (division of Macmillan Publishing Co.), 1980.

Rothberg, Robert R. *Corporate Strategy and Product Innovation.* New York: The Free Press (division of Macmillan Publishing Co.), 1976.

Salb, Joan G. *Retail Image & Graphic Identity.* New York: Retail Reporting Corporation, 1995.

Schultz, Don E., and Dennis G. Martin. *Strategic Advertising Campaigns.* Chicago: Crain Books, Crain Communications Inc., 1979.

Schultz, Don E., Stanley Tannebaum, and Robert F. Lauterborn. *Integrated Marketing Communications.* Lincolnwood, IL: NTC Business Books, 1992.

Shanks, Bob. *The Cool Fire.* New York: Vintage Books, Random House, 1977.

Sheth, Jagdish N., and S. Ram. *Bringing Innovation to Market.* New York: John Wiley & Sons, 1987.

Smith, James Allen. *The Idea Brokers.* New York: The Free Press, div. Macmillan, Inc., 1991.

Souder, William E. *Managing New Product Innovations.* Lexington, MA: Lexington Books, 1987.

Tregoe, Benjamin B., and John W. Zimmerman. *Top Management Strategy.* New York: Simon and Schuster, 1980.

Urban, Glen L., and John R. Hauser. *Design and Marketing of New Products.* New York: Prentice-Hall, 1980.

Weilbacher, William M. *Brand Marketing.* Lincolnwood, IL: NTC Business Books, 1995.

Wind, Yoram J, Vijay Mahajan, and Richard N. Cardozo. *New-Product Forecasting.* Lexington, MA: Lexington Books, 1981.

Wind, Yoram J. *Product Policy: Concepts, Methods, and Strategy.* Reading, MA: Addison-Wesley Publishing Company, 1982.

Yankelovich, Daniel. *New Rules.* New York: Random House, 1981.

About the Author

George Gruenwald is a corporate growth and development consultant specializing in the identification and hands-on implementation of new business and new products opportunities for many of the world's largest corporations.

From 1972 to 1984, he was successively president, chairman, chief executive, and chief creative officer of Campbell-Mithun, Inc. (now Campbell Mithun Esty), a major advertising agency with an international reputation for successful new products marketing development. Mr. Gruenwald has worked in the subject field of this book with more than 50 of the world's largest companies, including almost one-third of the top 100 U.S. advertisers.

Previously, Mr. Gruenwald was founder and chief executive of Pilot Products, Inc., a new products marketing development service; Advance Brands, Inc., a sales and distribution service; and was a founding officer of North Advertising Incorporated (now Grey Advertising). Earlier, he was a new products brand and advertising manager at Gillette's Personal Care division; creative director at Willys-Overland Motors (now Chrysler's Jeep division), and assistant to the president of UARCO Incorporated.

Mr. Gruenwald frequently speaks on new products for private industry, trade and professional associations, and universities. His commentary on marketing and new product development has been published by the American Management Association, American Marketing Association, Association of National Advertisers, as well as *Advertising Age, Marketing News, Business Start-Ups, Intrapreneurial Excellence,* etc., and many major newspapers.

He is the author of *New Product Development—Responding to Market Demand* (1992), *New Product Development Checklists* (1991), *New Product Development—What Really Works* (1985), and the subject of the 1989 business video interview *New Product Development,* in which he shares his "Seven Steps to Success" in developing and launching new products and services.

Mr. Gruenwald was a corresponding task group member of the "Engineering Stages of New Product Development," a cooperative effort of the National Institute of Standards and Technology and the National Society of Professional Engineers, under which inventors and small businesses may receive technical and financial support to bring their energy-saving ideas to market.* (An inventor, Mr. Gruenwald holds the Venture Group® trademark.)†

A 14-year member of the Public Broadcasting Service (PBS) board and its executive committee, Mr. Gruenwald has headed committees and task forces on Future Service Opportunities and on Technology Applications.

His interests in nutrition and health led to his election as a trustee of the Linus Pauling Institute of Science and Medicine as well as a member of the External Advisory Committee of the Linus Pauling Institute at Oregon State University.

During World War II, he was a public relations writer and editor for the allied air forces in the Mediterranean theater of operations. He has a bachelor of science degree from Northwestern University's Medill School of Journalism, and was among the first alumni inductees into its Hall of Achievement, established in 1997 to commemorate Medill's 75th anniversary.

---

* The NIST/NSPE definitions were to be applied in the operation, management, and evaluation of the Department of Energy/National Institute of Standards and Technology (DOE/NIST) Energy-Related Inventions Program (ERIP).

† Registered Service Trademark U.S. Patent Office 920358.

Index